The 25 Issues That Shape American Politics

This book is organized to examine the major subjects taught in American politics through the lens of twenty-five hot button issues affecting American politics and policy today. These key issues reflect the ideas, principles, concerns, fears, morals, and hopes of the American people. The authors argue that these issues are the heart and soul of the American political system, serving as the basis for the disagreements that drive citizens, public servants, and elected officials into action.

Features of this Innovative Text

- Examines 25 issues in light of the 2016 presidential election and beyond.
- Up-to-date chapters reflect important developments in the arenas of money and politics, immigration, health care, race relations and civil rights, gun control, and gay rights in particular.
- Includes international coverage with recent and ongoing events surrounding Iran, Syria, Israel and Palestine, and China.
- A chapter on Russia puts recent developments in Syria, Ukraine, Crimea, and the "near abroad" in context with US foreign policy.

Michael Kryzanek is Emeritus Professor of Political Science and Special Assistant to the President of Bridgewater State University. He is the author of books on American politics, US foreign policy, and Latin American politics. Dr. Kryzanek received his undergraduate degree from Marquette University and his Ph.D. from the University of Massachusetts, Amherst. While on the faculty, he received awards for teaching and research, including the Lifetime Achievement Award.

Ann K. Karreth is Assistant Professor of Politics and International Relations at Ursinus College. Dr. Karreth's primary research interest is in African democracy and international development. She has published articles in numerous journals and book chapters. She teaches courses in comparative politics, research methods, public policy, and American foreign policy. Dr. Karreth received her undergraduate degree from Boston College and her Ph.D. from the University of Georgia.

Praise for the Second Edition

In an era of "fake news" and "alternative facts," students are ever more in need of balanced and empirically sound explorations of the many major issues confronting the United States. This book delivers exactly that. Our national agenda is crowded; this book helps students soundly examine it.

Steven E. Schier, *Carleton College*

In this innovative and timely book, Michael Kryzanek and Ann Karreth give readers a fresh perspective on key issues in American politics, covering everything from national security and terrorism to health care and gun rights. The authors bring each topic to life with highly informative discussions that supplement the standard approach to American politics. This book is sure to be a valuable addition to introductory and advanced undergraduate courses.

Michael Parkin, *Oberlin College*

This book provides an excellent survey of the range of issues structuring political debate in the contemporary American polity. Considering all sorts of questions – domestic and international, economic and cultural – Michael Kryzanek and Ann Karreth expertly summarize the key arguments on all sides of these important debates, with an admirable sense of fairness and balance. In addition, the pedagogical tools provided and referred resources in each chapter will be very helpful for students who want to dig deeper in their own explorations of these complex topics.

Matthew Wilson, *Southern Methodist University*

Michael Kryzanek and Ann Karreth's well-organized and accessible text substantively navigates contemporary issues and provides students and scholars with deeper insight into the crucial divisions that characterize and animate American political life.

Jay Steinmetz, *University of Oregon*

The 25 Issues That Shape American Politics

DEBATES, DIFFERENCES, AND DIVISIONS

Michael Kryzanek
Bridgewater State University

Ann K. Karreth
Ursinus College

Routledge
Taylor & Francis Group

NEW YORK AND LONDON

First published 2018
by Routledge
711 Third Avenue, New York, NY 10017

and by Routledge
2 Park Square, Milton Park, Abingdon, Oxon, OX14 4RN

Routledge is an imprint of the Taylor & Francis Group, an informa business

Library of Congress Cataloging-in-Publication Data
A catalog record for this book has been requested

ISBN: 978-1-138-65471-6 (hbk)
ISBN: 978-1-138-65475-4 (pbk)
ISBN: 978-1-315-62305-4 (ebk)

Typeset in Palatino
by Apex CoVantage, LLC

To Grace, Noah, and Caleb Sabo

and

Mae Karreth

CONTENTS

PREFACE

There are various ways to study American politics. There is the traditional, institutional approach, in which the Constitution and the three branches of government are explained and analyzed in order to better understand the foundation upon which American democracy has been built. Then there is the policy or process approach, which accents the way the political system works from the initial inputs or demands of the citizenry all the way through the final outputs or public policies. There have also been approaches to the study of American politics that stress the importance of examining the role of elites, groups, and key players who influence the final outcomes of government policymaking. All of these approaches are excellent explanatory methods for understanding what is arguably one of the most complex and complicated political systems in place in the world today.

However, there is also another approach to understanding American politics that serves as the basis of this book. American politics is driven and shaped in large part by a wealth of issues that reflect the ideas, the principles, the concerns, the fears, and the hopes of the American people. Issues in many respects are at the heart and soul of the American political system; the institutions of government respond to the issues; the process of policymaking is a response to the issues; and elites, groups, and players all seek to influence the manner in which the issues are addressed and resolved. There would be no American politics without issues, and without issues there would be nothing for the American people to support or reject and to demand that their elected representatives act upon in the policy arena.

Because the issue universe in American politics is so pervasive and critical to the functioning of American democracy, it is natural that there will be arguments over how best to deal with these matters. Many of the issues that make their way to the front burner of American politics are entangled in controversy and filled with pro and con positions. The fact that these issues are political in nature means that they stimulate intense partisan pressure. As a result, it is accurate to state that the political issues often shape the national agenda, the policy process, and the political fortunes of politicians and political parties. Moreover, because many of these issues percolate from the American public through polls, organized campaigns, or direct contact with public officials, they also foster intense debate, sharp differences, and deep divisions within the country.

This book, *The 25 Issues That Shape American Politics: Debates, Differences, and Divisions*, is thus designed to describe not just the key issues currently at the center of the national political arena, but to present the positions of both sides that form the arguments and serve as the basis for the disagreements that drive the political position to action. Each of these issues is what political pundits often describe as hot button, which means that they are important to the life and future of the country and they create ongoing ideological and partisan discussion.

PEDAGOGICAL FEATURES

Each of the issues is presented in a similar format with (a) a section on background, (b) a description of the issue from the various sides in the policy argument, and (c) the sources of the differences and the divisions that have arisen in the national conversation. Each issue also has key quotes from those leaders associated with the issue debate, along with important data and information that further flesh out the issue and contribute to the differences and divisions. Finally, each chapter concludes with a debate topic, some critical thinking questions, key Internet sites to visit, and helpful books to read.

ACKNOWLEDGEMENTS

The 25 Issues That Shape American Politics: Debates, Differences, and Divisions has been a joy to write, especially the opportunity for father and daughter to collaborate on this important description of the American political process. Both of us have developed our issue chapters based on our interactions with students in the classroom, collegial discussions in our respective political science departments, and endless opportunities to listen to the voice of American citizens. We owe a profound debt of gratitude to inquisitive students, patient colleagues, and the opinions and actions of all those Americans who make democracy a true treasure of governance.

We also want to take this opportunity to thank all those we love who supported us during this writing journey. To our wonderful spouses, Carol and Johannes, thanks for being there and cheering us on; to all the members of our extended family—Laura, Kathy, and Jim and the little ones, Grace, Noah, Caleb, and baby Karreth; to Jennifer Knerr and William Sudry at Routledge, thanks for your assistance and wise advice; and to those who worked on the final draft and put the manuscript in readable shape, thanks for your efforts. This book has been a work of love and dedication. We hope you enjoy it and that it will help you to understand issues that define our politics and our way of life.

Michael Kryzanek
Whitman, Massachusetts

Ann K. Karreth
Philadelphia, Pennsylvania

INTRODUCTION
Are We a Nation United or Divided?

Alexis de Tocqueville, the famous observer of American life during his journeys here in the 1830's, said the following about the way we as a people approach politics.

> The political activity that pervades the United States must be seen in order to be understood. No sooner do you set foot upon American ground than you are stunned by a kind of tumult . . . It is impossible to spend more effort in the pursuit of happiness.[1]

"Tumult" is indeed an appropriate word to use to describe the political environment in this country as Americans express their opinions, advance their causes, and seek to bring change. The issue arena in the American political system is expansive and dynamic with a range of highly charged concerns that often reflect a public that has firm beliefs and passionate resolve. It is not an exaggeration to claim that we as a nation are in a constant state of political debate as we air our differences and accent our divisions with stunning regularity. As a result, the governing system is marked by tension and confrontation as political leaders and ordinary citizens participate in a difficult decision-making process.

Despite our reputation as a nation that does not vote with great frequency (we are at the bottom of the list of voter participation, usually just ahead of Switzerland), Americans are joiners of groups, advocates of causes, avid volunteers, and generous givers to charities. Much of this participation is at the local level and usually involves issues or concerns that are not national in scope or controversial in nature. But when it comes to political issues that galvanize public opinion and energize the American people, there is an ever-growing and highly competitive interest group sector with as many as 30,000 registered organizations and millions of dues-paying members seeking to influence the government and shape public opinion. These interest groups are part of what has come to be called a pluralistic society as competing groups representing critical issues seek to change the political landscape of American society. This competition was viewed by the early founders like James Madison as a check on the likely excesses of the majority, but in contemporary times the explosion of interest groups advocating for particular issues or causes has fostered a political climate best described as a series of constant debates marked by passionate differences and deep divisions.

On the Record

James Madison, outlining his political philosophy and the impact of factions (groups) on the American system in Federalist #10 said the following:

> The latent causes of faction are thus sown in the nature of man; and we see them everywhere brought into different degrees of activity, according to the different circumstances of civil society. A zeal for different opinions concerning religion, concerning government, and many other points, as well as of speculation as of practice; an attachment to different leaders ambitiously contending for preeminence and power; or to persons of other descriptions whose fortunes have been interesting to the human passions, have, in turn, divided mankind into parties, inflamed them with mutual animosity and rendered them much more disposed to vex and oppress each other, than to cooperate for the common good.

Throughout our political history we have often taken great pride in the fact that despite our differences over critical and emotional issues, compromise and consensus prevail and partisan and ideological disagreements fade as all the parties to a policy dispute come together and support the agreed-upon solution. But in recent years American political life compromise and consensus have been overshadowed by unbending intransigence among issue proponents and policy gridlock in the halls of Congress. Not only has the issue arena become overheated with more and more areas of concern and citizen demands making their way into the governing arena, but politics has become a relentless campaign to push and pull government toward a specific policy goal. In many cases there is little room for compromise and consensus; instead, two rival camps poise for complete victory rather than "half a loaf." When a law is passed, an executive order issued, or a judicial decision rendered, there is often little sense of finality as both issue camps dig in their heels and continue their campaigns for total victory.

There has been much made of the issue tensions and confrontations that mark contemporary American politics. The operative phrase today is that America is a "divided nation"—Democrats versus Republicans, red states versus blue states, conservatives versus liberals, evangelicals versus seculars. At the core of the divisions stirring up the political pot are the issues, which serve as the focus of partisan debates and define electoral differences. In the era of the Internet, mass media, and sophisticated marketing strategies, Americans are bombarded with partisan blogs, competing talk radio shows, 24/7 cable news programs, and direct mail campaigns, all designed to inform but also infuriate as they seek to build a case for their particular issue perspective. Although the vast majority of Americans stay on the fringes of these issue divisions, those that do take an interest have plenty of ammunition in order to solidify their position and advance their cause.[2]

It is important to state that the view of a "divided America" is not without its skeptics and detractors. On many issues, polling data point to a broad public consensus, or at least an apathetic reluctance to be drawn into a debate about differences. American politics may not be so much divided, so the argument goes, as held captive by partisan ideologues and issue proponents who have effectively captured the national consciousness while the vast silent majority remains on the sidelines. For example, on some issues such as background checks for those seeking a gun permit, the strong opposition of the pro-gun rights National Rifle Association does not mesh with an overwhelming percentage of Americans (92%) who favor background checks as a common sense reform.[3] The politics of the center and moderation still have relevance in American politics, despite the passion that can surround a particular issue. The claim is made that all this talk of constant debates, irreparable differences, and deep divisions is the stuff of ideologues controlling the political dialogue in this country and the media pumping up the political "noise" all in an effort to gain attention.[4]

The key to understanding the current political landscape of American politics and the impact of critical issues on the governing process and governing decision-making is to develop a "picture" of the American people. What are the characteristics of national life that best define us? What do we stand for or believe in? Are there any generalizations about American national life that can be made with a degree of certainty? Simply said—who are we? This is, of course, an enormously broad series of questions that are not easily answered. But there are some measures of American national life that can help us better understand the American public and thereby give us some clues about the issue environment that is created from these characteristics, beliefs, and generalizations.

One approach is to develop a demographic profile of the American people, basically a data driven definition that describes who we are. Recent data compiled by the US Census Bureau showed that the United States is a nation of approximately 324 million people, making this country the third-largest globally with about 4.6% of the world's population. Population growth in the United States has increased by 85% since 1950, a considerable increase compared to other industrial countries like Germany and Italy, which have experienced meager population growth. Although fertility and mortality rates have remained fairly constant over time, the impact of immigration has had a profound effect on population increases in this country and is projected to be the key to population growth well into the remainder of this century.[5]

But more than the overall population numbers, data shows that, besides becoming bigger, we are also becoming "older." Since the 1950s the United States has been involved in a profound demographic change: rapid population aging. Where in 1950 the population of the United States was represented by a pyramid with the wide base made up of young people and the tip of older Americans, by 2050 the pyramid is predicted to become a rectangle as more and more seniors, who are part of the post-World War II baby boomer generation, live longer while the fertility rate remains constant. By 2050 it is estimated that one in every five persons in the United States will be 65 or older.

Potentially more influential from a demographic standpoint is the rise of the Millennial Generation—those born between 1980 and 2000. There are currently an estimated 83 million in this generation. The Millennials are likely to become the largest generation in the US labor force. Americans under the age of 20 now make up 27% of the total population, while those over 65 currently make up nearly 13% of the total population. Not surprisingly, there is a generation gap between the baby boomers and the Millennials that contributes to differences and divisions in culture, politics, values, and vision.[6]

Census data also show that America is becoming racially and ethnically diverse. As a result of immigration and higher fertility rates among non-whites, American society is changing and will continue to change in terms of its racial and ethnic make-up. Currently 81% of Americans responded in census questionnaires that they are white, followed by 12.6% African-American and 3.7% Asian-American. The important conclusion of the study was that the percentages of African-Americans and Asian-Americans are expected to increase significantly in the coming decades, and Hispanic-Americans will likely be viewed as a unique racial/ethnic group. Currently, the 81% white American figure includes the Hispanic population, which currently is not recognized as a separate racial category by the US Census Bureau. Americans of Hispanic origin thus are grouped with the white population. But when separated out from the white category, census data show that 50.4 million people can be identified as Hispanic or about 16% of the population. In real terms, African-Americans, Hispanic-Americans, and Asian-Americans make up almost a third of the current population in the United States.[7]

This demographic picture of the American people has profound implications for issue formation and policy development in the coming years. Because of an expanding, aging, and diverse population, concerns over Social Security, health care policy, intergenerational distribution of governmental resources, immigration, and racial and ethnic integration are certain to rise to the top levels of the national issues agenda. The government will be faced with enormous pressure from groups and the general public over how to address the challenges that will emanate from the changing demographic profile of American society. Since many of these issues will require the setting of budget priorities and dealing with highly sensitive race, ethnic, and class relationships, the changing character of America's population is a critical ingredient in shaping national politics.

Another means of better understanding the political landscape of American politics and the link to important policy issues is to examine the national electorate. How Americans vote and what they say about the reasons behind their votes give powerful clues to defining public opinion, not just toward candidates for office, but also by defining what voters believe these candidates stand for or what they promise to achieve once in office. To get a better understanding of the political landscape and issue formation in American politics, polling done by the *Washington Post* in 2015 showed that 35% of Americans identified as conservatives, 25% as liberals, and 41% as moderates. There are some signs that those identifying as liberal have increased their ranks in recent years, a trend that some feel will continue in large part because of the growing influence of Millennials who often share many of the beliefs held by liberals.[8] Many of the Millennials who side with liberal values are increasingly adopting the political label of progressive, a political category that accents the importance of reforming our democratic system by limiting the influence of moneyed interests and corporate power.[9]

Although the mainline political categories of Conservative, Liberal, and Moderate are labels that have imprecise meanings, it is safe to state that Conservatives have generally been associated with smaller government and government deregulation of business, less taxation, and a strong defense posture in the world. Liberals are in general supportive of government action to solve national problems and value personal freedom and privacy rights. Moderates, as the word would suggest, are somewhere in between Conservatives and Liberals, which means that they may see some benefit from government action and regulation, support some but not all personal freedoms and privacy issues, and are cautious about, but not opposed to, government taxation and spending.

Clearly from the poll results on the ideological positions of the Americans, the Moderates are the dominant force in the political arena, balancing off the Liberal left and the Conservative right. Some would say that the Moderates are indecisive and uncommitted, while others will stress the fact that the Moderates are merely in the great traditions of compromise and consensus as they seek a middle ideological road. But what the influence of the Moderates means in American electoral politics is that political candidates must shape their positions on a range of national issues that play to the center of the ideological spectrum. This centrist view of American politics and the American citizenry was put to a hard test during the 2016 presidential election as Donald Trump was supported by approximately 46% of the electorate who did not easily fit into the traditional political categories. These Trump supporters challenged the long-standing positions held by the Republican Party in areas such as trade, immigration, and foreign and military policy.[10] In a real sense, in the 2016 election America became a country even more divided by Conservatives, Liberals (Progressives), Moderates, and the Trump supporters. This division has called into question the centrist character of American politics and American life.

Polling data has also provided a list of what concerns the American citizenry. These lists of issue concerns often provide another clue about what Americans are thinking, what they value, and how they see the direction that the country is going in. In data compiled by the Gallup organization in 2012, the top issue concerns were the national economy, health care, the national budget and debt, and foreign policy, particularly as applied to the wars in Iraq and Afghanistan. But by 2015, as a result of terrorist attacks in this country, the issue concerns shifted somewhat as terrorism topped the list followed by the economy, jobs, budget deficits, health care costs, and crime. In the 2016 presidential campaign, new issue concerns associated with race relations, immigration, trade, and presidential temperament were added to the list.[11] In the days after the election of Donald Trump as President, the Pew Research Center conducted another poll that found that the top five priorities of the American people were terrorism (76%), the economy (73%), education (69%), jobs (66%), and health care (64%).

It is important to point out that examining issue politics through demographic data, ideological positions, or polling priorities provides the popular side of the American political landscape. What is just as important, if not crucial, to understanding the way issues drive politics and government in this country is the professional side of issue politics, namely the influence that special interest groups play in setting the policy agenda and shaping the final outcome of public decision-making. The process of American politics is increasingly driven by the interest group sector, which is not only large and ever expanding, but enormously powerful with a range of influence "tools" at its disposal in order to sway government. From campaign funds to small armies of expert staff members and lobbyists to sophisticated public relations and marketing strategies, the interest group of today is a formidable participant in the governing process. Many of the issues that will be discussed later are championed by huge interest group organizations that have the capacity to inundate Congress and the Executive branch with email, mobilize grassroots demonstrations, and spend money lavishly on the Internet, television, newspapers and radio advertising, and television commercials. The old adage about one person fighting city hall and single-handedly bringing about change is rarely achieved in this country; the politics of change is now the domain of a well-financed interest group that fights city hall or Congress or the president, and many times wins.

Special interests that act to advance specific issues or issue agendas come in many shapes and sizes. Economic groups such as the US Chamber of Commerce, representing the business sector, and the AFL-CIO, the major labor organization, are concerned with a broad range of issues. The Chamber may concentrate on tax, trade, and regulation issues but would also weigh in on issues such as immigration reform and affirmative action in hiring. The AFL-CIO would concentrate on labor rights and safety issues, but also be involved in issues such as the impact of globalization on job security and energy independence. Professional groups such as the American Medical Association, which represents physicians, would concentrate its efforts on health care reform and research funding, while the National Education Association, which is the primary group lobbying for teachers, would speak for its membership on education issues such as testing and teacher standards related to the No Child Left Behind Act. Also of importance are social groups such as the American Association of Retired Persons, the largest interest group operating in the political arena, which naturally is concerned with Social Security and Medicare as well as pocketbook issues such as the cost of energy.

These so-called umbrella groups that address a wide range of national issues are also joined by single-issue groups that, as defined, direct their energies and resources toward achieving a specific issue objective. The National Rifle Association has for years been one of the most effective groups active in national government as it zealously protects Second Amendment rights against any legislation that would limit gun ownership. The highly contentious abortion issue has fostered a number of active groups such as Planned Parenthood, a strong supporter of abortion rights, and the National Right to Life Committee, which is the primary anti-abortion organization. Racial and ethnic groups have also formed in order to champion issues critical to their constituencies. African-Americans are represented by the National Association of Colored People (NAACP) as they seek government programs to address poverty and welfare reform, while the Hispanic community is led by the League of United Latin American Citizens (LULAC), which has been in the forefront of the challenges to immigration reform and discrimination against legal and illegal migrants. Finally, numerous groups have been formed in recent years that advocate on behalf of conservation and environmental preservation. Groups such as the Sierra Club and the National Resources Defense Council are active in the areas of global warming, pollution, and energy independence.

FYI

The influence of interest groups is often judged by their ability to raise and spend money on candidates and campaigns. Below are the top ten interest groups recognized as having the most influence in shaping legislation and organizing grassroots support.

1. The National Rifle Association
2. The United States Chamber of Commerce
3. The American Medical Association
4. The American Association of Retired Persons
5. Americans for Prosperity
6. MoveOn.Org
7. American-Israel Political Action Committee
8. American Federation of Labor and Council on Industrial Organization (AFL-CIO)
9. National Abortion Rights Action League
10. National Association for the Advancement of Colored People

Source: Center for Responsible Politics

American politics is dominated by the twenty-five issues that make up this book, and political parties, ideological movements, and government are often embroiled in policy debates over these key issues. But just about every facet of national life has an organization advocating for a particular cause or objective. From the Tobacco Institute and the National Whiskey Distillers Council to the Gay and Lesbian Alliance Against Defamation and the National Organization for Women, the issue arena is highly specialized and ever-changing. It is thus no wonder that the American political system suffers from issue overload as it is bombarded by public opinion, lobbyists, and well-organized campaigns, all designed to get the attention of governmental leaders, all passionate about advancing their particular issue through the maze of national decision-making.

The connection between the issues that dominate American politics and the maze of government is an essential part of the policy process in the United States. The Founders purposely did not make it easy for a specific issue concern to be transformed into public policy. Not only was government divided into three competing and powerful governing bodies, but also, within those governing bodies, there were numerous institutional checks and balances, partisan roadblocks, state and federal turf wars, and bureaucratic wrangling. To take an issue through this maze often would take years, suffer many setbacks and delays, and endure inevitable compromises that were the result of fierce bargaining and political deal-making. Foreign observers of the American political system often wondered how anything got done within this maze. In fact, James Bryce, a British observer, wrote in 1888 that "there is in the American government . . . a want of unity. The Sailors, the helmsman, the engineer, do not seem to have one purpose or obey one will so that instead of making steady way the vessel may pursue a devious or zigzag course, and sometime merely turn round and round in the water."[12]

The sailing analogy used by Bryce, suggesting that the American political system is often adrift or at least moving in different directions, accurately depicts the challenges faced by proponents of a particular issue. Unlike parliamentary systems where there is government based on party majority and disciplined voting, the American presidential/separation of powers system cannot guarantee that a political promise made to a specific issue constituency can be translated into a public policy. The American political system is a captive of a contentious confluence of party, group, public opinion, money, and media, all contributing to what Bryce called "a want of unity" and leading to that "zig zagging" and frequent turning "round and round in the water." As we will see, issues such as immigration reform, gun legislation, and global-warming initiatives have suffered the fate of endless delay and legislative death because the American political system is not designed to be efficient, speedy, and effective.

Political scientists have attempted to make sense of the American political system and the issues and their proponents and opponents that seek to "zig zag" through the troubled waters of the policy process. Although the core steps in the traditional policy process model of American politics may vary a bit and have different titles, there is general consensus about the following stages in the way the American political system transforms problems into solutions:

1. Setting the Political Policy Stage in the Environment of American Political Culture
2. Identifying the Problem by Citizen Initiative, Media Campaigns, or Interest Group Activity

3. Getting the Problem on the National Political Agenda
4. Developing a Policy among Key Governing Elites
5. Making the Policy into Law—the Black Box of American Government
6. Implementing the Policy through the Bureaucratic Establishment
7. Evaluating the Policy through Congressional Oversight and Bureaucratic Examination

Data Bank

There are 23 separate ways to delay or kill a bill in the United States legislative process.

Before even the policy process begins, it is essential to recognize that the values, the beliefs, the behavior patterns, the prejudices, and the fears that exist within the character of the American public and American institutions will shape the manner in which national issues and national problems are handled. When the American public expresses its views on a particular issue directly to government officials or in a larger public opinion forum, that expression is often influenced by the dominant public culture that exists in the country at the time. For example, the political culture of the United States has often been described as fundamentally based on personal freedom, individualism, and inalienable rights. Therefore an issue such as abortion would likely be framed by the American people in terms of this culture of freedom, individualism, and rights—the rights of a woman to control her body versus the rights of the fetus that is in her body.

The American political culture, however, is not just about freedom, individualism, and rights; there are other aspects at work in the political environment that can shape the feedback of the people. The American political culture is also one that is guided by principles associated with equality, fairness, tolerance, and community spirit. Therefore, matters related to race relations would be profoundly influenced by these values and beliefs as proponents of policies like affirmative action and gay rights, which are designed to protect or enhance racial and gender fairness, and would thereby accent this aspect of our national political culture.

In order for the policy process to begin in earnest and move toward some action, the American people have to show that they are concerned or angry about what they see around them and make a demand on government. This can be in the form of a letter or email to an elected representative, conversational links on Internet sites related to the issue, interest group pressure, or demonstrations that seek to bring further attention to the issue. Government institutions and the political leaders who run those institutions are not going to respond to a single complaint, but if they see that a particular issue has wide interest and that there is a growing demand for action, then they will be forced to pay attention. Politicians read public opinion polls regularly and check their Twitter or Facebook accounts, and many of their actions related to a pressing national issue is the result of listening to the people either directly, through polling, or social media.

No list of issue demands, however, gets anywhere in the American political system without key elites becoming involved. Political party leaders and activists, think tank experts, congressional committee staffers, and interest group lobbyists are the keys to taking the public demand forward. An issue needs institutional or organizational representation to provide it with the "lift" necessary to carry it through and around the obstacle course that is our separation-of-powers governing process. Political parties and their connection to elections and control of the governing institutions of Congress and the Presidency are critical supports. Party leaders and activists can make a particular issue a priority and champion a cause as a way of winning votes and expanding power. Think tanks provide the brainpower to assist decision-makers in seeing the costs and benefits, the strengths and weaknesses of a proposed policy. Congressional committee staffs know the ins and outs of the legislative process and are key advisors to their bosses, who eventually will cast a vote on the proposed policy. Finally, interest groups and their professional lobbyists are vital players in the process because as professional advocates they can provide the organizational tools necessary to carry the issue through the process.

The black box of decision-making, better known as government, is where national issues become captive to the complexities of the American governing system. As stated earlier, nothing runs smoothly in American government, and more than likely issues will end up zigging and zagging their way through extended Congressional hearings, bitter partisan battles, frequent presidential disagreements, and endless bureaucratic second-guessing. The issue will be in the hands of Congressional party leaders and lobbyists, but just because there are powerful advocates for a particular cause does not insure that the process will be any easier, since there will be Congressional party leaders and lobbyists opposed to the issue who are just as adamant about using the system to clog up the machinery of government as the proponents are to make the machinery work smoothly. The black box is appropriately named since it is difficult to see what is really going on, even though hearings, debates, and votes are public. But it is what is going on behind the scenes among Congressional party leaders and lobbyists that often times make the difference as to whether an issue lives to move forward or is a victim of the system. When success is achieved it is often because deals are struck, compromises are made, middle ground is occupied, and key players are satisfied about the eventual shape and direction of the issue legislation.

If the issue makes it through the black box, it becomes an output of government, a public policy that is designed to address a need, solve a problem, expand a right, prohibit a practice, or change a direction. This is often a proud moment of government as a president, backed by smiling legislators, signs a bill into law and hands out the complimentary pens that were used in the ceremony. Speeches are given, credit is distributed, and promises are made about the positive impact that the policy will have on the country. The long road of a public demand has been traversed as one group won and the other lost in the high stakes game of issue politics in American government.

The public policy is made law, but that does not end the process as the bureaucracy is charged with implementing the legislation, which often gives these non-elected officials considerable influence in determining exactly how the policy solution will be put into place. Specific rules and regulations will need to be drafted, budgets drawn up, new tasks will likely have to be given to government employees, and perhaps an organizational structure will need to be created in order to ensure that the general wishes of the decision-makers are carried out. Once the bureaucrats have had their turn at the process, the policy is implemented, but the process does not end there as all those people at the beginning of this long chain of events will be watching to see if indeed the new legislation is working and whether the decision made in the black box of government has lived up to its promises. The long road to a policy may be over, but along the way it has likely exhausted the participants, taken years to accomplish, and may look a lot different from what was proposed at the start.

The Founders coined the term E Pluribus Unum, "From Many, One" to emphasize that their goal was to create a country where the many units, in this case the individual states, would work together for the national good and remain united. E Pluribus Unum can also be used to describe the challenge that comes from the "tumult" of issue voices and causes as described by de Tocqueville and the "zig zagging" that occurs in American politics as issues enter the decision-making black box. We indeed are a nation of many voices, many concerns, many advocates, and many visions. But we also are a nation that can easily become immobilized and directionless as our political system becomes inundated with contentious issues and unbending issue groups. The First Amendment clearly gives each and every one of us the right to peaceably assemble and petition the government for a redress of grievances. But the question that must be asked is: At what point do all the debates, all the differences, and all the divisions that accompany issue formation and issue advocacy compromise the need for "Unum"—unity?

The contentiousness of American politics and the unbending nature of issue-driven partisanship have led in recent years to governmental gridlock that has overwhelmed the policymaking system. One study shows that gridlock has doubled since 1950 as 71% of the major issues went unlegislated in the 2011–2012 period; there was scant change in that figure in the years following 2011–2012. One pundit even gave this political malaise a term—gridlockracy—to show how our democracy has fallen prey to a governmental system that has great difficulty in making public policy.[13]

This gridlockracy has also had a negative impact on public trust. A Pew Research Center poll in 2014 found that only 24% of Americans stated that they trust government compared to 36% in 2005, 33% in 2000, 44% in 1986, 54% in 1971, and 73% in 1958. As the report concluded, "a continuation of this gridlock will likely continue the decline in public trust, a key foundation of democratic government."[14]

James Madison applauded the rise of factions that represented diverse interests, issues, and causes, but there is also the common good, the national interest, and the general will that the Founders were seeking when they dreamed of a nation of E Pluribus Unum. As we explore more deeply the twenty-five issues that shape American politics, it will be important to remember the alternatives—"tumult" and "zig zagging" rather than From Many, One.

The Great Debate

The American political system, which accents debate, differences, and divisions is a constructive means of developing and implementing public policy or a dangerous and destructive flaw in the way Americans do politics and governing.

Debate Topic

Discuss how you and others view the American system with its zig zagging and its quality of "tumult."

Critical Thinking Questions

1. Can it be possible to solve complex national problems in a diverse, pluralistic, and interest group dominated political system as currently exists in the United States?
2. What recommendations do you have to help bring more efficiency to the American policymaking process?
3. Does the American political system work for the benefit of the nation or for special interests?
4. How can we as American citizens ensure that the common good is being addressed rather than narrow interests?
5. Would the United States be better off with a parliamentary form of government rather than the current presidential system?

Connections

Local organizing is increasing and having an impact on not just local politics, but on bringing issues to the national policy scene. See the website of Local Victory, which advises Americans on how to develop grassroots organizations. See www. localvictory.com

One of the more active groups seeking to make the American political system work and be open to the public is the Center for Responsive Politics. Its website is http://www.opensecrets.org

Check out the websites of the key public policy players in American government—the House of Representatives, www.house.gov; the Senate, www.senate.gov; the president, www.whitehouse.gov

Common Cause, a political reform group, which has as its mission statement "Holding Government Accountable," is one of the leading advocates of political reform. Its Internet site can be reached at www.commoncause.org

One of the most influential grassroots organizations in recent American politics is the Tea Party. Visit its site at www.teapartypatriots.org

A Few Books to Read

Cigler, Allan J. and Burdett Loomis, *Interest Group Politics*, 8th edition (Washington, DC: CQ Press, 2011).

De Tocqueville, Alexis, *Democracy in America*, 2 vols. (New York, NY: Penguin Classics, 2003; 1835).

Gupta, Dipak, *Analyzing Public Policy: Concepts, Tools and Techniques*, 2nd edition (Washington, DC: CQ Press, 2010).

Hamilton, Alexander, James Madison, and John Jay, *The Federalist Papers*, ed. Clinton Rossiter (New York: New American Library, 1961).

Putnam, Robert D., *Our Kids: The American Dream in Crisis* (New York: Simon and Schuster, 2016).

Notes

1. James Bryce, *The American Commonwealth* (New York, NY: Penguin Classics, 2003; 1888).
2. The divisions in American society are the subject of the book by Bill Bishop and Robert G. Cushing, *The Big Sort: Why the Clustering of Like-Minded America Is Tearing Us Apart* (Boston, MA: Houghton Mifflin, 2008). Bishop and Cushing contend that the growing isolation of Americans is creating extreme and divisive policy positions.
3. See my discussion of center politics in Michael Kryzanek, *Angry, Bored and Confused, a Citizen Guide to American Politics* (Boulder, CO: Westview Press, 1999).
4. "The Changing Demographic Profile of the United States," US Census Bureau, August 6, 2013.
5. See "Immigration's Impact on Past and Future U.S. Population Change," Pew Research Center, September 28, 2015.
6. See Scott Keeter and Paul Taylor, "The Millennials," Pew Research Center, December 11, 2009.
7. See "Changing Patterns in U.S. Immigration and Population," The Pew Charitable Trust, December 18, 2014.
8. See "Millennials in Adulthood," Pew Research Center, March 7, 2014.
9. Ibid.
10. Derek Thompson, "Who Are Donald Trump's Supporters, Really?" *The Atlantic*, March 1, 2016. See also Luke Timmerman, "Who Are Trump's Supporters? Not Who You May Think: Meet My Friend J," *Forbes*, November 9, 2016.
11. See "Public Policy Priorities Reflect Changing Conditions at Home and Abroad," Pew Research Center, January 15, 2015.

12. See Dawson Church, "Gridlockracy," December 8, 2014, www.huffingtonpost. com/dawson-church/gridlockracy-gridlokruhse_b_6281362.html

13. "Beyond Distrust: How Americans View Their Government," Pew Research Center, November 23, 2015.

14. Bryce, op. cit.

1

TERRORISM **AND** HOMELAND **SECURITY**

Issue Focus

No function of government is more important than the protection of the homeland from invasion or threats to national security. The attack on America on 9/11 underscored the importance of homeland security and the need to develop the institutions, policies, and procedures that will heighten national security and the safety of the homeland. To meet the challenges the nation faces from external and domestic terrorist threats, the Department of Homeland Security was established in 2001. The department is a huge and expansive bureaucracy that is often under intense scrutiny with high expectations to ensure that America does not experience terrorist attacks either from organized groups or so-called "lone wolf" individuals. Guarding the homeland is an enormous task as even one attacker can inflict devastating death and injury. When there are failures in the system of homeland security, when there are questions about the legality of the policies, or when there is the perception that this country is inadequately protected, questions are inevitably raised about whether our homeland is indeed secure.

Chapter Objectives
This issue chapter will seek to:
1. Examine the government institutions that are charged with protecting the country from threats—domestic and foreign—as well as natural disasters and pandemics.
2. Discuss the policies put in place by the government to address the threats and protect the American people and American assets.
3. Present the public debates, policy differences, and national divisions that have arisen in the United States and the most appropriate, effective, and legal approaches to protecting the homeland.

SOME BACKGROUND

As President George W. Bush stated in the aftermath of the terrorist attacks on the United States, "9/11 changed everything." Not only did it produce heightened public anxiety about the prospect of new attacks and alter much of the national security infrastructure throughout the United States, it also profoundly changed the course of American foreign policy in the Middle East. In response, the Bush administration launched a global war on terror, but aimed first at al Qaeda training camps in Afghanistan, where the masterminds of the attacks had their base of operations. The Taliban Islamic radicals that controlled Afghanistan would also be a target since they had welcomed Osama bin Laden and his al Qaeda fighters and provided them with the protection they needed to engage in their war against the United States. Preparations for a military strike against al Qaeda and the Taliban moved quickly, and support from the American public was overwhelming for a retaliatory strike against Afghanistan.[1] Within months of 9/11, the United States had launched such a strike and had achieved considerable success in driving the Taliban out of key areas of the country, including the capital of Kabul, and destroying the al Qaeda base camps along the rugged, mountainous Afghanistan-Pakistan border.

The relative ease with which the United States dismantled the Taliban regime and destroyed al Qaeda's base of operations emboldened the Bush administration to move against Iraq and its leader, Saddam Hussein. By November 2001, Bush and his national security team were discussing the prospects of an invasion of Iraq and the removal of Saddam Hussein. The Iraqi leader had been a thorn in the side of the United States since his invasion of Kuwait in 1990 and because of his refusal to allow United Nations' inspectors to examine, without restrictions, the status of his weapons-of-mass-destruction program in the areas of nuclear, chemical, and biological agents. Because the Bush administration believed that Iraq could develop into a key ally to terrorist groups and provide them with the means to wage further attacks against the United States, the invasion was given the highest priority.[2]

The now-famous, lightning invasion of Iraq in April 2003 quickly tumbled Saddam Hussein from power and created within the Bush administration a heightened sense of euphoria as it envisioned the transformation of Iraq into a functioning democracy and a pro-United States stabilizing force in the Middle East. But as the United States turned from becoming a liberating force that was greeted with initial goodwill to an occupying force that gradually faced heavily armed insurgents and homegrown al Qaeda terrorists, the initial policy of a pre-emptive strike and invasion of Iraq became the source of unending debate in Washington and, indeed, throughout the United States.

When Barack Obama assumed the presidency in 2009, he quickly got to work on his campaign promise of ending the war in Iraq. His administration had felt that President Bush's strategies of strong-armed regime change, occupation, and nation-building were flawed and, in reality, made the United States less safe by effectively radicalizing those who believed the United States was conducting a war on Islam. By the end of his first term as president, Obama had withdrawn the majority of US troops from Iraq, drawing heavy criticism from conservatives who believed that it endangered the stability of the country and the region. In nearby Afghanistan, Obama chose to increase troop presence, arguing that the more significant threat to US national security came from Taliban and al Qaeda groups operating in the mountainous region on the Afghan-Pakistan border. During his second term in office, however, President Obama decided to pare down US troop presence in Afghanistan as well.

In addition to their "boots on the ground" approach to counterterrorism, the Obama administration's war on terror also included the use of more covert activities, such as drone strikes and special operations aimed at taking out the key strategic outposts of terrorists groups. President Obama's use of covert action proved successful in taking down 9/11 mastermind, Osama Bin Laden, in a secret raid on his Pakistani compound. Nevertheless, his strategy of withdrawal from Iraq and Afghanistan has proven more controversial, as it has not only allowed the Taliban to make significant territorial advances in recent years in Afghanistan, but it has also created a political vacuum in Iraq, facilitating the rise of sectarian violence and—as some have argued—has even paved the way for the rise of the Islamic State.

The war on terror has also been fought at home as the government has taken numerous steps after 9/11 to ensure that an attack on the United States will never happen again. Strengthening homeland security occurred on a number of levels, some organizational and bureaucratic, others more intrusive and controversial. In 2001 the Bush administration quickly went about creating a new cabinet level agency, the Department of Homeland Security, which sought to streamline the disparate sectors of intelligence gathering and protection of vital resources and installations. The new department combined bureaucratic entities from twenty-two individual agencies, including the Coast Guard, the Federal Emergency Management Agency (FEMA), the Secret Service, and Immigration and Customs Enforcement (ICE). The Secretary of Homeland Security was given extraordinary access to the president and wide powers to put in place government assets that would be capable of meeting the growing global terrorist threat.[3]

As constituted, the Department of Homeland Security has a number of responsibilities and mission objectives. At its core, the mission of the department is "protecting the territory of the United States from terrorist attacks and responding to natural disasters." From this mission statement, the department is required to perform a wide range of functions, including internal evaluations of the state of homeland security, protection of national assets, response to attacks and disasters, and cooperation with federal, state, and local agencies and private entities to assure that the nation has in place the means necessary to prepare for and respond to terrorist attacks and natural disasters. To accomplish this task, Homeland Security has developed various programs, networks, and advisory systems designed to provide a broad range of assessments on the current state of national preparedness and the vulnerabilities that exist, along with action initiatives designed to ensure that the nation, its citizens, its infrastructure, and its economic structure are secure.[4]

The next step in the process of ensuring national preparedness is prevention and protection. To achieve these goals, the department has put in place two critical programs that address key targets that are likely on the terrorists' list. The Container Security Initiative (CSI) is directed by the US Customs and Border Protection (CBP) and is charged with developing measures that will protect the ports of the United States and, in particular, monitor the container traffic that enters the ports on a daily basis. In addition, Homeland Security has established the National Infrastructure Protection Plan (NIPP) that works with state and local authorities to devise plans that will ensure that bridges, roads, tunnels, water treatment plans, nuclear power and electric generating facilities, and water reservoirs are properly secured and monitored. The Department has also initiated a First Responders program that is designed to train and equip fire, police, and emergency medical personnel, who would be the first on the scene of an attack, and has worked with states and local communities to provide funding for the purchase of necessary equipment.[5] Finally, Homeland Security has placed extensive budgetary resources into research— from agriculture to bio-defense to behavioral aspects of terrorism—and the development of new technologies, which will assist the country in combating the terrorist threat.[6]

The most comprehensive and active sector of Homeland Security is in the area of immigration and border security. The Coast Guard, the Customs Services, the Border Patrol, and the Transportation Security Agency (the 50,000 ubiquitous airport screeners) are but some of the most visible government organizations that are at the front lines, ensuring that terrorist agents or materials that could be used in an attack do not enter the United States. In many respects, the whole area of immigration control and border security is the most difficult challenge the Department of Homeland Security faces as thousands of people from foreign countries enter the United States legally and illegally every day, and millions of travelers yearly use domestic and international airlines.[7]

FYI

The United States Border Patrol is responsible for patrolling 6,000 miles of Mexican and Canadian international land borders and over 2,000 miles of coastal waters. Founded in 1924, the Border Patrol has over 21,000 agents (with thousands more called for by President Trump). Border Patrol agents train for 13 weeks at the Federal Law Enforcement Training Center in Artesia, New Mexico. Nearly half of the Border Patrol agents are Hispanic-Americans. Once they complete their training, the agents then are assigned to one of twenty enforcement sectors near the borders with Canada, Mexico, and the Caribbean. Besides the more traditional enforcement techniques such as binocular surveillance and horseback patrols, officers now use drones, heat sensors, and night-vision equipment to capture illegal immigrants crossing the border. In addition, the rugged SUV remains the primary means of chasing down those who would enter the United States illegally. Since 1924, 123 officers have been lost in the line of duty.

Source: Border Patrol website

Today the Department of Homeland Security is the backbone of our domestic anti-terror strategy. However, because defending the homeland can come in conflict with personal freedom and other constitutional protections, and actions taken by various government agencies in the name of homeland security can raise citizen concerns, there have been numerous court challenges and ongoing political disputes.

DEBATES, DIFFERENCES, AND DIVISIONS

The tactics used to fight terror and protect the homeland in the United States have frequently changed throughout the Bush and Obama administrations, but in many ways, the strategy has remained the same. When President Obama assumed the office of the presidency in 2009, he vowed to dismantle much of the architecture of the war on terror put in place by the Bush administration following the September 11th attacks. The administration believed that the Bush era counterterrorism tactics—which included the use of torture, the establishment of secret prisons worldwide, and widespread surveillance—had not only compromised American values and moral integrity but had also been counter-productive in confronting terrorist threats and, thus, had made America less safe. In his first days in office, President Obama issued an executive order that effectively closed CIA "black sites," a network of clandestine prisons around the world where enemy combatants could be detained and, allegedly, interrogated via extralegal means (President Bush—who established the sites through a presidential directive in 2001—had insisted that the interrogation techniques used at such sites were lawful). In another executive order, Obama clamped down on the use of torture by barring any "officer, employee, or other agent" of the US government from using interrogation techniques that are not in line with methods listed in the US Army manual.[8]

But even as the Obama administration went about dismantling some of the most controversial aspects of Bush's counterterrorism approach, he encountered difficulty in carrying through one of his most significant campaign promises, the closing of Camp Delta at the Guantanamo Naval Base in Cuba. The US government had established the detainment complex in 2002, shortly after the invasion of Afghanistan. International human rights organizations and numerous civil liberties groups in the United States accused the US military personnel at Camp Delta of using torture methods in violation of established international war standards. As information filtered out of Camp Delta that prisoners were being subjected to a form of interrogation called water boarding, the debate intensified across the United States, including the halls of Congress, over a permissible means of finding out key information from detainees.[9]

Because water boarding involves simulating the drowning experience by continuously pouring water over the detainee's face until he or she submits to answering questions, many critics of this policy stated that it was a violation of international agreements and placed the United States in the company of torturers. Bush administration officials denied the statement that water boarding was torture and stressed the importance of gaining valuable information from detainees. When asked about water boarding, then Vice-President Cheney stated, "We don't torture. That's not what we're involved in." Attorney General Michael Mukasey, who was less clear about water boarding, said,

"There are some circumstances where the current law would appear clearly to prohibit water boarding, but other circumstances would present a closer question." As for President Bush, his position was clear: "We do not condone torture. I have never ordered torture. I will never order torture. The values of this country are such that torture is not a part of our soul and our being."[10] But the use of water boarding had gained considerable attention in the US media and among the American public, raising serious questions about whether the United States condoned torture.

With the electoral victory of Barack Obama, there was much anticipation in Washington, and indeed around the world, about the potential closing of "Gitmo" (the airfield designation code for Guantanamo Bay). Quickly after the inauguration, Obama signed an executive order directing that Camp Delta be shut down. His decision to do so immediately created a deep political divide in Washington as Republican critics demanded to know what the president's plans were for the 245 detainees remaining at Camp Delta. There was concern among many in Washington that the release of detainees would be a serious threat to US national security. Senator John Thune of South Dakota explained, "The American people don't want these men walking the streets of America's neighborhoods."[11] Incidentally, lawmakers were also wary of the electoral consequences of supporting the closing of Gitmo, since many assumed detainees would simply begin fighting again after their release, and therefore, an attack on the homeland would leave lawmakers with blood on their hands. In attempting to downplay the consequences of the prison closing, Obama and his Secretary of Defense Robert Gates promised that detainees would be dispersed to federal prisons throughout the country or sent to prisons in foreign countries.[12] But this pledge did little to allay fears, as Senator Thune added, "The American people don't want these detainees held at a military base or federal prison in their back yard, either." The partisan division over the detainees became so intense that Congress denied funds for the closing of Camp Delta, as Democrats joined Republicans in a huge setback for the Obama administration.

The international politics involved in closing the US facility at Guantanamo Bay proved just as heady for the White House. Securing transfers of detainees to foreign detention centers required much "diplomatic pressure and financial bargaining" on the part of the administration, and these efforts often failed. Bulgaria and Yemen agreed to accept detainees only after relocation expenses and other financial incentives were negotiated. Similarly, while Germany was asked to accept nine Gitmo detainees, they agreed to the transfer of only two.[13] The political difficulties that came with attempting to close Gitmo never eased. During his eight years as president, Obama failed to make good on his most spirited campaign pledge, even though the number of detainees at Guantanamo had shrunk to just seventy-six in 2016.[14]

The handling of terrorist detainees has also created constitutional and institutional confrontations among the White House, Congress, the Supreme Court, and the American people during both the Bush and Obama administrations. In particular, the debate has concerned the right of detainees to have access to legal representation and, ultimately, a fair trial. The position of the executive branch dating back to 2002 was that the detainees were "unlawful combatants" who were outside the jurisdiction of civilian courts. Lawyers for the detainees complained that any individual held in a facility of the United States was entitled to challenge his or her detention, often termed the right of habeas corpus. As the issue of detainee rights worked its way through the federal court system, eventually the US Supreme Court issued a decision.

In Rasul v. Bush (2004), the Court in a 6–3 ruling stated that the terrorists had habeas corpus rights and further that detainees could file challenges in US district courts concerning their status as detainees. Later, in Hamadan v. Rumsfeld (2006), the Supreme Court, in a 5–3 decision, stated that the military commissions established by the Bush administration without Congressional approval were unconstitutional and that the procedures laid out in the Geneva Convention on the legal rights of detainees did apply to the "enemy combatants" held at Guantanamo. After years of legal jockeying, in 2008 the Supreme Court, by a vote of 5–4, overturned a Court of Appeals decision upholding the Military Commissions Act that says the guarantee of habeas corpus does not apply to those "without property or presence within the United States." The high court, however, stated that, indeed, detainees had the right to challenge their imprisonment before a federal civilian court, thus opening up the floodgates of petitions for trial by detainees and dealing the Bush administration a stunning defeat.[15] The controversial ruling (Boumedienne v. Bush) heightened legal activity as many of the detainees pressed the courts to hear their cases, and supporters of detainee rights rushed forward to advance the cases of those held without opportunity to have their case heard in court.[16] By 2011, the *Washington Post* reported, most detainees had "won their cases in lower courts."[17]

While the Obama administration had staunchly advocated for constitutional protections for detainees, it seemed to backtrack in 2012 when the Justice Department released a new set of rules that limited lawyers' access to detainees who had lost their initial habeas corpus petitions, citing security necessities. Obama's Department of Justice maintained that, "in the absence of active habeas petitions, lawyers do not need guaranteed access to their clients or to classified information necessary to pursue their claims," even when critics pointed to a lack of any credible evidence that classified information had been disclosed during the thousands of attorney-client visits that had transpired in past years.[18]

Obama also created controversy when he signed the National Defense Authorization Act in 2013 that expanded the power of the federal government to conduct anti-terror activities domestically. In particular, the bill renewed his power to apprehend and indefinitely detain those suspected of terrorist activities, even US citizens. Critics slammed the act as unconstitutional in that it effectively suspended the right of habeas corpus for American citizens. Obama expressed reservations about the bill, saying in a statement, "The fact that I support this bill as a whole does not mean I agree with everything in it," admitting that he had "serious reservations with certain provisions that regulate the detention, interrogation and prosecution of suspected terrorists."[19] Nonetheless, it was signed, leaving some Americans to ponder if the United States was reverting back to the secretive and abusive days of the Bush-era War on Terror.

While many Americans on the left condemned the Obama administration for its false promises on Guantanamo and its disregard of the rights of detainees, others criticized it for refusing to seek accountability for those in the Bush administration that had instituted the torture techniques used in Camp Delta. The torture issue continued to divide members of Congress as Democrats pushed for hearings that would bring Bush Justice Department officials to testify about their justification for the use of torture techniques such as water boarding. Assistant Attorney General (and later an Appeals Court Justice) Jay Bybee, White House Counsel John Yoo, and CIA General Counsel John Rizzo, among others, were targeted by Democrats as the chief supporters of the use of "enhanced interrogation techniques." There was also talk of a so-called Truth Commission to determine the extent of the Bush administration's support for the interrogation techniques, with the veiled threat of possible prosecution of key officials. President Obama showed little interest in these hearings or in a Truth Commission, fearing that it would divide the country and turn the attention of Washington policymakers, and indeed the country, away from his economic and domestic agenda.[20]

Another major component of the war on terror and the protection of the homeland has been an ever-expanding domestic surveillance program, designed to investigate and monitor those individuals in the United States who were deemed potential or real terrorist threats. Within weeks of 9/11, Congress overwhelmingly passed (and President Bush signed) the USA Patriot Act, which provided the government with wide powers to search the personal records, cell phone conversations, Internet communications, and other information of those who were viewed as "enemy combatants." By defining these individuals as enemy combatants, the Patriot Act established a new and controversial level of extra-constitutional powers, as the FBI was given expanded legal discretion to engage in these searches. At the same time Congress also created the Foreign Intelligence Surveillance Court, which was authorized to approve the searches. As constituted, the federal judges on the court meet in secret and legitimize the actions taken by the government under the Patriot Act.

Right from the outset, the Patriot Act was the target of civil libertarians, lawyers groups, and a number of institutions such as libraries and colleges. Critics of the act stated that there was little debate over the legislation and little consideration given to the impact of the Patriot Act on constitutionally protected rights. In total, twelve existing laws were amended with significant changes, which greatly expanded the powers of government to interfere in an area that in the past was deemed private. In particular, so-called "sneak-and-peak" provisions of the new law allow law enforcement officials to conduct surreptitious searches and seizures using a new standard of "reasonable necessity" and permit authorities the option of not notifying the target of the searches that a search and seizure action has been taken. Both of these investigatory powers were changes from established Federal Rules of Criminal Procedures but were deemed necessary to gather information of suspected terrorists.[21]

Initially public opinion was solidly in favor of the legislation, as many Americans wanted the government to take aggressive action to protect the homeland from a terrorist threat, even if it meant a lessening of individual liberties. But support for the Patriot Act has waned after numerous public critiques of the dangers of expanded government investigatory power. Moreover, the American public seemed to turn against domestic surveillance programs in 2013 after former National Security Agency (NSA) contractor, Edward Snowden, leaked classified documents that revealed a massive and secretive global surveillance program under the direction of the NSA. The fallout from the Snowden affair was immediate, with some labeling the whistleblower a hero and others stamping him a traitor, while the US Department of Justice charged him with two counts of violating the 1917 Espionage Act. Nonetheless, in response to his disclosures, many Americans—as well as citizens in nations where counterterrorism officials have cooperated with NSA programs—became more skeptical about a grand bargain between their security and their privacy.

The Patriot Act and the NSA's surveillance program have also triggered political battles between the White House and Congress and within the halls of the Capitol. The Democrats have consistently favored rewriting the Patriot Act, or at least changing it significantly, to limit the power of the president to conduct such practices as unlimited roving surveillance or to demand business records of suspected terrorists. Facing formidable pressure from Democrats, President Bush agreed to seek judicial approval for wiretaps and email monitoring and promised that he would abide by established procedures. Facing that same pressure, the Obama administration took action to institute serious reform of the government's surveillance powers. In June 2015, President Obama signed the USA Freedom Act, which included stipulations that removed the authority of the NSA to collect bulk records of Americans' telephone records and added measures of transparency to the way that the government collects information. The reform, however, was only a small part of a much larger act that was a direct derivative of the original Patriot Act—which had expired the day before its passing—and contained many of its same provisions. In fact, the expiration of the Patriot Act was the result of a congressional standoff in which Republican Senator (and presidential candidate) Rand Paul had used the filibuster to prevent the renewal of what he called "the most unpatriotic of acts." On the Senate floor, he advocated for "an open rebellion," asking his colleagues, "Do we really want to live in a world where the government has us under constant surveillance?"[22]

While Obama had taken steps to reign in the authority of those agencies charged with protecting the Homeland, many of Obama's critics on the left argue that the president had, in fact, "presided over a vast increase in domestic and foreign surveillance through the NSA."[23] In doing so, he has betrayed his commitment to constitutional principles by effectively expanding the so-called "national security state."[24] For one, the Obama administration chose to retain Keith Alexander as chief of the NSA. Alexander, a three star general, had headed the agency since 2005 and was widely criticized for the creation of the NSA's metadata surveillance program, which involved secretly tracking every phone in the United States. The reappointment of Alexander did little to calm the fears of Americans that their privacy was being violated in the name of counterterrorism efforts. Other critics pointed to Obama's complicity in expanding surveillance globally by supporting such initiatives as the SOMAL-GET mission, a covert program in which the United States illegally obtained access to communications networks in the Bahamas in order to "tap, record and store cellular data" for the purpose of intercepting narcotics traffickers and human smugglers.[25] While Obama had declared that "in a dangerous world, government must have the authority to collect the intelligence we need to protect the American people," his critics pointed out that the SOMALGET mission had little to do with actual counterterrorism efforts, since Americans face no real threat of terrorism originating from the stable Bahamian democracy.[26] More concerning to civil libertarians in America, however, was that, in their view, Obama had taken few steps to ensure oversight of the surveillance state. As James Banford explained in a *Foreign Policy* article, Obama once threatened to veto a bill that "would have required him to brief all members of congressional intelligence committees about covert operations" and has used the Justice Department to intimidate whistle blowers in the intelligence community.[27]

Data Bank

The number of undocumented immigrants who have been deported (or "removed" in the language of the US Border Patrol) has been an issue of some debate during the Obama presidency and, once again, during the Trump presidency. Using data from the Border Patrol from 2011–2016, the numbers are listed below:

    2011–396,906
    2012–409,844
    2013–368,644
    2014–577,295
    2015–235,413
    2016–240,255

Source: US Border Patrol website

While Obama's support for mass surveillance at home was heavily criticized (especially by liberals and libertarians), assessments of Obama's counterterrorism efforts abroad have been mixed. Some point to his notable

"War on Terror" victories, such as the 2011 CIA-led raid on an Abbottabad, Pakistan compound that led to the capture and killing of 9/11 mastermind, Osama bin Laden. Others claim that, in addition to taking out al Qaeda's central node and key operative, the Obama administration was successful in significantly weakening the entire al Qaeda network structure by implementing a 30,000 troop surge in Afghanistan in 2009. Furthermore, many argue that Obama's overall counterterrorism orientation of utilizing drone strikes and covert operations to target terrorist command posts (such as high technology raids conducted by the Army's "Green Berets") has been a shrewd and effective tactic. These types of "surgical strikes" eliminate the need to engage in "boots on the ground" counter-insurgency missions, which so often result in a quagmire.

Still others highlight his overseeing of an historic pact with the Islamic Republic of Iran (as well as the permanent members of the U.N. Security Council, Germany, and the European Union), which negotiated a reduction in Iran's capacity to enrich uranium and permitted inspectors from the International Atomic Energy Agency to monitor its facilities in exchange for the lifting of international sanctions on the regime. Signed in 2015, the Joint Comprehensive Plan of Action (JPCOA)—known colloquially as the Iran Deal—advances US national security interests by limiting the proliferation of nuclear materials in the increasingly volatile region of the Middle East. In doing so, its proponents argue, the Iran Deal has made important steps in furthering America's long-standing nonproliferation agenda and, ultimately, protecting the homeland.

But for each of these victories, critics have pointed to Obama administration policies that have endangered US national interests, weakened our position in the world, and, ultimately, have made the American public less safe. While Obama scored a political victory in ending an unpopular war by withdrawing a majority of US troops from Iraq in 2010, the United States left a political vacuum in Baghdad that resulted in renewed sectarian violence across the country. Conservative detractors accused the Obama administration of creating a breeding ground for fundamentalist groups in Iraq and essentially paving the way for the rise of ISIS, a group that has terrorized populations throughout the West with its attacks on civilians. Also, while President Obama could be credited with taking down the notorious Osama bin Laden, his critics argue that US strategy in Afghanistan has ultimately failed. After the United States began reducing its troop presence in Afghanistan, the Taliban simply regained control of strategically important territory in the country. Moreover, critics from both the left and the right have heavily criticized the administration's use of drone warfare and secretive operations. Conservatives argue that Obama relied on the use of drones simply because he was unwilling to put "boots on the ground" to fight terrorists abroad (in Syria, for example), and that such fecklessness has only destabilized the region further. Obama's opponents from the left argue that Obama's use of drones has proven counterproductive to his desire to "win a war of wills and ideas" because of collateral damage from strikes that have unintentionally hit civilian targets, potentially radicalizing those populations.[28] Obama, they argue, was just as aggressive in the "War on Terror" as his outwardly "hawkish" predecessors, merely conducting his war in the shadows and, thus, avoiding scrutiny. Finally, many have questioned whether Obama's Iran Deal truly benefits our national security interests, since the removal of sanctions makes available a pool of funds that the Iranian regime could use to support terrorist groups like Hezbollah that have actively worked to destabilize its neighbors. In short, each of these foreign policy endeavors have been subject to significant scrutiny, with many arguing that Obama's counterterrorism efforts have threatened the interests of the United States in the Middle East, a region of immense geostrategic importance.

The most fervent critic of Obama's counterterrorism policies was his successor to the presidency, Donald J. Trump. Trump's electoral success had much to do with his ability to channel the fears of the American public about terrorism and homeland security to his own political advantage. The billionaire businessman was enormously effective on the campaign trail in portraying American borders as porous and American leadership as feeble in the face of what conservatives coined "radical Islamic terrorism," a term Trump criticized President Obama for refusing to use. President Trump's narrative was dark: not only had our failing homeland security infrastructure allowed potential terrorists onto our soil but had also permitted criminal elements from Central and South America to pour over our southern border, leading to a marked increase in crime in our communities. In statements to the media and at rallies across the United States, Trump promised that he would implement deportations of undocumented immigrants and impose restrictions on the ability of Muslims from abroad to enter the United States "until our country's representatives can figure out what's going on."[29] Other conservatives were also highly critical of the state of homeland security under the Obama administration, in particular his decision to expand an initiative admitting refugees of the drug war in Guatemala, Honduras, and El Salvador into the United States. Republicans lambasted Obama for exacerbating a border crisis with a misuse of his authority that, as Republican Congressman Robert Goodlatte explained, essentially rewards "individuals who have no lawful presence in the United States with the ability to bring their family members here."[30]

On the Record

President Trump's initial appointment to head the Department of Homeland Security, General John F. Kelly, in his testimony before the House of Representatives Committee on Homeland Security, presented his views on protecting our borders. A portion of his testimony follows:

As a nation, control of our borders is paramount. Without that control, every other form of threat—illicit drugs, unauthorized immigrants, transnational organized crime, certain dangerous communicable diseases, terrorists—could enter at will. DHS was created to prevent terrorist attacks against the United States. . . . Achieving this priority begins with physical obstacles like a border barrier and supporting infrastructure and surveillance capabilities. In this effort, I am committed to executing President Trump's plan to secure our southern border with effective physical barriers, advanced technology, and strategic deployment of law enforcement personnel. While the presence of physical barriers and additional technology is essential, it must be bolstered by the persistent patrol and vigilance of dedicated men and women of DHS.

Source: February 7, 2017, US Capitol.

After winning the presidency and securing a majority in both the House and the Senate, Donald Trump has attempted to make good on his campaign promises. Shortly after taking the oath of office in January 2017, President Trump signed an executive order that limits travel to the United States of all refugees as well as individuals from seven majority Muslim countries, including Iran, Somalia, Iraq, Libya, Sudan, Syria, and Yemen. The order immediately caused chaos and confusion at major US airports as Customs and Border Protection officials attempted to carry out the order without clear instructions. In addition, the order fueled immediate outrage, as well as spirited protests, as stories about the relatives of American citizens being detained at airports circulated across the media. Many argued that the "Muslim Ban" was not only unconstitutional but fundamentally Anti-American, averse to the values of religious freedom that the country holds dear. The Trump administration vehemently denied that the order was meant to single out Muslims; rather, it was designed to protect our national security by relieving our overburdened homeland security infrastructure. Moreover, they argued, the countries subject to the ban had already been designated as terrorist "hotspots" and subject to some travel restrictions during the Obama administration. Almost immediately after its issuance, the order faced legal challenges and was ultimately suspended by US District Judge James Robart in Seattle. The US Supreme Court, in June 2017, stated in a unanimous decision that it would review the travel ban in October, but in the meantime, access to the United States from the seven countries has been limited to those who have family members in the United States or a job offer or academic appointment. President Trump claimed a victory with the decision, stating that the court upheld his ban, but the victory was only partial and critics of the ban wait for their day in court in October to show how the ban was based on religion, not national security. The fate of President Trump's executive order is uncertain. Nonetheless, it is clear that the Trump administration will be taking a different approach to counterterrorism and homeland security than its predecessor.

The Great Debate

At the heart of the debate about how best to secure the homeland is the issue of the proper balance between personal freedom and national security.

Debate Topic

Can we protect the country from a terrorist attack and still remain an open and free democracy?

Critical Thinking Questions

1. Has the government gone too far in restricting personal rights to protect the homeland from terrorist attacks?
2. What role, if any, should the American public play in protecting the homeland from a terrorist attack?
3. Do you believe that water boarding is torture? What interrogation techniques should be permissible?
4. What rights should foreign terrorist detainees have under the US Constitution?
5. Is the use of drone strikes a more effective approach to counterterrorism than sending soldiers into harm's way to perform counterinsurgency missions? Given that drone strikes carry the potentiality of civilian casualties, is it a more just approach?

Connections

The first place to start to understand homeland security is at the Department's website: www.homelandsecurity.gov

The website of the National Counterterrorism Center offers many resources on US counterterrorism efforts. It can be accessed at www.nctc.gov/index.html

The American Civil Liberties Union has been the most outspoken critic of the US national security state. Its website can be accessed at www.aclu.org

The University of Maryland's Global Terrorism Database (GTD) collects information on terrorist events around the world. View the website and data at http://start.umd.edu/gtd/about/

The Journal of Homeland Security and Emergency Management is a useful guide to the latest research and opinion on domestic security issues. See www.degruyter.com/view/j/jhsem

Some Books to Read

Bobbitt, Philip, *Terror and Consent: The Wars for the Twenty-First Century* (New York: A.A. Knopf, 2008).

Greenwald, Glenn, *No Place to Hide: Edward Snowden, the NSA, and the U.S. Surveillance State* (New York: Macmillan, 2014).

McChrystal, Stanley, Tantum Collins, David Silverman, and Chris Fussell, *Team of Teams: New Rules of Engagement for a Complex World* (New York: Penguin, 2015).

Mueller, John and Mark Stewart, *Chasing Ghosts* (New York: Oxford University Press, 2016).

Yoo, John, *War By Other Means: An Insider's Account of the War on Terror* (New York: Grove Press, 2007).

Notes

1. For background on the run-up to the Afghanistan invasion see Bob Woodward, *Plan of Attack* (New York: Simon and Schuster, 2004).
2. For background on the preparations for the invasion of Iraq see Robert Draper, *Dead Certain: The Presidency of George W. Bush* (New York: Free Press, 2007).
3. See the Department of Homeland Security website, www.dhs.gov
4. www.dhs.gov/files/programs/preparedness.shtm
5. www.dhs.gov/files/programs/critical-infrastructure.shtm
6. See statement of Bradley I. Buswell, "Undersecretary (Acting) Science and Technology Directorate Department of Homeland Security," US House of Representatives, Committee on Appropriations, Sub-Committee on Homeland Security, March 26, 2009.
7. www.usatoday.com/news/washington/2004-12-27-homelandUSAT_x.htm
8. See "President Issues Executive Order Banning Torture and CIA Prisons," *The American Journal of International Law*, Vol. 103, No. 2 (April, 2009), pp. 331–334.
9. For a discussion of the reform of Abu Ghraib prison see a study conducted by the Carnegies Endowment for Peace at www.carnegieendowment.org/arb/?fa=show$article=22772
10. These quotes were presented in the *Washington Post National Weekly Edition*, February 18–24, 2008, p. 9.
11. David Herszenhorn, "Funds to Close Guantanamo Denied," *The New York Times*, May 20, 2009.
12. Sheryl Gay Stolberg, "Obama Would Move Some Detainees to U.S.," *The New York Times*, May 22, 2009.
13. Connie Bruck, "Why Obama Has Failed to Close Guantanamo," *The New Yorker*, August 1, 2016.
14. Charlie Savage, "2 Guantanamo Prisoners Are Transferred to Serbia," *The New York Times*, July 11, 2016.
15. *Hamadan v. Rumsfeld* 126 S. Ct. 2749 (2004).
16. For a discussion of the court decision regarding detainee rights in civilian court see Ronald Dworkin, "Why It Was a Great Victory," *New York Review of Books*, August 14, 2008, pp. 18–21.
17. Baher Azmy, "Obama Turns Back the Clock on Guantanamo," *The Washington Post*, August 16, 2012.
18. Ibid.
19. Julia Azari, *The Presidential Leadership Dilemma: Between the Constitution and a Political Party* (Albany, NY: SUNY Press, 2013), p. 201.

20. For background on this issue of the Bush torture policy see "Investigation into the Office of Legal Counsel's Memoranda Concerning Issues Relating to the Central Intelligence Agency's Use of 'Enhanced Interrogation Techniques' on Suspected Terrorists," a report by the Office of Professional Responsibility, Department of Justice (February 19, 2010). For a discussion of this report see David Cole, "They Did Authorize Terror, But. . .," *New York Review of Books*, April 8, 2010, pp. 42–43.

21. Charlie Savage, "Judge Rules Against FBI on Data Gathering," *Boston Globe*, September 7, 2007, p. A2.

22. Jordain Carney, "Paul Wages Patriot Act Filibuster With Call for an 'Open Rebellion,'" *The Hill*, May 20, 2015.

23. Michael Boyle, "President Obama's Disastrous Counterterrorism Legacy," *The Guardian*, August 5, 2013.

24. For more, see Dana Priest and William M. Arkin, "A Hidden World, Growing Beyond Control," *The Washington Post*, July 19, 2010, http://projects.washingtonpost.com/top-secret-america/articles/a-hidden-world-growing-beyond-control/print/

25. James Bamford, "Every Move You Make," *Foreign Policy*, September 7, 2016.

26. Lindsey Grudnicki, "President Obama on Privacy and Civil Liberties: A Retrospective," *The National Review*, June 10, 2013.

27. Bamford, "Every Move You Make."

28. Boyle, "President Obama's Disastrous Counterterrorism Legacy."

29. See "Donald J. Trump Statement on Preventing Muslim Immigration," December 7, 2015, www.donaldjtrump.com/press-releases/donald-j.-trump-statement-on-preventing-muslim-immigration

30. Julie Hirschfeld Davis, "U.S. to Admit More Central American Refugees," *The New York Times*, July 26, 2016.

2

THE **MIDDLE** CLASS **AND**
THE **AMERICAN** DREAM

Issue Focus

The United States is a country of great diversity—ethnic, racial, religious, language—yet in the area of socio-economic class, Americans often describe themselves as being in the middle. There are certainly Americans who reside at the bottom of the economic scale, mired in poverty, and there are those who make up the wealthy, the so-called 1%. Because being middle class is so pervasive as an identifying characteristic of American life, it is important to examine the current status of this socio-economic construct and its relationship to the political and government systems. The middle class in the United States is indeed changing, and those who are part of this segment of our society are increasingly playing a significant role in defining the challenges faced by this country. In many respects the future direction of the United States will be determined by how those in governing power respond to the challenges faced by the middle class.

Chapter Objectives
This issue chapter will seek to:
1. Describe the current economic and financial condition of the American middle class and the impact those changes have had on their political behavior and outlook for the future.
2. Discuss how the two most recent major candidates for the presidency, Hillary Clinton and Donald Trump, responded to the changing character of middle-class life through their statements and policy proposals.
3. Evaluate the short-term and long-term influences of the middle-class crisis on American democracy and the American dream of prosperity and financial security.

One of the foundational explanations of the American experience is that this country is a land of opportunity where those who live here can make their dreams come true. With hard work, determination, and a personal commitment to use their innate talents, Americans, whether immigrants or those who have lived here for generations, can succeed individually, in groups, and within a family unit.[1] As a corollary to this view of the American dream is the belief in the growth and strength of the middle class. Although often difficult to define with precision, the middle class is comprised of those millions of Americans who live with a modicum of comfort and security and have incomes and wealth above those defined as poor; they are small business people, skilled trades men and women, factory workers, and professionals;

they own homes, send their children to college, enjoy vacations, and are able to build a retirement nest egg. While not wildly rich, the American middle class validates our capitalist system with its ability to generate new opportunities and new wealth and, in the process, provide a solid economic center that engenders hope in the future.[2]

This foundational explanation for the American experience is now under attack as the American dream slips into irrelevancy and the middle class undergoes a disturbing transformation, shedding the comfort and security of the past to be replaced with uncertainty, a narrowing of opportunities, financial distress, and a loss of faith in the future. Over the last twenty years, and especially since the economic collapse of 2009 and the Great Recession, many Americans who make up the broad middle class have lost their jobs, their homes, their savings, and most of all, their confidence in the economic system that had in the past worked for them. According to a study funded by the Russell Sage Foundation, "the inflation-adjusted net worth of the typical household, one at the median point of wealth distribution, was $87,992 in 2003. By 2013 it had declined to $84,500."[3]

This drop in wealth for those Americans in the middle class is not just a set of numbers generated by academic studies, it has real everyday consequences. What this drop has meant for many Americans in the middle class is a real life validation of the old adage of living paycheck to paycheck— that is, if there is a paycheck. Neal Gabler, in an article in *The Atlantic*, talked about the financial impotence of the middle class and their fiscal fragility when faced with a household crisis. Using responses to Federal Reserve Bank and Pew Charitable Trust surveys and his own experience, Gabler found that many Americans are having serious problems finding the money to pay for essential expenses like an emergency room visit or a car repair payment. These surveys found that 55% of American households did not have enough liquid savings to replace a month's worth of lost income, and 71% were concerned about "having enough money to cover everyday expenses."[4] Gabler, although a prize-winning journalist and writer, admitted that there were times in recent years when he was part of the 47% of Americans who responded in the Federal Reserve Bank study saying they would have to borrow funds or sell a possession in order to come up with the money to cover a $400 expense.[5]

Because of this precipitous drop in household wealth and the real life consequences of financial impotence, there is mounting evidence that the middle class as we have traditionally understood this social group is indeed shrinking. The Pew Charitable Trust study is especially revealing. From 2000 to 2014 the share of adults living in middle-income households fell in 203 of the 229 US metropolitan areas examined. The study found that, in many cases, the decrease in the size of the middle class was substantial, dropping as much as 4–6 percentage points. The Pew study also concluded that their findings pointed to the need to redefine the middle class because it may no longer be characterized as a majority of the American population.[6] In fact, the American middle class, by most measures, has lost the distinction as the most affluent of social groups in the world. Those in the middle class in many of the advanced industrial countries have either tied the United States in terms of median income (Canada) or are closing the income gap (Great Britain, the Netherlands, and Sweden) and may indeed surpass the United States if the trend of middle class decline in this country continues.[7] In 2014 the US Commerce Department set $130,000 as the benchmark income level for middle-class status for a family of four. Median income in 2014 was about half that amount.[8]

One of the key underlying sources of the demise of the American dream and the shrinking of the middle class in the United States is the growing level of income inequality. Simply put, while those at the high end of the income scale have seen enormous growth in income in recent years, those at the bottom of the income ladder and those in the middle have seen only modest growth, if not stagnation. Congressional Budget Office data show that from 1979 till 2005 the mean after-tax income of the top 1% of Americans increased by an inflation-adjusted 176%, while the middle quintile rose by 21%. Those Americans in the bottom quintile rose only 6%. This shift of wealth to the 1% has only increased in recent years. Writing for the Harvard Business Review in 2015 William Lazonick stated, "Five years after the official end of the Great Recession, corporate profits are high, and the stock markets are booming. Yet most Americans are not sharing in the recovery. While the top .1% of income recipients—which include most of the highest-ranking corporate executives—reap almost all the income gains, good jobs keep disappearing, and new employment opportunities tend to be insecure and underpaid."[9]

Data Bank

Income Range for Middle-Income Households

	Lowest	Lower Middle	Middle	Upper Middle
2014	$31,402	$41,868	$125,608	$188,412
2010	$31,042	$41,389	$124,169	$186,253
2000	$33,314	$44,418	$133,256	$199,884
1990	$29,651	$39,533	$118,603	$177,905
1980	$26,486	$35,313	$105,942	$158,913
1970	$23,610	$31,479	$94,439	$141,659

Source: Pew Research Center Analysis of the Current Population Survey, Annual Social and Economic Supplements, 1971, 1981, 1991, 2001, 2011, 2015.

The challenges faced by the American middle class coupled with the growing level of income inequality has had a marked effect on the political system, especially in the recent campaign for the presidency. In 2016 both

Hillary Clinton and Donald Trump used the plight of the middle class as talking points designed to advance their candidacy and presented policy prescriptions that they viewed as remedies to level the economic and financial playing fields. Clinton's major challenge in the primary season was from Senator Bernie Sanders of Vermont, who effectively characterized the economic system as "rigged" in favor of Wall Street and major corporations and Clinton as beholden to financial elites evidenced by her highly paid speeches to major banking institutions like Goldman Sachs. Sanders gained popularity among the young and the disaffected middle class who had been hit hard by the Great Recession and were mistrustful of Clinton's sincerity as a champion of the middle class.[10]

Because of the effectiveness of the Sanders message Clinton began to embrace policy positions that were designed to appeal to Americans who experienced the stresses of a system that favored the wealthy. Clinton presented an eight-point policy proposal designed to, as she stated, "give the middle class a raise." The eight points of the proposal were:

1. Cut middle class taxes and raise taxes on the wealthy
2. Make college affordable
3. Raise the minimum wage
4. Support unions
5. Rebuild infrastructure
6. Boost manufacturing jobs
7. Invest in clean energy
8. Lower childcare costs

Source: Hillary Clinton campaign website

On the campaign trail, Clinton emphasized the college affordability, minimum wage, and equal pay components as she sought to increase her appeal to younger voters, the working poor, and women. Specifically, Clinton promised to develop a program through the states to provide free college tuition to those who meet acceptance standards. In the area of minimum wage, she supported a gradual increase, starting at $12.00 and working up to $15.00 an hour. In the equal pay component, she often castigated Republicans who fought against legislation that would foster greater pay equality in the workplace. By taking stronger positions on middle-class issues like college tuition, minimum wage, and equal pay, Clinton eventually won the Democratic nomination but not before Sanders and his supporters pushed her to take so-called progressive stances and lessen her ties to big money elites on Wall Street and corporations.[11]

Trump, on the other hand, developed a campaign strategy that played to the anxieties and anger of the middle class in states hit hard by job losses in a globalized economy and criticized the failure of Democrats to pay attention to the needs and aspirations of white Americans. Trump effectively pushed aside Republican candidates during the primary season with his positions on stopping illegal immigration, renegotiating trade agreements, and claiming that if elected he would be the voice of those left behind in the middle class. Trump touted his reputed business acumen and negotiating skills to convince middle-class voters that he could bring change to the stagnant Washington political environment and grow the American economy in ways that shifted economic and financial benefits to the long-forgotten, white middle class.[12]

In one of his major speeches to the Detroit Economic Club entitled "An America First Plan: Winning the Global Competition," Trump outlined his economic plan, with particular emphasis on how he would respond to the deteriorating condition of the American middle class. The major points of that address are:

1. An across-the-board income tax cut with special emphasis on cuts that benefit the middle class.
2. An economic plan to "jump start" the American economy that would add millions of jobs by lowering corporate tax rates.
3. An end to many business regulations that add to the cost of doing business and retard hiring.
4. Trade reform, especially enforcing controls on Chinese currency policies and returning jobs to the United States.
5. Energy reform that enhances opportunities for workers in coal-producing states.
6. Childcare policies that allow families with children to deduct from their income taxes the average cost of childcare.

Source: Trump campaign website

Of special interest to Trump's promise to the middle class was his opposition to the North American Free Trade Agreement (NAFTA), negotiated by President George H.W. Bush and signed by President Bill Clinton, as a major source of lost jobs in the manufacturing sector, especially in the Rust Belt states of Indiana, Michigan, Ohio, Pennsylvania, and West Virginia. He further took aim at the Trans Pacific Partnership agreement (TTP) signed by President Obama but not approved by the US Senate. The agreement was designed to further trade opportunities in Asia (China was not included) but was viewed by Trump as a "bad deal" that would hurt the American economy and the middle class. In both instances, Trump talked about bringing manufacturing jobs back to the United States and linked Hillary Clinton to the globalized economy through her husband's support for NAFTA and her early support for the TTP. Both agreements he claimed robbed the white working class of jobs as manufacturing went south to Mexico or east to Asia. Trump also presented a tax plan that he claimed would create 25 million new jobs and increase the nation's GDP by an annual rate of over 3%. Further, he offered a childcare proposal presented by his daughter Ivanka Trump that was designed to appeal to middle-class mothers. Still, the core of his relief for the middle class remained in the areas of trade, immigration, and jobs.[13]

On the Record

Hillary Clinton said the following about the middle class:

> I'm running for president because every day Americans and their families need a champion, and I want to be that champion. I want to make the words middle class mean something again.

Donald Trump said the following about the middle class:

> The hedge fund guys are getting away with murder . . . The middle class are getting absolutely destroyed. This country won't have a middle class.

Sources: Clinton and Trump campaign websites

FYI

The Ten Metropolitan Areas That Lost the Most in Economic Status from 2000–2014

Some metropolitan areas in the United States did experience gains in middle-class status due in large part to special job-creating circumstances—energy-based economies, information technology, and tourism—but the ten metropolitan areas below suffered the greatest loss of middle-class status during the period studied.

Rocky Mount, North Carolina
Rockford, Illinois
Detroit-Warren-Dearborn, Michigan
Mansfield, Ohio
Fort Wayne, Indiana
Michigan City-La Porte, Indiana
Hickory-Lenoir-Morganton, North Carolina
Jackson, Michigan
Goldsboro, North Carolina
Springfield, Ohio

The common denominator in the above ten metropolitan areas that suffered the greatest loss in economic status—often termed a shrinking of middle-class status—was a decline in manufacturing and manufacturing jobs. These metropolitan areas, many in the Midwestern Rust Belt, were hit hard by the movement of jobs overseas or the replacement of jobs through technological advances.

Source: Pew Research Center, 2016, "America's Shrinking Middle Class: A Close Look at Changes Within Metropolitan Areas."

If there is a core explanatory condition that explains the support for Donald Trump and the divisiveness present in American politics and national life it is anger, specifically middle-class anger. It is not just that individual income has flatlined in the last twenty years, or that those without college degrees have a much higher degree of unemployment, or that inequality is getting worse; anger has entered the psyche of American life, especially among the middle class. In January 2016, *Esquire* magazine, in collaboration with NBC, interviewed 3,000 Americans and asked them a range of questions about their attitudes and beliefs about the current state of this country and their own lives. Two questions that were particularly revealing were the following:

"About how often do you hear or read something in the news that makes you angry?"

Among whites, 73% said that they get angry at least once a day. The most angry were those in what was described as the middle of the middle class—earning between $50,000 and $75,000.

The second question related to the American dream:

"Do you think the American dream—if you work hard you'll get ahead—is alive and well?"

Among the respondents, 52% stated that this vision of America once held true but not anymore. Those respondents between 45 and 64, particularly white males, showed the least confidence in the American dream.[14]

This anger and loss of confidence in the American dream has not only contributed to the divisiveness and partisan intransigence in American politics but also has had a deleterious impact on American democracy. The conventional wisdom related to the middle class in politics and national life is that this large group of citizens served as the "glue" that held the political system together. The middle class was viewed by political scientists and political pundits as the solid center of American democracy, the stabilizing force that both parties sought as the key not just to victory but also to ensuring a stable political system. The term middle is not just an economic condition used to describe financial circumstances but a description of the quality of moderation that being in the middle suggests. Moderate politics that shifted only a short distance from the moderate right to the moderate left, from moderate conservatism to moderate liberalism, were the mode in which politics was defined.[15]

But after eight years of divisiveness and intransigent partisanship in American politics during the Obama presidency, the middle class is no longer a dependable stabilizer of our democratic system. In fact, the middle class is the source of all the anxiety and anger that fostered the Tea Party, the Occupy Wall Street movement, the candidacy of Bernie Sanders, and the rise of Donald Trump. The American middle class is now not a moderating force that brings our political system to the center but one that tears the system apart as those in the middle demand to be heard, demand change, demand throwing out the governing elites who have let them down and ignored their needs. This middle-class disenchantment has reshaped American politics, creating great uncertainty as candidates no longer have a reliable and moderating influence on the political system.

If the American political system and, indeed, American democracy is to restore the moderation and stability of the middle class, it may be enabled by a recent change announced by the US Census Bureau. The Census Bureau announcement in September 2016 that median household incomes had increased substantially for the first time since 2007 was one of the first tangible signs that the economy was rebounding in a way that would assist the struggling middle class. Median income—the level at which half of the households are above and half are below—rose to $56,500 in 2015, a 5% increase of nearly $3,000 from 2014. Incomes rose for every age and demographic group with non-Hispanic whites gaining 4.4%, Hispanics 6%, and low-income families 8%. Coupled with the steady drop in the unemployment rate and the resulting competition for workers, wages in the United States rose in the 2014–2015 period, contributing to the bump in the median income.[16] As Chris Christopher, an economist at a forecasting firm in Lexington, Massachusetts, stated about the increase, "The middle class, is finally, finally, gaining a bit of traction . . . it's been a long slog."[17] Most economists saw the increase as likely to continue on into next year.

Nevertheless, the good news on the substantial rise in median household income was balanced by continued troubling data on income inequality. The Census Bureau found that income inequality increased by 5.5% since 1993, which translated into only marginal gains in the overall financial condition of most Americans. Should the median income numbers continue to rise for an extended period of time, the middle class may indeed find that their economic status has improved, but one positive data point is not sufficient to change the mood of the increasingly angry middle class. Robert Shapiro, a senior fellow at Georgetown University's School of Business and a former undersecretary of commerce during the Clinton administration stated, ". . . there are still many Americans in their prime working age who have fallen behind in this century as manufacturing jobs have waned and the economy has focused on high-technology, degree-based jobs. They lost their jobs, and lost the value of their houses during the last recession, and more recent gains haven't been enough. For those people they're still not back to where they were and they are still angry."[18]

The fate of the American middle class and, indeed, the American dream remains unclear. The message of anger and anxiety within the middle class has certainly been transmitted throughout the political system. Politicians within the two major parties, ideological pundits, and the Washington elites know that the divisions in our country are less that of party or ideas or age and more about the economic gaps between those who have prospered and those who have been left behind. Americans in the vast middle class have defined their country in ways quite different from the past, and the election of 2016 is evidence that those seeking public office and governing power will need to develop policy prescriptions that respond to the concerns of a segment of society that is marked by uncertainty and instability.

Indeed, whole paradigms of national economic and political life will need to be reexamined. Globalization with its emphasis on the unrelenting spread of free trade at the expense of traditional job security and employment stability will undoubtedly be seen anew through a new critical lens, a middle-class lens. Pay structures, whether equal pay for women, minimum wage increases, or most importantly, staggering income inequality that separates the 1% at the top in Wall Street and corporate boardrooms from the average man and woman on Main Street are ripe for review. Further, the long-neglected immigration conundrum about the impact of the undocumented on the American economy will need to be resolved.

Perhaps the most challenging issue for the US government and, indeed, the American public will be about redistribution policies. Part of the Trump victory in the 2016 election was related to the perception of many in the middle class, especially the lower middle class, that the Obama administration, and even those administrations before his presidency, paid far too much attention and distributed scarce resources to the poor, minorities, and new arrivals, both legal and illegal. While a good case can be made that government policies have in the past helped the middle class, such as the home mortgage deduction and Medicare, the perception among those in the middle class who voted for Trump was that the Democrats and Hillary Clinton had forgotten them. In the coming years, the policy battles faced by the Trump administration regarding redistribution initiatives for the middle class through tax cuts and job growth will be front and center in the political arena.[19]

If this country continues to lose the glue that the middle class has provided the economic and political systems, then the partisan, ideological, and demographic divisions will only deepen and further weaken our nation. James Carville, Bill Clinton's campaign advisor during the 1992 election, coined the now-famous, political call-out "It's the Economy, Stupid." Although a bit brash in content, Carville knew that the economic condition of the American economy drove politics and political decisions. But what he didn't know at the time was that the state of the American economy can also destroy traditional politics and foster a decline of American democracy. Of all the issues presented in this book, the current state and future direction of the American middle class is at the core of defining what our democracy is and will become.

The Great Debate

There have been many proposals forwarded by candidates for the presidency and other national and state government offices that focus on assisting and advancing the middle class—increasing the minimum wage, free college tuition, equal pay for women, tax cuts, and jobs expansion.

Debate Topic

As you look at these proposals in areas such as trade agreements, equal pay reforms, minimum wage increases, and tax cuts, what policies do you feel will best benefit the struggling middle class in this country?

Critical Thinking Questions

1. Why did government leaders in Washington fail to take steps to respond to the plight of the American middle class?
2. Is it realistic for those members of the middle class who lost their jobs in manufacturing to enter a new workforce based on high technology?
3. Is the anger expressed, especially by white males of the middle class, a short-term condition or a new behavior pattern that will affect our national political system?
4. Does the American dream still exist or is it a myth with little contemporary relevance?
5. How would you define your socio-economic status and your confidence in your future?

Connections

The most frequently quoted study on the middle class comes from the Pew Research Center, http://pewsocialtrends.org/2016/05/11/americas-shrinking-middle-class-a-close-look-at-changes-within-metropolitan-areas/

A public policy approach to the plight of the American middle class can be found in Trevor Beltz, "The Disappearing Middle Class: Implications for Public Policy and Politics," http://scholarship.claremont.edu/cmc_theses/412/

Two media-generated commentaries on the American middle class that are helpful are:

"Middle Class Shrinks Further as More Fall Out Instead of Climbing Up"—www.nytimes.com/2015/01/26/business/economy/middle-class-shrinks-further-as-more-fall-out-instead-of climbing-up.html

"Middle-Class Betrayal? Why Working Hard Is No Longer Enough In America"—www.nbcnews.com/feature//in-plain-sight/middle-class-betrayal-why-working-hard-no-longer-enough-america-n291741

For an international perspective, see the following link from the German magazine *Der Spiegel*—"A Superpower in Decline: America's Middle Class Has Become Globalization's Loser," www.spiegel.de/international/0,1518,439766,00.html

Some Books to Read

Bartlett, Donald L. and James B. Steele, *The Betrayal of the Middle Class* (New York: Public Affairs, 2012).

Carville, James, *It's the Middle Class Stupid* (New York: Blue Rider-Penguin, 2012).

Faux, Jeff, *The Servant Economy: Where America's Elite Is Sending the Middle Class* (New York: Wiley, 2012).

Hacker, Jacob and Paul Pierson, *Winner-Take-All Politics: How Washington Made the Rich Richer and Turned Its Back on the Middle Class* (New York: Simon and Schuster, 2010).

Stiglitz, Joseph, *The Price of Inequality: How Today's Divided Society Endangers Our Future* (New York: Norton, 2012).

Notes

1. The term "American Dream" was first coined and discussed by James Truslow in his book *The Epic of America* (New York: Blue Ribbon Books, 1931).
2. The definition of the American middle class was discussed in the groundbreaking study of social class in America by C. Wright Mills. See C. Wright Mills, *White Collar: The American Middle Class* (New York: Oxford University Press, 1951). See also Richard Fyre and Rakesh Kochhar, "America's Wealth Gap Between Middle-income and Upper-income Families is Widest on Record," Pew Research, December 17, 2016.
3. "Are You in the Middle Class? Try Our Income Calculator," Pew Research Center, May 11, 2016.
4. See Fabian T. Pfeffer, Sheldon Danzinger, and Robert F. Schoeni, "Wealth Levels, Wealth Inequality, and the Great Recession," Russell Sage Foundation, June, 2014. See "Changes in U.S. Family Finances From 2010–2013; Evidence From the Survey of Consumer Finances," *Federal Reserve Bulletin*, Vol. 100, No. 4 (2014), pp. 1–164.
5. Neal Gabler, "The Secret Shame of the Middle Class," *The Atlantic*, May, 2016.
6. "America's Shrinking Middle Class; A Close Look at Changes Within Metropolitan Areas," Pew Research Center, May 11, 2016.
7. See David Leonhardt and Kevin Quealy, "The American Middle Class Is No Longer the World's Richest," *New York Times*, April 22, 2014.
8. "Income and Poverty in the United States," U.S. Department of Commerce, September, 2015.
9. William Laconick, "Profits Without Prosperity," *Harvard Business Review*, November, 2015.
10. Bernie Sanders, "A Rigged Economy," November 8, 2015, www.berniesanders.com
11. Larry Light, "Hillary Clinton's Bid for the Economic Hearts of the Middle Class," *Time*, August 13, 2016.
12. Evan Halper and Lisa Mascuro, "Now Trump Has His Chance to Change Washington, But It Might Change Him Instead," *Los Angeles Times*, November 9, 2016.
13. See "Trump Spoke Out Against Free Trade Deals," Speech in Monessen, Pennsylvania, June 28, 2016 as reported in *Time*, June 28, 2016.
14. See "American Rage," The Esquire/NBC Survey, January 3, 2016.
15. See Ryan Lizza, "The Center Is Dead in American Politics," *The New Yorker*, October 21, 2015.
16. Quoted in Christopher S. Ragaber and Jesse J. Holland, "American Got a Raise Last Year for 1st Time Since 2007," *AP: The Big Story*, September 13, 2016, www.bigstory.ap.org
17. Deidre Fernandes and Evan Horowitz, "Incomes Leap for First Time in 8 Years," *Boston Globe*, September 14, 2016.
18. Quoted in Boston Globe, "Incomes Leap for First Time in 8 Years," op. cit.
19. See Jerry Z. Muller, "Capitalism and Inequality: What the Right and the Left Get Wrong," *Foreign Affairs*, March/April, 2013. See also "Inequality: Fat Tails," *The Economist*, January 7, 2017.

3 GLOBAL **WARMING** AND **CLIMATE** CHANGE

Issue Focus

Policy issues are often categorized as domestic or foreign, but with the concern over global warming and climate change the issue range has expanded to the entire planet. Dealing with the effects of global warming and climate change has thus become an issue with governments from around the world seeking ways to form policies and agreements that stem the advance of an environmental threat that can have an impact on weather extremes, species protection, degradation of vital natural resources, and perhaps most important, economic security and prosperity. Despite strong scientific evidence concerning global warming, there is also skepticism in some circles about the data and proposed policies to deal with this challenge to the planet.

Chapter Objectives
This issue chapter will seek to:
1. Define global warming and the range of its impacts on environmental and climate conditions.
2. Present the contentious debates over the sources of global warming and the effect that public policies may have on the national economy and consumer choices.
3. Discuss the short- and long-term potential of global warming to change the planet and the way humans live on it.

SOME BACKGROUND

In 2006 former Vice-President Al Gore helped to develop and narrated a documentary entitled *An Inconvenient Truth* and followed up the movie with a book by the same title. Gore's *An Inconvenient Truth* was basically a sophisticated slide show on the impact of global warming. Gore took viewers on a tour of regions of the world that had been dramatically affected by the warming of the planet. Gore's slide presentation showed, for example, how many of the glaciers had been significantly reduced within a relatively short period of time (20–30 years), and that if the trend were to continue, the glaciers would likely disappear within this century. The slide show was an immediate box office success (Gore, along with his collaborators on the project, would eventually win an Academy Award), and he later won the Nobel Peace Prize for his work alerting the world to the dangers of global warming.[1]

As a result of *An Inconvenient Truth,* combined with regular dire warnings from the scientific community, global warming has entered the daily lexicon of conversation. As commonly defined, global warming is the gradual increase in the global temperatures caused by the emission of gases that trap the sun's heat in the earth's atmosphere (often termed the greenhouse effect). Gases that contribute to global warming include carbon dioxide, methane, nitrous oxides, chlorofluorocarbons (CFCs), and halocarbons (the replacements for CFCs). The carbon dioxide emissions are primarily caused by the use of fossil fuels for energy such as coal, oil, and natural gas.

It is important to point out that some level of greenhouse gas emission is essential because their absence would cause the earth's temperature to be around 0 degrees Fahrenheit, instead of an average of 59 degrees Fahrenheit. But as the level of greenhouse gases has increased, so has its impact on temperature and what many scientists believe are increasing incidents of extreme climate change such as changes in rainfall patterns, powerful storms, a rise in sea levels, and adverse impacts on plants, wildlife, and humans. Temperatures have increased by about 1.8 degrees Fahrenheit since pre-industrial times. Many scientists believe that global warming must stay below an increase of 3.6 degrees Fahrenheit because any temperature increase beyond that point would lock the world into a future of rising sea levels, severe droughts, and flooding, causing widespread food and water shortages.[2]

To see what many in the scientific community view as the impact of global warming on the planet and the potential it has for radically changing our world, the following specific examples of climate change provide a cautionary note on where we may be headed:

2016 was the warmest year in recorded history.

Ice in the Artic is disappearing fast. By 2040 the region may have its first completely ice-free summer.

Glaciers and mountain snows are increasingly melting. Glacier National Park in Montana has just 27 glaciers; there were 150 in 1910.

Over 14 million acres of spruce trees in Alaska and neighboring British Columbia have either died or are at risk from bark beetles, which are now thriving in the much warmer regions of North America.

By 2100 average sea levels will be 2.3 feet higher in New York City, 2.9 feet higher in Hampton Roads, Virginia, and 3.5 feet higher in Galveston, Texas.

In 2013 there were 11 weather and climate disaster events with losses over $1 billion each. In total, these event losses were over $110 billion.[3]

Defining global warming has never been much in dispute, nor has there been any difficulty of finding an ever growing list of examples of how warming has affected the planet. But what has caused a storm of controversy are the issues of whether human activity, particularly economic and consumer activity, is the root cause of the warming trend and whether public policy measures should be taken in order to limit or curtail the human activity causing the warming trend. Passionate debates have dominated the economic, social, and political arenas over how best to respond to global warming and whether global warming is a major threat to the planet that must be dealt with immediately or a natural occurrence that does not require changes in lifestyle, a restructuring of economic activity, or massive governmental intervention. However, because global warming may have the potential to radically change the planet and threaten humankind, the issues of how seriously to take this warming trend and how best to deal with the impacts strike at the heart of how we live, how we grow economically, and how we look at the future.

DEBATES, DIFFERENCES, AND DIVISIONS

The scientific community is largely in agreement that global warming is the result of human activity. Many of the scientific societies and leading scientific journals have come to a consensus on the causes of elevated greenhouse gases and the resulting presence of global warming. The prestigious United Nations Intergovernmental Panel on Climate Change, which brought together the leading scientists in the world working on global warming, issued a widely discussed report in 2007 that stated clearly and without reservation that global warming is human-made and that, if significant corrective measures were not taken soon, the planet would face devastating consequences.[4]

The key findings of the U.N. Panel are as follows:

1. Warming of the climate system is unequivocal, as is now evident from observations of increases in global air and ocean temperatures, widespread melting of snow and ice, and rising global average sea level.
2. Most of the observed increase in globally average temperature since the mid-20th century is very likely due to the observed increase in the human emission of greenhouse gases.
3. Global warming and sea level rise will continue for centuries, even if greenhouse gases were to be stabilized.
4. The probability that this is caused by natural or climate processes alone is less than 5%.
5. The world temperature could rise by between 2 and 11.5 degrees Fahrenheit during the 21st century.

In 2009 the warnings of the U.N. Panel were validated by a group of environmental scientists meeting in Copenhagen, Denmark. The conclusion of these experts was that sea levels appear to be rising nearly twice as fast as previously predicted in the 2007 study. The Greenland and Antarctic ice caps are melting at an accelerating rate, with sea levels rising to a level at which low-lying regions will face catastrophic flooding, and in the process, devastate coastal cities such as New York, Miami, and Boston by 2050 and beyond. Recent studies from the Goddard Institute for Space Studies, the National Climate Data Center in the United States, and other international data centers continue to point out the increased short-term and long-term dangers from global warming.[5]

But scientific consensus has not curtailed opposing views on the source of global warming and the measures that should be taken in order to save the planet. Critics of the prevalent view, who make up a minority of the scientific community, state that scientists who support mainline global warming are ignoring alternative theories on the sources of the build-up of greenhouse gases and the positive applications of global warming on the planet. Furthermore, the critics state that the scientific majority are blindly following the consensus in order not to be ostracized in their profession and shut out from research grants. At the heart of the opposing view on global warming are questions about the accuracy of temperature readings that include urban areas where higher levels of heat are generated, variations in global temperature over time despite rising carbon dioxide levels, and solar activity in which the sun's output has changed over the last 60–70 years, thus contributing to a warming of the globe.

Freeman Dyson, a Nobel Prize recipient and professor of physics at Princeton, is one of the most prominent critics of the global warming scientific community. In a column written in 2015 Dyson stated:

> The Intergovernmental Panel on Climate Change believes climate change is harmful; that the science of climate change is settled and understood; that climate change is largely due to the release of carbon dioxide into the atmosphere by industrial societies; and that there is an urgent need to fight climate change by reducing the emissions of carbon dioxide. The most questionable of these beliefs is the notion that the science of climate change is understood. The biggest of all climate changes has been the ice ages, which have covered half of North America and Europe. Ice ages happened repeatedly in the past and we are about due for another one to start. A new ice age would be a disaster far greater than anything we have to fear from climate warming. There are many theories of ice ages, but no real understanding. So long as we do not understand ice ages, we do not understand climate change . . . Another important thing that we do not understand is the possible effect of the sun on climate. The sun's magnetic activity is strongly variable, and it appears to be correlated with the earth's climate. When the sun is magnetically active, climate gets warmer. We do not know how much of the warming is caused by the sun. If the effect of the sun is large, any effort to control climate change by human activity is futile.[6]

The global warming skeptics like Dyson have been somewhat successful in turning the American public away from a concern over the impact of global warming and in questioning the accuracy of the data presented by the scientific community. For example, in 2015 a listing of policy priorities of the American people showed that Global Warming/Climate Change ranked 22 out of 23 issues, with only 38% of the respondents viewing the issue as important. Furthermore, in the 2016 presidential debates there was not one question from the moderators regarding global warming and no interest in discussing this issue by Hillary Clinton or Donald Trump. A majority of Americans do believe that the earth is getting warmer and that this warming trend may have an impact on climate change, but the dire warnings from the scientific community or the positions of political leaders do not appear to raise real concern or a major push for infrastructure projects to limit the impact of sea level rise, super storms, or droughts.[7]

These scientific disagreements have served as the basis for the ideological and partisan battles that fill the halls of Congress and the West Wing of the White House. Liberals and environmentalists who view global warming as a human-made calamity that requires swift and comprehensive controls on fossil fuels rely heavily on the scientific consensus and chide conservatives in and out of government for ignoring the overwhelming evidence of the connection between greenhouse gases and the activities of humans. Conservatives and the business community retort that there is sufficient question about the reliability of the scientific data to move with caution and that the lock-step movement of environmentalists to put a break on fossil fuels despite the economic results would lead to a meltdown of the American economy.

One of the most prominent and outspoken members of what has come to be called the "denier" movement regarding global warming is US Senator Jim Inhofe (R-OK). As Chair of the influential Environment and Public Works Committee, Inhofe has often publicly criticized the scientific community and their views on global warming and climate change. In 2015 he brought a snowball into the Senate chambers to show in his view the fallacy of global warming. As he stated at the time, "there is hysteria of global warming . . . and the hoax is that there are some people who are so arrogant to think they are so powerful that they can change the climate." Inhofe is not alone as a member of the "denier" movement as many conservatives and Republican Party leaders do not support the scientific findings that point to the dangers of not addressing global warming.[8]

But despite the disagreements among some members in the scientific community and the use by politicians to accent these disagreements as a strategy to influence public policy or to curtail any efforts to address global warming, there is no question that the United States is a critical player in the global warming debate and that much of the differences of opinion and the partisan divisions surrounding greenhouse gases and the proper public response to the warming of the planet have been at the center of national politics and have spilled over into the international realm as well. With the United States using about 25% of the world's resources, primarily fossil fuels, and the average American sending some 15,000 pounds of carbon dioxide emissions into the stratosphere each year (the United States is responsible for 18% of the world's carbon pollution), other industrialized countries and many less-developed nations have accused this country of perpetuating a national culture of energy wastefulness, following national policies that accent economic development over conservation, and moving slowly to embrace alternative fuel sources.[9] It is important to point out that the United States is not alone as a major contributor to emitting greenhouse gases. Currently, China is the number one carbon polluter with nearly 25% of the world's emissions.

FYI

Scientists believe that by 2100 13 million Americans living in heavily populated cities on or near the oceans will have to move inland in order to avoid the influx of water from a massive increase in sea levels. Already some cities are taking steps to protect their coastline and their citizens. In Boston, city officials are backing up street lights and traffic signals with solar power and supporting new building designs. Hospitals and other health care centers are raising the ground floor up to levels that reflect data from 500 years of flooding. In Miami, city officials are adding new pumping stations and raising roads and seawalls. These officials have also developed comprehensive plans to prepare vital infrastructure over the coming years to protect against rising sea levels.

Source: CBS Miami, March 31, 2016

In order to better understand the politics of global warming and the current tensions that exist in the United States over this controversial issue, it may be helpful to review the manner in which government has responded through public policies and actions. The United States took a major step toward reducing greenhouse gas emissions during the presidency of George H.W. Bush. Pledging to be the "environmental president," Bush pressed for the passage of the Clean Air Act of 1990. Despite opposition from members of Congress representing industrial states like Michigan and Ohio, Bush was able to fulfill his promise on clean air. The Clean Air Act placed stronger controls on fuel use by automobiles. The legislation required automakers to install pollution devices on cars to reduce dangerous emissions. The Act also addressed emissions from factories. Industrial plants that emitted a certain level of gases were required to install devices (commonly called scrubbers) that would clean the air. Paying for what many in the business community called the costliest clean air program in history, the yearly $2.5 billion price tag associated with the intent of the Clean Air Act was seen as a necessary step in order to address those areas of environmental regulation that had been neglected by past administrations. While some business leaders complained about the new level of regulation, the Clean Air Act of 1990 was viewed as a watershed of vigorous environmental policy.[10]

The victory of the Bush administration in its domestic environmental agenda was not easily transferable to the international arena. The Earth Summit in Rio de Janeiro, Brazil, in 1992 brought into view the debate between the United States and the less developed world over who would make energy sacrifices. The United States, along with 166 other nations, reluctantly signed a treaty that would require this country to place a limit on emissions of greenhouse gases at 1990 levels by the year 2000.[11] But while many less-developed countries doubted whether the United States would ever meet the requirements of the treaty, the Clinton administration began taking policy steps to achieve emission controls that met the emerging international standards. In Clinton's first term, a broad-based energy tax was proposed as a way of meeting this goal. Republicans opposed the measure, arguing that the administration really wanted the tax for the sake of deficit reduction rather than to prevent global warming. The tax went down to defeat.

In the second Clinton administration the debate over global warming, clean air, and greenhouse emissions became more strident as new pressure was placed on the United States by the less-developed world and European powers. In 1998 at another United Nations Conference on the environment held in Kyoto, Japan, the Clinton administration took a controversial stance supporting more vigorous emission controls as a way of responding to the threats from global warming. Vice-President Al Gore, representing the United States at the conference, linked the extreme weather conditions recently experienced in the world and the beginning of polar icecap meltdown as signs that the world community of nations must take serious measures in limiting emissions. Business leaders responded quickly to the Gore position, arguing that the economic vitality of the nation depended upon the continued productivity of our industrial base and that emission controls would cripple what had become, at the time, the longest and most sustained period of economic growth in US history. The lines between environmentalists and supporters of economic growth had been clearly drawn, with the government at the center of the debate. The Kyoto agreement, although supported by the Clinton administration, was never ratified by the United States Senate.[12]

On the Record

Pope Francis, writing in the Pontifical Academies of Sciences and Social Sciences stated,

In the fact of the emergencies of human-induced climate change, social exclusion and extreme poverty, we join together to declare that: Human-induced climate change is a scientific reality, and its decisive mitigation is a moral and religious imperative for humanity.

Source: Pontifical Academies of Sciences and Social Sciences

Once George W. Bush entered the White House, the emphasis on responding to global warming shifted from mandatory emissions controls to technological advances and voluntary compliance. As a sign that he was wary of the environmental policies of the Clinton administration, President Bush placed a hold on 175 regulations, many of which were designed to put greater controls on corporate practices that could heighten the release of greenhouse gases and other pollutants. Bush was acting out of concern that the Clinton administration had introduced far too many regulations that established unnecessary restrictions on the corporate sector, but critics countered that Bush was seeking to gut much of the progress made by the Clinton administration in using the regulations to protect the environment.

More evidence about the changed policy position of the incoming administration on greenhouse gases emerged as the Bush administration did not support the Kyoto Protocol and would not send it forward to the Senate for ratification. Although the Clinton administration also did not submit the Protocol to the Senate for fear that it would not pass, the Bush administration was clearly opposed to the Protocol, even though it had worldwide support. President Bush did, however, support the Clear Skies Initiative in 2002, which targeted power plant emissions of dangerous chemicals such as sulfur dioxide and mercury and sought a 70% decrease in these pollutants. Critics, however, were quick to challenge the president on the initiative because it failed to address carbon dioxide, the main source of greenhouse gases. The Bush administration countered the arguments against the Clear Skies Initiative by stressing that, instead of mandatory emission controls, an alternative plan that sought an 18% reduction in greenhouse gases over ten years was being put in place. The alternative plan was tied to a formula linking the amount of carbon dioxide emitted to the per dollar amount of gross domestic product. This formula was touted by the president as slowing the growth of greenhouse gases without endangering the economy. In a speech announcing the Clear Skies Initiative, President Bush predicted that his alternative proposal would take the equivalent of 70 million cars off the road. As he stated at the announcement, "This is a common sense way to measure progress. Our nation must have growth. Growth is what pays for investments in clean technologies, increased conservation and energy efficiency."[13]

Despite the president's reluctance to address the carbon dioxide emission issue with mandatory controls and his accent on a mix of voluntary compliance by businesses, gradual measures to address greenhouse gas build-up, and technological advances to replace fossil fuels, Mr. Bush faced a growing body of evidence that greenhouse gases were accumulating at rapid rates in the atmosphere and contributing to heightened temperature increases. In 2002 the Environmental Protection Agency (EPA) issued a Climate Action Report that linked global warming with human activity. With such reports and other data from academic and research sources, the White House began to concede that scientific conclusions on the influence of human-made sources of global warming could not be ignored. Nevertheless, the president continued to stress the dangers of mandatory controls on the American economy as contained in the Kyoto Protocol and, instead, pushed for voluntary initiatives.[14]

The Bush administration's position on global warming was weakened by a series of media reports that showed that oil and gas industry executives were closely involved in shaping government studies on global warming. Philip Cooney, a White House aide and former oil company executive, was accused by members of Congress and environmental groups of changing the language used in government studies to downplay the influence of human-made sources on global warming. Cooney and business groups such as the Global Climate

Coalition were viewed as aggressively seeking to influence the final drafts of government research. Also troublesome for the Bush administration were the public statements of James Hansen, the Director of the National Aeronautics and Space Administration's Goddard Center, who charged that the White House was misleading the American public and raising doubts about what he viewed as sound scientific research on the causes of global warming. Hansen stated that the Bush administration wanted public statements from government scientists that "fit predetermined, inflexible positions."[15]

Although President Bush did not embrace the scientific conclusions about the human-made sources of global warming, in his 2006 and 2007 State of the Union speeches he did address the importance of weaning America away from foreign oil and moving quickly to develop alternative sources of energy using the latest technology. By continuing to stress technology and alternative fuel sources, the president was staying true to his position that mandatory compliance, or other suggestions such as a carbon tax or gasoline surcharge, would only lead to serious economic consequences for the American economy. As the president said in his 2006 State of the Union address, "America is on the verge of technological breakthroughs that will enable us to live our lives less dependent on oil. And these technologies will help us be better stewards of the environment, and they will help us to confront the serious challenge of global climate change."[16]

President Bush's emphasis on oil independence rather than on mandatory emissions controls and his rejection of tax proposals designed to dissuade Americans from using carbon-based energy sources led him to propose drilling in the Arctic National Wildlife Refuge in Alaska. The administration's support for the drilling was based on its contention that only 2000 acres of the 19 million acre reserve would be used for drilling and that it would not disrupt the wildlife or harm the environment. Opponents of the drilling quickly responded that such drilling was dangerous to the wildlife in the area and would not yield the kind of oil reserves necessary to move us closer to oil independence.[17] In a series of procedural maneuvers in the Senate, Democrats were able to use the filibuster tactic to remove language supporting the drilling from Congressional legislation.

But President Bush's lukewarm position toward the dangers of global warming and his staunch opposition to mandatory emission policies gradually gave way to a willingness to move toward more aggressive and comprehensive policies that would address what more and more Americans were seeing as a looming threat to the planet. By June 2007, President Bush went on record at a European summit in support of reducing greenhouse emissions by 50% by 2050 (still voluntary, not mandatory) and agreed to work more closely with the United Nations to achieve that result. It seems that the president in this global warming debate had been "overtaken by events" as states like California and cities like New York began to implement strong measures to limit greenhouse gases. Governor Arnold Schwarzenegger of California signed a unique agreement with British Prime Minister Tony Blair that both would work to reduce greenhouse gases. In New York City, Mayor Michael

Bloomberg took the unprecedented steps of requiring taxi cabs to be hybrid autos and instituting a heavy tax on cars coming into the city. As of 2007, there were 522 mayors of American cities representing 65 million Americans who pledged to support the Kyoto Protocol's goal of reducing greenhouse emissions by 7% below 1990 levels by 2012.[18]

The clearest evidence that the president had been "overtaken by events" in the global warming debate was the movement of many high-level and high-profile business leaders who began a push to move toward a resolution of the emissions deadlock and take the country forward as quickly as possible to energy independence and a greening of America using alternative fuels and new technology. Jeffrey Immelt, the former CEO of General Electric, for example, made numerous public statements about his intention to take GE into a new generation of green technology and to accent more energy-responsible product development. CEOs such as Immelt were not without their critics, especially from worried shareholders concerned about the uncertainty of future profits if the company pursued an aggressive greening strategy. Oil and coal industries that worried over the future growth of their products opposed a more comprehensive and substantive energy policy.[19]

The position of the oil and coal industry over energy policy was damaged when, in 2015, evidence surfaced that Exxon Mobil knew as far back as the 1980s that climate change was caused by human activity and would reach "catastrophic levels." Instead of divulging its scientific findings, Exxon Mobil participated in an alleged disinformation campaign that questioned scientific studies on climate change. A probe led by New York Attorney General Eric Schneiderman sought to subpoena documents from Exxon Mobil concerning its scientific research that showed the connection between fossil fuels and climate change.[20]

Data Bank

Home-cooking stoves used in the less-developed world are one of the top sources of carbon dioxide emissions. These stoves, which burn wood, dung or crop residue, produce black carbon, which is now considered as the source of 18% of carbon dioxide. Although "fixing" the carbon dioxide emission from fossil fuels will be a long and complex process, scientists claim that replacing the cooking stoves with more modern and efficient stoves that do not produce black carbon would produce a measurable decline in emissions in a relative short period of time.

Source: New York Times, April, 16, 2009.

Once in the White House, Barack Obama shifted gears quickly on the global warming issue and the impact on climate change. During the presidential campaign Obama promised to make the global warming threat a high priority and to put in place measures that would begin to aggressively attack the problem. On the campaign trail, Obama said, "Few challenges facing America and the world are more urgent than combating climate change. The science is beyond dispute and the facts are clear. Sea levels are rising, coastlines are shrinking. We've seen record drought, spreading famine, and storms that are growing stronger with each passing hurricane season."

Within days of taking office, Obama issued two executive orders: one that ordered the US Department of Transportation to increase automobile fuel economy standards and the other that ordered the US Environmental Protection Agency to begin developing a feasibility study that would allow individual states to enforce their own greenhouse gas policies. Finally, in April 2009, Secretary of State Hillary Clinton announced that the United States would take the lead in negotiating a global warming treaty, saying, "The United States is fully engaged and determined to lead and make up for lost time both at home and abroad . . . we are back in the game."[21]

President Obama echoed these renewed efforts to move quickly and comprehensively to deal with the impact of global warming at the international climate conference in Copenhagen, Denmark, in 2009. Obama warned that, "[T]he time we have to reverse this tide (of global warming) is running out." Yet despite his enthusiasm for taking aggressive action, his administration was unsuccessful in forming a comprehensive national bill to deal with greenhouse emissions. Again, disagreements over the impact of tough regulations on key resource areas such as coal-fired power plants and the automobile industry stalled the bill in Congress. Nevertheless, despite this failure to achieve a major legislative breakthrough, American consumers and businesses, backed by government-sponsored subsidies, moved toward installing solar panels and wind turbines as public opinion began to see the benefits of conservation and acceptance of alternative energy sources.[22]

During the second Obama administration, the primary focus was on achieving an international agreement that would set rules and target dates for significant reductions in fossil fuel emissions. In a lead-up to an international conference in Paris in 2015, the Obama administration and the Chinese government, led by its president Xi Jinping, agreed to cut emissions up to 28% from 2005 levels. China also agreed to establish a program often termed "cap and trade" in which it would sell permits to companies allowing them to pollute on a limited basis over a shorter period of time. President Xi pledged to begin reducing emissions no later than 2030.[23]

The agreement between the United States and China created the momentum for the Paris Summit. In December 2015, 195 nations reached an historic accord to combat global warming. The agreement committed the signatories to lowering greenhouse gas emissions to limit the impact of climate change. President Obama hailed the agreement as the "best chance to save the planet we have . . . together we have shown what is possible when the world stands as one."[24]

The major elements of the agreement were:

1. A long-term goal to make sure global warming stays well below 3.6 degrees Fahrenheit and to pursue efforts to limit the temperature rise to 2.7 degrees Fahrenheit.

2. An agreement to set targets for reducing greenhouse gas emissions every five years.
3. A five-year review of the targets to be established, with the hope of updating the targets and examining progress toward the targets.
4. An agreement that a level of "flexibility" in meeting the targets will be acknowledged, especially in poorer countries. No penalties would be issued to those countries that fail to completely meet their targets.
5. Richer countries would be encouraged to provide financial support to help poor countries reduce their emissions.[25]

Despite the euphoria associated with the agreement, which was formally implemented in 2016, some in the scientific community were not convinced that the targets could be achieved in time and would have to be adjusted. In order to achieve the goal, zero greenhouse gases would have to be emitted by 2070, or about 7 billion tons of carbon dioxide—a daunting task. The goals of the Paris Agreement were made less secure with the election of Donald Trump, who described the science of global warming as "bunk" and pledged to take the United States out of the Paris Agreement. Trump was true to his promise for, in June 2017, he announced that the United States would pull out of the Paris Agreement, citing job losses and a drain on the economy. Although the decision by Trump to get out of the Paris Agreement would not come into effect until 2020, there was widespread denouncement of the new position of the United States. European allies, in particular, were outraged over Trump's refusal to acknowledge climate change and the dangers of global warming. Environmental critics in the United States were equally concerned that the United States had given up its leadership position in the efforts to lessen carbon emissions. Nationally, conservatives were elated over Trump's decision, while many state and local governmental leaders pledged to honor the Paris Agreement no matter what direction the Trump administration had taken the country on this key domestic and international policy issue.

The decision by President Trump to pull out of the Paris Agreement combined with his appointments of pro-oil and gas officials at the Environmental Protection Agency and the Energy and Interior Departments pointed to an administration that was determined to deny the recommendations of the international scientific community, the United Nations, and the nearly 200 countries that signed the Agreement (the United States joined Syria and Nicaragua as the three countries officially opposed to the accord). Trump's key cabinet appointments in key environmental areas such as Energy, the EPA, and Transportation fostered great concern in the scientific community that their warnings about the impact of global warming would be ignored.

Joined with these debates and public policy initiatives is the fundamental issue of how much of a sacrifice the American people are willing to bear and what that sacrifice will mean in terms of their quality of life. In an analysis by the *Washington Post*, legislation and executive branch regulations that sought to reduce US fuel emissions by 60% in the next twenty years would require enormous changes to the American consumer and corporate land-scape. Automakers would have to double gas mileage, builders would have to overhaul building codes to allow for greener structures, and utilities would have to raise electric bills by 25% or more just to initiate the development and implementation of new energy-saving technologies. The *Post* study concluded that as many as one million wind turbines would have to be built, 400 new power plants using advanced technology would need to be placed on line, and enough solar panels to cover half the state of New Jersey would be required. The cost for all this revamping of the American energy system would cost trillions and necessitate significant tax and rate increases that would have a marked impact on the pocketbooks of Americans. Even if the United States started immediately on a comprehensive plan to revamp its energy system and energy use, it would take decades to put into place an effective response to the ever-expanding march of global warming.[26]

However, alongside these warnings, there continue to be those who question the wisdom of dealing with global warming by drastic and expensive public policies. Global warming skeptics such as Danish Professor Bjorn Lomborg question the practicality of spending billions, if not trillions, of dollars on programs to reduce greenhouse gases, when in his view the threat is not only distant, but also taking major policy actions would be devastating to the world's economy. Lomborg's position is summed up in this quote, "The cost and benefits of the proposed measures against global warming is the worst way to spend our money. Climate change is a 100 year problem, we should not try to fix it in 10 years."[27]

The policy responses on how best to deal with the impact of global warming on the planet are thus coming from all directions. The debates, differences, and divisions that marked this issue in the past are slowly but surely being replaced with a cautious national consensus that a comprehensive national energy plan of action must be taken now rather than by piecemeal adjust-ments and the promise of new technological breakthroughs. Despite President Trump's decision to pull out of the Paris Agreement, an ever-growing num-ber of Americans are worried about the impact of the decision and concerned about the future of the planet if corrective measures are not taken. Even though there remain legitimate concerns that stiff controls on emissions would lead to economic dislocations, those concerns are now in competition with a growing public realization that the effects of global warming may be much more seri-ous to humankind than the prospect of a possible economic slowdown.[28]

As a result, some form of balance between growth and conservation must be reached in the United States and, indeed, around the world, and efforts to develop and introduce new technologies that replace fossil fuels must be advanced with greater speed. There are still many unknowns about global warming and the growing levels of greenhouse gases in the stratosphere, but there is little doubt that humans have contributed to this crisis and that humans will have to take steps to respond effectively to the crisis and protect the planet we share.

The Great Debate

There remain a large number of Americans who either do not believe in global warming as a serious environmental threat or are not convinced that comprehensive measures need to be taken in order to respond to the impact of global warming on climate change. In light of the fact that global warming and climate change are not major policy priorities articulated by the American people, the following debate topic is appropriate:

Debate Topic

Is it necessary for the United States to take major steps to respond to global warming and climate change?

Critical Thinking Questions

1. Do you believe that the impact of global warming is an immediate threat to our planet's survival?
2. How do you respond to the conservative position that the answer to the rise in global temperatures is an unexplained condition that does not require drastic measures but rather adaptation to a new climate reality?
3. Is it realistic and practical for the American public to move away from carbon-based energy sources toward new sources of energy?
4. Why is global warming not higher on the priority list of critical national and international challenges despite overwhelming scientific proof?
5. What are your policy recommendations for dealing with global warming and climate change?

Connections

The National Aeronautical and Space Administration provides a reader and helpful guide to global warming and climate change. See "Global Climate Change: Vital Signs of the Planet" at www.climate.nasa.gov

There are a number of websites that deal with climate change; one of the best is from the Natural Resources Defense Council. See "Global Warming 101" at www.nrdc.org

For a wide-ranging discussion of the consequences of climate change, see the website from the Union of Concerned Scientists, "Confronting the Realities of Climate Change" at www.ucsusa.org

Many interest groups are involved in responding to global warming. The Sierra Club is one of the leading groups: www.sierraclub.org/globalwarming

A website that highlights the views of global warming skeptics can be found at www.skepticalscience.com

Some Books to Read

Hansen, James, *Storms of My Grandchildren* (New York: Bloomsbury Publishing, 2009).

Lomborg, Bjorn, *Cool It: A Skeptical Environmentalist's Guide to Global Warming* (New York: Knopf, 2007).

Mann, Michael E. and Lee R. Kump, *Dire Predictions: Understanding Climate Changes, the Illustrated Guide to the Findings of the IPCC*, 2nd edition (New York: DK, 2015).

McKibben, Bill, *Fight Global Warming Now: The Handbook for Taking Action in Your Community* (New York: Holt Paperbacks, 2007).

Nordhaus, William, *A Question of Balance: Weighing the Options on Global Warming Policies* (New Haven, CT: Yale University Press, 2008).

Notes

1. Al Gore, *An Inconvenient Truth* (New York: Rodale, 2006).
2. See "The Consequences of Climate Change," NASA, 2014, www.climate.nasa.gov
3. The Environmental Protection Agency has a comprehensive presentation of the impacts of climate change in the United States and the world. See www.epa.gov/climate-impacts
4. For background on the 2007 report see "As Climate Risks Rise, Talks in Paris Set Stage for Action," *New York Times*, November 30, 2015.
5. Ibid.
6. As quoted in the *Boston Globe*, December 4, 2015. See also Dennis Behreandt, "Global Warming Skepticism," *The New American*, 2007, www.jbs.org/node/2879
7. "Gallup: Americans Still Rank Climate Change as Low-Priority Concern," March 24, 2016, www.climatechaangedispatch.com.
8. See *Washington Post*, March 1, 2015.
9. See www.climateactiontracker
10. See the Clean Air Act in its entirety on the EPA website, www.epa.gov/air/caa
11. See "UN Conference on Environment and Development Proceedings (Earth Summit)," www.habitat.igc.org
12. See a critique of the Kyoto Accords in Clive Cook, "Sins of Emission," *Atlantic*, April, 2008, pp. 32–33.
13. The Clear Skies Initiative is explained and evaluated at www.cbsnews.com/stories/2002/06/03/tech/main510920.shtml
14. See www.epa.gov/climatechange
15. For a discussion of the dissent and controversy in the Bush administration over global warming policy see http://news/bbc.co.uk/1/hi/world/americas/4075985.stm
16. See http://www/whitehouse.gov/stateoftheuion/2006
17. See Justin Blum, "51–49 Vote Backs Arctic Oil Drilling," *New York Times*, March 17, 2005.
18. "Urban Greening," *Washington Post National Weekly Edition*, June 18–24, 2007, p. 33.
19. See Gregg Estabrook, "Hot Prospects: Who Loses and Who Wins in a Warming World," *The Atlantic*, April, 2007.

20. *Bloomberg News*, November 10, 2015.
21. See "Clinton's Speech at the UN Climate Change Conference, December, 2009," Council on Foreign Relations, December 17, 2009.
22. See "Obama's Speech to the Copenhagen Climate Summit," *The Guardian*, December 18, 2015.
23. *New York Times*, November 30, 2015.
24. *Boston Globe*, December 13, 2015.
25. Ibid.
26. "As Leaders Celebrate Climate Deal, Stark Numbers Loom," *Boston Globe*, December 14, 2014.
27. Bjorn Lomborg, "Climate Rhetoric Does Real Damage," *Boston Globe*, December 12, 2016.
28. See Veerabhadran Ramanathan, Jessica Seddon, and David G. Victor, "The Next Front on Climate Change," *Foreign Affairs*, March/April, 2016, pp. 135–142. For an update on survey data related to the Paris Agreement see Frank Newport, "Public Opinion and Trump's Decision on the Paris Agreement," *Gallup*, Polling Matters, June 2, 2017.

4

HEALTH CARE AND HEALTH CARE REFORM

Issue Focus

To most Americans, health is a high priority, if not their highest personal concern. Access to health care services, cost factors, quality of care, and the knowledge that a serious medical condition will be addressed in a timely manner are at the core of the health care debate in the United States. Added to these concerns is the proper role of government in this nation's health system. Because this issue is so personal, and in recent years involves the increased intervention of government, health care and health care reform are hot-button issues in American politics.

Chapter Objectives

This issue chapter will seek to:

1. Explain the current state of health care and the challenges facing all sectors of the health care industry in the United States—patients, medical professionals, hospitals, and insurance companies.

2. Discuss the various policy options designed to address health care and health care reform.

3. Examine the disagreements over the extent that government should become involved in dealing with health care and health care reform.

SOME BACKGROUND

Just about everyone has heard the words, "your health is everything." Well, in American politics, health care and health care reform are the "everything" on the domestic issue agenda. Health care has rocketed to the top of the policy concerns of the American people and has become an issue that is central to electoral politics and partisan competition. In many respects, the health care issue is a perfect storm of challenges for the American political system and, indeed, for all the major players that make up the health care industry—from hospitals to doctors to insurance companies to the patients. We Americans take great pride in our health care system, and many of us have come to expect that health care should be viewed as a basic right, even though the costs of that health care are skyrocketing. But our pride in the health care system and our view that we should be entitled to quality care, no matter the cost, has run up against the realities of the marketplace and the fact that our system is not without its limitations and its breakdowns. As we shall see, there is much that needs to be done to fix our health care system.

From a dollars-and-cents perspective, the US health care system is the costliest in the world. The United States currently spends $3 trillion annually, approximately 17% of its national income, on health care; that 17% is equivalent to $9,500 for each man, woman, and child in this country. It is estimated that health care costs will rise to $4 trillion by 2019, taking almost 21% of the gross domestic product (GDP). In the way of comparison, France is the country with the next highest expenditure in terms of GDP at 11.6%, followed by the United Kingdom at 8.8% of GDP. The high cost of health care in the United States is the result of a number of factors: Americans are number one among the advanced industrial countries in terms of use of prescriptions, and Americans have the highest rate of high tech procedures—MRIs, CT scans, and PET scans. The costs related to surgical procedures are enormous as well. When compared to other countries, for example, bypass surgery in the United States, on average, costs $75,000, $30,000 more than second-place Australia.[1]

Although the United States spends a substantial portion of its national wealth on health care, millions of Americans are without health benefits. Before President Obama's Affordable Care Act (the ACA, often termed Obamacare) was implemented in 2010, an estimated 47 million Americans were without health care coverage. Since then, over 11 million Americans, previously without coverage, signed up for health insurance. With this increased health insurance coverage, about 90% of the total population in the United States now has health insurance, either through their employers or through government sponsored and supported health care.[2]

The health care debate often returns to the matter of costs and the effect on the economy and businesses, large and small. In 2015 the average health care cost per employee was $12,041, with employee premiums rising yearly by 10% and with out-of-pocket deductibles in many company insurance plans approaching $1000 per family member each year. As a result of these heavy health care coverage costs, many businesses are scaling back their benefits or denying them to their employees, thus further increasing the ranks of the uninsured. These cutbacks have often led to difficult contract negotiations with unions and retirees from unions who resist any reduction or elimination of existing health care coverage. In 2011 General Motors spent $655 million on health care for its employees and their families. General Motors executives often claim that health insurance costs translate into an additional $1,500 to the cost of their cars and trucks.[3]

Rising health care costs have also had serious financial impacts on local governments and hospitals. Many local communities, from cities to small towns, have been faced with rising premiums for their employees at a time when homeowners and businesses are enduring higher taxes for public services. While, in the past, most of the issues of town finances were salaries for employees, currently salary issues have been joined with the cost of health care premiums and the move by government officials to cut back on the community's share of the insurance coverage. With respect to hospitals, the issue is the use of the emergency room by the uninsured, which not only places enormous demands on the staff, but leads to prohibitive costs that many small-size hospitals have been unable to carry. Hundreds of small- and medium-size hospitals have either closed or have had to merge with larger hospitals in order to survive, in part because of the costs related to emergency care of the uninsured.

But besides the issues of coverage and cost, there is also growing evidence that the health care system, despite its reputation for technological sophistication and a high level of expertise, has serious deficiencies. Nearly 100,000 Americans die each year from medical malpractice. Moreover, the distribution of medical professionals is heavily weighted toward urban areas, leaving many in rural locations with inadequate or completely absent care, and the endless and complicated paperwork that accompanies a visit to the doctor or the hospital has left patients both frustrated and angry. There is also the growing concern among health care professionals that the issues of coverage and costs have placed the challenges of dealing with chronic illnesses like cancer, diabetes, and obesity in the background. Organizations such as the Partnership to Fight Chronic Disease have stressed the importance of placing greater emphasis on disease control and eradication. Kenneth Thorpe, the founder of the Partnership, stated in 2007 that "for too long, the national debate has been focused on access and who gets covered. But what we should be talking about is how we can drive costs down and provide better care."[4]

There is no doubt that health care policy and health care reform are "hot" issues and their importance as a critical national priority is growing. But responding to the challenges of health care in America has, in the past, been subject to an ideological and partisan stand-off with only piecemeal solutions and policy gridlock. With Americans now living longer and therefore placing greater strains on health care providers, it goes without question that the push for reform will remain a "hot" issue for years to come.

Data Bank

Some of the key health indicators for the United States are:

> Life expectancy—all Americans—78.8 years
> Life expectancy—males—76.4
> Life expectancy—females—81.2
> Infant mortality—6.1 deaths per 1,000 births
> Number of doctors per 1,000 patients—2.6
> Annual physician visits—4
> Percent of population, 65 and above, with two or more chronic conditions—68%

Source: US Census Bureau, Center for Disease Control, American Medical Association.

DEBATES, DIFFERENCES, AND DIVISIONS

Fixing the health care crisis in the United States is not something new. For years, beginning in the 1970s, Senator Ted Kennedy of Massachusetts was seeking to implement a universal medical coverage system in the United States modeled after the systems in Europe, but his efforts never were able to gain Congressional support and were criticized by health care interest groups, insurance companies, and medical doctors who were opposed to what they viewed as a turn toward socialized medicine and big government intervention. But as the problems associated with health care continued to worsen, especially in the area of the uninsured, President Clinton established the Task Force on National Health Care Reform in 1992, which was charged with recommending legislation that would reform health care in the United States.

On the Record

President Obama's speech on health care reform to the American Medical Association, June 15, 2009:

Members of the American Medical Association, my fellow Americans. I am here today because I do not want our children to still be speaking of a crisis in American medicine fifty years from now. I do not want them to still be suffering from spiraling costs we did not stem, or sicknesses we did not cure. I do not want them to be burdened with massive deficits we did not curb or a worsening economy we did not rebuild. I want them to benefit from a health care system that works for all of us; where families can open a doctor's bill without dreading what's inside; where parents are taking their kids to get regular check-ups and testing themselves for preventable ailments; where parents are feeding their kids healthier food and kids are exercising more; where patients are spending more time with doctors and doctors can pull up on a computer all the medical information and latest research they'd ever want to meet that patient's needs; where orthopedists and nephrologists and oncologists are all working together to treat a single human being; where what's best about America's health care system has become the hallmark of America's health care system.

The formation of the Task Force ran into immediate controversy as the First Lady, Hillary Rodham Clinton, was appointed to lead the group. After extensive study from experts in the area of health care and whirlwind tours around the country to gather first-hand information from those Americans who had been negatively affected by the system, the Task Force presented a complex 1,000-page proposal that required employers to provide insurance coverage to their employees through Health Maintenance Organizations (HMOs) that would be closely monitored and regulated by the government. Immediately, the proposal, which became the Health Security Act, ran into a storm of opposition as many of the sectors affected by the plan complained that the bill was heavy on bureaucratic intervention and limited patient choice. A massive campaign was waged, funded by conservatives and opponents of a government-directed health care insurance system. In what is now a famous ad campaign launched to help scuttle the Clinton Health Security Act, a middle-class couple, named Harry and Louise, sat in front of the cameras and bemoaned the reform effect as too complex and bureaucratic. The ad was paid for by the Health Insurance Association of America.[5]

With key interests opposed to the bill and the Democratic majority in the Congress not enamored with the Clinton proposal, the Health Security Act was scuttled. Senate Majority leader George Mitchell introduced a compromise measure that sought to weaken the government's involvement and delayed the requirement that businesses provide the insurance until 2002. But even these changes were not enough to push the legislation through a skeptical Congress. The power of the hospital insurance industry was so intense, and the perception of the American people that big government was going to control their health care was so widespread, that the bill never made it through the legislative process. Furthermore, in 1994, the Republicans took power in the House and Senate, thus further destroying any hopes of bringing government-directed health care reform to a vote. Many critics blamed Hillary Clinton for the failure of the Health Security Act, particularly her inability to work with Congress and respond effectively to the interest group and media attacks. However, the key to the defeat of the Clinton health care reform was the fact that the proposals were too complex and bureaucratic and relied too heavily on government involvement.

FYI

The Canadian Single Payer Health System

The United States is the only industrialized nation that does not have a government sponsored and supported health care system. The so-called single payer system, which is in place in Canada, is often viewed as a model for the United States. Currently, Canada directs 9% of its Gross Domestic Product toward the national health care system. All Canadians are covered by the single payer system and receive an identification card that they take to the hospital for verification. Because of the single payer system, Canadians do not pay directly for their health care, but provincial taxes are considerably higher in Canada than they are in the United States. Although Canadians take great pride in their health care system, there are some problems such as long waits for operations, a low-tech style of medical care, and considerably lower pay for doctors and nurses, which has caused a brain drain of medical personnel to the United States and trips across the border to obtain more high tech medical care.

Source: "What If America Had Canada's Healthcare System," *The Atlantic*, October, 2014.

Health care issues remained in the background through the remainder of the Clinton administration and well into the Bush years as the country turned toward managed care plans, which included health maintenance organizations (HMOs that provide care from a network of participating doctors for a set fee), point of service plans (HMOs that allow members to choose doctors from outside their plan), and preferred provider organizations (PPOs or health care organizations that provide a wider network of physicians and hospitals to their clients). From 1993 through 1997, each of the health maintenance options grew significantly while the traditional fee-for-service plans declined in popularity. With HMOs and their various offshoots, the pooling of administrative resources, the developing of health professional resources, and the set fee created for a time an answer to the burgeoning health care demands of the American public and the ever rising costs of hospital stays, medical technology, testing, and doctors' visits. These answers turned out to be incomplete, short-term solutions to the health care crisis facing America.

The Clinton administration was able to make some headway with respect to health care reform. In 1996 President Clinton signed into law a measure that would allow Americans to keep their health insurance when they lost or changed their jobs or when they started a new business. Most importantly, the bill also required that insurance companies keep providing coverage to those who got sick while holding valid policies. Later that year, Congress, at the urging of the president and enormous public pressure, passed legislation requiring that insurance companies provide at least two days of hospital care for mothers giving birth. There had been an outcry over the practice known as "drive-through deliveries" as insurance companies and managed care operators sought to trim hospital costs. Then in 1997, President Clinton's Advisory Commission on Consumer Protection and Quality in the Health Care Industry proposed a Patients' Bill of Rights that was designed to provide Americans with some rules and expectations as they interacted with the health care system and managed care operators. The Patients' Bill of Rights was never enacted into law; rather, it became a set of guidelines that individual states and individual HMOs adopted.[6]

But as the country moved further and further into managed care, criticism of the system and its limitations increased significantly. Patients complained about the decrease in the amount of time that doctors spent with them, the difficulty of seeing specialists, and the numerous instances of health plans denying claims or referrals. Health care in the United States became the target of patients and doctors who viewed the system as too focused on the bottom line, controlled by accountants and less and less interested in the quality of care for the patient. The HMO system had indeed kept the cost of health care down, or at least controlled, but in the process it created new problems that struck at the heart of the doctor-patient relationship. As Bill Gradison, the president of the Health Insurance Association of America stated, "The public said to do something about health-care inflation, and we've been largely successful in doing that. Now, patients are saying, "Hold on, we don't like the way you're doing it.""[7]

With the HMOs under fire and the American public complaining about coverage and cost, it was inevitable that the health care system would enter the political arena. By 2007, as the campaign for the presidency began to take shape and the number of uninsured continued to rise, talk of universal coverage for Americans once again rose to the top of the domestic policy agenda. Although health care reform was viewed as a national issue, the intense disagreements and partisan gridlock that characterized the issue for so long caused reform efforts to begin to percolate at the state level. States began addressing the gaps and the inequities in the current private sector system of insurance coverage and moved toward universal health care programs. Massachusetts, for example, became the first state in the nation to mandate that each of its citizens have health care coverage. State officials in Massachusetts established a highly visible and aggressive public relations program to alert citizens to the new program and to warn them that failure to sign up for the program would lead to the loss of a tax deduction on the state income tax form. While many Massachusetts residents without health care benefits hailed the program, there were critics who pointed out that premiums, even for narrow preventive care, were still too high for many low income workers ($7,000 annually for a family of three).[8]

The movement of Massachusetts to develop a universal health care program and the interest of other states like California spurred political leaders running for the White House to present their own proposals that would be national in scope. Hillary Clinton, on the campaign trail for president, reprised her role from 1993 to present a health care insurance plan that would require all businesses to provide their employees with coverage. Employees would be required to purchase the insurance from their employer or through a program much like that used by federal employees. Those unable to purchase the coverage because of low incomes would be provided with tax credits. Businesses, especially small businesses that in the past feared the financial impact of providing health care to their employees, would also receive tax credits to ease the burden. In order to deal with the opposition from insurance companies, the Clinton proposal accented that millions of new clients would buy the health coverage and, because they would likely use the coverage in a preventive manner, not just for emergencies, Clinton was confident that the insurance companies would enjoy new-found profits.[9]

Clinton promised that, if elected, she would use the power of government to keep health care costs down, but she said that the level of regulation and intervention by the federal government would not be as expansive as the 1993 version of universal coverage. Clinton's plan stressed the importance of mandatory health care insurance much like the Massachusetts plan. Clinton added that, under her plan, there would not be any denial of insurance coverage for a pre-existing condition. In order to pay for the new health insurance, tax cuts established by the Bush administration for those Americans earning over $250,000 would be repealed. The cost of the Clinton health care plan was placed at $110 billion a year. Her Democratic opponent at the time, Barack Obama, diverged somewhat from her health care proposal by not accenting mandates but rather by placing more emphasis on child health care.[10]

On the Republican side, health care reform and universal coverage barely resonated among the presidential candidates and their supporters. Most of the candidates placed health care reform far down on their list of national priorities, and when they did talk about health care, their position was that market-based and tax-related solutions were the only answer, not government-directed programs. Mitt Romney, on the campaign trail in 2007, for example, derided the Clinton health care plan saying, "Hillary care continues to be bad medicine . . . in her plan we get Washington-managed health care. Fundamentally, she takes her inspiration from the bureaucracies." When the Republicans did talk from a policy perspective about health care, they accented health care vouchers that Americans would be encouraged to purchase or the establishment of high risk pools for the uninsurable to provide catastrophic care. For his part, President Bush in his 2007 State of the Union address did talk about ending the tax exemption on employer-based health insurance and stressed that, "free market, profit-driven health care" were the best ways to deal with the health care demands of the country.[11]

Despite its opposition to government-directed national health insurance, the Bush administration directed its attention to a prescription drug program administered through the Medicare system. On January 1, 2006, the government launched its Medicare Part D initiative that aimed to subsidize the cost of prescription drugs for the 21 million eligible Medicare recipients. The prescription drug plan aimed to assist those seniors who were the poorest and most prone to illness with low-cost coverage for medications. Those retirees in the Medicare system with higher incomes were given the option of purchasing prescription plans that required out-of-pocket premiums with deductibles and co-payments. The aim of Medicare Part D was to provide prescription drug coverage at a low cost, but getting the program off the ground became difficult as many seniors were confused as the coverage was channeled through a number of participating insurance companies who each had their own eligibility rules and coverage regulations.

Although the Bush administration allocated over $400 million to introduce the plan to the American public, at the early stages of the program only a fraction of those eligible signed up for the subsidized program. There were complaints about long waits for telephone assistance, poor communication between the Medicare administration and local pharmacies, and most importantly the so-called "donut hole "exemption. For example, in the Medicare Part D program, seniors would pay a $250 deductible and then 25% of the cost of drugs up to $2,250. But after that amount of expense has been reached, the recipients receive no subsidy until they begin to spend $3,600. At that plateau, seniors would pay $2 for generic drugs and $5 for preferred drugs. Yet it is that gap or donut hole between $2,250 and $3,600 that angered many seniors and senior advocates. Stories of many seniors going to pharmacies and finding out that they had exceeded their coverage and were now in the donut hole ran rampant and created frustration and anger among seniors. Eventually, however, after all the various communication and insurance problems were ironed out, many more seniors signed up for the reduced drug cost program, and by

2007 the program was receiving positive reviews, even though the donut hole coverage issue remained.[12]

The Bush prescription drug program was criticized by Democrats in Congress and senior advocates as too weighted to benefit the insurance and pharmaceutical companies and HMOs. Critics alleged that the legislation was drafted by insurance and pharmaceutical lobbyists working with key Republican representatives in the House, such as former Louisiana congressmen Bill Tauzin, and then jammed through Congress by the leadership in the dead of night without the opportunity for debate or amendments. Representative Tauzin eventually left Congress and took a job as the president and CEO of the Pharmaceutical Research and Manufacturers of America, one of the leading lobbying groups representing the drug industry.

The Medicare Prescription Drug Improvement and Modernization Act of 2003, which established the Medicare Part D program, was seen by critics as another example of the Bush administration's attempt to privatize health care in the country by encouraging seniors to sign up for private prescription plans. Initially, the plan was touted as a cost-saving measure with the estimated bill at $400 billion over 10 years, but within months of the passage of the bill, the costs jumped to $534 billion, and many opponents of the privatization initiative predicted that the costs would increase even higher, especially since drug costs were rising above the level of inflation (in 2005 the White House raised the estimate of the program to $1.2 trillion over ten years).[13]

There were some clear corporate winners in the new prescription drug system. The profit returns to the pharmaceutical industry were estimated at $139 billion, with the insurance companies and HMOs also reaping huge gains. The legislation passed by the Republican-controlled Congress prohibited any group from purchasing agreements and volume discounts with the drug companies as was the case with the Veterans Administration. The result of this prohibition was that the drug companies and their allies in the insurance industry and HMOs were protected from government-sponsored competitive pricing arrangements. So while Medicare recipients gained some new benefits (minus the donut hole issue), and criticism died down as enrollments went up, it was the private sector that became the clear profit winners in this new prescription drug initiative.

The different approaches to health care in this country were made even more vivid during the 2007 Congressional debate over the State Children's Health Insurance Program (SCHIP). The program provides insurance coverage to 6.6 million children from families who are above the federally defined poverty level but do not have the money to purchase health benefits. A bipartisan Congress approved, by wide margins, a bill to increase the SCHIP program by $35 billion over the next five years and add over 4 million new children to the program.[14] President Bush threatened a veto of the legislation and offered his own proposal that would increase SCHIP funding by $5 billion over 5 years. The president stated that he was opposed to the large increase presented by Congress because it would place too many children into a government-based health insurance program. The increase in the SCHIP program was to be funded by a jump in the federal cigarette tax, which was not palatable to some Republicans, who saw a tax, no matter what the source or the outcome, as unacceptable.[15]

Many observers of the Congressional debate and the president's threatened veto saw the battle over SCHIP funding as a prelude to an electoral battle over national health care that was certain to be part of the 2008 campaign. As *Washington Post* columnist E.J. Dionne stated, "If a proposal with broad bipartisan support that is friendly to state governments and covers the most beloved group in society—children—can't avoid being gutted for ideological reasons, what hope is there for a larger health compromise?"[16] Although President Bush was in no mood to compromise over the program, many members of Congress, both Democrats and Republicans, were reluctant to turn down a bill that was designed to improve the health of young children. Those in favor of the SCHIP program and its expansion vowed that they would continue to press for health insurance for children. President Bush eventually vetoed the SCHIP legislation, and the House and Senate were not able to override the veto as Republicans stood by their president despite the anticipated criticism from voters in their home state and district. Eventually the SCHIP program was extended to 2009 but without any increases in funding to the states. The title of the SCHIP program was later changed to CHIP.

As the debate over health care reform continued into the Obama administration and the differences and divisions became sharpened between Democrats and Republicans, there was no shortage of policy recommendations on how best to provide coverage to the uninsured, keep costs down, and provide quality care to the patients. Early on in the Obama presidency, many Democrats suggested that spending caps be instituted as a way of controlling runaway costs. This policy prescription ran counter to the market system in this country, and as a result, most of the representatives of the insurance, pharmaceutical, and hospital industries expressed opposition, saying in part that such caps would deter research and make the medical profession unattractive as salaries and salary raises would be controlled by government agencies.

President Obama was determined to break through the opposition to comprehensive health care reform and make reform one of the key policy priorities of his administration. As a first step, Obama called a health summit at the White House and brought together a wide range of health care professionals. At the summit and later in other public pronouncements, Obama signaled that the core of his reform was the so-called public option, a government program akin to Medicare that would compete with the private insurance industry and provide a low-cost health care package to those currently without medical insurance. Other aspects of the reform effort would address issues such as denial of insurance for pre-existing conditions, bureaucratic waste, and the burgeoning cost of health care to employers, both large and small. There was also the commitment on the part of the Obama plan to provide continuous health care coverage to those unemployed and the opportunity for families with children up to 26 years of age to remain on a family plan.[17]

As the Obama health care reform plan evolved, the concept of a public option focused on creating competition among insurance providers and enrolling many of the uninsured with low cost insurance as a way of keeping premiums down and limiting yearly increases in the percent of GDP directed to health care. In theory, the Obama proposal was based on signing up healthy young people by large numbers who would compensate for the costs related to those insured requiring expensive health care. Furthermore, those Americans who did not purchase the heavily-subsidized health insurance from the government would be subject to a tax penalty. This tax penalty was seen as a means of getting people to sign up for the government program and ensure the viability of the health care reform.

Republican leaders in the health care debate were staunchly opposed to the public option part of the Obama proposal and offered their own solutions to the reform by presenting policy recommendations that accented personal responsibility for medical coverage. Some Republicans suggested that Americans should be offered the opportunity to purchase their own insurance in a way similar to buying life or car insurance. To soften the cost factor, Republicans offered proposals that provided tax incentives, private savings accounts, and deductions as a way of keeping the government out of the health care business. Republicans argued that their approach would create more market competition, lead to a reduction in insurance costs, and offer individuals an incentive to take better care of themselves because individuals would be footing the bill for their own health care.

At the heart of the Republican proposal was the medical savings account. The accounts work in a manner similar to retirement plans as citizens can contribute a sum of money (initially proposed as $2600 for an individual and $5,150 for a family) to a tax-deductible account and use that money to pay for medical bills that were not part of any government-sponsored program. The objective of the medical savings account was to encourage Americans to provide for their own health care just like they provide for their own retirement (minus any government-sponsored Social Security).[18] Critics of the savings accounts pointed out that many low-income Americans and those entering senior status might not be able to afford to place money aside for health care and that only those who are wealthy could take advantage of this opportunity.

By June 2009, the health care reform issue began to take shape. In a major address to the American Medical Association, President Obama laid out some of the key elements of his plan. Obama sought to link health care reform to the national economy as he stressed that if no changes were made to the manner in which medical care was delivered and paid for, both the business sector and the government would face costs that could easily keep the nation in a recession and further add to the national debt. Obama continued to stress the importance of the public option of his health care reform package, but he also tried to gain support from doctors by emphasizing the importance of taking care of patients rather than dealing with insurance companies to get approval for tests and procedures and then being reimbursed for their work. Obama also talked about his position on malpractice insurance and the need to establish a national medical database to bring greater efficiency to a bureaucratically weighed down system of medical care. After the speech, Republicans shot back that they would not accept any public option health care reform and stressed that the Obama plan would be cumbersome, severely weaken the private sector insurance industry, and place a forced tax on Americans who did not participate in the program.[19]

The debate over health care reform finally entered the legislative arena in March, 2010. The Obama reform effort fostered not only a fight between Congress and the White House, Democrats and Republicans, conservatives and liberals, but also among an army of lobbyists representing the insurance industry, hospitals, pharmaceutical corporations, doctors and nurses associations, health care activists, and the emerging Tea Party anti-big government movement. It became clear early on in the debate that there would be substantial differences on the bill between the House and Senate and indeed within the two political parties.

Although the Republicans were united in their opposition to the public option and what they viewed as inevitable tax increases and government bureaucracy, the Democrats were faced with disagreement among their members over issues such as whether abortions and access to free contraception would be covered in the new reform bill, whether insurance would become mandatory, and whether businesses would be penalized for not providing health insurance to their employees. The Obama administration also introduced a two-tier system of health benefits: 1) a federal government exchange that permitted potential insurance buyers to sign up online or in person for insurance that was low-cost and offered a number of insurance company options, and 2) a link to state-controlled Medicaid programs that were subsidized by the government and offered those poor Americans deemed eligible an opportunity to get health insurance.

After weeks of partisan wrangling, a Senate version of the health care reform bill passed that served as the basis for a future agreement with the House. Republicans attacked the Senate bill as filled with secret deals that mollified conservative Democrats and much too expensive (one estimate put the cost as $1 trillion over ten years). The Republicans' message did strike a chord with the American people as support for the overhaul waned. A sizeable majority saw the bill as another example of big government, more taxes, and a denial of personal freedom. Reform initiatives, such as eliminating preexisting conditions for insurance coverage, continuation of coverage to the unemployed, and the opportunity to extend coverage to families with children under 26, were lost in the campaign to stop the legislation.

On March 23, 2010, President Obama signed the Affordable Care Act—soon to be called Obamacare—a comprehensive reform of health care that had been sought since the administration of Harry Truman. The vote in the House of Representatives, 216–212 in favor, showed the narrow support for the Senate-driven legislation. The Affordable Care Act did phase in some of the more controversial tax policies and mandates until 2014 along with other regulatory issues that were raised by the Republicans in the House of Representatives.[20]

Since its passage, the Republican-led Congress has tried 56 times to repeal Obamacare, all unsuccessful as President Obama used his veto power.

Despite the failure to repeal Obamacare, the reform effort had great difficulty being implemented. In its first enrollment year, there was a massive breakdown of the federal exchange system as the government-contracted Internet site broke down or created huge delays. Eventually, 11 million Americans did sign up for the insurance, supporting the administration's contention that this reform would continue to be popular and meet the sign-up goals that guaranteed a financially secure program. Nevertheless, Obamacare continued to be viewed as unpopular by a majority of Americans and the Republicans used this view to continue their fight to repeal the Affordable Care Act.

Obamacare continued to face stiff challenges to a successful implementation. In 2012, in a landmark decision, the Supreme Court sided with some states that were opposed to accepting the extension of the Affordable Care Act through Medicaid. With this judicial victory, over 20 states, most with Republican governors, refused to participate in the Medicaid extension program. The impact of this decision by the governors was that millions of Americans were denied the opportunity to access health exchanges and purchase low-cost health insurance. Besides the opposition of Republican governors, many of those in these states viewed the extension of Obamacare through Medicaid as having long-term fiscal challenges as subsidies from the federal government were for a limited time and would then place the burden on state tax resources. With 20 states not participating through the Medicaid program, the implementation of Obamacare was left to the federal-based exchanges and thus it was made much more difficult for poor people to access the new health law.[21]

The trials of implementing Obamacare did not end with the Supreme Court decision. Religious organizations, particularly in hospitals and universities associated with the Catholic Church, challenged the option of free contraception on the basis of personal conscience and government intent to force policies that violated personal religious beliefs. There was also growing disenchantment among Americans who lost their private insurance because it did not meet the requirements of Obamacare. Also, many small- and medium-sized businesses complained that the requirement to provide health care to their employees severely impacted their companies and forced them to downsize the number of employees.[22]

Perhaps the biggest challenge to Obamacare came in 2016 when a number of insurance companies dropped out of the program, citing declining profits, thus leaving potential participants in the program with fewer options and higher costs. The decision by some insurance companies worsened late in 2016 when the government announced that premiums for Obamacare would increase by an average of 25%, an announcement that rattled the administration and gave the Republicans and their candidates a new opportunity to challenge the law and repeal it if victorious in the presidential election. Despite the fact that the costs of premiums had leveled off in the previous years of the program and the overall cost of health care had decreased, the premium increase emboldened opponents of Obamacare. Nevertheless, sign-ups for Obamacare continued at a brisk rate and the administration and its supporters both in Congress and in the country pledged to make the program work with appropriate "fixes" rather than scuttle the landmark legislative legacy of the president. The future of Obamacare remains uncertain, despite its record of expanding health coverage to millions of Americans, and the next four years of the Trump presidency may define more precisely how this health care reform will function.[23] Even before President Trump took office, Republicans were calling for a repeal of Obamacare, despite the fact that they had difficulty articulating what specific health care plan would replace the Affordable Care Act. The Republicans were opposed to the mandated tax penalty, the Medicaid subsidies, and the rising cost of premiums, but they were criticized by health care experts for not developing a way to insure the uninsured.

The Republicans saw their opening on repealing and replacing Obamacare with the election of Donald Trump, who sought early on to live up to his campaign pledge to repeal and replace the Affordable Care Act. But despite majorities in both the House and Senate and promises by legislative leaders such as Speaker of the House Paul Ryan, the efforts to end Obamacare were stymied by ideological conflicts within the House membership. Staunch conservatives (dubbed the Freedom Caucus) were adamant in pushing for a complete repeal of the ACA but had little in the way of a replacement other than promises of greater freedom, competition, and lower premiums. Members of the Freedom Caucus were adamant in their refusal to engage in compromise efforts that kept in place some of the popular provisions of the ACA such as guarantees of coverage for pre-existing conditions and a range of other medical procedures. Also, the Freedom Caucus was determined to get rid of the Medicaid subsidies that provided the poor with insurance coverage. Health experts and the non-partisan Congressional Budget Office examined the proposal and stated that upwards of 24 million Americans would lose their coverage or be unable to pay for higher premiums and deductibles under the Republican plan.

As the stand-off between the Freedom Caucus and moderates within the Republican House membership continued and became more caustic, public opinion showed heightened support for Obamacare and skepticism that the Republican plan would improve health care and access to health care. Support for the ACA was joined by pressure from major interest groups such as the American Association of Retired Persons and the American Medical Association along with grassroots groups who were angry with the Republican proposal. Demonstrations in many congressional districts with Republican representatives created a public relations nightmare.

For his part, President Trump engaged in an effort to end the dispute, but he was unable to change minds and arrive at a deal that could provide a legislative victory and a validation of his campaign promise. As the repeal measure went to the floor of the House for a vote, it was clear that Speaker Ryan and his leadership team did not have the votes to pass the legislation, and so after weeks of negotiating and promises of repeal and replace, the vote on the ACA was taken off the floor, ending at least for a time the Republican effort to end the Affordable Care Act. This failure of the Republicans to repeal and replace Obamacare was a huge political blow to President Trump and the Republicans and revealed the deep divisions within the GOP in Congress over how to end what was becoming an increasingly popular health care program.

The Republicans, however, were not ready to give up. The leadership team went back to the members and made some additional changes to the Medicaid subsidies, leaving more decisions on the program up to the states and making even deeper cuts in the program for the poor. The bill, the American Health Care Act of 2017, kept the protection for pre-existing conditions, which was widely supported by public opinion. The bill also provided tax credits for families to purchase health insurance, a favorite Republican solution to funding health care. The changes and compromises gave the Republicans in the House the votes they needed, yet the bill barely passed the House (217–213) and went forward to the Senate where an equally contentious fight among the Republicans began. After weeks of seeking to gain the votes for a repeal and replace of the Affordable Care Act, the Republican leadership failed to get the necessary votes for passage and adjourned for the summer, unable again to end Obamacare.

A legislative journey that began with the administration of Harry Truman was certain to face legislative challenges, if not outright repeal. As has always been the case with health care reform in this country, the most recent leg of the journey has been filled with "starts and stops" and deep, deep partisan and national divisions.

The Great Debate

Health care reform has proven to be a difficult and controversial policy problem to resolve. In many respects, it is the most contentious policy issue in the United States. Part of the problem with reforming health care is the basic issue of how best to deliver medical care—through a market-based system with little or no government involvement or a government directed, subsidized, and regulated system. Then there is the issue of access—should every American receive health care and how is universal health care achieved?

Debate Topic

Is health care in the United States a basic right that should be available to all Americans, despite the cost, the regulation, and the inevitable role of government?

Critical Thinking Questions

1. Why is the United States the only industrialized country not providing universal health care?

2. Some have said that Americans should solve their health care crisis using tax breaks, incentives, and personal savings accounts. Do you agree?
3. Should health care benefits be part of an employment package or should the employee be responsible for his or her own health coverage?
4. Should Americans be forced, through mandated-care programs, to buy their own health insurance coverage through the government?
5. How are you planning to deal with the cost of health care in the coming years?

Connections

A helpful guide to the Affordable Care Act can be found at www.healthcare.gov

A non-partisan consumer site that serves as a watchdog of the health industry in the United States can be found at www.healthinsurance.org

The American Medical Association is active in the debate on national health care and other health care policies: http://www.ama-assn.org

Forbes, a business magazine, provides a listing and examination of major health insurance companies. The site is at www.forbes.com/HealthInsurance

Massachusetts has the nation's first state-directed, mandated health care program. The program, called the Commonwealth Connector, is explained at www.mahealth connector.org/

Some Books to Read

Blackman, Josh, *Unprecedented: The Constitutional Challenge to Obamacare* (New York: Public Affairs, 2013).

Brill, Steve, *America's Bitter Pill: Money, Politics, Backroom Deals and the Fight to Fix Our Broken Health Care System* (New York: Random House, 2015).

Dawes, David, *150 Years of Obamacare* (Baltimore, MD: JHU Press, 2016).

Jonas, Steve, Raymond Goldsteen, and Karen Goldsteen, *An Introduction to the U.S. Health Care System*, 7th edition (Berlin: Springer Publishers, 2007).

Reece, Richard, *Understanding Obamacare: Travails of Implementation, Notes of a Health Reform Watchdog* (New York: Westbow Press, 2014).

Notes

1. Robert Pear, *New York Times*, December 3, 2015.
2. Reed Abelson and Margot Sanger-Katz, *New York Times*, September 16, 2016.
3. For background on the issue of health care and competitiveness see Lee Hudson Teslik, "Health Care Costs and U.S. Competitiveness," Council on Foreign Relations, March, 2012, www.cfr.org/publication/13325
4. For Kenneth Thorpe's comments, see "PFCD Executive Director Ken Thorpe Testifies Before Health Reform Leaders," December 10, 2008. See www.fightchronic disease.org

5. See David Broder, "Our Broken Health Care System," *Washington Post*, July 15, 2004. Also David Broder, "An Urgent Case for Fixing Health Care," *Washington Post*, May 29, 2005. Also a discussion of the 1993 Health Security Act can be found in an article in the *New York Times*; see Adam Clymer, Robert Pear, and Robin Toner, "The Health Care Debate, What Went Wrong? How the Health Care Campaign Collapsed," *New York Times*, August 29, 1994.

6. See Bipartisan Patient Protection Act, Senate Bill 1052, 107 Congress, 2001–2002, www.congress.gov

7. Interview with Bill Gradison, "William Gradison: Insights Into the Past and Future of Health Care Policy-Making," *Business Insurance*, October 29, 1997.

8. See www.mahealthconnector.org/portal/site/connector

9. The various positions of the candidates running for the presidency in 2008 can be found in an article by Perry Bacon Jr. and Anne Kornblut, "A Reformer, Reformed," *Washington Post National Weekly Edition*, September 24–30, 2007, p. 13.

10. Ibid.

11. www.whitehouse.gov/2007/stateoftheunion

12. See Henry Aaron, "Prescription Drug Bill: The Good, the Bad, the Ugly," *Brookings*, January 15, 2004.

13. "Millions Not Joining Medicare Drug Plan," *Washington Post*, February 21, 2006.

14. See "Bush Vetoes Children's Health Insurance Bill," *Boston Globe*, October 4, 2007.

15. Ibid.

16. *Washington Post*, September 26, 2007.

17. For an overview of the Obamacare legislative process see "History and Timeline of the Affordable Care Act," *eHealth*, September 22, 2016, www.resources.ehealthinsurance.org

18. For the Republican alternatives to Obamacare see Ashley Craig, "Here Are 10 Republican Alternatives to Obamacare," *Opportunity Lives*, February 13, 2015, www.opportunitylives.com

19. See also the Republican position as stated in its party platform, "Republican Party on Health Care," *On The Issues*, 2012, www.OnTheIssues.org

20. Robert Pear and David M. Herszenborn, "Obama Hails Vote on Health Care as Answering the 'Call of History,'" *New York Times*, March 21, 2009.

21. Robert Pear, "State Level Brawls Over Medicaid Reflect Divided GOP," *New York Times*, December 27, 2015.

22. Greg Stohr, "Religious Objections on Obamacare Get U.S. Supreme Court Review," *Bloomberg Politics*, November 6, 2015.

23. See the analysis of the third year of Obamacare in *The Economist*, November 7, 2015.

5

IMMIGRATION **AND** IMMIGRATION **POLITICS**

Issue Focus

No issue in this book creates such strong opinions among the American people as how the United States should deal with its illegal immigrant population. One of the founding principles of American political culture is the importance of holding to the rule of law, yet the United States is a nation made up of immigrants, some here illegally, who often contribute to the general economy and enrich society with their diversity. Those immigrants who come to the United States as undocumented have touched off a furious debate as to how to properly match the American governing principle of the rule of law with the reality of millions of illegal immigrants who are part of the national economy.

Chapter Objectives

This issue chapter will seek to:

1. Explore the extent of illegal immigration into the United States and the reasons for the migration of undocumented workers.

2. Examine the benefits and drawbacks of illegal immigration on the American economy; federal, state, and local services; and the impact on the melting pot culture, traditionally a key foundation of the US immigration culture.

3. Discuss the pros and cons of the policy responses of federal, state, and local governments to illegal immigration.

SOME BACKGROUND

There is perhaps no more passionate issue on the American political agenda than illegal immigration into the United States. Although this country is a nation of immigrants and the Statue of Liberty calls out "give me your tired, your poor, your huddled masses longing to be free," when it comes to those from far-away nations who enter this country illegally, the welcome sign is taken down. Public opinion polls consistently show that Americans remain open to those foreigners who follow the immigration laws and enter this country through the established channels. But when it comes to those immigrants who climb a fence from Mexico into California, arrive by a broken-down fishing boat from Haiti, or travel long distances from Central America, Brazil, or China, the popular reaction is usually negative and the solution direct—imprisonment or deportation.

The issue of illegal immigration into this country, however, is not so cut and dried, and the solutions not so direct. Up to twelve million illegal immigrants (this is the working estimate, but officials admit that they do not have any valid means to measure who is in this country illegally) are currently residing in this country, and they come here in search of work—work that is not that difficult to find, especially in low-wage jobs such as landscaping, roofing, or meat packing, along with restaurants and hotel service jobs. Some of these illegal immigrants eventually return home with sufficient money to start a business or build a new home, but many stay and blend into American society, hoping that they will not be arrested by immigration officials and forced to go back to certain poverty (and in some cases death) back in their country of origin.

The issue of the growing presence of these illegal immigrants in the United States has entered the political process as government officials from local town governments to the US Congress and the president have weighed in on how this country should respond to this influx of workers. There has been no shortage of solutions to illegal immigration from securing the border with Mexico with cement and steel walls; using the United States military, Coast Guard, and state national guards to beef up patrols; fining and arresting employers who knowingly hire the undocumented; and staging massive roundups of those here illegally. In the 2016 presidential campaign, Donald Trump secured his victory in the Republican primaries with his pledge to build a wall along the Mexican border to restrict access to the United States. He even claimed that the Mexican government would pay for the wall. This promise by Trump resonated with many in the Republican electoral base and other Americans who revealed a nativist backlash to illegal immigration.[1]

On the Record

Donald Trump's most memorable and controversial statement in the 2016 presidential campaign was his position on building a wall separating the United States and Mexico as a means of limiting access to illegal immigrants entering this country. His statement was:

> I will build a great wall—and nobody builds a wall better than me—and I'll build them very inexpensively. I will build a great wall on our southern border, and I'll make Mexico pay for that wall.

Source: Trump campaign website

Although there are clear differences and divisions over illegal immigration, there seems to be one thing that is common to the debate, and that is the passion that Americans express about these 12 million workers. It seems that every American has taken a position on what to do about these workers and their families, many of whom have been born in this country. The debates surrounding these new arrivals to our country have raised a range of questions and concerns about who we are as a people, how we will be able to maintain our diverse ethnic and racial identity, and whether we remain committed to offering the American dream to a new generation of immigrants, despite their status.

These questions and concerns exist within the economic and social context of globalization, which has changed the rules not only on trade, aid, and investment, but also on work and workers. While, in the past, the movement of people seeking work in a foreign country was largely seasonal and limited to a few economic sectors, globalization has intensified the need for labor (usually cheap, unskilled labor) and has created a huge army of international workers drawn to advanced, industrialized countries like the United States. Unless globalization undergoes a radical transformation in the coming years, or countries like the United States shut down their borders, this international work force will continue to travel in search of jobs and greater income, whether they possess proper documentation or not.[2]

DEBATES, DIFFERENCES, AND DIVISIONS

There is no more divisive and contentious aspect of the debate over illegal immigration into the United States than the economic consequences of the 12 million undocumented people living and working in this country. Broadly speaking, the issue is whether the illegal immigrants are a drain on the national economy as they take jobs away from Americans, depress wage scales, and heighten the costs of education, health care, and crime, or whether they are contributing members of the American economy as they pay taxes, spend on consumer goods, and perform work functions in which Americans have shown little interest. There is no limit to the positions of either side in this argument, and reams of data and analysis have been brought to bear by advocates on either side of the debate.

Those who criticize illegal immigration and its impact on the national economy stress that undocumented workers siphon taxpayer dollars away from vital services. Data from federal and state sources show that the cost of providing health care, education, and other social services for illegal immigrants was $113 billion in 2014. The average cost of the 1.8 million school-age children of illegal immigrants was estimated at $7500 per child or $11.2 billion. States such as Texas, New Mexico, Arizona, and California have had to face the economic challenges of providing assistance to illegal immigrants, with some hospitals forced to deal with closings or bankruptcies from federally mandated programs that require free emergency room services to those here illegally. At the federal level, the costs of supporting illegal immigrants is centered in Medicaid payments (medical assistance to the poor), food assistance, the federal prison system (where illegal immigrants are held awaiting decisions on their status), and federal aid to local school districts.[3]

Also at issue in terms of social welfare spending at the state and local levels are the so-called "anchor babies"—an estimated 300,000 babies born to parents of illegal immigrants who are, by birth in the United States, automatically American citizens. These "anchor" babies add to the cost of hospital care and eventually to the educational systems of cities, towns, and counties. The language in the 14th Amendment to the constitution states that "all persons born or naturalized in the United States" are granted citizenship. Many critics say that language should be changed to curb the anchor baby practice of coming to the United States illegally and then giving birth to a child who gains citizenship rights and social welfare and education support.[4]

On the other side of the illegal immigration debate regarding economic costs is the position taken by those who claim that there is a positive economic impact from the undocumented immigrants that goes well beyond what they may cost the taxpayer at the federal, state, and local level. The undocumented population, for example, pays federal and state taxes, along with rents, bank fees, and mortgages as well as purchasing a whole host of consumer products and paying sales tax. According to a study done by the conservative CATO Institute, removing undocumented workers would take $250 billion out of the national economy each year, 10% of Nevada's workforce population would evaporate, and three million more people in California would either be forced to return to their country of origin or migrate elsewhere.[5] A further study by a UCLA economist and political scientist, Raul Hinojosa Ojeda, estimated that, over a ten-year period, the removal of the undocumented population would cost the United States economy $2.6 trillion, with the hotel, restaurant, construction, home improvement, and farming (especially harvesting) industries hit hard.[6]

Data Bank

Numerical Size and Share of the Foreign-Born Population in the United States—1970–2014

	Size of Immigrant Population (millions)	Immigrant Share of Total US Population (%)
1970	9.6	4.7
1980	14.0	16.2
1990	19.8	7.9
2000	31.1	11.1
2010	40.0	12.9
2014	42.4	13.3

Source: Migration Policy Institute/Data from US Census Bureau

Those on either side of the illegal immigration debate present their data and their arguments in campaigns seeking to gain the attention of the White House, Congress, and the American public opinion. Some advocacy groups fill the Internet and other media outlets with economic and budgetary reasons to put a stop to illegal immigration, while others tout the advantages of these workers, not just in terms of cheap labor, but in the numerous ways that they contribute to the local, state, and national economy. There is so much information and advocacy surrounding the illegal immigration debate that there is no clear body of evidence that provides with certainty whether illegal immigration provides real employment benefits to this country or is a serious drain on our governmental, social, and cultural resources. What remains is the passion as both sides battle it out over these 12 million workers. As with most critical domestic policy issues, the national controversy over illegal immigration is directed at the White House and Congress.

The contemporary policy process related to illegal immigration begins with the administration of George W. Bush. The Bush administration took a number of steps to limit the flow of illegal immigrants into the United States as pressure mounted in the Republican Party and Congress to stem the flow of undocumented migrants entering the United States, especially from Mexico. The $2 billion Strategic Border Initiative (SBI) was launched early in his administration and was presented as the "most technologically advanced border security initiative in American history." The SBI was a mix of video surveillance of border entry points, robotic drones, and heat-sensing devices designed to enhance the ability of the Border Patrol to spot the movement of illegal immigrants from Mexico. Then, in 2006, the US Immigration and Customs Enforcement Agency began a renewed effort to raid businesses that had hired undocumented workers. Finally, in 2006, Congress passed the Secure Fence Act, which funded (at the cost of $2 billion) a 700-mile fence that was fifteen feet high, with the critical section of the fence erected from Calexico, California to Douglas, Arizona, the prime entry area for illegal immigrants.[7]

In his 2006 State of the Union address, President Bush called for a comprehensive immigration plan that would "address the problem of illegal immigration and deliver a system that is secure, productive, orderly and fair." Although the president accented the need to secure our borders, he also proposed a guest worker program and the opportunity for current illegal aliens to work toward gaining full citizenship status. President Bush's proposal sought to balance the pressure from his own party, which pushed for sealing the border with Mexico, and business interests, which wanted to continue the practice of hiring immigrant laborers. Because the president's plan for immigration reform was critical to the political debate that ensued throughout 2006 and 2007, it is instructive to present the core proposals that he presented to Congress. Those proposals are as follows:

> An increase in the numbers of Border Patrol agents along with National Guard units to heighten surveillance, install barriers, and patrol access points.

A further expansion in funding of the president's Secure Border Initiative and its emphasis on using high-tech methods of surveillance and detection.

An expansion of "expedited removal" so that captured illegal aliens can be sent back to the country of their origin more quickly.

An increase in detention facilities, which would allow Border Patrol agents to incarcerate larger numbers of illegal aliens.

The training of 1500 state and local police officials to work with federal officials to protect the border.

A tougher stance on workplace enforcement and stiffer fines for employers who knowingly hire illegal aliens.

A strengthening of the ability of the Department of Health and Human Services to develop a more sophisticated database to determine whether illegal aliens have acquired Social Security cards.

The development of a tamper-proof identity card for every legal foreign worker so that businesses can verify the legal status of their workers.

The creation of a Temporary Worker Program that a) allows employers to hire workers only for jobs that Americans have not taken and only for limited terms of time in the United States (thus with the understanding that these workers will return home), and b) issues Temporary Worker status only when the economy warrants it.

A program that allows illegal immigrants the possibility of earning citizenship status by paying a penalty for their illegal entry, learning English, paying their taxes, passing a background check, and holding a job continuously for a set number of years. When these requirements are met, the illegal alien will be considered for citizenship but must go to the "back of the line." There will be no amnesty, but rather an emphasis on citizenship, loyalty to the United States, and assimilation into American society.[8]

FYI

90% of the over 21,000 Border Patrol agents are stationed in various enforcement sections along the 1,951 mile border with Mexico. In 2015 the Border Patrol apprehended 188,122 illegal immigrants at our southern borders and returned them to their homeland. This level of apprehension was an 18% decline from 2014 and the lowest since 1969, suggesting to some that interest by those without documentation is no longer as strong as in the past. Moreover, Immigration and Customs and Enforcement police have stepped up deportation efforts of undocumented immigrants thus further limiting cross border movement to the United States.

Source: US Border Patrol web site

President Bush's immigration reform package had something in it for everyone from the "secure the border" group to the "let them stay" group. But it was the last proposal dealing with the possibility of earning citizenship that caused the most fury and became the key focus of the political debate in Congress and, indeed, the country. Republicans in Congress, especially those from border states, were furious with the proposal for a so-called "pathway to citizenship," stating that such a program would reward illegality and likely increase the prospect of immigration. Democrats, on the other hand, saw the proposal as a good step forward toward resolving this contentious issue by setting the bar high and requiring illegal immigrants to take certain steps toward citizenship, including going to the end of the line and waiting until legal immigrants received proper documentation.

What appeared to some to be a reasonable compromise proposal by the president set off a firestorm of opposition from the Republican-controlled Congress. Representative James Sensenbrenner from Wisconsin introduced the Border Protection, Anti-Terrorism and Illegal Immigration Control Act, which was in stark disagreement with the president and rejected the guest worker and pathway to citizenship proposals. Besides pushing for the border fence, Sensenbrenner went even further by advocating that illegal immigrants face felony, not misdemeanor, charges for crossing into the United States, requiring that they face mandatory detention after being apprehended and that employers face increased fines (up to $40,000) for hiring undocumented aliens. As Representative Sensenbrenner said of his bill, "With the border controls and the enforcement of employer sanctions, the jobs for illegal immigrants will dry up . . . and if you can't get a job because employer sanctions are enforced, my belief is that a lot of the illegal immigrants will simply go back home."[9]

The Sensenbrenner bill not only diverged significantly from the White House proposal, but also from work being done in the Senate, where a spirit of compromise existed among Democrats and Republicans. With Senators Kennedy of Massachusetts and McCain of Arizona taking the lead and bringing together a broad coalition of Democrats and Republicans, the Senate was fashioning the Comprehensive Immigration Reform Act, which incorporated the guest worker program and the controversial pathway to citizenship. Because the Senate bill was viewed by many as a middle-of-the-road proposal, the essential elements of the legislation are provided below:

A speed up in the construction of the 700-mile border wall and the hiring of an additional 18,000 new Border Patrol agents.

The creation of a database that would allow employers the opportunity to verify the status of job applications.

The formation of a "guest worker" program that would allow some 400,000 illegal immigrants currently without proper documentation to live and work in the United States for up to three two-year terms.

In, addition, the Senate bill provided for the creation of a "Z" visa that would allow undocumented immigrants who arrived before January 1, 2007, and who identify themselves as here illegally, to enter a citizen track after paying a fine of $5,000, returning to their homeland for a period of time, undergoing a background check, and having no criminal record. The "Z" visa would be valid for four years and renewable for another four years while the immigrant applied for citizenship status. Those applying for and gaining the "Z" visa would be placed at the end of the line of those being considered for United States citizenship. Only spouses and minors of illegal immigrants would be eligible to apply for the "Z" visa, not extended family members.[10]

Further, the Senate bill provided for the development of a "merit system" for awarding permanent resident status (the green card) that would require proof of English proficiency, attendance at civics classes, and education courses designed to improve work skills.

The bipartisan coalition members in the Senate were convinced that they had presented a viable alternative to the stringent House position and the president's proposal, especially with the introduction of the "Z" visa and its demanding requirements for citizenship. But opponents of the Senate version of immigration reform mounted a vigorous media and grassroots campaign using talk radio, mass mailings, and Internet networks to place enormous pressure on the Senate and its compromise. The public pressure against the Senate version was so intense that the bipartisan coalition broke apart, and the bill died an early death. With the House refusing to endorse the Senate version, and the Senate incapable of fighting back the wave of public opinion, comprehensive immigration reform was put aside in favor of piecemeal policies such as the border fence and more vigorous enforcement of employer hiring practices.

Into this presidential and congressional mix over illegal immigration reform was added the growing presence of the Latino community in the national debate. During the debates in the House and the Senate, millions of Latinos throughout the United States protested in largely peaceful demonstrations in most of the major cities in the country. The demonstrations showed the enormous grassroots organizational power of the Latinos (fueled in part by Spanish language television and radio stations). In April 2006, in over 102 cities, crowds that varied from 100,000 to 500,000 protested the Sensenbrenner bill and endorsed the concept of a pathway to citizenship in the Senate bill. The demonstrations reached a high point on May 1 when the Latino protestors staged the "Great American Boycott" that was designed to remind Americans of the important economic impact of immigrants, legal and illegal, on the national economy.[11]

The boycott did not appear to have much of an effect as many immigrants went to work (some fearing retribution from their bosses) and most continued their normal buying habits. There was also a backlash from many Americans who were bothered by the fact that many demonstrators carried Mexican flags and displayed signs with slogans such as "We Are the Only Owners of the Continent." Nevertheless, despite the points of controversy surrounding the demonstrations, the message was loud and clear that Latino "power" in the American political system could not be ignored and that the Latino community throughout the country had the capacity to band together to make their voices heard on the illegal immigration issue.

With the immigration reform legislation battle in stalemate, the debate over illegal immigration did not come to an end, but was refocused in different directions, primarily at the state and local level. Nineteen states passed various forms of employer sanction laws that penalized those who knowingly hired illegal immigrants. Some of the states with such legislation like Nevada wrote the bills with language that was so general and expansive that prosecution of employers would be difficult, if not impossible. In Nevada, a massive building boom was in place for years and illegal immigrants were known to form a sizeable portion of the workforce. The Nevada legislature and the business community thus created a bill that was unenforceable and thus would not limit the building boom.

In neighboring Arizona, however, the legislature passed a stiff employer sanction bill called the Fair and Legal Employment Act. The legislation established the power of the state to suspend for 10 days or, after numerous offenses, revoke business licenses of those firms who hired illegal immigrants without proper documentation. The purpose of the law was to create an anti-illegal immigration climate and force undocumented migrants to leave the state. Anti-illegal immigration groups pushed hard for the legislation as they claimed widespread support from small businesses, contractors, and farmers. One state representative in Arizona summed up the position of the supporters of the legislation when he said, "Illegal immigrants have no business being here, none. Shut off the lights, and the crowd will go home. I hope they will self-deport." But before the bill was officially implemented in January 2008, immigration groups supportive of illegal aliens went to federal court to challenge the law as beyond the scope of state power. The argument was made that immigration is a federal matter and the states do not have the right to punish employers who hire illegal immigrants. David Selden, who represented a coalition of business interests (who likely benefited from illegal workers), stated, "It's only the federal government that has the authority to decide who is an illegal alien." According to Selden, "state and local government can only take action against a business after the federal government has determined that a worker is in the country illegally."[12] The federal court agreed with Selden's argument.

There have also been attempts at the local level to control illegal immigration. In Hazelton, Pennsylvania, Mayor Lou Barletta enforced the city's new Illegal Immigration Relief Act that imposed fines on landlords who rented apartments and houses to illegal immigrants. The law also denied business permits to companies that hired undocumented workers. The law further required tenants to register with the city and pay for a housing permit, which would be granted contingent on compliance with the law. The Hazelton law was similar to over 90 such ordinances around the country that sought to limit illegal immigration into communities by controlling housing rentals and sanctioning landlords and businesses. Mayor Barletta pushed for the new law as a result of a crime wave in Hazelton that he attributed to the rising population of illegal immigrants. Although Hazelton is a city of only 30,000, it had become increasingly popular for immigrants leaving Philadelphia and New York City to find employment.[13]

The Hazelton Illegal Immigration Relief Act was the subject of a lawsuit brought by Hispanic advocacy groups who contended that the city did not have the authority to restrict illegal immigration through housing and employment sanctions. Again the argument forwarded by these groups was that the federal government has the sole power to regulate immigration and that the Hazelton law violated the due process and equal protection clauses of the Fourteenth Amendment. The suit against the Hazelton law reached federal district court, and the presiding judge found that the Illegal Immigration Relief Act violated federal laws and was a usurpation of the government's exclusive control over matters related to immigration. Although the judge's ruling affected only Hazelton, it showed again that the failure of Congress and the president to enact comprehensive immigration reform sparked efforts at the state and local level to control illegal immigration, even though the authority to do so is not within the boundaries of the constitution.

But while federal courts have shut down attempts at the state and local level to place restrictions on illegal immigrants either in employment or housing, the issue of providing driving licenses to undocumented immigrants has taken center stage. Twelve states, including California, have passed legislation permitting illegal immigrants to apply for and receive driver's licenses. In California, 605,000 licenses were granted to undocumented immigrants in 2015 as a result of Assembly Bill 60. The argument for the law is that it increases safety on the California roads because drivers, whether in the state legally or illegally, must pass tests in order to get the license and are more likely to be insured. Although the California license states clearly that "federal limits apply," meaning that law enforcement officers in other states are not required to accept the license as valid identification, the law has clearly provided a measure of legitimacy to those in the state illegally.[14]

While much of the anti-immigrant legislation at the state and local level occurred during the George W. Bush administration, the election of Barack Obama did little to quiet the controversy, although attention was drawn toward the deep recession, which also forced a return of many illegal immigrants to Mexico and Central America as job opportunities declined. Obama did push for greater border security, including $27 billion in his 2010 budget for stronger controls of illegal Mexicans entering the United States, preventing employers from hiring illegal immigrants, and improving bureaucratic roadblocks to settling longstanding immigration issues of those applying for citizenship. The administration also directed the Department of Homeland Security to use Section 287(g) of the Immigration and Nationality Act to train local police officials to enforce immigration laws. Although this decision pleased state and local officials who were thereby given the authority to work with federal officials to track down illegal immigrants, human rights groups complained that many of the arrests were arbitrary and that too many immigrants in the country legally were harassed. These complaints prompted the Obama administration to establish a policy position that raids on factories and other work places in search of illegal immigrants would be limited, if not abandoned, as a way of lessening the tensions between Hispanics and the government.[15]

In President Obama's second term the immigration debate shifted to a range of issues such as

- the mass exodus of unaccompanied minors from Central America crossing the border,
- popular anger over the failure to deport illegal immigrants who committed serious crimes,
- the status of creating so-called sanctuary cities to protect the undocumented population,
- the use of executive orders by the president to by-pass the unwillingness of Congress to deal with the undocumented, and
- the electoral politics heading into the 2016 elections, which featured not just anti-Mexican rhetoric by Donald Trump but also talk of mass deportations and attacks on the Muslim community, including a proposed ban on Muslims coming into the United States.

Obama's second term was indeed a time of intense debates, differences, and divisions over illegal immigration.

Beginning in 2014, the gang-related violence in Central America, especially in El Salvador and Honduras, led thousands of young people to travel across Mexico and enter the United States. The United States was caught unprepared for the influx of these young migrants who feared for their lives if they stayed behind. In June 2014 alone, over 10,600 unaccompanied youths crossed the border into the United States. The influx required that the US Department of Health and Human Services, working with the Department of Homeland Security, provide temporary shelter in states like Texas and California. President Obama asked for an additional $400 million to deal with the youth influx. Governors in the southwest, such as Texas Governor Greg Abbott, maintained a state National Guard presence to dissuade additional youths from entering the United States.[16]

Congressional critics of the Obama administration's response to the Central American youth forced the government to take more aggressive action to stem the tide of migrants by increasing the number of Border Patrol agents, working with Central American governments to encourage them to control their own borders, and cooperating with the Mexican government to launch its own Southern Border Program to monitor their border with Guatemala and Belize. The United States provided over $150 million in technical aid to Mexico to help track and contain the migrant flow.

These measures initially limited the movement of the Central American youths to the United States, but in late 2015 and 2016 (spurred on by a fear of a Trump presidential victory) a new influx of undocumented youths began a new trek to this country. In October to November 2015, 10,500 youths entered the United States and again fueled the anti-immigrant fires in the American political arena. Republicans in Congress and in the states blamed the Obama administration for allowing porous borders and lax security while the Hispanic community viewed these youths as creating a humanitarian crisis that required the United States to act to allow them into the country as refugees seeking political asylum.

Partisan politics around the immigration issue intensified in July 2015 as a 32-year-old California woman, Kathryn Steinle, was allegedly killed by a San Francisco man, Juan Francisco Lopez Sanchez, with numerous convictions and five deportation citations. Lopez Sanchez was allowed to remain in San Francisco because that city is designated by municipal law as a sanctuary city, which establishes a limited level of cooperation with federal immigration officials and provides a safe haven for illegal immigrants, in this case even one with an extensive criminal record and five deportation citations. San Francisco city officials justified their sanctuary policy as one way of cooperating with the Hispanic community to protect illegal immigrants in the country. The city cooperated with the federal Immigration and Customs Enforcement Agency only when a warrant was issued. Critics of the sanctuary policy of San Francisco angrily stated that the sheriff of that city went out of his way to protect Lopez Sanchez and should have notified the federal authorities after he was arrested for an outstanding warrant.[17]

The murder of the California woman set off a barrage of political outrage over what was claimed to be excessive liberal efforts to protect illegal immigrants and respond to the Hispanic community, who are opposed to what they see as excessive police and federal enforcement policies against illegal immigrants. Increased pressure also was placed on President Obama not only to renounce the sanctuary city policy but also to speed up deportations of illegal immigrants who have committed crimes. Despite the criticism of Obama on deportations, his administration has been far more aggressive in deporting illegal immigrants with criminal records and, in 2016, initiated a new effort to expand deportations, which currently are at about 230,000—a significant drop from a high of 409,000 in 2012.[18]

Tensions between the White House and the Republican Congress intensified considerably in late 2015 and into 2016 as the Obama administration sought to protect its executive order, implemented without Congressional approval, to protect 5 million immigrants (in most cases the immigrant parents of US citizens or permanent residents) from deportation through the program known as Deferred Action for Parents of Americans (DAPA). Twenty-six states were successful in convincing a federal Appeals Court to block the executive order on DAPA, with the result that the Obama administration sought relief from the Supreme Court, which agreed to hear the case. Republicans lambasted the president for bypassing Congress and issuing the order, but the administration relied on what it believed was its power under the constitution to control and direct immigration policy in this country. In 2016, in a case brought by the state of Texas, a divided Supreme Court (4–4 as Justice Antonin Scalia's death had created a situation in which a tied court was bound to accept a lower court decision) upheld a lower federal court decision that issued a preliminary injunction against implementation of DAPA.[19] In 2017 the Trump administration announced that it would be ending the program.

Although unconnected to the DAPA suit and executive authority was the issue of what the administration called the Deferred Action for Childhood Arrivals (DACA). DACA was designed to protect from deportation youths brought to this country illegally before their 16th birthday and before June, 2007. It would allow those eligible to receive renewable two-year work permits and exemption from deportation. The executive action protects some 720,000 young illegal immigrants from deportation and allows them to live and work in the United States. DACA was the Obama administration's attempt to resurrect, in another form, the failed DREAM Act. Formally known as Development Relief and Education for Alien Minors, the DREAM Act is a program to protect from deportation the children of illegal immigrants who were brought to this country at an early age and have sought to remain here to pursue their education and job opportunities. The initial DREAM Act failed to pass Congress. A federal court injunction delayed implementation of an expanded program announced by the Obama administration until 2016.[20] At numerous times during the campaign and while in office, President Trump pledged to support the DREAMERS, but in September of 2017 he directed his Attorney General Jeff Sessions to announce that DACA would be recinded but not implemented for six months, thereby giving Congress time to act on the future of the program. A number of states, such as California, have instituted their own version of the DREAM Act by giving educational assistance to enter college—financial aid, scholarships, and grants—to these children.

The most contentious debate that highlighted the differences and divisions in American society started with presidential candidate Donald Trump, who in the wake of the mass killings in San Bernadino, California, by two sympathizers of the jihadist group ISIL, called for a ban on travel to the United States by Muslims. Trump's outspoken stance on Muslim visitors to this country and his later calls for the closing of certain mosques and perhaps even special identification cards for Muslims endeared him to his supporters, but at the same time created a national conversation on how this religious minority, many of whom were recent legal migrants to this country, should be treated.[21]

In the wake of the Trump attacks on Muslims, there was a spike in anti-Muslim attacks and discrimination as many state governors sought to reject any acceptance of Muslim refugees from the conflicts in the Middle East into the United States. Despite these attacks and prohibitions on Muslims, many Americans were outraged by Trump and his diatribes against the followers of Islam as they emphasized the constitutional guarantees for the free practice of religion, the unlawful singling out of religious groups for special treatment, and the attempt to end, even for a time, the legitimate travel of Muslims to this country. A number of other Republicans denounced Trump while President Obama made numerous supportive statements about Muslims, including a visit in 2016 to a mosque to show solidarity with those who practice Islam. Nevertheless, the seeds of suspicion were sowed by Trump's remarks, opening up a discussion that at times reflected our tolerance and respect for diversity, while at other times showed our penchant for prejudice and nativism.

The issue of illegal immigration into the United States with all its complexities and divisions touches the core of the American experience. The guiding principle of being an American is the assimilation of peoples from all over the world from the early Pilgrims to the migrants from Latin America, Asia, and the Middle East. Some of these arrivals, like those on the Mayflower, did not have proper documentation; in fact, they just arrived unannounced and uninvited. Others such as the huge wave of European immigrants during the period from 1880–1920 benefited from a national policy that officially welcomed a new workforce that dreamed of unlimited economic opportunities and the assurance of personal security.

What differentiates these early arrivals from the immigrant arrivals of today is not just that over 12 million are undocumented and come here by crossing borders illegally, but that many Americans are concerned that the concept of the "melting pot" no longer has value. The so-called Mexicanization of some parts of California and the Southwest, where whole sections of cities and towns are enclaves of Mexican life with few signs of linkage to the United States, has caused a backlash among many resident Americans who are angry over bilingualism, protection of illegal immigration rights, and open displays of Mexican nationalism. There is thus the resulting fear among many Americans that, over time, the Mexican immigrant population will form two nations with little common heritage and no concept of a national "melting pot."[22]

Prominent thinkers and writers like the late Harvard University professor Samuel Huntington and television commentator Patrick Buchanan have written books that raise disturbing questions about the latest wave of arrivals on American shores. Huntington, in his book, *Who Are We? The Challenge to America's Identity*, states that the new arrivals from Mexico in particular have not assimilated into the American identity and have little loyalty to the United States. Huntington praises the Anglo-Protestant ethic that, in his opinion, is the foundation of our society and laments that these values of liberty, equality, the rule of law, and individual rights have not been embraced by recent immigrants. He sees Mexican immigrants as seeking separation from resident Americans and showing little interest in the American way of life.[23] Buchanan, in his book *State of Emergency*, is much more threatening in his prediction about the impact of illegal Mexican immigration into the United States. As he says, "If we do not get control of our borders by 2050 Americans of European descent will be a minority in the nation their ancestors created and built. No nation has ever undergone so radical a demographic transformation and survived." Buchanan even goes so far as to suggest that some Mexicans in America dream of the day when they become the controlling majority in states like California, Arizona, New Mexico, and Nevada, which were taken by the United States after the Mexican-American War in 1848.[24]

Those Americans who fear the impact of undocumented migrants, primarily from Mexico, were pleased when President Trump signed executive orders to begin the building of a wall along the over 2,000-mile border with Mexico, crack down on illegal immigrants, and take away federal funding from cities that have declared themselves sanctuary cities. Agents for

Immigration and Customs Enforcement (ICE) stepped up their apprehensions of illegal immigrants as criminal threats, although some of those arrested and headed for deportation had minor violations. The aggressive arrests by ICE agents prompted some illegal immigrants to seek asylum in churches and some big city mayors to defy the actions of the government, especially when such arrests broke up families. Although the response to these measures was predictable from the Hispanic community and Mexico, the president was undeterred in implementing his campaign promises to secure the border and punish those big city mayors for their sanctuary city policies. Trump's signature promise to build a wall along the border stalled in Congress without funding, but bids to construct the wall were sent out and design plans were presented and made public. As for the Mexican government, it continued to state that Mexico would not pay for the wall.

Although comprehensive immigration reform is yet to be addressed, the divisive national debates continue and the juggernaut of globalization continues with its requirement that work and labor be flexible and open. Nevertheless, calls for militarizing the border, increasing deportations, or creating a hostile environment for illegal immigrants continue to be popular among a vast majority of Americans. However, a counterweight to this opposition to reform is the reality of the growing influence of the Hispanic community. Politicians from both parties recognize that the Hispanic voting bloc is critical and policy actions that alienate Hispanics could translate into defeat at the polls.

Ideally, government, business, interest groups, and the American people will arrive at some middle ground on this difficult issue. Meanwhile the passion that has driven the debate over illegal immigration has not abated; it has only intensified, creating a political landscape fraught with division both in the political arena and in American society.

The Great Debate

With 12 million illegal immigrants living in the United States, public policies that lessen the political and social tensions are difficult to achieve. One of the solutions proposed by the Obama administration and others is the creation of a pathway to citizenship for these immigrants. The pathway, as presented, would not be automatic as those undocumented residents would be required to go to the "end of the line" as they apply, pay all back taxes, show that they do not have a criminal record, and in some proposals, show that they have a working knowledge of English.

Debate Topic

Should illegal immigrants be granted a pathway to citizenship with rigid application requirements but no punishment for their original illegal entry into the United States?

Critical Thinking Questions

1. How would you resolve the fact that there are an estimated 12 million illegal immigrants in the United States?
2. Should immigrants who are here legally be required to learn English and should the United States government make English the official language of our country?
3. Do you believe that illegal immigrants are a drain on the United States and local economies or a benefit?
4. Many critics of illegal immigration are outraged over the so-called "anchor babies," born in this country but with illegal immigrant parents, which gives them automatic citizenship. Is this good government policy?
5. Some critics of existing immigration policy are in favor of mass deportations of illegal immigrants. Is this policy proposal realistic?

Connections

A valuable resource for understanding the border control problem is the website of the US Border Patrol: www.cbp.gov/xp/cgov/about

A list of pro and con groups associated with the illegal immigration debate has been developed by the non-profit organization, the United States Immigration Support. Its site is at www.usimmigrationsupport.org

A support group for illegal immigrants is the Immigrant Solidarity Network; its website is at www.immigrantsolidarity.org

Immigration Watchdog is an organization that monitors the illegal immigration controversy. Visit the site at http://immigrationwatchdog.com

The Center for Comparative Immigration Studies at the University of California at San Diego is recognized as having a reputation for solid and non-partisan research on immigration. Its site is www.cis-ucsd.org

A Few Books to Read

Brown, Donathan and Amardo Rodriquez, *When Race and Policy Collide: Contemporary Immigration Debates* (Santa Barbara, CA: ABC-CLIO, 2014).

De La Torre, Miguel, *The U.S. Immigration Crisis: Toward an Ethics of Place* (Eugene, OR: WIPF and Stock, 2016).

Gonzalez III, Joaquin Jay and Roger Kemp, *Immigration and America's Cities: A Handbook on Evolving Services* (Jefferson, NC: McFarland, 2016).

Eckstein, Susan Eva and Adil Najam, *How Immigrants Impact Their Homeland* (Durham, NC: Duke University Press, 2013).

Romero, Fernando, *Hyperborder: The Contemporary U.S. Mexico Border and Its Future* (Princeton, NJ: Architectural Press, 2007).

Notes

1. The issue of illegal immigration is addressed in Donald Trump policy positions on his campaign website. See www.donaldtrump.com
2. The link between globalization and immigration is discussed by George J. Borjas in an article entitled "Immigration and Globalization: A Review Essay," *Journal of Economic Literature*, Vol. 53, No. 4, (2015), pp. 961–974.
3. This data was from a study sponsored by the advocacy group the Federation for American Immigration Reform. The Federation takes a stand against illegal immigration. See the study, "The Fiscal Burden of Illegal Immigration on the United States," Federation for American Immigration Reform, July, 2011.
4. Pamela Constable, "For Illegal Immigrants With Babies the Anchor Pulls in Many Directions," *Washington Post*, September 20, 2015.
5. This data was contained in an opinion article in the Boston Globe by Marcela Garcia entitled "The US Economy Runs on Immigrants." See *Boston Globe*, January 17, 2016.
6. Ibid.
7. "Two Sides of the Border Fence," *Washington Post National Weekly Edition*, October 23–29, 2006. Also see, "Fighting the Fence," *The Economist*, June 14, 2008.
8. See "Bush Call for Changes on Illegal Workers," *CNN*, January 8, 2004, www.cnn.com/2004/ALLPOLITICS/01/07/bush.immigration/index.html
9. Charles Buffington, "Immigration Issue Splits GOP," *Washington Post*, May 27, 2006.
10. The McCain-Kennedy bill is analyzed in an editorial in the *New York Times*, See: "Enter McCain-Kennedy," *New York Times*, May 14, 2005.
11. Teresa Watanabe and Hector Becera, "How DJs Put 500,000 Marchers in Motion," *Los Angeles Times*, March 28, 2006.
12. Quoted in Mary Jo Pitzi, "Agreement Heard Against Employer Sanction Law," *Arizona Republic*, November 15, 2007. See also Randall Archibold, "Arizona Enacts Strengthened Law on Immigration," *New York Times*, April 24, 2010.
13. John Hurdle, "Judge Strikes Down Town's Immigration Law," *New York Times*, July 26, 2007.
14. The California Assembly Bill 60 can be found at https://leginfo.legislature.ca.gov
15. The controversy surrounding the 287(g) authority is examined in Susan Jones, "ICE Scraps 287(g) Program That Allowed Local Police to Enforce Immigration Law," *CNS News*, December 26, 2012.
16. Jerry Markon and Joshua Partlow, "Unaccompanied Minors Crossing Borders in Greater Numbers," *Washington Post*, December 17, 2015.
17. Sanctuary cities and criminal activity are examined in "A Delicate Balance," *The Economist*, July 11, 2015, p. 32–33.
18. Jeff Jacoby, "Mass Deportations Would Leave America Poorer," *Boston Globe*, March 24, 2016.
19. For background on this case see "Supreme Court to Review Key Immigration Case," *Boston Globe*, January 20, 2016.
20. See "Obama to Take Legal Fight Over Immigration to Supreme Court," *Boston Globe*, November 11, 2015.
21. Charlie Savage, "Trump's Plan to Bar Foreign Muslims Might Survive a Lawsuit," *New York Times*, December 9, 2015.

22. For background on the issue of Mexicanization see Robert Pastor and Jorge Castenada, *Limits to Friendship: The United States and Mexico* (New York: Knopf, 1988).

23. Samuel Huntington, *Who Are We? The Challenge to America's Identity* (New York: Simon and Schuster, 2004).

24. Patrick Buchanan, *State of Emergency* (New York: Thomas Dunne, 2006).

6

TAXING **AND** SPENDING

Issue Focus

The lifeblood of any government is revenue and what political leaders decide to do with that revenue. Collecting taxes and then spending those taxes on national priorities is one of the core functions of American government. As can be expected, when taxes are collected from the American people and American business, the reaction is often displeasure, if not anger, at having to hand over their earnings to the government. However, there is just as much displeasure and anger at the manner in which tax dollars are spent as government decides where to channel revenue, especially if the government spends more money on policies and programs than it takes in from taxpayers. These issues of taxing, spending, and debt have become contentious issues in contemporary American politics.

Chapter Objectives
This issue chapter will seek to:
1. Explore recent tax policies in the United States and the effect of these policies on the American taxpayer.
2. Examine government spending priorities and the impact of spending on deficits and the national debt.
3. Discuss the different approaches to tax and spending policies taken by Democrats and Republicans.

SOME BACKGROUND

The old adage that the only certainties in life are death and taxes points out the centrality of the issue of paying the government "its due" and the government establishing policies that determine what citizens and corporate entities will be required to transfer to the Treasury of the United States. Although setting tax rates and collecting taxes is a fundamental requirement of any government and one of the primary responsibilities of citizens, the relationship between the American people and their government when taxes are the subject becomes strained and contentious; there is an inevitable certainty that debates, differences, and divisions will follow over who should pay and how much should be paid to the treasury. The difficult relationship that exists between the government and the American people over taxes and tax policy is best shown in public opinion polls when respondents are asked to name their least favorite government agency. Their response is usually the Internal Revenue Service (IRS), which has as its primary function collecting corporate, personal income, and other excise taxes. As in the Bible, tax collectors remain even today one of the least respected occupations in our society.

The issue of taxation has its origin in the early days of the revolutionary era when the colonists resisted the policies of the British to extract money from them through the Stamp Act and later the Townsend Act in order to pay for foreign debts. The rallying cry of "No taxation without representation" has become part of Americana and underscores the importance that taxation has played in shaping our political culture. Later in the revolutionary period western farmers engaged in what came to be called Shay's Rebellion as they challenged the authorities over new taxes placed on their farms. Although the rebellion was put down (after the government had to raise private funds to pay its soldiers), popular resistance to unfair or imposed taxes continued.

Once independence was achieved and the new country sought to establish a fiscally sound government, there remained problems in raising taxes as the major sources of funding for the national government were excise taxes on land ownership and trade transactions, highly speculative government held bonds, and lines of credit from foreign allies. The early Federalist Party disappeared from the political scene in large part because of scandals associated with bond speculation and excise taxes on western farmers. There were also constitutional issues about the power of the national government to establish banks free of taxation by the states. In one of the most important Supreme Court decisions in the history of this country, Justice John Marshall took the side of the federal government in McCulloch v. Maryland and validated the right of the central government to establish a national bank without facing taxation from the state of Maryland. Moreover, Marshall upheld the right of the federal government to tax and conduct other fiscal matters under its constitutional implied powers that reached beyond its stated or enumerated powers.

But the most serious and controversial development regarding taxation occurred during and after the Civil War as the country needed additional revenue and began turning to the income tax as the most direct manner of taxing citizens. In 1862, a law was passed requiring that those Americans with incomes above $600 would pay a 3% tax, while those with incomes over $10,000 would pay a tax of 5%. Although the law was abolished in 1872 and the courts argued for years over whether any income tax had to be apportioned among the states based on their census, pressure remained to use income as the primary means of raising revenue. Therefore, in 1913, the Sixteenth Amendment was passed by the states establishing the income tax as the law of the land and allowing Congress the responsibility of setting and raising rates.[1]

As the country developed into a world power and the government, especially during the New Deal era under President Franklin Delano Roosevelt, assumed greater domestic responsibilities to respond to the needs of the poor, the aged, and the infirmed, the need for additional revenue increased. Raising taxes during wartime or in order to pay for what was considered a social good was less controversial during the Depression and World War II era. But as government got bigger and budgets to run the United States entered the trillion dollar range, support for tax increases began to wane and presidents and presidential candidates ran on platforms that pledged to resist new taxes. Public opinion polls from the 1980s onward, when anti-tax and less government president Ronald Reagan took office, showed that Americans were averse to tax increases and wanted their government to cut government spending rather than take more money out their pocketbooks.[2]

While opposition to tax increases began to dominate the domestic policy scene, special interest politics entered the realm of fiscal affairs as the US tax code became the target of constant lobbying to gain specific credits, exemptions, deductions, or incentives that would diminish the tax burden or perhaps even eliminate it. In response to this pressure, Congress has made regular additions and adjustments to the US tax code and, in the process, contributed to the most complex tax laws in the world. The US tax code spreads to thousands of pages of arcane rules and regulations and a growing professional industry of tax preparers and accountants who have responded to the need for interpreting the law and using the law to legally avoid the tax bill. Taxation thus has become not just a tool of fiscal management for the country, but also a political and ideological minefield as tax policy is often embroiled in partisan struggles over who would pay taxes, who could avoid paying taxes, and what areas of income, profit, property, or stocks would receive special benefits.

The combination of growing aversion to taxes coupled with the scramble to gain tax benefits and advantages contributed to a growing awareness of the fairness issue. The question of who should pay the largest share of taxes was asked with greater frequency by Americans. Middle-class taxpayers complained about carrying the largest burden of taxation at the expense of the wealthy and corporations, while the wealthy and corporations responded that they pay enormous tax bills and that heightened taxation only punishes wealth accumulation and restricts economic growth. Liberal Democrats, in particular, jumped on the tax fairness bandwagon as they regularly chastised conservatives and, in particular, Republicans in Congress for passing legislation that provided generous tax advantages to those at the highest income levels in the nation. Claims that taxes were responsible for growing income inequality and that a class war was being instigated by unfair tax policies were heard with greater frequency in Congress and on the campaign trails.[3]

Data Bank

In 2016, Americans paid approximately $3.34 trillion in federal taxes and $1.64 trillion in state and local taxes, for a total tax bill of $4.99 trillion, or 31% of national income. In 2016, Tax Freedom Day was on April 24th, 114 days into the year. This is the day that represents the time during the calendar year when tax obligations to the federal government end.

Source: Tax Foundation

It should come as no surprise that when the government sets policies that are designed to remove money from people's pocketbooks or corporate ledgers such policies become a major issue area and that debates, differences, and divisions will follow. Most Americans would agree that government is a necessary evil and that many services of government are absolutely essential for the good of the country. But paying for those essential services is where problems arise. Consequently, taxation has become one of the most contentious issue areas of public policy. Every American would agree that he or she owes the government its "due,"; the question though is, how much "due"?

DEBATES, DIFFERENCES, AND DIVISIONS

Talk of taxes and tax policy in the modern era is best begun with the election of Ronald Reagan in 1980. Reagan ran for and won the presidency on a platform of lower taxes and less government. His plan, dubbed "Reaganomics," was a decided shift away from the dominant model of economic policy that had been in place since the New Deal days of Franklin Delano Roosevelt. Rather than emphasize the role of big government and ever-expanding taxes, Reagan talked about the importance of stimulating the economy by huge tax cuts and sharp reductions in government spending, except for expenditures related to national defense. The theory supporting Reagan's position on taxes and spending as the key to economic growth was what came to be called "supply-side economics." Supply-side stressed the importance of creating business demand rather than consumer demand by shrinking the tax burden on the corporate sector and those with high incomes. By providing corporations and high income citizens with significant tax breaks, Reagan believed that the economy would grow faster, and by cutting back on government spending, the need for more borrowing to cover federal expenses would diminish and thus lessen the need to raise interest rates.[4]

In 1981, Reagan won an early victory on tax cuts when Congress shared his position and passed a measure that reduced the average tax rate by 23%. In 1986 Reagan was able to push through a much more ambitious tax policy with the passage of the Tax Reform Act, which eliminated more than twelve tax brackets replacing them with just two (15% and 28%). The Tax Reform Act also cut certain personal exemptions and standard deductions and removed millions of poor people from the tax rolls. Corporations also benefited by a reduction in the top rate from 46% to 34%, but lost out with the repeal of the investment tax credit and the closing of a number of favorable loopholes in the tax code. By the time Ronald Reagan left office, income tax rates, especially at the high end, dropped significantly as the top personal tax bracket was reduced by 42% in seven years. During the Reagan years, the tax cuts helped businesses to expand investments in new equipment and buildings, while creating a financial boon for investors in the stock market.[5]

But there was a price to pay for supply-side economics as the loss of revenue coupled with continued government spending, particularly in national defense, created ever-growing federal deficits averaging between $150 billion and $250 billion each year during the Reagan presidency. The ballooning deficits and the skewing of the tax breaks toward business and the wealthy spurred critics to describe supply-side economics as really "trickle- down economics" with barely a trickle of tax relief for the majority of Americans and, worse yet, contributing to a growing trickle of national debt that future generations of Americans would have to deal with. As the Reagan administration left office in 1989, the debate over who benefited from supply-side economics and the downside of steep revenue losses began in earnest with Democrats increasingly calling for middle class tax cuts and a kind of "soak the rich" policy that reduced the tax benefits enjoyed by the wealthy and corporations.[6]

Ronald Reagan's successor, George H.W. Bush, will always be remembered for his rallying cry of "Read my lips, no new taxes." Seeking to emulate Reagan's approach on tax policy, George H.W. Bush continued to emphasize the supply-side approach that changed the American political economy. But by 1990 Bush faced an ever-growing federal deficit and was openly critical of Reaganomics, even to the point of calling it "voodoo economics." Faced with the growing deficit, Bush recanted his promise of no new taxes and increased the income tax to the great displeasure of his conservative base and the American voting public. George H.W. Bush lost the 1992 presidential election to Bill Clinton for a number of reasons, including a downturn in the economy, but the failure of Bush to keep his famous promise of "Read my lips, no new taxes" weakened his traditional voting base and showed him to be trapped in the political culture of tax cuts created by his predecessor Ronald Reagan. It may have been economically sound to raise taxes in order to deal with out-of-control deficits, but the idea of tax cuts had caught on among conservatives and the business community, and Bush, to his regret, went against the conservative-business tide.[7]

The election of Bill Clinton in 1992 brought the first Democrat to the White House since Jimmy Carter in 1976. Clinton ran on a platform of strengthening the American economy by pushing for free trade agreements and budget restraint. But one of his most controversial economic positions was a tax increase on the wealthy. As a Democrat, Clinton believed that the Reagan-Bush years had concentrated too many tax breaks at the high end of the income scale and that it was time to give low- and middle-income Americans some tax relief. In 1993 despite overwhelming Republican opposition, Congress passed the Omnibus Budget Reconciliation Act, which raised taxes on the top 1.2% of the wealthiest Americans, while giving tax reductions to 15 million low-income people. The Clinton initiative also provided for tax breaks to small business operators who, in the past, had been overlooked as the Republicans concentrated many of their corporate cuts on large enterprises. Clinton also used the legislation to develop a series of budget goals designed to rein in the government spending that was creating an ever-growing federal deficit. Clinton's goal was to reduce the federal deficit by 50% during his administration.[8]

In the last few years of his presidency, Bill Clinton was able to move the federal expenditure ledger from a deficit to a surplus, the first time that had occurred since the administration of Lyndon Johnson in the late 1960s. In 1998 the surplus was $69 billion; in 1999, $126 billion; and in 2000, $236 billion (and in a carryover from his administration there was a surplus during the first fiscal year of the Bush administration as well). Clinton would tout his deficit reduction efforts (helped in large part by defense spending that declined as a result of the end of the Cold War), along with the revenue received from his tax hike on the rich, but critics pointed out that Clinton merely benefited from a strong economy with low unemployment, a sizzling stock market, and high consumer spending levels. Whatever the reason, Clinton and the Democrats reminded the American people that it was possible to control government spending and not be burdened by huge government deficits as occurred during the Reagan and Bush presidencies.

The return of the Republicans to power after the victory of George W. Bush in the 2000 election meant also a return to supply-side economic policies. Bush wasted no time in having his Economic and Tax Reconciliation Act of 2001 passed by the Congress. The centerpiece of the legislation was a one-time rebate to the American taxpayer, with what the president described as a "typical family of four" receiving around $1,600.[9] But while the president touted the tax rebate and his concern over helping the average American family deal with the financial demands of everyday life, his tax policy continued to accent a reduction in income tax rates, which in most cases benefited those in high-income brackets. A joint study from the Urban Institute and the Brookings Institution in 2006 found that the 2001 tax cuts gave on average $118,000 in tax benefits to .3% of the American households with incomes of $1 million or more, while in contrast households in the middle 20% of the income range received $740.[10]

The Bush tax bill was not only about tax rate reduction. The president's bill also linked the tax cuts with a significant drop in the capital gains tax, which is applied to the profits that individuals acquire as a result of the sale of stock and property. The capital gains tax was reduced from 28% to 15% and was further evidence of the Bush administration's position of using tax policy to benefit those with higher incomes. Bush even returned to Congress in 2003 and sought to move the timetable for reduction of the capital gains tax forward more quickly because he was convinced that reducing the tax on stocks and property would further stimulate the economy. The Republican Congress supported the new timetable, along with tax reductions on dividend income. Finally, the tax legislation also repealed the estate or so-called "death tax" on inheritance income over $250,000, which Democrats roundly criticized as an unnecessary change in the tax code that only benefited a miniscule number of Americans at the highest income levels in the country. Republicans, however, found the estate tax an infringement on the right of Americans to keep the wealth accumulated within the family and away from the revenue-seeking Internal Revenue Service. Economist Paul Krugman summed up the argument about the skewed nature of the tax cuts:

> The reality is that core measures of both the 2001 and the 2003 tax cuts mainly benefit the very affluent. The centerpieces of the 2001 act

were a reduction in the top income-tax rate and elimination of the estate tax—the first by definition, benefiting only people with high incomes; the second benefiting only heirs to large estates. The core of the 2003 tax cut was a reduction in the tax rate on dividend income. This benefit, too, is concentrated on very high-income families."[11]

After the passage of the 2001 tax legislation, the Bush administration sought to have the cuts and other measures become permanent after the law expired in 2010. The extension of the legislation became a point of contention between Republicans and Democrats who fought over not just the impact of the cuts on the American economy, but also the long term impact on the federal deficit. It was estimated that making the tax cuts permanent would cost the government $3.5 trillion over ten years and contribute to a furthering of the federal deficit, which from 2001 to 2006 has increased by $2.3 trillion. President Bush pushed aside the criticism of the tax cuts and their impact on the federal deficit when he said in 2006, "You cut taxes and the tax revenues increase." This classic supply-side argument endeared President Bush to those who viewed his tax policies as stimulating growth, enriching Americans, and eventually having a positive impact on the federal deficit as a strong economy created new jobs and new wealth, and with that, new sources of revenue.

But with the tax cuts implemented during the Bush presidency, the $6 trillion in the surplus achieved during the later years of the Clinton administration quickly faded away and deficit spending returned. As a result of the Bush rebates, further tax cuts in later years, the prescription drug program, and of course, the wars in Afghanistan and Iraq, the surplus was transformed into a $3 trillion deficit. The disappearance of the surplus prompted Democrats in Congress and liberals, who worried about the fate of numerous social programs threatened by the shift in revenue to wealthy taxpayers and the Defense Department, to conclude that the Bush administration was purposely seeking to downsize the federal government and "starving" it of revenue so new programs could not be introduced, such as a universal health care plan and additional money for education and social welfare.

Despite the criticism of those in Congress who feared the long-term impact of budget deficits, President Bush held steady to his position that the tax cuts, coupled with strict cost cutting measures in the federal budget, would turn government revenue collections from red to black. In a major address in July, 2007, President Bush said that his tax policies had indeed achieved the desired impact on the budget deficit. The president stated that the deficit had been reduced by more than $200 billion since 2004 and had settled at $205 billion for the fiscal year 2007–2008. Moreover, Bush stated that the deficit was at 1.5% of Gross Domestic Product, the lowest in forty years. With a continuation of his tax cutting policies and budget constraints, Bush promised that by 2012 the deficit would be wiped out with a surplus of $33 billion. Democrats immediately accused the president of using "accounting gimmicks" and understating the costs of the Iraq war, the rise in Social Security and Medicare costs, and what they viewed as a weakening economy.[12]

FYI

The Office of Management and Budget, which is an agency under the direction of the White House, publishes a yearly breakdown of the federal budget dollar, where the revenue comes from, and where it goes. Below is the breakdown for 2014.

Where Revenue Comes From

46.2% from individual income taxes
33.9% from Social Security and Medicare taxes
10.6% from corporate income taxes
3.1% from excise taxes
6.3% from other sources (gifts, estate taxes, custom duties)

Where the Revenue Goes To

24% to Social Security
25% to Medicare, Medicaid, the Children's Health Insurance Program, and the Affordable Care Act
16% to national defense and international security
10% to safety net programs
6% to interest on debt
19% to all other federal programs: veterans and retirees, transportation, education, science, and foreign aid

Source: Center on Budget and Policy Priorities

Discussing the debates surrounding tax policy in the United States and pointing out the differences and divisions is not a simple matter of Democrats versus Republicans, liberals versus conservatives. Today, most public opinion polls will point to the fact that Americans are opposed to tax increases and support candidates for office who are not tax-and-spend proponents. Most politicians are afraid to use the "T" word in running for office and pledge that they will address the spending side of the federal ledger, not the revenue-generating side. But saying that, it is possible to show that liberal Democrats, who often represent those Americans of the lower and middle classes, support tax policies that are progressive in nature, meaning that tax revenues should fall most heavily on those individuals who make more money. If there are to be tax increases, then those increases should be shouldered by the rich. Liberal Democrats also support tax policies that target tax breaks that benefit corporations at the expense of the working man and woman. In running for the presidency in 2008, Barack Obama stressed that, if he were victorious, he would implement a tax policy that would decrease the tax burden of 95% of the American public, while increasing the tax burden on the top 5%.

Republicans, on the other hand, not only oppose tax increases but also any increase that would be progressive in nature. Their position is that taxes at the high end of the income scale should be either held constant or, more appropriately, reduced because reductions at this income level will translate into greater investment, greater purchases, and greater savings. At the corporate level, there is substantial support for the position of the Republicans who see taxation policies that seek to limit exemptions or reduce incentives as unfriendly to businesses and stymie their ability to invest and grow. The argument made by the Republican proponents of low corporate taxes and expanded exemptions and incentives is that this is how jobs are created, new factories built, and new research conducted that pushes the economy forward. Attempts to hike corporate taxes, so the argument goes, create only disincentives for businesses and weaken their ability to compete both domestically and in the global marketplace.

Taxes and tax policy will always remain a key policy area in American politics, and that was no different when Obama took office in 2009. Early in his presidency, Obama targeted American firms that established tax havens outside the United States to lessen their corporate tax burdens and, in the process, deprived the government of billions in revenue. Although business groups complained that any legislative effort to close the overseas tax havens would have a negative impact on the competitiveness of US corporations, Obama was adamant that the tax code needed to be changed as a matter of fairness, job creation, and patriotism. Corporate leaders fired back that what was needed was a reduction in taxes on businesses in this country, which has one of the highest rates among advanced industrial countries.

On the Record

Tax avoidance has become a major policy issue in the United States as individuals and corporations transfer their money and profits "offshore" to banks and holding companies to avoid paying US federal and state taxes. In April 2015, President Obama addressed this issue of tax avoidance:

> many (corporations) are aided and abetted by a broken tax system, written by well-connected lobbyists on behalf of well-heeled interests and individuals. It's a tax code, full of corporate loopholes, that makes it perfectly easy for companies to avoid paying their fair share. It's a tax code that makes it all too easy for a number of individuals and companies to abuse overseas tax havens to avoid paying any taxes at all. And it's a tax code that says you should pay lower taxes if you create a job in Bangalore, India, than if you create one in Buffalo, New York.

Source: White House web site, 2015

Even though President Obama railed against offshore tax havens, his main focus upon taking office was dealing with the Great Recession. Obama relied on what has commonly been termed Keynesian economic strategies, in large part a stimulus to the economy achieved by large scale government spending, even if that would mean deficit spending and increased debt. In February 2009, Congress, over Republican objections and little bipartisanship, passed the American Recovery and Reinvestment Act, a $787 billion stimulus bill. The president lauded the legislation as a jobs bill. As he stated at the time, "Our goal at the heart of the plan is to create jobs. Not just any jobs, but doing the work America needs done—repairing our infrastructure, modernizing our schools and hospitals and promoting the clean, alternative energy sources that will help us finally declare independence from foreign oil."[13] Republican critics of the bill cited the Act as an example of Democrats creating big government programs, enlarging the debt, and not targeting the bill toward tax relief for small business and corporate investment.

As the American economy struggled to move out of the Great Recession with little job growth in 2009 and a weak GDP, the Obama administration turned its attention in 2010 toward financial reform. With Wall Street big banks, investment houses, and hedge funds often viewed as the culprits in the crash of the economy, Democrats developed a sweeping financial reform bill. Called the Dodd-Frank bill, named after Connecticut Senator Chris Dodd and Massachusetts Congressman Barney Frank, the bill established an independent consumer watchdog bureau to protect borrowers in the areas of home mortgages, credit card interest rates, and other lending. The bill also sought to rein in major financial institutions through new regulatory powers.[14]

Again with scant Republican support, the Dodd-Frank bill narrowly passed, but President Obama called the legislation a step forward that would "protect consumers and lay the foundation for a stronger and safer financial system, one that is innovative, creative, competitive and far less prone to panic and collapse." Republicans saw the bill as another example of intrusive government that would harm corporate and banking competitiveness and ultimately limit job growth. Senate Majority Leader Mitch McConnell of Kentucky summed up the Republican objection to the bill by stating, "The White House will call this a victory . . . But as credit tightens, regulations multiply, and job growth slows even further as a result of this bill, they'll have a hard time convincing the American people that this is a victory for them."[15]

Gradually, job growth in the first Obama term began to move upward with an average of 200,000 new jobs created each month by 2011. Critics, however, were not impressed with these job numbers, since they did not reflect the number of Americans who had given up looking for work or were engaged in temporary and irregular part-time employment. Nevertheless, the official rate of unemployment did begin to drop from a high of 9.8% in January, 2010, to 8.0% in 2013. As President Obama prepared to begin his second term, he claimed that the American economy was on the rebound, while the Republicans remained unconvinced that little had changed as millions of Americans remained jobless or had given up hope for a new job.

During President Obama's second term, fiscal policy moved front and center of the policy debate. Republicans, who gained control of both the House and Senate, turned their attention to the federal budget and, in particular, the usually routine process of extending the debt ceiling. Starting in 2011 and reaching a crisis level in 2013, Republicans threatened to shut down the government by refusing to extend the debt ceiling, which had reached a level of $16.394 trillion. The debt ceiling allows the government to pay past bills incurred and approved by Congress. Usually, Congress passes the debt ceiling extension without controversy in large part because the credit rating of the US government is a critical ingredient of our economic standing in the world. Failure to pass the debt ceiling would likely mean a default and a review of the credit rating of the US government from the highest level, AAA. Republicans argued that the debt ceiling should be raised only if government spending was cut significantly and that failure to take budget cutting measures should lead to a government shutdown in order to end what was viewed by conservatives as out-of-control government spending and business-as-usual practices with respect to automatically passing a debt ceiling increase.[16]

The White House and Congress during 2013 engaged in a long and drawn out confrontation over the debt issues with temporary fixes, extensions, short-term appropriations, and an arcane legislative maneuver called sequestration. Budget sequestration is a legislative procedure that caps the size of the federal budget in the official departmental categories of spending. The result of sequestration is automatic cuts in departmental budgets as the Treasury Department holds back the funds to the government. Sequestration was first used in the 2011 budget and debt ceiling debate and became part of the Budget Control Act of 2011. The cuts from sequestration were estimated to be $1.2 trillion over a ten-year period beginning in 2013 and ending in 2021, and if implemented thoroughly, would reduce the budget by $4 trillion. The cuts were in all discretionary spending areas (not including Social Security and Medicare). The sequestration deal with the White House was often viewed as a "chopping block" approach to budgeting by the Congress in agreement with President Obama. Public policy areas such as education, job training, housing, science research, and veterans services were all affected. The cuts instituted the lowest level of non-defense discretionary spending since the Eisenhower administration. Although Congressional leaders did eventually approve a partial and temporary reduction in sequestration, the impact of the budget reductions remains significant.[17]

With sequestration cutting the federal budget and no agreement on debt ceiling approval, the confrontation between the Obama administration and Republicans in Congress led to a sixteen-day shutdown of government between October 1 and October 16, 2013. With an estimated cost to the US economy of $10 billion, 800,000 government workers were furloughed. As Congressional leaders and the White House jockeyed for an advantage in the shutdown, the crisis over government spending and the debt ceiling created real uncertainty in international stock markets and credit rating agencies. On October 16th, Congress and the White House agreed to a temporary spending bill. Tea Party and other anti-spending groups were outraged over the Republican leadership agreeing to the resolution to temporarily resolve the impasse, but the financial and corporate sectors were relieved that the government was back in business. Nevertheless, animosity in Congress ran high over the failure to stop raising the debt ceiling and continuing to pass interim spending bills.[18]

On October 17th, President Obama signed off on the compromise, ending the shutdown. Although this was a piecemeal resolution, the conservative faction in the Republican House of Representatives vowed to fight on against the debt limit extension and the continuation of the sequestration budget caps. Senator Ted Cruz of Texas called the compromise a "terrible deal" and Kentucky Representative Thomas Massie admitted that the Tea Party movement in the House had achieved little and got a "goose egg" for their efforts.[19]

The National Debt

The national debt in late 2016 was $19.7 trillion, up from $18.1 trillion in 2015, and $17.8 trillion in 2014. In the year 2000, the national debt was $5.8 trillion. The current national debt translates into $58,321 per person.

Source: Data from the Congressional Budget Office, 2016 and the Board of Governors of the Federal Reserve Bank, 2016

In 2015 and 2016, fiscal policy shifted to a more cooperative level as President Obama and Speaker of the House Paul Ryan worked out a $1.1 trillion budget that took the government through an entire year of funding, a practice that had been missing from the federal government since Obama took office. The deal not only funded government and raised defense and domestic spending but also extended some tax credits for solar energy and childcare, preserved a number of business tax breaks, and lifted a long established ban on exporting US crude oil, while delaying two Obamacare taxes on expensive personal health care plans and medical devices. Both the Democrats and Republicans got something out of the budget deal, but more importantly, both sides reached an agreement that created a measure of stability to the federal government and the national economy. Speaker Ryan best summed up the budget deal when he stated, "in a divided government you're going to have some concessions, that's what compromise is about."[20]

If there is a downside to the spirit of budget compromise in the deal between Obama and Ryan, it was that the spending bill with the tax credits and cuts increased the deficit by an estimated $544 billion with a ten year estimate of an additional $9.4 trillion. While Obama was credited with decreasing the yearly deficit, in large part due to sequestration by some $439 billion in 2014, the new era of cooperation did little to deal with the staggering national debt and gave continued support to conservatives who saw the United States as just "kicking the can down the road" by not addressing spending in a way that approached a balanced budget and a significant lowering in deficits and debt.

As President Trump approached the 100th day of his presidency, he presented an overview of a proposed tax reform package that would be sent to Congress. The president promised to cut the corporate tax rate from 35% to 15%, eliminate the estate tax, close numerous loopholes, provide for tax credits for childcare, and increase the individual and marriage deductions. Trump and his economic team stated that this tax package would increase growth and personal prosperity, while critics saw the tax changes as largely benefiting corporations and the wealthy with little benefit going to the middle class. Because the American tax code is 70,000 pages with enormous levels of complexity and special interest opportunities to legally evade taxes, it was likely that the efforts of President Trump to make major changes to the tax code would be extremely difficult.

It is not possible to talk about tax policy in the United States without spending time talking about spending policy, or simply the budget of the federal government. The federal government spends annually approximately $2.7 trillion. With such a large yearly expenditure, what the government spends has a definite impact on the national economy. Much of what the government spends annually is classified in the category of non-discretionary funds, money that must be paid to Americans for various entitlement programs such as Social Security and Medicare. After the government pays interest on the money that it borrows, what is left is for national defense and other discretionary programs from funding the Federal Bureau of Investigation to the NASA space program to the interstate highway system. It is the discretionary spending that becomes the core of the partisan debate over national priorities and budgetary decisions. Although the federal budget, which is over 1200 pages and is contained in three huge books, is a mass of financial data and expenditure statements, it is in reality a blueprint of how the government defines what is important for the country and what scarce resources (the taxpayers' money) should be spent on.

President Obama's final budget proposal for fiscal year 2017 called for $4.2 trillion in federal spending, a four percent increase over 2016. In the area of discretionary spending, the budget proposed $1.15 trillion. The discretionary budget showed decreases in most areas except veterans' benefits, education, and international affairs. Mandatory spending in areas such as Social Security, transportation, and Medicare experienced proposed increases of five percent. In the area of defense spending, the 2017 budget set aside $622.6 billion. Combined with veterans' benefits, this area of discretionary spending made up 61% of the budget. By far the largest segment of the budget was in mandatory programs. Social Security, unemployment compensation, and labor appropriations (i.e., training programs) made up 33% of the budget or $1.39 trillion, while Medicare and other health programs made up 28% of the budget at $1.17 trillion. Interest on the national debt was $303 billion or 7% of the budget.[21]

The partisan and ideological differences and divides that occur over the federal budget are often concentrated in the areas of national defense spending and social welfare programs. Democrats are ever on the alert to determine whether the Defense Department is spending money lavishly and foolishly on new weapons systems. Cost overruns for new weapons are often at the center of the debates concerning national defense spending. Republicans, on the other hand, keep close watch over the expenditures of the Departments of Health and Human Services, Education, and Housing and Urban Affairs. Each of these departments contain many of the social programs that Republicans see as bloated and fostering a climate of dependence on government handouts rather than on personal responsibility.

Since the federal budget, except for those few years during the Clinton administration, has been out of balance and building huge national debts, there have been frequent Congressional efforts to insert into the system of spending decisions a requirement for a balanced budget. Although the budget process in the United States includes a long and complex interaction among the White House Office of Management and Budget, the Congressional Budget Office, and numerous executive and congressional committees and working groups, the final spending product is as much a political decision as a rational economic deliberation. To ensure that budgets were indeed balanced, political solutions have been attempted in the past that sought to build a budget document where spending was in line with revenue. Efforts to create a Balanced Budget Amendment to the constitution, the attempt by presidents to seek a specific line item veto as a budget check, and even the impoundment of approved spending measures by presidents have all met with failure. Budget decisions continue to be influenced by partisan policy positions, constituency pressure, and ideological objectives.[22]

Spending decisions have been highly publicized in recent years. One of the more controversial aspects of budgetary politics and practice center on the issue of earmarking, a legislative tactic in which a member of Congress or a group of members identifies a specific project as necessary for their home district and state and then proceeds to move that project through the legislative process without open debate and with little concern over the impact of that project on the overall budget. In 1995, there were 1,439 such earmarks costing the taxpayers $10 billion, but by 2005 the number of earmarks had risen to 13,997 with a cost of $27.3 billion. In 2006 the cost of earmarks was placed at $29 billion. While many of these projects were worthy as they funded research centers and medical facilities, others were laughable such as the $500,000 for the Teapot Museum in Sparta, North Carolina, and the $233 million so-called "Bridge to Nowhere" linking a sparsely populated island in Alaska to the mainland.

Billions of dollars in earmarked projects continue to move through the Congress despite the efforts by some members such as Senator Tom Coburn of Oklahoma and former Representative, now Senator Jeff Flake of Arizona. Both men have repeatedly scolded their colleagues for inserting earmarked projects into appropriations bills or even bills with little if any connection to the project as a way of moving them forward without any sort of legislative oversight. The efforts of Coburn and Flake have had some impact on the ear-marking process, and the Democrats who took over power in 2008 pledged to create legislative guidelines for the earmarking process and be more vigilant when such projects are pushed through without debate. In the end, however, it is just too tempting for a member of Congress to say to his or her constituents back home, or to a special interest, that a pet project was funded, even though that project and hundreds of others were, in effect, budget busters. Recent data for FY 2014 and 2015 show a slight decrease in earmarks from 109–105, but the total cost rose by 56% from $2.7 billion to $4.2 billion.[23]

Taxes and spending issues, despite their complexity, have really been quite simple to define in terms of political issues. Either taxes go up or taxes go down, either the rich benefit or the middle and lower classes benefit, and either the money citizens pay to the government is prioritized toward national defense or toward social welfare. Much of the debate, differences, and divisions have been over these relatively simple options. There are always discussions of tax reform such as simplifying the tax code with a flat tax (a set percentage of taxation without all the deductions), moving to a European value-added tax (a form of a sales tax where a particular good is taxed at every stage of its production and distribution), or establishing a national sales tax and ridding the country of the income tax. There have even been discussions about instituting a national lottery that would generate the money needed to run the government. But these reform efforts fall by the wayside as there has been too much invested in the current system and too many interests that benefit from maintaining the status quo. What happens, thus, is that the president and Congress tinker back and forth with the tax code and with the spending priorities making short-term decisions that benefit one group over the other or accent one priority over another. This kind of political tinkering with taxation and spending is unlikely to change.

The Great Debate

The debate over who should carry the heaviest burden of taxation in the United States remains a politically charged issue. Wealthy individuals and corporations fight increases in tax rates, whereas middle class Americans grumble over the tax burden they carry and the unfairness of the current system.

Debate Topic

As a means of providing revenue for programs deemed necessary for the public good, what should be the proper manner/formula used to distribute the tax burden in this country?

Critical Thinking Questions

1. If you were asked to provide the president with a list of spending priorities for the United States, what would those priorities be?
2. Critics say that cutting taxes, while popular, has led to regular budget deficits and a growing national debt. Where do you stand on the tax cut versus deficit/debt issue?
3. Do you think the United States should follow a tax policy that places a far greater burden on the rich as is the case in many European countries?
4. Earmarks are often designed to support special projects in a region or state and are pushed by members of Congress in response to citizen pressure. Is there anything wrong with this practice of "bringing home the bacon"?
5. What steps should be taken in order to achieve a US balanced budget? Is a balanced budget amendment the answer?

Connections

To gain a more precise understanding of the United States budget, check out the website of the Office of Management and Budget. The site summarizes the yearly budget of the government: www.whitehouse.gov/OMB

To gain a congressional perspective on government spending and overall economic policy matters, visit the website of the Congressional Budget Office at www.cbo.org

The Concord Coalition is a non-partisan watchdog group that takes stands on matters of United States fiscal policy: www.concordcoalition.org

Grover Norquist is the most visible opponent of taxes and tax increases. His group, Americans for Tax Reform can be reached at www.ATR.org

The American Tax Institute provides solid research on tax policy and its impact on the nation and the nation's economy. See http://americantaxpolicyinstitute.org

Some Books to Read

Burman, Leonard and Joel Slemrod, *Taxes in America* (New York: Oxford University Press, 2012).

Johnson, Simon and James Kwak, *White House Burning* (New York: Vintage, 2013).

Rasmussen, Scott, *The People's Money, How Voters Will Balance the Budget and Eliminate the Federal Debt* (New York: Simon and Schuster, 2012).

Schmitt, Jesse Albert, *Legal Offshore Tax Havens: How to Take Legal Advantage of the IRS Code and Pay Less in Taxes* (New York: Atlantic Publishing, 2008).

Wessel, David, *Red Ink: Inside the High-Stakes Politics of the Federal Budget* (New York: Crown Business, 2013).

Notes

1. A short history of the United States tax system can be seen at the US Treasury website. See US Department of the Treasury, Resource Center, "History of the U.S. Tax System," December 5, 2010.
2. For polling data on America's response to taxes, especially in the Reagan era, see Taxes: Gallup Historical Trends, www.gallup.com
3. A debate over tax policy, income inequality and wealth accumulation between conservative commentator Dinesh D'Sousa and liberal journalist E.J. Dionne provides a solid overview of the issue of who carries the tax burden in the United States. The debate can be seen at www.slate.com/id/3665/entry/24002
4. Reaganomics is explained by conservative economists William A. Niskanen and Stephen Moore in "Supply Tax Cuts and the Truth About the Reagan Economic Record," Policy Analysis No. 261, CATO Institute, October 22, 1996.
5. An analysis twenty years later of Reagan's Tax Reform Act can be found in analysis by Andrew Chamberlain, "Twenty Years Later: The Tax Reform Act of 1986," The Tax Foundation, October 26, 2006.
6. Paul Krugman of Princeton and a New York Times columnist has been a longtime critic of Reaganomics. See his view on the impact of the Reagan tax policy at Paul Krugman, "The Myth of Reagan's Miracle," *New York Times*, February 18, 2013.
7. The criticism of the tax increase by President George H.W. Bush is discussed in Jack Germond, *Mad as Hell: Revolt at the Ballot Box* (New York: Warner Books, 1993).
8. For a easily understandable discussion of the complex tax and budget bill known as the Omnibus Budget Reconciliation Act see http://answers.com/topic/onmibus-budget-reconciliation-act-of-1993
9. For the Bush tax policy positions see Chris Edwards, "Tax Policy Under President Bush," CATO Institute, August 14, 2006.
10. See "New Tax Cuts Primarily Benefiting Millionaires Slated to Take Effect in January," *Center for Budget Priorities*, September 19, 2005.
11. See Paul Krugman, "Now That's Rich," *New York Times*, August 22, 2010.
12. The transcript of President Bush's speech can be found at "Bush Stresses Taxes and Trade in Speech," *CNN Money*, January 30, 2007.
13. See David Herszenhorn and Carl Hulse, "Senate Passes $787 Billion Stimulus Bill," *New York Times*, February 11, 2009.
14. See Brady Dennis, "Congress Passes Financial Reform Bill," *Washington Post*, July 15, 2010.
15. Ibid.
16. Jackie Calmes and Jonathan Weisman, "Obama and G.O.P. Issue Challenges on the Debt Limit," *New York Times*, January 14, 2013.
17. See the coverage of the government shutdown by CBS at www.cbsnews.com/feature/government-shutdown/
18. A helpful timeline of the shutdown was developed by Eric Krupke of National Public Radio, "How We Got Here: A Shutdown Timeline," October 17, 2013.
19. Eric Werner and Andrew Taylor, "GOP, Obama Tepidly Back Budget Deal," *Boston Globe*, December 17, 2015.

20. Jake Sherman and John Bresnahan, "Paul Ryan Tells GOP: Budget Deal A Partial Victory," *Politico*, December 14, 2015.

21. See The President's Budget for Fiscal Year 2017 prepared by the Office of Management and Budget at www.federal-budget.insidegov.com

22. See "Balanced Budget Amendment: Pros and Cons," Peter G. Peterson Foundation, June 20, 2012.

23. The Center for Responsive Politics publishes through its website, OpenSecrets.org, a listing of earmarks for each session of Congress.

7
SOCIAL SECURITY AND MEDICARE

Issue Focus

Although many Americans are wary of government intervention in their lives, they welcome the two most popular public programs in the history of the United States—Social Security and Medicare. Designed to provide a level of income and medical security for seniors, both of these programs have mushroomed in cost in recent years as the baby boomer generation reaches retirement age and often requires greater health care needs. The question of what the government will do to respond to the fiscal challenges of these programs is one of the greatest public policy challenges of this century.

Chapter Objectives
This issue chapter will seek to:
1. Explain the formation of Social Security and Medicare as key social welfare programs initiated by the US government.
2. Discuss the serious financing challenges facing Social Security and Medicare.
3. Describe the various proposals designed to address the future funding shortfalls in both Social Security and Medicare.

SOME BACKGROUND

In 1940 Ida Fuller of Brattleboro, Vermont received her first Social Security check of $22.54. For the next thirty-four years of her life, she continued to receive a monthly check for that amount. In total, Ida Fuller received nearly $21,000 in Social Security benefits. Although she had contributed only about $22 in payroll taxes, since the new program had started only four years before she retired, Ida Fuller became the first American to be able to count on the help of the government in her retirement. Social Security was one of the landmark New Deal programs developed during the administration of Franklin Delano Roosevelt and was designed to provide Americans with a safety net of benefits to make their lives more secure. For much of its life, Social Security has been a fiscally sound program that has had enormous support among the American people and is still considered the most successful social program initiated by the United States government.

Sixty-eight years later, Kathleen Casey-Kirschling became the first baby boomer (those Americans born after 1946) eligible to receive her initial Social Security check. Because Casey-Kirschling was 62 and retiring early, she received only 75% of what she would have received if she waited to 66, the full retirement age. Casey-Kirschling, a seventh-grade teacher from New Jersey, is part of what has come to be called the "silver tsunami"— over 80 million Americans who will become eligible to receive Social Security benefits in the coming years. Casey-Kirschling is starting an entitlement trend that has the potential to create economic havoc. By 2017 the Social Security program will pay out more benefits than it receives in taxes, and by 2041 experts estimate that the money in the Social Security Trust Fund, which is the repository of the taxes paid to provide retirees with their benefits, will be depleted.[1]

On the Record

President Franklin Delano Roosevelt in 1935 at the signing of the Social Security Act said the following:

This law represents a cornerstone in a structure which is being built but is by no means completed—a structure intended to lessen the force of possible future depressions, to act as a protection to future administrations of the government against the necessity of going deeply in debt to furnish relief to the needy, a law to flatten out the peaks and valleys of deflation and inflation—in other words a law that will take care of human needs.

The chief problem facing Social Security is the graying of America. In 1900, for example, one in twenty-five Americans was 65 years or older, but by 2040 the number will be one in four. At the present time, the baby boomer generation is the fastest growing segment of the American population. At the same time, there is a shrinking workforce in the United States. In 1970 there were 3.7 workers per beneficiary paying taxes into the Social Security system, but by 2040 there will be 2 workers per beneficiary paying taxes. The clear result will be that the Social Security system will generate less revenue just at the time that the number of recipients is on the rise, a perfect storm of fiscal and social welfare challenges. Although Congress, starting with the Reagan administration, began to cut back on generous yearly cost-of-living adjustments indexed to the inflation rate and extended the retirement age, the fiscal challenges continued with little sign of relief. By the early 1990s it was becoming evident to Washington policymakers that population growth was driving the Social Security system and determining its destiny.[2]

The Population Challenge to Social Security

Population Growth By Age Group—1995–2040
Under 20 years of age—5% growth
Age 20–64 years of age—24% growth
Age 65 and older—112% growth

Number of Workers Per Social Security Beneficiary 1970–2070
1970–3.7 workers per beneficiary
1990–3.4 workers per beneficiary
2010–3.0 workers per beneficiary
2030–2.0 workers per beneficiary
2070–1.8 workers per beneficiary

Source: National Commission on Retirement Policy

While the Social Security challenges are indeed considerable, there is an even greater challenge coming in the health care related to the "silver tsunami." In 1964 the administration of Lyndon Johnson initiated a number of social programs designed to address poverty, health care, and aging in order to attain what he termed a "Great Society." One of the most significant initiatives was the introduction of Medicare, a medical insurance program targeted to seniors (over 65) and disabled youth as a health companion to Social Security. Part A of Medicare covers hospital stays and is funded through payroll taxes. Part B is for doctors' visits and is paid through a combination of general revenue and premiums paid by the recipients. In 2006 Part D was added, a prescription drug program that provides seniors with drugs at a reduced cost.

Like Social Security, Medicare started with modest outlays of federal dollars but has mushroomed to the point where it too is in financial difficulty. By 2050 it is estimated that Medicare will account for between eight and nine percent of the entire United States federal budget. While many experts believe that their projections about when the Social Security Trust Fund will be depleted have remained fairly constant at around 2040, the projections of when Medicare becomes a full-blown fiscal crisis have continued to drop. In 2004 those who study Medicare financing dropped their projection about when the Medicare financing crisis would hit from 2026 to 2019. But in 2015 a report from the trustees of the Medicare program stated that because of the reforms implemented through the Affordable Care Act the Medicare Hospital Insurance Fund will be able to pay 100% of the cost of hospital coverage through 2030. Yet with every year the doomsday clock related to Medicare is recalculated as health care costs skyrocket and the percentage of national gross domestic product tied to Medicare continues to edge upward.[3]

One of the more controversial aspects of the trust funds in Social Security and Medicare is that for the last twenty years surpluses in the Social Security Trust

Fund have been invested in US government bonds. Since the Reagan administration, the Social Security Trust Fund, which is currently $2.8 trillion, has experienced a surplus and, as a result, Congress has issued Treasury bonds and then transferred the surplus to regular government appropriations. The bonds are repaid with interest when they mature. This practice continues today, especially as government deficits expand. To some critics of this practice, especially seniors, this transfer is viewed as a "raid" on the contributions of those who paid into the system. At present, this practice of using surpluses to issue bonds and then transferring the surplus to cover normal operating expenses of the government has not posed a problem. But when the Trust Fund begins to go into deficit as the "silver tsunami" waves forward and the cost of health care takes a higher and higher percentage of gross domestic product, the Treasury notes will be called in. It is at this juncture, probably around 2040 (but likely sooner) that the government will have to find the money to deal with the deficit that was masked by the borrowing. This borrowing shortfall will then have a major impact on regular government spending and will likely force talk of new taxes or more borrowing.[4]

Today, Social Security and Medicare are at the center of a national debate, not just over how to deal with out-of-control costs and the possible bankruptcy of key social welfare programs, but also the wisdom of huge government sponsored and funded entitlement initiatives. With Roosevelt's New Deal and Johnson's Great Society, the federal government assumed the responsibility of providing for the retirement and health care of seniors. Before the Great Depression, this country responded to social welfare concerns on a more personal and local level. The family unit, the church or synagogue, the neighborhood, and a network of charity organizations were the primary sources of assistance to those who needed a helping hand or a long-term safety net. During the heyday of Democratic dominance in Congress, especially in the 1960s and 1970s, the government continued the tradition as provider of last resort. Huge government outlays, new taxes, and large bureaucracies were the result.

But the recognition that future population pressures on Social Security and Medicare are inevitable forced the government to think about alternatives to providing financial security to retirees and medical assistance to seniors. Social Security and Medicare remained the foundations of this country's entitlement system, but new ideas and new proposals entered the political arena as talk of privatization of retirement savings, new forms of medical insurance, and restrictions on benefits and eligibility for benefits became more commonplace. However, any time two long-serving federal programs that are popular and provide a large dose of financial security face criticism or new options, political and popular tensions are sure to follow. It is these tensions and the debates, differences, and divisions that feed them that have fostered one of the most difficult policy challenges of our time.

DEBATES, DIFFERENCES, AND DIVISIONS

When a public policy has the potential to wreak financial havoc on the United States Treasury and bring uncertainty to millions of Americans, it follows that political leaders will enter the fray and introduce their vision of how to fix what is broken or will break. But in terms of Social Security and Medicare, there is an added component to this policy challenge. The threat from Social Security and Medicare is not just financial, it is generational. If the experts are right and some twenty or thirty years from now the two major programs designed to provide a financial safety net for America's seniors implode, then the burden of providing for their retirement pensions and medical insurance will likely fall on those who are still working. The only way out of this box is to advance controversial proposals that delay access to or drastically scale down benefits, which hits hard at seniors. The other more traditional options are more borrowing or higher taxes, both of which place a significant financial burden on the younger generation. In short, the Social Security and Medicare funding dilemmas are about how best to take care of grandma and grandpa in their senior years, but it is also about how much of the financial burden their grandchildren will have to bear in order to ensure that Social Security and Medicare remain solvent.

In some respects, the challenge of Social Security is at present more manageable and less threatening then Medicare. The issue with Social Security is a matter of funding. Although the program may go into deficit down the road, it can be fixed with a minimal tax increase, more borrowing, or a sustained and vibrant economy that would pump money into the government's coffers. While new taxes or borrowing are not attractive, and depending on solid economic growth in the long run is uncertain, experts and political leaders at present are not supporting drastic measures such as extending the age when benefits can be received to 70 or drastically reducing benefits such as eliminating the yearly cost-of-living increases. Both of these measures would likely meet with stiff opposition from seniors and groups representing seniors such as the American Association of Retired Persons.[5]

The key in the projected shortfall in Social Security is whether young workers would be willing to pay higher taxes, even if those taxes were relatively small, in order to keep the program going. There is general agreement that in the next 25 years the financing problem will be manageable and that payroll tax increases will not be necessary. But further into the future, by 2075 for example, the Trust Fund shortfall may rise to $20 trillion and could require tax increases of as much as 54% in payroll taxes along with serious cuts in benefits. This is obviously a long way off, but it does point out that Social Security is a ticking time bomb that, when it does go off, will have a devastating impact on young workers who will be asked to pay the price to take care of retirees.[6]

FYI

Social Security, more formally known as the Old Age and Survivors and Disability Insurance Trust Fund (OASDI), is the program that provides old age, survivors, and disability insurance to eligible Americans. The program is funded by contributions from workers and their employers

(continued)

FYI   (continued)

through a payroll tax that is equivalent to 6.2% of covered wages. The Internal Revenue Service collects the taxes and deposits the contributions into the trust fund. The revenues in the trust fund pay for the benefits to eligible pensioners. As a result of a change in the law in 1983, a retiree must be 67 years old to receive full benefits. The trust fund associated with Medicare is called the HI (Hospital Insurance) Fund. Like the Social Security Trust Fund, the HI Fund also is used to collect Medicare payroll taxes similar to Social Security. In 2004 the assets of the Social Security Trust Fund were $1.6 trillion. As for the HI Fund, in 2004 the total assets were $183 billion. The significant difference between the Social Security Trust Fund and the HI Fund shows why Medicare is considered in more imminent danger of financial distress.

Source: "Social Security and Medicare: The Impending Fiscal Challenge," Report from the Kansas City Federal Reserve Bank, 2006

Even though the Social Security financial crisis may be a long way off and involves not just dollars and cents but also potential generational tensions, that does not mean the political system is ignoring some short-term fixes. Much of the policy debate surrounding Social Security stems from Republicans in Congress who have waged a public relations campaign touting the benefits of privatizing the retirement system and creating individual savings accounts. With individual savings accounts, the worker's retirement benefits would depend on how much he/she contributed to his/her own account over the lifetime of employment and more importantly how well the savings account performed since the contributions would be placed in various types of investment mechanisms such as mutual funds, annuities, bonds, and the stock market. Under this system, there would be no payroll taxes and the emphasis would be on personal responsibility, rather than a government sponsored and administered program.[7]

Despite the accent on personal responsibility in preparing for retirement, the individual savings account proposal was not without its detractors. A bipartisan National Commission on Retirement Policy advocated for a go-slow approach suggesting that only 2% of the payroll tax be shifted into the accounts with workers receiving a range of investment options. But more conservative members of Congress advocated for a two-thirds shift in payroll taxes to the individual savings accounts. Supporters of the plan were convinced that the Social Security system is headed for a breakdown and the only way to effectively provide for retirement benefits is to move quickly and comprehensively to privatization. The Republican position raised opposition from many economists and congressional budget analysts who agreed that there would be transition costs associated with a shift to individual savings accounts as money would have to be found to cover existing Social Security pensions during the time that the system was moving toward partial privatization.[8]

But the real opposition to the individual savings accounts came from Democrats who viewed the proposal as financially risky, since workers would be asked to make investment decisions that they might not be prepared for and then hope that their return would not be threatened by a downturn in the stock market or any other economic slowdown that affected their investment. Inherent in this position from the Democrats was that the government provides workers with a guaranteed stream of pension money without the hassles and fears that come with personal investment. The Democrats also stated that the individual savings accounts were merely a way of enhancing the business of Wall Street investment firms who would enjoy a land office business as workers flocked to them to start their retirement accounts. Even the investment firms expressed some reluctance because of all the new administrative and start-up costs that would be incurred as the system attracted millions of new clients. Nevertheless, critics of the privatization proposals stated that, after a period of transition, the investment firms would be the real winners, while the workers would be forced to pay brokerage fees and then be subject to potential market volatility that could compromise their retirement nest egg.[9]

Data Bank

In 2014, 24% of the federal budget—$870 billion—was directed to payments for Social Security, which averaged to a monthly payment of $1,329 for each recipient (56 million recipients). Social Security also provided benefits to 2.3 million spouses of and children of retired workers, 6.1 million surviving children and spouses of deceased workers, and 10.9 million disabled workers and their eligible dependents. On the Medicare side, there are four programs under this umbrella program: Medicare—hospital care up to 80% coverage, Medicaid—hospital coverage for the poor, Children's Health Insurance Program (CHIP)—a Clinton era initiative to provide assistance to children of poor families, and the Affordable Care Act—subsidies for those applying for insurance coverage. Like Social Security, Medicare and its subsidiary program account for 24% of the federal budget or $836 billion dollars for its 55.5 million recipients. Together, Social Security and Medicare account for 17.5% of the entire GDP of the United States.

Source: Center for Budget Priorities

While the Republicans have been pressing for privatization of Social Security through the individual savings accounts, Democrats, besides criticizing these accounts, have launched their own short-term solution to deal with the future financial insolvency of the retirement policy. At present, all earnings of American workers up to $90,000 are taxed for Social Security purposes at

12.4%. But every dollar earned above the $90,000 mark is exempt from taxation, which benefits high wage earners. Removing the cap would, according to the Congressional Budget Office, close the funding gap over the next 75 years. The earnings gap would, in effect, raise the payroll tax of the high income earners by 1.9%, a small increase with a major impact on Social Security solvency. In 2005 President Bush expressed an interest in raising the cap on income above the $90,000 mark, but wealthy seniors raised objections to the payroll tax increase. The payroll cap increase has remained on the backburner of Social Security reform.[10]

From a worker point of view, however, the reforms proposed by Republicans and Democrats are not just about dollars and cents or public versus private pension programs. Rather, a key issue is whether the retirement age will be boosted in the coming years as a way of further delaying the financial breakdown of the Social Security Trust Fund. More and more Americans are seeking to retire at an earlier age, as was the case with baby boomer Kathleen Casey-Kirschling. Should the retirement age for receiving benefits be increased beyond 67, there would likely be a public outcry. Currently, many Americans retire early, take a smaller percentage of their Social Security benefits, and work part-time to supplement their income until they reach 67. But any policy change that would increase the retirement age to 70, as some political leaders have suggested, would force seniors to radically change their postwork plans.

Pushing the retirement age forward to 70 creates other problems. Studies from the General Accounting Office show that those American workers who remain on the job beyond the time that they are eligible to receive Social Security benefits are more susceptible to work-related injuries and require disability payments to cover the impact of the injuries. But many businesses are increasingly supportive of raising the retirement age to receive Social Security benefits because they see an experienced and conscientious workforce among the seniors who can be tapped for part-time employment. Businesses have also supported an extension of the retirement age as a possible answer to the illegal immigration issue. Should the government vigorously enforce existing laws regarding the presence of illegal migrants in the workplace and diminish the number of these workers, the alternative would be to rely on those in their late 60s and perhaps early 70s as "replacement workers."

As most experts who have studied both Social Security and Medicare predict, it is the latter program that is in fiscal crisis mode and requires quick and comprehensive reform. As stated earlier, the Medicare trustees continue to push forward the year when the program goes in the red. With a modest cost of .7% of GDP in 1970 to a ballooning 2.6% of GDP currently, it is a certainty that the year when Medicare goes into deficit will continue to drop. With health care costs rising yearly above the national inflation rate and the addition of the new prescription drug program causing new fiscal pressures (the cost of the program from 2006 to 2014 was estimated by the Bush administration to cost $872 billion), there is no relief in sight from the reality of a deficit under the current structure of the program.[11]

Medicare Costs As % of Gross Domestic Product

2010–3.7%
2020–4.5%
2030–6.2%
2040–8%
2050–8.5%
2060–10%
2070–11%

Source: Report of the Medicare Trustees, 2016

But like Social Security, the looming crisis in Medicare is not on most Americans' radar screens, and politicians usually avoid the problems by admitting there is a fiscal challenge, but then make only vague promises to fix the inevitable shortfall. The problem with Medicare reform is that most Americans, and certainly most politicians, have a short-term outlook. Polling data on national priorities often finds Medicare reform far down the list, yet Medicare remains a popular program. A recent poll by the Kaiser Foundation in California found that 58% of the respondents said that Medicare was most important to them.[12] But while Americans depend on and politicians proudly point to Medicare as a success, when a crisis looms in the distance, reforms are put off for another day.

One of the key reasons why Medicare stays in the background of public opinion and is avoided like the plague by politicians is that reform efforts will be much more controversial and include considerable changes in the manner in which health care for seniors is delivered and paid for. The options available to policymakers are generally fraught with sacrifice and, if implemented, would create a groundswell of citizen outrage. Of course, one of the obvious answers is to raise taxes (the Democrats naturally would target the rich) or require larger premiums (which some Republicans have supported), but to do so would require hefty increases that are certain to create opposition. But the other options are no more attractive. There have been proposals to reduce the services provided by Medicare, which usually pays for 80% of hospital and nursing home stays (within a set period) and services such as ambulance transportation, diagnostic tests, laboratory services, and emergency room visits. But a cutback in these services or a reduction in the percentage that the program would pay for would, without question, place an enormous financial burden on seniors. There have also been some doomsday scenarios regarding health care delivery as a result of the financial shortfalls in Medicare. Rationing of medical services has been raised as a possible outcome with seniors either having to wait long periods of time for procedures or being part of a triage system where doctors and nurses determine the order of care rather than a speedy response to a medical condition.[13]

The doctors and hospitals have also not been immune to the reform initiatives as there have been proposals to limit or reduce the reimbursements that Medicare provides hospitals and doctors for services provided. For years, hospital executives have been complaining that the government has been shortchanging them in Medicare reimbursements. As a result, hospital income has been reduced forcing, according to the hospital executives, the closing or the merging of hospitals. Doctors as well have complained that Medicare payments to them for medical services rendered have been reduced, cutting into their incomes and making it less attractive to become involved in a practice that caters to seniors. In recent years, there has been some level of reimbursement adjustment for hospitals and doctors, but down the road it is anticipated that the matter of Medicare reimbursements to hospitals and doctors will be central to the debate over how to save the senior health program.[14]

One of the potentially divisive proposals to reform Medicare in the short run was presented by the Bush administration in 2007. The president, as part of his fiscal 2008 budget, proposed that seniors making more than $80,000 would pay higher premiums and deductibles for the prescription drug program. In effect, the proposal advocated for a "means test" that would be required for participation in the costly drug program.[15] Republicans in the Senate championed the proposal, but it was defeated on its first try. The AARP worked vigorously against the change, saying that it would erode the incomes of seniors. Despite the defeat, the White House stressed that the change to a means test would save $10 billion over five years, but more importantly, it secured the concept of means testing as a new factor in providing Medicare benefits.

In 2006 economists from the Federal Reserve Bank in Kansas City presented a lengthy study entitled "Social Security and Medicare: The Impending Fiscal Challenge." Their conclusions point not only to the enormity of the problem but also the urgency for remedial action. Below is an excerpt from the conclusion of their study:

> The government's fiscal challenge is to ensure the long-run viability of both programs. Under current law, the dedicated sources of revenue available to the government are woefully inadequate for financing the benefits promised to current and future beneficiaries. The present value of the government's future obligations over the next 75 years is estimated to be $35.6 trillion. As a result, the government would need to increase revenues, reduce spending, or increase borrowing by running larger budget deficits. However, the cumulative value of the larger budget deficits would need to be $35.6 trillion in present value terms, which is significantly larger than the nation's federal debt—the cumulative sum of past budget deficits of $7.4 trillion at the end of 2004.[16]

As for President Obama, he did push Congress to accept his recommendation to provide a one-time $250 benefit to retirees in his 2015 budget, similar to the amount he provided in his Recovery Act in 2009, as a way of easing the burden on seniors upon retirement. Republicans were opposed to such a payment on grounds that it would expand the deficit since the initial $250 benefit would cost $14 billion. The White House also pushed for a measure that would provide easy access to Social Security benefits and programs to those workers who did not have retirement plans through their employer: about 75 million Americans. Called "myRA," the program was designed to set up automatic enrollment in 401K-type retirement accounts with no upfront fees or processing costs. Obama's call for greater benefits for retirees was criticized not only by Republicans but also some economists who pointed to polling data that showed most retirees satisfied with their retirement and not in need of new benefit increases.[17]

Despite President Obama's firm commitment to provide assurances that seniors would have adequate retirement benefits and health care security, his last year in office was a time in which candidates for his position took the center stage with respect to these two popular but costly programs. During the 2016 presidential campaign, Democratic candidate Bernie Sanders proposed complete Medicare coverage for all seniors, a regular cost of living increase for Social Security recipients (in 2015–2016 there was no COLA for recipients), and aggressive measures to bring down the cost of prescription drugs, which in many cases are beyond the reach of many poor and middle class Americans. Sanders campaigned on a platform of moving toward a government-controlled, single payer system as is found in most European countries. Sanders' rival, Hillary Clinton, ran on a platform of building on the current programs for Social Security and Medicare and not making radical changes to systems that she felt could be reformed and extended. Republican candidates paid little attention to the Social Security/Medicare issue, restating their desire to move to a personal responsibility approach based on tax credits and private saving accounts as the most cost-effective means to provide retirement and health care benefits to retirees.[18]

The unwillingness of the White House and Congress to reform the costs associated with Social Security and Medicare did abate a bit as the budget deal struck by President Obama and the Republicans in Congress in 2015 led to some minor but significant changes in spousal benefits for Social Security recipients and a fiscal "fix" to the Social Security Disability Insurance (SSDI) program, which was threatened by insolvency. In a bipartisan move, the Obama administration and Congress agreed to shift billions from the Social Security Trust Fund to the SSDI in order to keep it afloat. Republicans, who in the past condemned such "raids" on Social Security as money was taken from one program to fix another, agreed to the transfer in large part because they did not want to be seen as being against supporting the financial needs of those who depend on disability payments.[19]

With the election of Donald Trump, Republicans, led by Speaker of the House Paul Ryan, took aim at Medicare, suggesting that Congress would seek to overhaul Medicare and move to a new financing system that lessened the role of government and created Medicare "exchanges" where private companies would compete with the traditional government-run Medicare program to attract customers. Ryan claimed that Medicare was "going broke" because of Obamacare, a claim denounced by Democrats who stated that the Affordable Care Act actually strengthened the program and extended its solvency. Democrats immediately pounced on Ryan's Medicare proposal and pledged that they would fight to protect senior citizens and the government program.[20]

Unlike the issues that have been presented so far, the problems and challenges of dealing with the fiscal woes of Social Security and Medicare are currently not creating intense debate, partisan differences, and social divisions; they are only distant concerns that will be addressed in another decade. But once the "silver tsunami" of Social Security and the mind-boggling cost increases associated with Medicare come into play, these two programs will rise to the top of the list of political issues facing the political system and, indeed, the entire country. The best that can be hoped for is that, true to the American political tradition, we will somehow muddle through and create a patchwork of fixes—public, private, or both—that carry the programs forward. But the unknown about dealing with Social Security and Medicare is: Will there be a generational divide, and will the solutions presented to deal with these two vital programs foster difficult debates and serious differences between young and old? The future of Social Security and Medicare is in the hands of those young people who will be asked to make decisions about those older than them, and those decisions may require major sacrifices and radical changes in the way the United States government operates.

Former Illinois Senator Everett Dirksen once talked about federal expenditures and said, "a billion here, a billion there, after a while it becomes real money." With Social Security and Medicare, it is not a "billion here and a billion there"; rather, it is $35.6 trillion in obligations over the next 75 years. This financial obligation is truly mind-boggling and shows clearly why reforming the financial structures of Social Security and Medicare are so important, even though the impact of impending bankruptcy and debt is years away. If the American public faced the prospect of such a huge financial liability in their households, even if it were years away, they would most likely take some corrective action, but right now both the American public and their political leaders are in the traditional policy mode so common in our political system, putting off till tomorrow what needs to be dealt with today.

The Great Debate

In many respects the fiscal reform of Social Security and Medicare is a generational challenge with the prospect of younger Americans paying more in taxes in the future to cover the costs of these entitlement programs, especially as more and more seniors are being added to the retirement rolls and thus eligible for Social Security and Medicare.

Debate Topic

To what extent should the younger generation pay for the pension and health care needs of seniors? Is this a generational obligation for the common good or an undue burden on younger Americans?

Critical Thinking Questions

1. Should the government act now to reform Social Security and Medicare instead of "kicking the can down the road" and leaving it up to future leaders as is happening now?
2. In terms of Social Security, do you feel that Americans should be responsible for their own retirement benefits or should we rely on the government taking care of the funding?
3. In terms of Medicare, are you in favor of limiting health care services for seniors through some sort of means testing or significant increases in premiums and deductibles?
4. If Social Security is the so-called "third rail of American politics"—immune from change or significant reform—then how can the government resolve the future funding problems?
5. One of the most serious proposals for reforming Social Security is extending the retirement age at which benefits can be collected to 70. Is this a wise recommendation?

Connections

The major advocate for seniors in both the Social Security and Medicare policy debates is the American Association of Retired Persons. See www.aarp.org

The National Commission on Retirement Policy is one of the key sources of information and policy alternatives related to reforming Social Security and Medicare. The Commission is associated with the Center for Strategic and International Studies. See www.csis.org

The Social Security Administration is a critical source of information on the program. See www.ssa.org

The Centers for Medicare and Medicaid Services (CMS) is the key source for information on the program. See www.cms.org

The government website for Medicare is www.medicare.gov

Some Books to Read

Aaron, Henry, *Reforming Medicare* (Washington, DC: Brookings Institution Press, 2008).

Altman, Nancy and Eric Kingson, *Social Security Works! Why Social Security Isn't* (New York: New Press, 2015).

Clark, Robert, Marilyn Moon, Timothy M. Smeeding, and Robert Louis Clark, eds. *Economics of an Aging Society* (New York: John Wiley and Sons, 2004).

Oberlander, Jonathan, *The Political Life of Medicare* (Chicago: University of Chicago Press, 2003).

Shaviro, Daniel, *Making Sense of Social Security Reform* (Chicago: University of Chicago Press, 2001).

Notes

1. "First U.S. Baby Boomer Applies for Social Security," *Reuters*, October 15, 2007, www.reuters.com/article/latestcrisis/idusn15383509
2. "Finances of Social Security and Medicare Deteriorates," *New York Times*, May 2, 2006.
3. See Trustees Report and Trust Fund for 2016 at Centers for Medicare and Medicaid Services, www.CMS.gov
4. Steve Vernon, "Let's Debunk This Social Security Myth," *CBS News*, July 6, 2016. Vernon explains the use of surplus Social Security funds and the issuing of bonds that gain interest. www.cbsnews.com
5. See the position of the AARP on Social Security reform at its website, "Keep Medicare and Social Security Strong," November 17, 2016, www.aarp.org
6. Robert Pear, "Social Security Underestimates Future Life Spans, Critics Say," *New York Times*, December 31, 2004.
7. See the Republican position of Social Security Reform at www.ontheissues.org/Social_Security.htm#RepublicanParty
8. See "The 21st Century Retirement Security Plan: Final Report of the National Commission on Retirement Policy," Cornell University ILR School, March, 1999.
9. "Democrats Mobilizing on Social Security," *Washington Post*, February 15, 2002.
10. "Upper-Income Seniors: Pay More," *Washington Post National Weekly Edition*, December 15–21, 2007.
11. "Social Security and Medicare: The Impending Fiscal Crisis," Federal Reserve Bank of Kansas City Economic Review, First Quarter, 2006.
12. The Kaiser poll and other data regarding support for Medicare can be found in an article entitled, "Medicare as Reflected in Public Opinion," *Journal of American Society of Aging* (June 9, 2015), pp. 1–5.
13. See Alice Rivlin, "Why Reform Medicare? The President's and Other Bipartisan Proposals to Reform Medicare," Report of the Brookings Institution, May 21, 2013.
14. See Adrianna Anderson, "Medicare Reimbursement," July 28, 2015, www.Medicare.com. See also "Medicare's Physician Payment Rules and the Sustainable Growth Rate," Statement of Donald B. Marron before the Subcommittee on Health Committee on Energy and Commerce, US House of Representatives, July 25, 2006.
15. "Means Test Sought for Medicare Drug Plan," *Washington Post*, October 5, 2007.
16. Social Security and Medicare: The Impending Fiscal Challenge: 2006 Annual Report of the Board of Trustees of the Federal Hospital Insurance and Federal Supplementary Medicaid Insurance Trust Fund, May 1, 2006. (pdf).

17. The position of the Obama administration on "Seniors and Social Security" can be found on the White House website under the above title. See www.white house.gov. See also an article critical of Obama's Social Security Policy by Robert Samuelson, "Obama's Social Security Failure," *Washington Post*, June 12, 2016.

18. Bernie Sanders' position on Medicare for all can be found at his website, https://berniesanders.com

19. Emily Brandon, "How the Budget Deal Changes Social Security," *US News Money*, November 13, 2015.

20. Alison Kodjak, "Paul Ryan's Plan to Change Medicare Looks a Lot Like Obamacare, All Things Considered," National Public Radio, November 26, 2016.

8 RACE RELATIONS AND RACIAL POLITICS

Issue Focus

There is little doubt that in the history of this country the most divisive issue has been race relations. From the days of the slave trade when Africans were forcibly brought to American shores to the deep national differences over slavery that led to the Civil War and to the Civil Rights movement in the 1950s and 1960s, the United States has often been defined in terms of how it deals with racial discrimination and how it moves toward creating a nation that advances equality for all its people. The election of Barack Obama as the country's first African-American president signaled a turning point in race relations, but many in the African-American community continue to face racial bias and see the struggle for civil rights as an ongoing process of acceptance and social justice.

Chapter Objectives
This issue chapter will seek to:
1. Describe the struggle of African-Americans for civil rights and the evolution of the civil rights movement in the United States.
2. Examine the current debates over government policies designed to ensure racial equality, the differences in approaches to eradicating racial discrimination, and the race-based divisions that still remain in American society.
3. Discuss the current status of race relations in the United States as a result of the election of President Barack Obama.

SOME BACKGROUND

America has often been called a nation of immigrants, but America is also a nation of former slaves and indigenous natives who were either brought here against their will or were forcibly pushed out of their ancestral homelands in order to make way for the white man. The history of race relations in this country, especially with respect to African-American slaves and Native Americans, is disturbing and sad. The slaves brought here from West Africa to work in the fields of the South were not only denied their basic civil and human rights, but they were also treated as simple property easily bought and sold by landowners anxious for inexpensive labor. The natives who occupied this country before the white man landed were often treated as unwanted interlopers who could be moved from place to place in order to accommodate the white man's dream of extending the frontier westward. In both cases, the slaves and the natives were expendable and many endured the cruelest treatment.

Over time, with the natives worn down from fruitless wars against the white man and relegated to reservations, the struggle for civil rights shifted to the millions of slaves who made up large segments of the population in southern states. The Civil War, which was fought in large part over the issue of slavery, ended with a victory by the North and the promulgation of the Thirteenth Amendment, abolishing slavery; the Fourteenth Amendment, promising "equal protection of the laws"; and the Fifteenth Amendment, granting voting rights to former slaves. But after the war and the issuance of the Civil War Amendments, discrimination and segregation continued in the United States. In many of the southern states, so-called Jim Crow laws were instituted which effectively made former slaves second-class citizens and shut them out from any equal treatment in the white man's world. Blacks faced new roadblocks to full citizenship, and those who questioned the separate system were many times the victims of unfair justice and, worse yet, physical intimidation, beatings, and public lynching.

It was not until the post-World War II era that blacks made an organized and aggressive effort to change the face of race relations in the United States. Using the courts, economic boycotts, civil disobedience, and public demonstrations, blacks began the civil rights movement in this country. The National Association for the Advancement of Colored People (NAACP) became the primary voice of the movement representing the interests of black people in state capitals, the halls of Congress, and at the Supreme Court. Young lawyers like Thurgood Marshall, who argued the key school desegregation case before the Supreme Court (Brown v. Board of Education of Topeka, Kansas), religious leaders like Dr. Martin Luther King, Jr., who started the famous Birmingham boycott, and ordinary citizens like Rosa Parks, who bravely refused to give up her seat to a white man and move to the back of the bus, stepped forward to rally the people to take action against discrimination and segregation.[1]

The push for equal treatment and the breakdown of the racial barriers that existed in this country were not easily accomplished. Political leaders and governmental officials in southern states steadfastly refused to acknowledge the inherent injustices of discrimination and segregation and did all in their power to stop the civil rights movement. Federal marshals had to be brought into Mississippi to ensure that local officials would not block blacks from registering to vote. In Alabama, Governor George Wallace stood in the doorway of the University of Alabama to stop blacks from enrolling. In the US Congress, southern senators used filibuster techniques to stop legislation that would end discrimination and segregation.

Stiff public resistance to civil rights activism, primarily in the South, took the form of church burnings, executions of demonstrators and organizers, and widespread police brutality. This culture of hate often targeted prominent officials of civil rights organizations. Dr. Martin Luther King, Jr., the leader of the civil rights movement and the inspirational voice of black America, was assassinated in Memphis, Tennessee in 1968 as he prepared to demonstrate in favor of that city's garbage men, who were on strike. King's assassination set off days of rioting in many of the major cities and made clear the anger and division that existed between white and black America over the issue of race relations and civil rights.[2]

While the death of Dr. Martin Luther King, Jr. pointed out the hatred that still lingered in this country, the civil rights movement achieved some notable successes, including the passage of the Civil Rights Act of 1964, a landmark piece of legislation that placed the federal government as the guarantor of an open and equal society in key areas such as housing, transportation, employment, and accommodations. In 1965 Congress passed the Voting Rights Act that tore down the barriers that had been put in place in the South and elsewhere to deny blacks the right to vote and compete fairly for public office.[3] Both of these bills were followed by other civil rights laws and bureaucratic regulations that moved the United States away from discrimination and, in effect, ended the era of racial segregation. Much needed to be done in order to ensure that political and social rights for black America were expanded to include economic opportunity and fair distribution of economic benefits, but by the beginning of the 1970s, the civil rights movement had become a force to be reckoned with and an accepted part of the process of moving America from two separate countries to one.[4]

On the Record

Now I say to you today, my friends, even though we face the difficulties of today and tomorrow, I still have a dream. It is a dream deeply rooted in the American dream. I have a dream that one day this nation will rise up and live out the true meaning of the creed: 'We hold these truths to be self-evident, that all men are created equal.'

Dr. Martin Luther King, Jr.: speech at civil rights march on Washington, August 28, 1963.

In the forty years since the death of Dr. Martin Luther King, Jr., the civil rights movement has pushed forward with a wide agenda for change. Black leaders who have followed in the footsteps of Dr. King, such as the Reverend Jesse Jackson and the Reverend Al Sharpton, have charged that America remains a nation where there remains discrimination, perhaps more subtle and less oppressive, but discrimination nonetheless. They and other leaders from a new generation of African-Americans continue to point out that black people face daily challenges in finding jobs, purchasing homes, dealing with the police, and enduring racist comments and attitudes. The struggle for racial equality in the minds of many African-Americans is by no means over, and the remedies for ensuring that African-Americans are treated equally has caused new debates and fostered new differences and divisions in this country. It is those debates and those new differences and divisions that we now discuss.

FYI

Some Important Dates in the Civil Rights Movement

1954—Supreme Court declares school desegregation unconstitutional.

1955—Rosa Parks refuses to move to the back of the bus in Montgomery, Alabama.

1957—Arkansas Governor Orval Faubus uses National Guard soldiers to block nine black students from attending Little Rock High School. President Eisenhower sends in federal troops to protect students and ensure integration of the high school.

1960—Four black college students begin sit-in at lunch counter in Greensboro, North Carolina.

1962—President Kennedy sends federal troops to the University of Mississippi to ensure that James Meredith, the school's first black student, can enroll and attend classes.

1963—Dr. Martin Luther King, Jr. delivers "I Have a Dream" speech in Washington.

1963—Church bombing in Birmingham, Alabama, kills four black girls.

1964—Congress passes Civil Rights Act after 75-day filibuster by southern senators.

1965—March from Selma to Montgomery, Alabama, to demand protection for voting rights.

1965—Malcom X assassinated.

1965—Riots in the Watts section of Los Angeles.

1965—Voting Rights Act signed into law.

1968—Martin Luther King, Jr. assassinated in Memphis, Tennessee.

1978—Supreme Court rules in the Bakke decision that medical school admission policies that set aside positions based on race are unconstitutional.

1983—Martin Luther King, Jr. federal holiday is signed into law.

1990—President George H.W. Bush vetoes a civil rights bill that he views as imposing racial quotas on employers. A watered-down version of the bill eventually passes.

1996—The Supreme Court rules that race cannot be used in creating congressional districts.

2003—The Supreme Court found that an affirmative action point system designed to enhance the chances of minorities getting into the University of Michigan was unconstitutional.

2006—Despite Republican opposition, the Voting Rights Act of 1965 was re-authorized.

2008—Barack Obama was elected the first African-American president of the United States.

(continued)

FYI   (continued)

2014–2015—Police killings of unarmed black men set off violent protests and rioting.

2015—Massacre of nine black church members in Charlestown, South Carolina, by white supremacist.

2015—South Carolina Governor Nikki Haley orders all Confederate flags on state property to be removed.

2015—Black Lives Matter movement forms and challenges police shootings of blacks.

2017— Neo-Nazi, white supremacist rally in Charlottesville, Virginia leads to violence with one dead and twenty injured.

DEBATES, DIFFERENCES, AND DIVISIONS

Although what is often termed de jure discrimination (discrimination based in law) is now largely a memory, there remain in America examples of de facto discrimination (discrimination that is the result of inequities of power and everyday examples of bias). For example, US Census data point to a striking gap between blacks and whites in terms of income. In a study done in 2014, the Census Bureau found that the median household income of African Americans was $35,398, while for whites the median household income was $60,256. Furthermore, the percentage of African-Americans in poverty, again using US Census data in 2014, was 27.4%, while the percentage for whites was 11%. There has indeed been evidence of a vibrant and expanding African-American middle class, but compared to the white middle class, the percentage is quite small. In recent studies the percentage of black households defined as middle class was 38.4% compared to 60% of all race-defined households. Despite recent gains for the black middle class, data from the Great Recession era of 2008–2009 showed that black families lost 50% of their wealth during that period. As a result of this economic downturn, in 2011 the typical white household had a net worth of $91,405 compared to the black household with a net worth of $64,460.[5]

Data Bank

Comparing the Black and White Economic Experience

Home Ownership
73% of white households own their own homes—44% of black households own their own homes.

Education
34% of white adults finished college—21% of black adults finished college.

Life Expectancy
Life expectancy for a white baby born in 2010 was, on average, 78.9 years;
a black baby born in the same year could be expected to live, on average,
75.1 years.

Unemployment Rate
Based on data from 2013, white unemployment rates have been, on average, 6.6%, while unemployment rates for blacks were, on average, 12.6%.

Source: US Census Bureau, NAACP, and The Urban League

The economic disparities that exist today between blacks and whites in
America have become the target of much of the action of the contemporary civil
rights movement. To remedy the disparities, African-American leaders remain
committed to the affirmative action policies that were instituted during the
administration of President Lyndon Baines Johnson. Affirmative action policies basically seek to ensure that minorities and women are not discriminated
against in hiring and promotion, and in order to ensure that such discrimination does not occur, federal regulations provide guidelines and requirements
that businesses and other institutions must follow to create a fairer hiring and
promotion playing field and to guarantee that there will be a level of diversity
in the workplace. But while the goals of affirmative action fall within the tradition of equal opportunity and anti-discrimination, the program to require
businesses and institutions to abide by the federal regulations and foster a
diverse workforce has come under intense scrutiny and passionate debate.

The opposition to affirmative action is based on the view that hiring,
admission, and promotion procedures should be guided by merit and achievement, not by a desire to right the wrongs of the past or to create a more diverse
workforce. Supporters of merit-based procedures for hiring, admissions, and
promotions argue that affirmative action often fosters a quota mentality as
employers and institutions show preferential treatment toward minorities and
women. Since affirmative action was implemented, there has been an ongoing debate about whether the federal regulations foster "reverse discrimination" as white males are allegedly denied jobs, admission, and promotions in
order to achieve a government-imposed directive. Proponents of the merit-
based approach believe that minorities and women should not advance in any
way because of the assistance of the government, but rather should use their
personal talents, skills, and initiative to succeed. There is great faith among
the merit-based proponents that the United States remains a nation of equal
opportunity if only the citizens, no matter their race, gender, or disadvantaged
state, work within the existing economic and social system.[6]

The supporters of affirmative action, particularly in the African-American
community, take issue with the critics of the policy. They make the argument
that there continues to be both subtle and overt examples of racism and discrimination that remain in American society and that without the pressure from
government, hiring, admission, and promotions in business and institutions

would be skewed toward whites. Leaders in the African-American community continue to battle those in government who would gut affirmative action and replace it with merit-based procedures. Although affirmative action guidelines continue to remain in place and are supplemented by state anti-discrimination policies, public opinion in support of the program has waned in recent years, and Supreme Court decisions have chipped away at the use of race as a key factor, especially with respect to admissions procedures at colleges, universities, and professional schools.[7]

Affirmative action policies have been challenged on a number of occasions, some making it all the way to the Supreme Court. Most of the significant decisions involved admissions policies at colleges and universities and professional schools. The landmark Bakke case (Regents of the University of California v. Bakke) in 1978 struck down a point system that allowed minorities with lower test scores to enter the medical school. The court saw the California system of allocating admission "seats" to minorities based on race was a quota system that was unconstitutional. The court, however, did uphold the principle of affirmative action, which aimed to create a diverse student body and compared the use of race as similar to choosing candidates for admission based on geographic considerations.[8] Since the Bakke decision, the Supreme Court has narrowed the circumstances in which preferential treatment of minorities is acceptable under the constitution. For example, in 1995 the court eliminated fixed quotas in the granting of government contracts, thereby reversing the decision in the Fullilove case in 1980, which provided for quotas to be used for minority-owned firms that competed for government contracts.[9]

In recent years, the issue of affirmative action again was situated in the university setting, this time at the University of Michigan and involving a point system that gave greater weight to students of color over whites who may have scored higher on standardized tests. The Supreme Court, in a close 5–4 decision in 2003 (Gratz v. Bollinger and Grutter v. Bollinger), struck down the point system as another example of unconstitutional quotas, but at the same time upheld a University of Michigan Law School admission policy that used race as one factor in its admission process.[10] In both cases, the justices did hold firm to the view that the university had a legitimate right to try and create a diverse student body, but in the case of undergraduate admissions, the court felt that the weighted point system that placed a higher weight on race was a violation of the equal protection clause of the 14th Amendment. The University of Michigan ruling at the undergraduate level forced many institutions of higher learning to abandon quota-like procedures and rely more on close examination of students' academic records, letters of recommendation, and extra-curricular activities.

Contemporary race relations in the United States have not only been linked to Supreme Court cases and state action. In 2006 Congress was embroiled in a debate over the reauthorization of the Voting Rights Act. The Voting Rights Act, which originally was made law in 1965, had reached its expiration point requiring reauthorization. Southern Republican legislators balked at approving the bill, stating that it singled out their region as the center of voting discrimination and irregularities and that the legislation would open the way toward federal ballots being printed in languages other than English. Some Republican legislators from Georgia and Texas were upset that voting irregularities in Florida during the 2000 Presidential election were being linked unfairly to their states since the reauthorization allowed the Justice Department to review any changes to voting procedures in nine southern states that had a history of voting discrimination.[11] Despite the rebellion among southern Republicans, the Republican leadership and President Bush pushed vigorously to end the stand-off, and in a Rose Garden ceremony, President Bush signed into law the Fannie Lou Hammer, Rosa Parks, and Coretta Scott King Voting Rights Act Reauthorization and Amendments Act of 2006.[12]

But the Voting Rights Act of 1965 continued to be a source of debate and significant change. In 2013 the Supreme Court, in a 5–4 decision, struck down Section 4 of the act by allowing nine states, primarily in the South, to change their election laws without prior federal approval. Supporters of Section 4 called it the "heart" of the act and saw the decision as a means of perpetuating voting barriers to blacks. The majority decision, written by Chief Justice John Roberts, stated that blacks no longer faced barriers to voting in those states with a history of discrimination. As Roberts wrote, "the country has changed."[13] The immediate result of the ruling was that states like Texas were free to enact voter identification laws that could limit black participation in elections (black leaders stated that many minorities do not have proper identification, especially elderly blacks). Other states were allowed to move forward with redistricting plans that effectively created representative districts that limited black voting power to the advantage of Republican candidates and incumbents.

While much of the struggle for equal treatment and equal opportunity has fostered intense debate and partisan wrangling in the institutions of government, it is in the everyday lives of African-American citizens that some of the most heated debates occur, revealing the continuing differences and divisions between black America and white America. One of the most serious examples of the deep divide between the races in recent years has been over racial profiling by local and state police departments. The term racial profiling refers to the use of certain race-based characteristics by law enforcement authorities in determining whether a person of color is likely to commit a crime. Police have justified the use of racial profiling as a means of preventing crimes or pursuing criminals who have allegedly committed a crime. Civil rights advocates such as the American Civil Liberties Union (ACLU) and representatives of the African-American community such as the NAACP have criticized the practice as racist and in direct violation of the Fourth Amendment guarantee against illegal search and seizure.[14]

More controversial than the profiling, especially in recent years, has been the shooting of unarmed black men by the police. In 2015, 100 unarmed black men were killed by police (37% of all unarmed people killed), including the highly publicized killing of teenagers Michael Brown in Ferguson, Missouri, Tamir Rice in Cleveland, Ohio, Laquan McDonald in Chicago, Illinois, and Freddy Gray in Baltimore, Maryland. The killings only intensified the racial divide in this country as many blacks viewed these killings as a continuation of long-standing police racism and brutality. Many whites defended police as having a difficult and dangerous task of deciding in a split second how to respond to a threat or perceived threat from an individual.

Despite the debate about proper police procedures, the deaths of unarmed black men stirred the black communities in many urban areas and spawned the Black Lives Matter movement that challenged police actions and demanded the firing of police officers responsible for the killings and comprehensive reforms of the manner in which police deal with members of the black community. In places like Ferguson, Missouri, and Baltimore, Maryland, the deaths of Michael Brown and Freddy Gray led to days of violent demonstrations and destruction of private property. In some cases city officials settled out of court for millions of dollars with the families of those killed by police, in some cases police officers involved in the killings were fired, and in others, officers were placed on trial for murder. The spate of killings in 2015 did appear to foster a willingness on the part of the police and city officials to create new ways of community policing and more effective ways of responding to a perceived threat from individuals. Nevertheless, the deaths of unarmed blacks left deep suspicions in the African-American community over what was viewed as police racism and callous concern for black youths.[15] Also in a number of cases where black men have been shot and killed by police, the officers involved were not charged.

Even more disturbing for the African-American community is the rise in hate crimes and examples of racial threats. Again, in recent years, there has been a marked increase in cross burnings and spray paintings of racial epithets on the homes and property of African-Americans. There has also been a rise in the presence of rope nooses placed at the homes of blacks or in schools where blacks are students. The nooses are grim reminders of the lynchings that occurred in the South of blacks who dared challenged the system of segregation. In response to such actions, states have passed hate speech laws based on their interpretation of the Supreme Court's doctrine of "fighting words." Under this doctrine the government can prohibit and eventually prosecute those individuals who engage in activities designed to foment fights or affect the public peace. As a result of this interpretation, individual states have passed hate crime laws, in large part to address racist activity or speech.[16]

Such laws, however, have stimulated wide debate over free speech issues and the growing influence of politically correct comments. While there has been debate over limiting speech that may offend certain racial groups on college campuses, the major concern in the African-American community has been over the cross burnings and spray painting. In 2003 the proponents of hate crimes laws won a victory in the Supreme Court as it upheld a Virginia law saying that the state has the right to limit cross burnings, which have a clear intent to intimidate a particular racial group. The court did not support the First Amendment claim that the law limited the ability of groups, like the white supremacist Ku Klux Klan, from publicly expressing their views.

The issue of racial hatred and white supremacy reared its ugly head again in the aftermath of the election of Donald Trump. Various racist groups such as neo-Nazis, the Ku Klux Klan, and members of organizations often described as the "alt-right" (for alternative right wing) became more visible with rallies, parades, and public speeches. Many of these groups stated that the election of Donald Trump gave them new opportunities to spread their beliefs. Although Trump publicly denounced the racist groups and their message, the number of violent hate crimes skyrocketed along with Nazi symbols that were spray-painted on churches, synagogues, and Islamic centers.[17]

In recent years, the anger of the African-American community has focused on the number of blacks incarcerated in prisons, in many cases for minor offenses, often related to drugs. One in four black men born since the 1970s has spent time in prison. Many African-American leaders place the blame for the high incarceration rate on the Crime Bill of 1994, signed by President Bill Clinton, which cut back on parole, provided grants to build prisons, and supported what became known as the Three Strikes provision, which sent offenders with three convictions to long prison terms. The impact of the Crime Bill on black incarceration had and continues to have a serious effect on not just the individuals in prisons, but also their families, which have been torn apart by the absence of a male bread winner and by seeing their husbands, fathers, and brothers in jail for extended periods of time for drug offenses.[18]

The huge increase in the United States prison population and its direct relationship to drug arrests and incarceration also has a racial component. According to data compiled by the NAACP, African-Americans constitute nearly 1 million of the 2.3 million individuals incarcerated, which is six times the rate of whites, even though 14 million whites and 2.6 million African-Americans report using an illicit drug. Whites, therefore, are using drugs at five times the rate of blacks, yet blacks are sent to prison for drug offenses at ten times the rate of whites.[19] According to data from the Sentencing Project, African-Americans serve virtually as much time in prison for drug offenses (58.7 months) as whites do for a violent offense (61.7 months). While African-Americans represent approximately 12% of the total US population, 38% have been arrested for drug offenses, and 59% of those in state prisons are serving time for a drug offense.[20]

The huge number of African-Americans in jails in this country has been most distressing to the black community as the incarceration has contributed to numerous socio-economic ills such as the breakup of families, the loss of income for families of those convicted, wage declines of ex-convicts when they return to the work environment, an inability to reintegrate themselves into the community, and a deep-seated hostility toward law enforcement and public officials. As Professor Glenn Loury of Brown University stated in his testimony before the Joint Economic Committee of Congress in 2007, "For these men (who have been imprisoned for long periods of time on drug-related charges), their links to family have been disrupted; their subsequent work lives will be diminished; their voting rights are often permanently revoked. They will suffer, quite literally, a 'civic excommunication' from American democracy. It is no exaggeration to say that, given our zeal for social discipline, these men will be consigned to a permanent non-white male nether caste."[21]

The disparity in the African-American prison population because of drug-related convictions was addressed by the United States Supreme Court in December 2007 when the justices, in a 7–2 ruling, granted trial judges more discretion to impose more lenient sentences for crack cocaine convictions, which are often the primary source of the extensive incarceration for African-American males. Justice Ruth Bader Ginsburg, writing for the majority, stated, "It would not be an abuse of discretion for a district court to conclude when sentencing a particular defendant that the crack/powder disparity yields a sentence greater than necessary."[22] The Supreme Court decision allowing greater discretion and likely greater leniency came as a result of growing outcries by the African-American community and the Congressional Black Caucus over Congressional penalties put in place in the Reagan administration that led to the "100 to 1" sentencing disparity, meaning that the possession of 5 grams of crack cocaine brought the same five-year prison sentence as the possession of 500 grams of powder cocaine. As a result of this decision, it was estimated that as many as 20,000 prisoners could petition to have their sentences reduced. The Bush administration and the two conservative judges who dissented in the case, Justice Clarence Thomas and Justice Samuel Alito, stated that placing such discretion in the hands of the trial judges would take away Congress's right to set guidelines and leave the current sentencing guidelines without much force or meaning.[23] It is important to state that, during the last two years of his presidency, President Obama did initiate a policy of reducing the prison time of some African-Americans jailed for minor drug offenses, but those released were only a small percentage of blacks behind bars, many of whom were incarcerated as a result of the Crime Bill of 1994.

The status of race relations in the United States at the present time must be considered hopeful yet discouraging. Much progress has been made on the political front from voting rights to the institutionalization of a wide range of civil rights. African-Americans are now at the highest levels of government as evidenced by Supreme Court Justice Clarence Thomas and Secretaries of State Condoleezza Rice and Colin Powell, and of course, President Barack Obama. African-Americans are also well-represented at the state and local levels including big city mayors, county commissioners, education leaders, and high-level law enforcement officials. Blacks still remain underrepresented in government, especially at the gubernatorial level, but they are not absent from the centers of political power as they once were before the civil rights movement pushed for change.

On the economic front there has also been some progress. Despite the considerable gap in income and other key indicators of wealth, there has emerged in the last twenty years a professional and middle class that holds out hope for other African-Americans about the prospects of making it in the

American economic and social sphere. There are now black CEOs of major US companies, black multi-millionaires, and many stories of rags-to-riches blacks using their entrepreneurial skills and hard work to become financial success stories. While there remain far too many blacks stuck in poverty, with the gap between the rich and the poor growing in this country, the success of some blacks holds out hope that moving up the economic ladder in the American system is not beyond the realm of possibility.

Of course, the election of Barack Obama as the 44th president in many respects "changed everything" in race relations in the United States. The election of Obama was viewed as a watershed event in the United States as it proved to many in the country that race is not a barrier to achieving the highest elected office in the land. Obama's victory energized the African-American community and filled many with new hope that an era of real racial harmony had arrived.[24] Despite the Obama presidency, there are still barriers to full equality in the African-American community and disappointment among some black leaders at his civil rights agenda. A Gallup poll in 2007 showed that whereas 75% of white Americans polled said that race relations were good, only 55% of blacks agreed. The percentage of blacks agreeing to the question was the lowest response since 2001 when 70% of blacks said relations with whites were good.[25]

Still, despite the election of Barack Obama to the presidency and some hopeful economic signs, especially among the black middle class, the recent spate of killings of unarmed black men by police and the protests that followed has soured the American public on the current state of race relations, and perhaps reveals an ominous future. A *Washington Post–ABC* poll in July, 2016, showed that six out of ten adults felt that race relations are bad (63%) while only 32% felt they were "generally good."[26] A Rasmussen poll in January, 2016, found that 50% of American adults thought race relations were getting worse, an increase of 6% since a similar poll was taken in 2015, and a 20% increase since 2014. Only 20% of the respondents to the Rasmussen poll felt that race relations were getting better.[27]

What is even more disturbing is that the 2016 presidential election unleashed increased racial discord, and Donald Trump made comments and took policy positions that were heavily criticized as racist in tone. Many on the liberal side of the political equation felt that Trump's slogan to "Make America Great Again" was a code phrase designed to appeal to whites who feared blacks, Hispanics, and Muslims. As for Trump, he often appealed to African-Americans by stating that under Democratic presidents little if any economic progress had been achieved and posed the question to black voters, "What have you got to lose?" by voting for him.[28]

The report card of race relations in the United States is thus filled with Cs and Incompletes as progress in creating a truly equal America is far too slow and filled with unmet goals. Taken over time, particularly since the Brown v. Board of Education case in 1954 and the civil rights victories of the 1960s, it is possible to state that considerable progress has been made in improving race relations in the United States. Blacks and whites generally get along (although often from a distance) and the days of race riots appear to be a bad memory. Yet so much needs to be done to erase the economic gap, the quiet discrimination, and the occasional outbursts of blatant racism. It appears safe to state that America will continue to have a race problem and will have to face the fact that much more needs to be done to bring blacks and whites together.

The Great Debate

A substantial majority of Americans now believe that race relations have deteriorated in the last four years, despite the election of Barack Obama. Although there are hopeful signs in terms of black middle class expansion and increased levels of African-American government officials, the killings of unarmed black men by police has heightened tensions between blacks and whites and led to a general racial unease between whites and blacks.

Debate Topic

How can the United States improve race relations in the coming years? What specific steps would you recommend to restore a more positive racial environment in America?

Critical Thinking Questions

1. Recent polling data suggests that younger Americans are "color blind." Do you agree?
2. Why do think that the largest percentage of poor people in the United States is African-American?
3. Is it fair to use affirmative action procedures to give preferences to minorities in hiring and admissions to colleges and professional schools?
4. Where do you stand on racial profiling by police of African-American men and the contention by blacks that DWB (driving while black) remains a racial problem in this country?
5. What policies would you recommend to improve relations between the police and the black community?

Connections

The premier advocate for African-Americans is the National Association for the Advancement of Colored People. Visit its site at www.naacp.org

A website that examines a range of issues and concerns of African-Americans is www.africanamericans.com

The Reverend Jesse Jackson's Rainbow Coalition is one of the more prominent social justice groups advocating for African-Americans. Its website is at http://www.rainbowpush.org

The National Urban League has been in the forefront of African-American community issues and is also a leading advocate for blacks. See www.nul.org

Government policy related to race relations and racial justice is centered at the US Commission on Civil Rights. Visit its site at http://usccr.gov

A Few Books to Read

Alexander, Michelle, *The New Jim Crow: Mass Incarceration in the Age of Colorblindness* (New York: The New Press, 2010).

Coates, Ta-Nehisi, *Between the World and Me* (New York: Spiegel and Grau, 2016).

Lowery, Wesley, *They Can't Kill Us All: Ferguson, Baltimore and a New Era in America's Racial Justice Movement* (New York: Little, Brown, 2016).

Obama, Barack, *Dreams of My Father* (New York: Broadway Books, 2004).

Ogeltree, Charles J. Jr., *All Deliberate Speed: Reflections on the First Half Century of Brown v. Board of Education* (New York: Norton, 2004).

Notes

1. For background on the struggle of blacks in America see Michael Klarman, *From Jim Crow to Civil Rights: The Supreme Court and the Struggle for Racial Equality* (New York: Oxford University Press, 2004).
2. See a compendium of King's speeches in Clayborne Carson and Kris Shepard, eds., *A Call to Conscience: The Landmark Speeches of Dr. Martin Luther King, Jr.* (New York: Time Warner, 2001).
3. A study of the black experience in the period of the civil rights movement is Andrew Hacker's *Two Nations: Black and White, Separate, Hostile, Unequal* (New York: Scribners, 1992).
4. See Taylor Branch, *At Caanan's Edge: America in the King Years, 1965–1968* (New York: Simon and Schuster, 2000).
5. This data was accessed from US Census data and the Pew Research Center, Social and Demographic Trends, by Race. See www.pewsocialtrends.org/2013/08/22/ See also the analysis of Laura Shin on race and household wealth, *10 Proposals for Eliminating the Racial Wealth Gap, March 27, 2015 Forbes*, March 27, 2015.
6. For a criticism of affirmative action and other government policies related to race relations, see Stephen Thernstrom and Abigail Thernstrom, *America in Black and White: One Nation, Indivisible: Race Relations in America* (New York: Simon and Schuster, 1997). For a comprehensive discussion supporting affirmative action see Thomas Nagel, "A Defense of Affirmative Action," Report from the Center for Philosophy and Public Policy, Testimony Before the Subcommittee on the Constitution of the Senate Judiciary Committee, June 18, 1981.
7. See Valerie Strauss, "Why We Still Need Affirmative Action for African Americans in College Admissions," *Washington Post*, July 3, 2014.
8. Regents of the *University of California v. Bakke* 438 U.S. 265 (1978).
9. *Fullilove v. Klutznick* 488 U.S. 488 (1980).
10. *Gratz v. Bollinger* 539 U.S. 306 (2003).

11. Carl Hulse, "Rebellion Stalls Extension of Voting Right Act," *New York Times*, June 26, 2006, http://nytimes.com/2006/06/22/washington/22vote.html?

12. "Voting Rights Act Renewed for 25 Years by President," *The Washington Times*, July 27, 2006.

13. Adam Liptak, "Supreme Court Invalidates Key Part of Voting Rights Act," *New York Times*, June 2, 2013.

14. See the discussion of profiling in American history in "What's at Stake" in Christine Barbour et al., *Keeping the Republic* (Washington, DC: Congressional Quarterly Press, 2006), pp. 207–208 and 261–262.

15. See Wesley Lowery, *They Can't Kill Us All: Ferguson, Baltimore and a New Era in America's Racial Justice Movement* (New York: Little, Brown, 2016).

16. The landmark decision related to hate crimes was out of Minnesota. See *R.A.V. v. City of St. Paul* 60 LW 4667 (1994).

17. See the analysis of the Southern Poverty Law Center in "Hate and Extremism," December 20, 2016.

18. See Ta-Nehisi Coates, "The Black Family in the Age of Mass Incarceration," *The Atlantic*, October, 2015, pp. 60–84.

19. This data comes from the Criminal Justice Fact Sheet of the NAACP, 2016. View this data under the title "Criminal Justice Fact Sheet," www.naacp.org

20. See Ashley Nellis, "The Color of Justice—Racial and Ethnic Disparity in State Prisons," June 14, 2016. See this study at www.sentencingproject.org

21. See "Hearing Before the Joint Economic Committee," Congress of the United States, October 4, 2007.

22. See *Kimbrough v. United States*, 06–6330, 552 U.S.

23. Ibid.

24. "Obama Presidency Nudging Views on Race, Poll Finds," *New York Times*, April 28, 2009.

25. See Joseph Carroll, "Whites, Blacks, Hispanics Assess Race Relations in the U.S.," *Gallup Poll*, August 7, 2007.

26. Krissah Thompson and Scott Clement, "Poll: Majority of Americans Think Race Relations Are Getting Worse," *Washington Post*, July 16, 2016.

27. "Voters Paint a Grim Racial Picture of America," *Rasmussen Reports*, August 26, 2016.

28. See Peniel Joseph, "Trump Has Normalized Our Worst Racial Impulses," *CNN Opinion*, September 27, 2016.

9 REFORMING EDUCATION

Issue Focus

The link between education and national development is clearly established in the United States. An educated workforce provides the foundation upon which the country can compete effectively in the new global economy and expand the level of prosperity to a growing number of Americans. However, because of the heightened importance of education in American life, public schools are facing intense scrutiny as critics point to a range of deficiencies from low test scores to increased dropout rates. As a result, new options for educating America's youth have come to the fore. What was once general agreement on the positive contributions of public education are today undergoing challenge and change.

Chapter Objectives
This chapter will seek to:
1. Describe the problems associated with public education in contemporary America, especially since the highly critical study *A Nation At Risk* was published in the 1980s.
2. Present the numerous federal, state, and local initiatives that have been developed to reform public education.
3. Discuss the obstacles to reform that remain as the United States seeks to develop an educational system that will respond to the challenges of the 21st century.

SOME BACKGROUND

In 1983 Ronald Reagan appointed a commission to examine the state of education in the United States. The commission came back with a scathing critique entitled *A Nation at Risk*. The report stated in part, "Our Nation is at risk. The educational foundations of our society are presently being eroded by a rising tide of mediocrity that threatens our very future as a Nation and a people." The attack on education in America was based on data that showed test scores were dropping significantly, while other countries, some far below the United States in national income, were making remarkable progress in preparing their students for the demands of an ever-increasing global economy. The report was designed to shock the country into taking bold steps to improve education and to address what many policy analysts felt was the most important public issue facing the country.[1]

A Nation at Risk stimulated a national conversation about what needed to be done in order to get the country's educational system back on track. Liberals talked about pumping billions of dollars into improving school buildings, hiring more teachers, and updating equipment and technology. Conservatives stressed that the public education system had to be completely changed and pushed for charter schools that were outside the domain of union influence, vouchers that allowed parents the financial flexibility to remove their students from a local school and go to another school, and, most importantly, high stakes testing that accented the importance of teacher and administrative accountability to reach certain benchmarks of academic success. Although there was no shortage of solutions to the education problem facing the United States, *A Nation at Risk* placed what happens in our schools and with our students at the forefront of a national policy debate.

In 2002 Senator Edward Kennedy of Massachusetts and Representative George Miller of California, both Democrats, worked cooperatively with the Bush administration to push through the landmark education bill entitled No Child Left Behind. The law was not only an example of bipartisanship in a policy area where there was general agreement that major reform was essential, but also it established teacher and school accountability through testing as the foundation of assessing educational progress. Those schools that did not show "adequate yearly progress" were deemed failing and would face both the stigma of poor quality education and a cut in federal funding. The No Child Left Behind Act was a major shift in the role of the federal government in education from requiring accountability standards to pledging more funding for schools at the state and local levels. In fact, the law quickly created a tense relationship between the federal government and the states who felt it was an intrusion on what had been their responsibility since the early days of the constitution.

Five years later, Kennedy and Miller were in the forefront of a legislative movement to overhaul No Child Left Behind and target the Bush administration and the Department of Education as failing to provide adequate budgetary resources for the law and for not understanding the special challenges faced by low-income, immigrant, and special-needs students. As Senator Kennedy said in his support for a reform of No Child Left Behind, "We still have the concept of accountability, but what we need to do is get away from labeling, get away from the punitive aspects and give help and assistance to the neediest schools. We're now on a pathway to make some sense on this." Both Kennedy and Miller were responding to a groundswell of opposition to the No Child Left Behind law as teachers, administrators, and parents complained about its rigid adherence to testing standards, and states and local authorities criticized the law for creating unfunded mandates as the federal government promised money to assist in implementing the standards and then held back on the appropriations.[2]

Public education in the United States has a proud heritage that dates back to Horace Mann in the 1830s and has remained since that time the dominant channel for providing young people with the skills they need to enter the world of work. Moreover, public education has often been viewed as the "great equalizer" as it has offered Americans of any race, color, creed, or religious affiliation the opportunity to expand their personal horizons and achieve their dreams. Today, however, public education is not only under attack as failing in its mission of preparing young people with the necessary skills to succeed in a highly competitive world, but it is also being challenged by numerous alternatives from the private sector, the religious community, and even home schooling. Americans remain committed to public education and often place it high on their list of policy priorities, but public education has become an issue where there is an endless supply of new reforms and new options and no shortage of contrarian views on how to fix an education system that many see as in desperate need of repair.

On the Record

As the first commissioner of education in Massachusetts, Horace Mann is often considered the father of public education in the United States. Mann was a tireless advocate for education and for its ability to improve the lives of the citizens of Massachusetts. I (MK) am also proud to say that he was the founder of my university, one of the first state institutions of higher learning in the United States. One of his most famous quotes about the value of education is cited below:

Education then, beyond all other devices of human origin is the great equalizer of the conduct of men, the balance-wheel of the social machinery.

Source: Bridgewater State University Archives

DEBATES, DIFFERENCES, AND DIVISIONS

Among all the proposals for education reform in the United States it is safe to say that the driving force behind the reform is standardized testing. One of the outgrowths of the *A Nation at Risk* report was the move by states to require students to take regular testing mechanisms to gauge their proficiency in key subject areas such as English, Mathematics, and Science. Many states have also made passing the tests a requirement for graduation, thus introducing the term high-stakes testing. The testing movement was based on the view among many legislators at the state and local levels that school systems had to be held accountable for certain established benchmarks of educational progress; the normal report card and parental visit were not sufficient. In the view of these leaders, there needed to be a statewide or school systemwide measure of proficiency that went beyond the grades given by the teacher or the verbal assessments of progress given to parents. So throughout the country a new educational industry was formed as state boards of education developed standardized tests and began administering them to the students. Along with the tests, state education policymakers created set curricula in the major content areas to ensure that students were learning the same material.[3]

Standardized testing quickly became the target of criticism from teacher unions, minority leaders, and opponents of a "one-size-fits-all" testing procedure. The position of the critics was that testing was not only unfair to minorities, those with special disabilities, and students with test-taking phobias, but also that the emphasis on creating standardized curricula forced teachers to "teach to the test," leaving little room for ancillary material related to the curricula, extended discussion, analysis of a topic, or the introduction of subject matter that was outside the established framework. Moreover, critics pointed to the fact that test scores were increasingly being used as the basis for merit pay for teachers and, as a result, fostered heightened competition among schools districts to achieve high scores—two objectives that teacher unions roundly oppose as fostering a learning environment that is more about scores than mastering a body of knowledge. The National Education Association (NEA) has become the primary voice of opposition against standardized testing, emphasizing that reliance on test scores as the focus of education reform ignores other proven strategies such as smaller class sizes, more services for at-risk students, increased teacher professional development, and more reliance on a range of assessments rather than test scores.[4]

Despite the criticism, advocates of standardized testing pressed forward and have been supported by state legislatures, the business community, and the federal government. Many states have, in fact, expanded their testing programs and required higher scores in order for a student to be defined as "proficient." What often drives the push for tougher standardized test scores are results from similar tests in other countries that compete with the United States. The mathematics and science standardized test scores, in particular, from other countries are used to show that the United States has to pick up ground and maintain its focus on accountability in order not to fall further behind many of the major industrial countries in the world. More importantly, support for standardized testing has become associated with a business approach that is based on measurable progress much like a profit and loss report or a quarterly dividend assessment. Learning must be data driven, so the argument goes, and reliance on subjective, teacher-controlled evaluations is not considered an acceptable method of determining proficiency in a subject area or the extent to which remedial action needs to be taken in order to improve proficiency in the subject area.[5]

FYI

An organization called the Program for International Student Assessment tests 15-year-olds from 30 of the major industrialized countries that are members of the Organization of Economic Cooperation and Development (OECD). The tests are in mathematics and science. In the most recent PISA study from 2012, the mean score for Mathematics placed the United States 35th among OECD countries—below the Slovak Republic and above

Lithuania; in the Reading category, the United States ranked 26th—above Iceland but below the United Kingdom; and in the Science category the United States ranked 29th—above France but below the Czech Republic. In all categories, countries such as China (with Shanghai separated out), Singapore, Hong Kong, Taiwan, South Korea, and Japan led the way in the PISA scores. On a positive note, the United States did show modest progress in the rankings related to mathematics and science proficiency.

Source: Data from Program for International Student Assessment

Following further along the business model that has influenced the debate on educational reform is the introduction of school choice, which is driven by a system of vouchers. In large part because of the dissatisfaction with the public school system, especially in the inner cities of this country, there has been a movement supported by parent groups, the business community, and conservative educational reformers to create the opportunity for students to move from a public school to a private or parochial school. The key to this process of moving out of a school district to what are perceived to be better schools is that the parents are given a financial voucher to cover the cost of most, if not all, of the tuition at the private or parochial school. What the voucher system also does, besides introducing choice to parents, is remove the equivalent of what the public school receives to educate the child who is leaving the system and transfer it to a private or parochial school. In the end, the voucher system empowers not only the parents but also provides a transfer of money from public education to private or parochial education.[6]

At present there has been only limited implementation of a school voucher system and no real impetus to expand this educational option. In the 1990s, only two states, Wisconsin and Ohio, started voucher programs, and in both states the issue headed to the state courts for a challenge led by teacher unions and groups that were concerned the doctrine of separation of church and state was being violated by using public monies to support religious schools. There has also been action on the federal level involving public support for private schools in situations not directly related to financial vouchers. In a series of cases in the 1980s and 1990s, the Supreme Court held that a parental tax deduction for education purposes was constitutional, even though the overwhelming majority of the deductions claimed by the parents were for expenses related to their children attending parochial schools. In the 1990s, the court also ruled in favor of a state providing a sign-language teacher, even if that teacher worked in a parochial school. In perhaps the most important decision, in 1993 in Agostini v. Felton, the Supreme Court ruled that the state of New York could provide remedial education instructors in parochial schools and allow them to teach on school property.[7]

The key decision regarding vouchers came in 2002 when the US Supreme Court in Zelman v. Simmons-Harris voted 5–4 that the Cleveland voucher system was constitutional.[8] The argument made by the majority of the justices was that the primary purpose of parental decisions about education for their children was a secular one, and the choice of a private or parochial school did not violate the principle of separation of church and state. But the victory by the proponents of vouchers has not spread across the country. In 2006 the Florida Supreme Court struck down the Opportunity Scholarship program that provided for vouchers. The court held that the voucher system violated the state constitution and upheld the principle of state money being used for non-public schools only. There have also been defeats of school vouchers at the ballot box. In California in 2000, by a vote of 70% to 29%, the voters of that state rejected an expansive voucher program that would have allowed the transfer of public money to a private or parochial school without regulations regarding the accreditation or need. Finally, in 2007, the voters in Utah rejected a $3,000 tuition subsidy. The Utah vote was considered important because of the conservative nature of the state and the heavy influence of the Mormon religion in the political arena.[9]

But the struggle to move vouchers into the front ranks of the school choice movement has taken a new tact. In New Jersey in 2007, parents in 25 underperforming public school districts filed suit in court rather than use a statewide referendum as in Utah. The suit argued that because the public schools are denying students their constitutionally mandated right to a quality education, the courts in New Jersey should refund the tax money paid to the local communities so that the parents could use that money to pay for tuition at a private or parochial school. Support for vouchers in New Jersey remains low, but advocates are hoping that in the future an activist court in that state will give a boost to the school voucher movement.[10]

Despite the setbacks and uncertainty associated with state-funded voucher programs, there has been an expansion of school choice initiatives supported by individual donors or private foundations. Most of these voucher programs are directed at inner city schoolchildren where opposition to public schools is greatest and where private and parochial schools have sought to carve out an educational niche designed to offer alternatives to parents. Also, private individuals and foundations have begun to establish separate schools in the inner city and provide students with tuition assistance or full scholarships. Besides Cleveland and Milwaukee, which has the highest number of privately funded choice schools, private groups and foundations have established choice schools in Dallas, Buffalo, Oakland, New York, and even in smaller cities such as Midland, Texas. In most of these cities, there has been proven success with these privately funded urban schools as inner city youths have, in many cases, excelled in the classroom and have gone on after graduation to attend two-year or four-year colleges.

Data Bank

In data from 2013, the national average for spending per pupil was $10,700, up from $9,963 in 2006. The state with the highest per pupil expenditure was New York with an allocation of $19,818; the lowest per pupil expenditure was in Utah with $6,555. The costs per pupil were adjusted to reflect regional cost differences. When data was separated out by school district, the highest expenditure per pupil was Boston, Massachusetts, at $20,502, with Jordan, Utah, at the low end with a per pupil expenditure of $5,708.

Source: US Census data and US Department of Education

In the wake of the difficulties faced by supporters of vouchers, supporters of school choice have pushed successfully to develop charter schools. Charter schools are non-religious public schools that offer parents and students choice, but are structured in ways that separate them from traditional public schools. Charter schools have fewer regulations, more flexible union contracts, and stress instructional innovation and parental involvement. The designation of a charter school means that the state or local school board grants a charter for a set period of time (usually three to five years) and must within that period show that it has met the mission goals that it has set in its application for the charter. The underlying relationship that drives the charter school movement is that, in return for more autonomy to experiment, there is an expectation of accountability and improved education.

The charter school movement started in the 1980s when Philadelphia designated a number of its underperforming schools as schools-within-schools and fostered a climate of innovation and autonomy. These schools were termed charter schools. Later, in Minnesota, charter schools were established that were based on the concepts of opportunity, choice, and responsibility. In 1991 Minnesota passed the first charter school law. By 1995 nineteen states signed laws establishing charter schools and implemented a process for schools to obtain a charter based on specific mission statements and mission objectives. In 2013 the number of charter schools surpassed 6000, a 7% increase. Since 2006 the growth rate for charter schools has increased by 47%. Nevertheless, despite growth, charter schools represent only 6% of the United States public school system as they compete with 98,454 public schools.

Despite its relatively small share of public education, the charter school movement has been supported at the federal level. President Clinton, in his State of the Union address in 1997, called for the creation of 3,000 charter schools. President George W. Bush continued his support with his 2002 proposal for $100 million for what he called the Credit Enhancement for Charter Schools Facilities Program. Since 1994 the US Department of Education has provided federal support of $6 million in assistance to states and communities to advance the charter school movement.[11] President Obama has been a strong supporter of charter schools, especially as they provide what he views as opportunities for inner city children to benefit from schools with longer school hours, extended school years, and more teacher and principal accountability. Data from 2015 show that the federal government contribution to charter schools reached $235 million as it provided grants to states and local communities. Projections for FY 2016 show that the federal government will expand its funding of charter schools.[12]

It is fair to state that the charter school option is catching on across the United States. Since many charter schools are small in size and often accent a particular mission such as international studies, music, or the environment, they are attractive to parents who are interested in a specialized curriculum. Parents also support charter schools because of new assessment techniques and more innovation with specialized educational experiences. Even teacher unions are proposing charter school options within existing public school systems that allow teachers the ability to experiment with new teaching styles and instructional methods. However, there continues to remain reluctance on the part of teacher unions and their supporters in state legislatures to fully embrace the charter school movement, and there have been efforts to limit the number of charters that would be made available to prospective groups anxious to start a new school. In a statewide referendum in Massachusetts in 2016, for example, voters rejected a measure to increase the cap on charter schools to 12 new schools as voters felt that funding for the traditional public schools would be impacted if budgetary support went to charters.[13]

Although vouchers and charter schools have garnered the bulk of the attention in the school choice movement, it is also necessary to comment on a third alternative to the traditional public school, and that is homeschooling. As the title implies, homeschooling is providing a child an education within the home setting, usually by a parent. The parent(s) must receive permission from the local school district or state authority to conduct a home school program with their child or children, which includes an examination of the curriculum that will be followed, the books used, and the testing that will be employed to determine progress. Despite these administrative hurdles, homeschooling has become increasingly popular with parents who are concerned with the decline in public education, the safety environment in the schools, and in many cases the lack of religious or values training in the traditional public schools.

The homeschooling movement began as a result of the work of education critics John Holt and Raymond and Dorothy Moore. Holt and the Moores wrote controversial books on how children learn and the limitations of the traditional public education system. Both argued formal schooling was harmful to the development of the child and that the nurturing attachments developed between parent and child, especially at the elementary level, were far better than those within the public school classroom. As a result of the work of Holt and the Moores and their aggressive promotion of their views, a new movement took hold based on home schooling and direct parental involvement in the education of their children. Moreover, as the evangelical religions gained increasing prominence in the United States, there was a significant exodus from the public schools, which were viewed as harmful to the moral and ethical development of children.[14]

Homeschooling has seen remarkable advancement as an educational alternative. United States Department of Education data show that from 1999 to 2003 the number of home-schooled students increased from 850,000 to 1.1 million. Data from 2012 showed that there were 1.8 million American students homeschooled with an average growth rate of 2% each year. The growth in homeschooling is not only because of the support of born-again Christians and those disappointed in public schools. The advantages of one-on-one tutoring in the home environment, the emphasis on student-paced learning, and the benefits of using, on a regular basis, the vast resources often available in the community such as museums, science reserves, colleges, and other institutions where field trips can be arranged have become increasingly attractive. Moreover, taken from a fiscal point of view, home schooling saves local public school districts an estimated $24 billion a year, although in many districts home-schooled children do participate in athletic, cultural, and support services that require financial expenditure by the school district.[15]

Homeschooling definitely has its critics, especially from public school educators who question the academic quality of parental teachers, the lack of socialization, and the concern over excessive emphasis placed on religious instruction at the expense of mainstream subject matter.[16] Yet the National Home Education Research Institute contends that home-schooled children do well on standardized tests and have little difficulty entering college and succeeding in the college environment. The apparent success of the home-school movement has begun to influence public opinion. A Gallup poll in 2002 showed that since 1981, when the movement was first getting off the ground, opposition to homeschooling dropped from 73% to 54%.[17] Homeschooling remains a school choice option with the least support among Americans with school-age children, but its support line continues to move upward, and its success rate in terms of providing solid education results can no longer be ignored.

Amidst all the school choice options and the controversy and disagreement that has accompanied them, the key to education reform in the United States remains in the public schools. Many states have made K-12 education a high priority and have directed increased funding to school systems. However, there continues to be issue disputes connected to fairness in terms of funding among rich and poor districts, the often rollercoaster effect of budgets with good years and bad years of legislative and community support, and the ongoing dispute over teacher competency, certification, and merit. Yet within this atmosphere of fairness, funding, and the workplace conditions of teachers, there are numerous examples throughout the country of real reform and effective change that brings hope to those committed to improving and revitalizing the public school system in the United States.

To look at the future of education reform in this country, New York City may become a model. Former Mayor Michael Bloomberg announced in 2007 that he intended to make all the public schools in the city charter schools. The current number of charter schools at the time was 60, but the students in those schools showed a remarkable level of academic improvement as autonomy and greater accountability turned a number of schools around, especially in poor neighborhoods such as the Bedford-Stuyvesant district in the Bronx. In 2002 less than 40% of students in grades 3 through 8 were reading and performing math problems at their grade level, but five years later the percentage had increased to 65% in math and 50% in reading. Moreover, graduation rates were the highest they have been in more than 20 years, and the entire New York school system outperformed other major urban school systems in the state such as Syracuse, Buffalo, and Rochester.[18]

The school reform effort began when Bloomberg got effective control of the New York City school system and quickly moved the headquarters from Brooklyn to a building next to city hall. Next he set up a report card system to evaluate public schools and gave out grades to each school that reflected their academic performance and the input of students, parents, and teachers. Those schools that got a high grade would get an increase in their budgets, principals would get a bonus, and teachers merit pay. Those schools that received a bad grade for two consecutive years would see a change—the principal might be fired and any new principal would have to submit a remedial school improvement plan. If the trend of the school continued downward after two more years, the school would be closed.

Besides centralizing control of the school system in City Hall and implementing a tough accountability program, Mayor Bloomberg also brought the private sector into the reform movement. Bill Gates of Microsoft, Eli Broad, a billionaire from Los Angeles with ties to New York (who established a $500,000 college scholarship fund), and numerous wealthy hedge fund leaders contributed millions of dollars to support experimental programs in the charter schools. With sufficient private funds, many of the key changes did not have to rely on public money, and thereby limited contentious partisan debate. The combination of mayoral control, local autonomy, accountability, and private financial support proved to be, at least in the short run, an effective road map for educational reform, especially in a diverse, urban setting where there are numerous pockets of poverty and violence.

But when Bloomberg left office, his successor, Bill DeBlasio, appointed Carmen Farina as Chancellor, and a different educational approach was developed. Farina downplayed standardized testing, developed closer ties to teacher unions, and placed less emphasis on charter schools. Farina's approach was not top down and stressed the importance of a "kid friendly" education environment. So far, the Farina approach has not been viewed as successful. She has been roundly criticized by Bloomberg supporters and parents who see a return to the old model. Farina's tenure shows the difficulty of sustaining models of education reform, especially in urban school districts.[19]

While urban school districts struggled with reform at the local level, there were a number of new initiatives designed to push educational achievement forward at the national level. During the Obama presidency, there was reason to hope that the reform effort would continue unabated. Secretary of Education Arne Duncan, the former head of Chicago public schools, pledged to push forward with charter schools, merit pay for teachers, and an effort to limit the gap between rich and poor schools. Obama and Duncan also proposed major changes in the No Child Left Behind law, particularly in the area of how schools are judged as a result of assessment tests. They proposed that the 2014 deadline for bringing every American child up to an agreed-on standard of universal proficiency in a series of key subjects should be eliminated and replaced with a national standard of "college and career ready." Obama clearly made education reform one of his top priorities and gave Secretary Duncan wide latitude to bring change to public schools. But as Obama and Duncan would come to realize, change in public education comes slowly and consensus on the proper path to reform is not easily achievable.[20]

During the second Obama administration, Congress and the White House worked cooperatively to fix a number of the problems associated with the No Child Left Behind Act. In December 2015, the legislation was revised. The revision retained the controversial high-stakes annual testing in areas such as mathematics and reading, but returned more power to the states to set educational goals and limit the time that students are required to prepare for the testing. The Republicans got what they wanted—more local autonomy—while the Democrats got assurances that there would not be unequal distribution of federal funding for minorities and disadvantaged students from state to state. In signing the bill, President Obama stated, "With this bill we reaffirm that fundamentally American ideal that every child—regardless of race, gender, background, zip code—deserves the chance to make out of their lives what they want."[21]

While there was surprising bipartisanship in reforming the No Child Left Behind legislation, there was a vast ideological gap in implementing at the state level the so-called Common Core curriculum guidelines. Citing the need for state educational districts to have national uniform guidelines on its curriculum that responded to the challenges of global competition and the need for a more prepared national workforce, the federal government pushed forward the Common Core framework. At first, a number of governors, including Republicans, accepted the Common Core as a needed reform if the United States was to prepare a 21st century student population. But quickly there was pushback from conservatives who saw Common Core as a dangerous federal intrusion into state and local educational standards and, in some cases, voiced concern that the federal government was standardizing educational curricula in a way that was viewed as liberal, secular, and historically and scientifically biased. Many of the Republicans running for the presidency in 2016 made opposition to Common Core part of their political platform, pledging, if elected, not to permit a Common Core curriculum to be advanced by the federal government. Even reform-minded educators raised questions about the Common Core as overly ambitious and out-of-touch with the realities of classroom instruction. What started out as a generally accepted reform of educational guidelines for the next generation of American students languished as states, conservatives, and a growing body of educators cast doubt on Common Core.[22]

Each of the education issues that we have dealt with so far are complex and create serious divisions in American politics and society. Educational quality and education reform, however, has become so controversial because many Americans recognize how important this key investment is to the future of the country. A wide spectrum of leaders from government to business to law enforcement to social workers realize that making education work and producing educated graduates is a critical ingredient for our national success in an ever-competitive world environment. It is because of the importance of education that there is such a multiplicity of alternatives for change and reform being presented on the local, state, and national stages. The American public recognizes that getting education right means that this nation will continue to remain vital, prosperous, and strong.

Public education has, without a doubt, been struggling for the last thirty years. The country where public education got its start and developed a model for the rest of the world has failed too many of its young people. In 2016 it was reported in a Gallup poll that only 9% of respondents were "completely satisfied" with public school education, 34% "somewhat satisfied," 35% "somewhat dissatisfied," and 20% "completely dissatisfied."[23] Much of the concern by the poll respondents was in the area of weak mathematics proficiency and too much time being relegated to remedial courses. There is plenty of blame to go around as to the reasons that public education has disappointed so many of its citizens.

Supporters of public schools were angered over the appointment by President Trump of Betsy DeVos as Secretary of Education. Devos is a staunch advocate of charter, private, and religious schools and no supporter of federal funding for public education. As Secretary of Education, she has also showed little interest in using her office to defend attacks on gay, lesbian, and transgender students or working to lessen the debt burden of college and university students. Public educators saw DeVos as unqualified for the job of Secretary of Education, while President Trump applauded her desire to move to a more private sector model of education.

There may be debates and differences and divisions over how to improve the schools, but there is no shortage of desire and energy to make the public education system work. Although the No Child Left Behind Act is currently the target of criticism and regular attempts at redesign, the title of this landmark legislation is appropriate. The American people, governmental leaders at all levels, and a wide range of community leaders agree that the United States cannot leave any child behind; it must do its utmost to ensure that every American has a quality education as a steppingstone to the opportunities we as a nation promise to all our citizens.[24]

The Great Debate

The cornerstone of education reform from the federal to the state to the local level is standardized testing as a key to determining proficiency of learning and accountability of teaching. Critics of this approach say that so-called high stakes testing is deeply flawed in terms of preparation time, teaching to the test, testing tied to graduation, and erratic funding to assist students who have difficulty passing the test.

Debate Topic

Should standardized testing remain as the foundation for assessing the academic progress of students in the United States?

Critical Thinking Questions

1. What factors do you see as responsible for the low ranking of the United States on international assessment scores?
2. Is the answer to better education in the United States more public money or more competition from charter schools?
3. Do you agree with the assessment in recent polls that show Americans feel public schools are doing a "fair to poor job"?
4. Have standardized tests improved the quality of education in this country?
5. What recommendations would you make to "fix "American public schools?

Connections

The United States Department of Education is a valuable source for policy discussions on public education. See www.ed.gov

The National Education Association (NEA) is the leading advocate for public education in the United States. Their website can be reached at www.nea.org

The case for vouchers is made by the organization Rethinking Schools Online. See www.rethinkingschools.org

The primary organization advocating for charter schools is Charter Voice. The website can be reached at http://www/publiccharterschools.org

The homeschooling movement is represented by the organization Homeschooling. The site can be reached at www.homeschool.com

A Few Books to Read

Abeles, Vicki, *Beyond Measure: Rescuing An Overscheduled, Overtested, Underestimated Generation* (New York: Simon and Schuster, 2015).

National Commission on Excellence in Education, *A Nation at Risk: The Imperative for Education Reform* (United States Government Printing, 1983).

Goldstein, Dana, *The Teacher Wars: A History of America's Most Embattled Profession* (New York: Anchor Books, 2015).

Ravitch, Diane, *The Death and Life of the Great American School System* (New York: Basic Books, 2010).

Robinson, Ken, *Creative Schools: The Grassroots Revolution That's Transforming Education* (New York: Penguin Books, 2016).

Notes

1. National Commission on Excellence in Education, *A Nation at Risk: The Imperative for Educational Reform* (United States Government Printing, 1983).
2. "No Child Left Behind Authors Work on a Revision," *Boston Globe*, July 16, 2007.
3. See the website of the Association of Test Publishers and their study entitled "Testing in Schools," 2017, www.testpublishers.org
4. A recent examination of testing can be found in Lynsey Layton, "Study Says Standardized Testing Is Overwhelming Nation's Public Schools," *Washington Post*, October 24, 2015.
5. The most comprehensive study of the international educational achievement gap can be found in Tony Wagner, *The Global Achievement Gap* (New York: Basic Books, 2010). See also Jal Mehta, "Why American Education Fails and How Lessons From Abroad Could Improve It," *Foreign Affairs*, May/June, 2013.
6. Paul Peterson and David E. Campbell, *Charters, Vouchers and Public Education* (Washington, DC: Brookings Institution Press, 2004).
7. *Agostini v. Felton* 521 U.S. 203 (1997).
8. *Zelman v. Simmons-Harris* 536 U.S. 639 (2002).
9. "Pro-Choice," *The Economist*, June 9, 2007.
10. Ibid., p. 38.
11. For an update and assessment of the charter school movement in the United States see, "After Freedom," *Economist*, August 27, 2016. See also, Roger Altman and Robert Hughes, "Making School Choice Easier," *New York Times*, December 7, 2015.
12. Valerie Strauss, "Obama's Real Education Legacy: Common Core, Testing and Charter Schools," *Washington Post*, October 21, 2016.
13. Shira Schoenberg, "Massachusetts Votes Against Expanding Charter Schools, Saying No to Question 2," *Mass Live*, November 2, 2016. Also see Shirley Leung, "Why It's So Hard to Vote Yes on Question 2," *Boston Globe*, November 4, 2016.
14. See a discussion of the National Home Education Research Institute in Isabel Lyman, "Homeschooling Back to the Future," CATO Institute, Policy Analysis No. 294, January 7, 1998. Also see Jason Bedrick, "Competition Is Healthy for Public Schools," CATO Institute, December 9, 2015.
15. See "Research Facts on Homeschooling," National Home Education Research Institute, March 23, 2016.
16. Rob Reich, "The Civic Perils of Homeschooling," *Journal of Educational Leadership*, Vol. 59, No. 7, pp. 56–59.
17. Linda Lyons and Gary Gordon, "Homeschooling: Expanding Its Ranks and Reputation," *Gallup Polling*, May 7, 2002.
18. "Six Books a Week," *The Economist*, May 10, 2008. See also "Red Ties and Boys Pride," *The Economist*, May 10, 2008, p. 40.
19. See Alexander Nazaryan, "Carman Farina, New York City's School Chief, and the Perils of School Reform," *Newsweek*, August 10, 2016.
20. Paul Manna, "The Three Rs of Obama's Education Reform," *Americas Quarterly*, Fall, 2010.
21. As reported in the *Boston Globe*, December 11, 2015.
22. Valerie Strauss, "Common Core Reading Pros and Cons," *Washington Post*, December 4, 2012.

23. "Education: Gallup Historical Trends," *Gallup Polling*, August, 2016.
24. Diane Ravitch has been a vocal critic of American education. See her current views on education reform and the progress made in Sara Mosle, "The Counterrevolutionary: How Diane Ravitch Has Upended the School Reform Movement," *The Atlantic*, September, 2013.

10 ABORTION RIGHTS

Issue Focus

The issue of a woman's right to control her own reproductive decisions versus the rights of a fetus has divided Americans for over forty years. This clash of viewpoints has been at the center of the national political debate since the landmark Supreme Court decision Roe v. Wade. There is little middle ground between the right of a woman to choose to abort a fetus and the right to protect life in the womb. Advocates on both sides of the debate have made this issue a litmus test of whether a state official, a member of Congress, a Supreme Court nominee, or a presidential candidate should be supported by the right-to-choose or right-to-life movement. This battle continues with little sign of letting up.

Chapter Objectives
This issue chapter will seek to:
1. Examine the long struggle between right-to-life and pro-choice groups over abortion rights in the United States.
2. Discuss the political and legal positions policy makers and jurists take concerning abortion rights.
3. Explore some of the new areas of controversy over abortion rights and the responsibilities of medical professionals regarding abortion counseling.

SOME BACKGROUND

In 1973 the Supreme Court outlawed most of the existing state abortion laws in its Roe v. Wade decision. In a 7–2 ruling regarding Texas law, the Court restricted state legislative interference in a woman's right to an abortion in the first three months of pregnancy, but did allow states to restrict, under certain circumstances, second and third trimester abortions. Almost immediately, the number of abortions performed in the United States increased dramatically. In 1981 there were 29.3 abortions per 1000 births, but by 2005 there were 19.4 abortions per 1000 births. In recent years, the number of abortions has declined somewhat. In 2007 the Centers for Disease Control reported that the number of reported abortions was 1.2 million, the lowest number since 1976. The downward trend has continued with a reported decrease in 2015 of more than 15% since 2010.[1] Despite the decline, data from the Guttmacher Institute showed that 1.1 million abortions were performed in 2011, a rate of 16.9 abortions for every 1,000 women of childbearing age.[2]

With the Roe v. Wade decision and the steady increase in legal abortions, the abortion rights debate in the United States began in earnest as state legislatures, Congress, and the courts took action that defined more precisely a woman's right to end her pregnancy. The intense passion over abortion rights continues on today as "pro-choice" and "right-to-life" groups mount national campaigns to either protect a woman's right to choose or protect a fetus's right to life. Despite the ruling in the Roe case and subsequent legislative and court action, the abortion rights debate has not been removed from the issue arena; it may move back and forth from a high priority to a lesser status in political circles, but it remains an issue that political parties, candidates for public office, and government officials cannot ignore.

A woman's right to an abortion has always been controversial in this country. Dating back to the 1820s, there were laws on the books in states controlling abortion rights and setting time limits on when abortions could be performed. By the early 1900s, however, most states had outlawed abortions and there was general agreement that abortion was an unsafe medical procedure that put women at risk. Even leading feminists at the time such as Susan B. Anthony and Elizabeth Cady Stanton were opposed to abortion as they turned their attention to other causes of equality such as gaining suffrage and breaking down other social and economic barriers to full equality. But as the United States moved into the 1960s, and the so-called sexual revolution began to take hold with its emphasis on personal freedom, more and more pressure was placed on public officials at the state level to expand abortion rights and allow women to control reproduction. By 1965, however, all states had passed restrictive laws banning abortion.[3]

With states refusing to make abortions available to women, it was up to the Supreme Court to take on this volatile issue. While the Supreme Court established a key legal precedent with its decision in the Roe case, it also created a firestorm of controversy as the nation debated not just the elements of the law, but the morality of allowing women to control the reproductive process in the early stages of pregnancy. The decision unleashed a torrent of opposition from religious groups (particularly the Catholic Church) that saw in the Supreme Court decision a rejection of life and a refusal to recognize the rights of the unborn fetus. Interest groups such as the National Abortion Rights Action League (NARAL) and the National Right to Life quickly began forming on either side of the debate. Kate Michelman of NARAL attributed the intensity of the debate to conservatives who were "driven by those who have never accepted reproductive rights as essential individual rights, and have seen the benefit of abortion as an organizing tool for a much larger social vision—a vision that rolls back civil rights gains, women's rights, rights of the disabled and environmental protections." Gary Bauer of the conservative American Values group placed the abortion battle squarely in the political arena when he stated, "the right to life is the most fundamental, natural human right upon which all other rights are based."[4]

The intensity of the social and political divisions over abortion have rights become so intense that yearly rallies and demonstration are held in January of each year to mark the Roe v. Wade decision. In this contentious environment, there were unfortunately numerous instances of confrontation and conflict as pro-life groups such as Operation Rescue staged sit-ins and other intimidating measures at abortion clinics to stop women from entering clinics to have abortions performed. There were also periods of violence as Planned Parenthood clinics were bombed in North Carolina and clinic workers were killed at a Planned Parenthood facility in Boston. In many states, legislatures put into place laws creating "safe zones" that separated pro-life protesters from those women seeking to enter abortion clinics. Pro-life advocates challenged these "safe zones" as violations of free speech, and in a stunning defeat for the pro-choice movement, the Supreme Court in 2014 struck down the Massachusetts buffer zone law. In recent years, the anti-abortion movement and the Republicans in Congress targeted Planned Parenthood, particularly in eliminating federal funding, but also charging that officials in the organization were engaged in the sale of fetal tissue and body parts. The charges proved unfounded.[5]

On the Record

Justice Blackmun, in defending his position overturning the Texas law that limited a woman's right to make reproductive choices said the following:

> The Court has recognized that a right of personal privacy, or a guarantor of certain areas or zones of privacy does exist under the Constitution . . . whether it be founded in the Fourteenth Amendment's concept of personal liberty and restrictions on state action . . . or as the District Court determined, in the Ninth Amendment's reservation of rights to the people, is broad enough to encompass a woman's decision or not to terminate her pregnancy.

Source: Roe v. Wade

The right to an abortion granted through Roe v. Wade quickly entered the political arena as members of Congress, state legislatures, and candidates for public office from local leaders to those running for the presidency took positions in support of a woman's right to choose or for a fetus's right to life. In the years immediately after the Roe ruling, candidates running for office, or long-time incumbents seeking reelection, often defined their campaigns around the abortion issue and were victorious, or went down to defeat based on their position on "choice" versus "life." The pressure from right-to-life proponents eventually influenced Congress to take action. In 1976 under the leadership of Representative Henry Hyde of Illinois, Congress passed legislation banning the use of public funds for abortions and removed insurance coverage for federal employees to obtain an abortion. Many states followed suit and removed public funding for abortions, thus limiting the availability of abortions for many American women.

Since Roe v. Wade, the Supreme Court has addressed a number of issues related to abortion and made some clarifying and limiting decisions. In the 1980s, state legislatures sought to make it difficult to obtain an abortion by requiring abortions to be conducted in hospitals rather than clinics. Also the courts declared that a 24-hour waiting period be instituted in hopes that women would change their minds about aborting their fetus after receiving information provided by the hospital about fetal development. In the most important decision regarding abortion rights, the Supreme Court in the 1992 decision Planned Parenthood v. Casey approved many of these restrictive regulations and trimmed back the trimester formula that was the core of the abortion rights decision in Roe v. Wade.[6] At the same time, the court validated as fundamental the right for a woman to have an abortion as consistent with the concepts of liberty and the right to privacy as suggested in the Due Process Clause of the Fourteenth Amendment. This change in Roe v. Wade was brought on by the viability issue because advanced medical technology enabled viability at five to six weeks earlier than 28 weeks or around the end of the second trimester. As a result, the court ruled that the 1973 formula of 28 weeks was obsolete, but the underlying principle of viability should remain as the basis for supporting abortions. The court clearly of viability emphasized that it was not overturning the right of women to seek abortions in this country. As the judges stated in their majority opinion, "If the right to privacy means anything, it is the right of the individual, married or single, to be free from unwarranted governmental intrusion into matters so fundamentally affecting a person as the decision whether to bear or beget a child."[7]

With abortion rights secure (at least for a time) with the Casey decision, attention turned to Congress where conservatives worked to achieve a ban on what was called partial birth abortions. Partial birth abortions which in the medical community are called intact dilation and extraction, are rare procedures usually performed to protect the life of the mother, in which the fetus is taken out of the womb and a saline solution is injected into the skull to end life. During the Clinton administration, partial birth abortion bills were vetoed as the president maintained his support for a woman's right to choose. But with the arrival of George W. Bush in the White House, the legislative dynamics changed. In 2003 a partial birth abortion ban bill was passed by Congress and signed by the president. The bill was initially blocked by a federal judge and the case went to the Supreme Court. In 2007 in a key decision (Gonzales v. Carhart), the Supreme Court by a 5–4 margin upheld the Partial Birth Abortion Ban Act, and the majority stated that the ban did not interfere with the precedents set with the Roe and the Casey decisions. Opponents of the ban saw the victory in the Supreme Court as a signal that abortion rights were under threat and that it was only a matter of time before a case dealing with a woman's right to an abortion would make its way to the court and face a new level of scrutiny.[8]

Actions on abortion rights were also taken at the state level as South Dakota, Nebraska, and Texas passed strict anti-abortion legislation that permitted no abortions and penalized doctors who performed the procedures by limiting their ability to practice medicine and defined those who had an abortion as committing a crime. In South Dakota in 2006, Governor Mike Rounds signed a law supported by anti-abortion advocates that would have made performing an abortion a felony. The law also allowed little leeway as it banned abortions, even if the mother's health was in danger. The law divided the state and initiated an intense referendum campaign to determine the will of the people of South Dakota. The referendum was eventually rejected by the voters but was seen nationally as representative of individual states seeking to end abortion rights without waiting for the federal courts to act.

DEBATES, DIFFERENCES, AND DIVISIONS

The abortion debate, as presented by Justice Blackmun in the above quote, has many sides—ethical, medical, philosophical, religious, and personal. But as an issue, the abortion debate was addressed on numerous occasions by the Supreme Court and became a lightning rod of partisan discord in Congress and the presidency, there are some critical elements to the abortion debate that are centered in the constitution and the interpretation of the constitution by the justices at all levels of the federal courts. Central to the disagreement over abortion is the privacy issue. Nowhere in the constitution is the word privacy used and no amendment to the constitution provides a specific right to privacy. But in Roe v. Wade and decisions leading up to that historic decision, justices on the Supreme Court in a real sense "found" the right to privacy as inherent in the constitution and based its decision to support abortion rights in part on the right to privacy.

In 1965 in Griswold v. Connecticut, the Supreme Court overthrew a Connecticut law that banned the use of contraceptives, saying that it violated the privacy rights of individuals seeking to purchase contraceptives. Writing for the majority, Justice William O. Douglas found that the right to privacy was created from the language and intent in the 1st, 3rd, 4th, 5th, and 9th Amendments. Douglas, using language that dissenters would later employ to question the constitutional validity of the decision language, stated that there existed, "penumbras, formed by emanations from those guarantees that help give them life and substance." In other words, the language contained in those five amendments signal that the Constitution does provide for the right to privacy. In particular, Justice Douglas used the 9th Amendment to support his case when he quoted its language that declares that "the enumeration in the Constitution of certain rights shall not be construed to deny or disparage others retained by the people." As Douglas suggested, just because the constitution does not specifically grant a right to privacy that does not mean the right was not intended to be provided to the American people.[9,10]

The abortion rights decision in Roe v. Wade not only created a firestorm of controversy over the Court's protection of a woman's right to choose, but it also led to a serious debate among constitutional scholars, especially those with conservative credentials, about whether there existed a right to privacy in the constitution. Justices and constitutional scholars who were often termed strict constructionists or supporters of original intent stated without hesitation that if the right to privacy is not mentioned in the constitution, then the right does not exist, therefore nullifying the founding principle on which Roe v. Wade was adjudicated. As the terms suggest, strict constructionists and supporters of original intent believe that the constitution must be viewed strictly as it was constructed by the Founders and that the original intent of the constitution can be determined only by the words used by those who wrote the document and its amendments.

One of the primary advocates of the strict construction and original intent perspectives on the right to privacy was former federal judge Robert Bork, who was unsuccessful in gaining Senate approval to the Supreme Court when Ronald Reagan nominated him in 1987. Bork was rejected in large part because liberal Democrats on the Senate Judiciary Committee were able to convince a majority of the members that Bork's views were out of step with a "living constitution" that expands rights and applies constitutional principles to modern day conditions and circumstances. Bork was unyielding in his rejection of the privacy rights that bolstered the Roe v. Wade decision and stressed that justices on the high court must be guided by the constitution as written, not as they would like it to be written or as they choose to interpret its language.[11]

Because the Supreme Court has been at the core of the abortion rights debate in this country, appointments to the highest court have become politicized as both Democrats and Republicans seek to influence the appointment process and ensure that justices are either pro-choice or pro-life. The failure of Robert Bork to win approval by the Senate was just the beginning of a long struggle over whether a shift in the balance of the Supreme Court to a pro-life majority would end abortion rights and overturn the precedent-setting Roe v. Wade decision. The partisan debate over abortion rights and judicial appointments came to a head during the hearings to approve or reject President George W. Bush's nomination of Samuel Alito to the high court. Alito was the president's replacement for Justice Sandra Day O'Connor, who in the past had supported abortion rights and joined the majority in the Casey decision. Liberal Democrats on the Senate Judiciary Committee viewed Alito as a quiet supporter of the pro-life position and sought to ascertain through tough questioning whether he would vote to overturn Roe v. Wade. Alito maintained his openness to both sides of the issue but would not make a public commitment on how he would vote on a case associated with abortion rights. Critics of Alito among pro-choice advocates, however, pointed to positions that Alito had taken as a federal judge in abortion-related cases that signaled his opposition to the judicial philosophy that was used in the Roe v. Wade case. This concern was born out in 2006 when Alito joined the majority, including Chief Justice John Roberts, who was also a Bush appointee, in upholding the Partial Birth Abortion Ban Law.[12]

Also part of the debate over abortion rights has been trying to set the proper balance between the rights of the mother and the rights of the fetus. Pro-choice advocates state that the right of the mother, who is a fully-formed human, must be considered more important than the right of the fetus whom they view as a "potential human." To deny a woman the right to an abortion, according to the pro-choice argument, would treat a pregnant woman as if she were less than a full person and elevate a fetus to the same status as the mother. Pro-life advocates, however, see the fetus as protected under the constitution because there is human life in the mother's womb. The fact that the fetus has not left the womb does not, in the view of the pro-life position, negate their inalienable right to life, and because of medical and scientific breakthroughs that impact viability, the call for fetal rights has become more pronounced.

But while the courts have yet to strike down a woman's right to an abortion, judicial decisions have indicated that a mother has the responsibility to protect the health and welfare of her unborn child. Court decisions and state laws have stated that fetuses have the legal right to begin life with a sound body and mind and that mothers cannot refuse hospitalization, intrauterine transfusions, or surgical deliveries that could assist the fetus in reaching full term and being delivered in a healthy state. While such decisions on the part of the courts and legislatures have not carried over into the debate over abortion rights, it does lay the legal groundwork for making the case for some degree of fetal rights. At present, however, the debate over the mother's rights versus the fetus's rights has come down on the side of the mother.

Data Bank

Abortion policy has, from the start, been the subject of regular assessments of American public opinion as each side in the debate has used polling data to support its position in the courts and in national and state legislatures. Below are two recent polling studies using different questioning approaches to determine the position of the American people toward abortion.

In 2014 a poll published in *Slate*, an online magazine, found the following results regarding American opinions on abortion:

Abortion should be prohibited in all circumstances—11%
Abortion should be permitted only to save the life of the mother—14%
Abortion should be permitted only in cases of rape, incest, and to protect the life of the mother—28%
Abortion should be legal for any reason but only in the first trimester—20%
Abortion should be legal for any reason up to the end of the second trimester—10%

Abortion should be legal for any time period—12%
5% had no opinion or did not answer

Source: Slate Poll, January 22, 2014

In another poll published by Gallup in 2015, Americans for the first time since 2008 stated in a statistically significant response that by a margin of 50%–44% they self-defined as pro-choice. A majority of women—54%—defined themselves as pro-choice versus 46% of men.

Source: Gallup Polls, May 29, 2015

If the controversy surrounding abortion and abortion rights has been largely in the political arena and before the federal courts, there is a social element—racial and economic—to the debate that cannot be ignored and is at the core of the pro-choice position. Many of those women who seek abortions are young minorities. Recent data from the Center for Disease Control show that African-Americans account for 37% of all abortions and black women are five times more likely to abort than white women. Data from the Center for Disease Control found that Hispanic abortions accounted for 25% of all abortions. Among white women the rate was 13 per 1,000 abortions.[13]

Many of the black and Hispanic women reported that their desire to have an abortion was related to the fact that they could not afford a baby or that the father had left the scene and they were unable to provide financially for the care of the child. Pro-choice advocates use this data to support their view that abortion is absolutely essential to provide poor black and Hispanic women with the option of terminating their pregnancies and not bringing a life into the world that would immediately be at an economic and social disadvantage. While pro-life supporters do not deny this data on race and economic status, they stress the importance of taking the baby to full term and then placing the child up for adoption.[14]

What complicates the racial and economic factors in the abortion debate is that, as a result of federal and state laws that do not provide for funding of abortions, many poor women do not have access to safe abortions, should they choose to terminate their pregnancy. Currently, only seventeen states offer coverage for poor women to have abortions, with California, Illinois, and New York being the largest states with health care provisions that cover abortions. In general, white women have higher incomes or a network of support that would allow them to pay for an abortion. Pro-choice supporters thus see the inequity in the current availability of abortion coverage as women of color are forced to travel long distances to states that have such benefits or carry an unwanted pregnancy to full term. Again, the pro-life position does not address the racial and economic disparity issues, but stresses the importance of fetal rights and the necessity of not terminating a pregnancy.[15]

FYI

The two major political parties have taken very different positions on abortion rights in their party platforms, revealing the vast differences that exist in political and governmental circles over this controversial issue.

The position of the Democratic Party as presented in its 2016 party platform:

We believe unequivocally, like the majority of Americans, that every woman should have access to quality reproductive health care services, including safe and legal abortion—regardless of where she lives, how much money she makes, or how she is insured. We believe that reproductive health is core to women's, men's, and young people's health and wellbeing. We will continue to stand up to Republican efforts to defund Planned Parenthood health centers, which provide critical health services to millions of people.

The position of the Republican Party as presented in its 2016 party platform:

The Constitution's guarantee that no one can "be deprived of life, liberty or property" deliberately echoes the Declaration of Independence's proclamation that "all" are "endowed by their Creator" with the inalienable right to life. Accordingly, we assert the sanctity of human life and affirm that the unborn child has a fundamental right to life which cannot be infringed. We support a human life amendment to the Constitution and legislation to make clear that the Fourteenth Amendment's protections apply to children before birth.

In a related abortion controversy, President Obama signaled early in his presidency that he was going to eliminate the "conscience clause" from federal regulations. On the last day of his presidency, George W. Bush signed an executive order protecting health care workers who object to abortion and other birth control practices on religious or personal conscience grounds. The decision by Bush invalidated fifty-four laws in thirty-seven states that provide for access to contraceptives and gave health care workers the right to refuse their medical services as a matter of conscience. The wording of the Bush regulation stated that abortion is properly defined as "any of the various procedures—including the prescription, most of the major medical dispensing and administration of any drug or the performance of any procedure or any other action—that results in the termination of life of a human being in utero between conception and natural birth, whether before or after implantation."

Obama's intention to reverse the conscience clause was supported by the major medical professional organizations such as the American Medical Association. These groups stated that doctors, nurses, and other medical professionals have an obligation to provide information that gives patients the full range of options available to them regarding contraception and pregnancy.

But some doctor groups that are linked to religious organizations and the Catholic Church criticized Obama for limiting what they viewed as the constitutional right of free speech and freedom of religion. These groups suggested that doing away with the conscience clause would be akin to moving to a totalitarian state.

Abortion rights entered into the health care reform debate surrounding the Affordable Care Act as pro-life Democrats joined conservative Republicans to demand that the bill not allow government-subsidized insurance to pay for abortions. In last-minute discussions with Democrats, President Obama pledged that he would sign an executive order banning any federal support for abortion, a move that helped swing pro-life members of the House of Representatives to vote for the bill.[16]

In his second term, President Obama faced intense pressure from religious groups over the portion of Obamacare that provided free contraceptives to those enrolling in the plan. The Catholic Church in particular challenged the contraceptive issue as it applied to Catholic hospitals and universities. The issue also got tangled in the religious liberty issue as many people of faith used the arguments in the landmark Hobby Lobby case that supported the concept of conscience in response to government programs or policies that were deemed against their religious beliefs.[17]

One of the most interesting cases involving Obamacare and religious liberty came from a suit filed by the Little Sisters of the Poor, an elder care charity, that asked the Supreme Court to protect them from the president's birth control mandate, arguing that the government should not force them to facilitate the coverage. As the lawyer for the nuns stated, "[I]t is ridiculous for the federal government to claim, in this day and age, that it can't figure out how to distribute contraceptives without involving nuns and their health plans." Although the Obama administration did agree to a so-called "opt out" provision in which religious groups or institutions would be required to sign a form stating their objections to the rule and then leave it up to the insurers through Obamacare on how to provide coverage, the nuns and other religious groups challenged the form itself saying it is a "substantial burden" and made them complicit in violating their religious beliefs.[18]

The intensity of the abortion debate was perhaps best viewed in the efforts of conservatives in Congress to defund Planned Parenthood, the federally subsidized organization that provides a range of health care, advice, and programs for women, including abortions. When an undercover video was released showing Planned Parenthood employees discussing the sale of fetal parts (which under current law is not illegal or unethical under the Uniform Anatomic Gift Act), Republicans in Congress immediately sought to defund Planned Parenthood, which received in FY 2015 $528.4 million—a combination of federal, state, and sometimes local government assistance, with the majority coming from the federal government. Although federal law prohibits use of federal funds for abortions (the abortions performed by Planned Parenthood clinics are funded by private sources and are about 3% of its services), the videos were used by conservatives to seek a complete defunding of the organization, even though the organization has been praised by women's groups for its work in cancer screening, wellness counseling, and a range of testing services. Despite harsh rhetoric from the floor of Congress and a media blitz, conservatives were not successful in their efforts to defund Planned Parenthood through a spending bill, although they pledged to continue their efforts as they were emboldened by the 2016 election results that placed Republican majorities in both the House and the Senate.[19]

The judicial battle over abortion rights shifted in 2016 to a case out of Texas—Whole Women's Health v. Hellerstedt—in which the state sought to require clinics that provide abortions to have surgical facilities and doctors to have admitting privileges at a nearby hospital. The case worked its way to the Supreme Court and, if approved, would have likely reduced the availability of abortion in Texas. But in a 5–3 decision (Justice Scalia, a staunch opponent of Roe v. Wade had passed away leaving only eight justices to decide the case) the court ruled that the law violated the constitution and reversed a lower court decision in favor of Texas law.[20]

Currently the abortion debate in the United States is in a "wait and see" mode. The appointment of Judge Neil Gorsuch to the Supreme Court is viewed by many in the pro-choice movement as a vote for ending abortion rights. At present no abortion rights case is on the Court's calendar but states and the pro-life movement are preparing to challenge Roe v. Wade in the near future. Gorsuch, in his confirmation hearing declined to take a stand on his view of Roe v. Wade is viewed by many conservatives as in the mode of the late Justice Antonin Scalia, who Gorsuch replaced.

However, should Roe v. Wade be overturned in the future, it is important to point out what such a decision would do at the state level. By striking down Roe v. Wade, states would then be free to set their own standards regarding abortion. Those states that now restrict abortions either through funding mechanisms or by not encouraging doctors or health professionals from starting clinics that perform abortions would certainly move quickly to build on an anti-Roe v. Wade decision coming from the Supreme Court. But those states that currently provide access and funding, especially large, liberal-leaning states like California, New York, and Illinois would likely not choose to limit a woman's reproductive rights established under current federal law. According to the Center for Reproductive Rights, in a 2004 study entitled "What If Roe Fell? The State by State Consequences" abortion rights appear secure in 20 states, but in the other 30 states, "women are at risk of losing their right to choose an abortion after a reversal of Roe."[21] A prelude to the future of abortion rights came in 2016 in Ohio. The bill passed by the legislature banned abortion as early as six weeks into the pregnancy. Republicans who worked to pass the bill cited the election of Donald Trump as part of their motivation to push for the tough abortion bill. Proponents of the pro-life position in other states are promising "an onslaught of pro-life legislation" in 2017. Currently, there are 18 states that have enacted various weekly time limits on abortion, with Ohio the most stringent.[22]

The result of an overturn of Roe v. Wade would thus likely be a compartmentalization of abortion rights in this country with many southern, midwestern, and mountain states forbidding abortions and other states on both coasts maintaining the right. Interestingly, what started out back in 1972 as a state issue that was overturned by a federal court may, if Roe is overturned, return the country to a time when states set abortion policy with the only difference being that there would not be a universal ban, as outposts of abortion rights would remain. The fate of Roe v. Wade is unknown, but what is certain is that the decision has divided America and will continue to divide America no matter what happens in the future.

The Great Debate

The struggle over abortion in the United States is rooted in the issue of rights—the woman's right to reproductive freedom or the fetus's right to life.

Debate Topic

In the battle over rights, does a woman's right to choose to have an abortion supersede that of the fetus in the womb?

Critical Thinking Questions

1. When does human life begin?
2. Should the fetus have constitutional rights?
3. Why do some consider it more important to protect a woman's right to choose an abortion than give birth?
4. If the Constitution doesn't mention privacy rights, do we have them?
5. What would be the consequences of overturning Roe v. Wade?

Connections

One of the primary advocates for women's rights, and in particular a woman's right to choose, is the National Organization of Women. See the NOW site at www.now.org

NARAL is the prime pro-choice organization in the United States. Its site is www.naral.org

The Pro-Life Action League is a pro-life organization in the United States. Its site is http://prolifeaction.org

National Right to Life is the oldest and largest pro-life organization advocating for an end to abortion. Its web site can be accessed at www.nrlc.org

Planned Parenthood is one of the primary organizations providing health-related services to women. View the site at www.PlannedParenthood.org

A Few Books to Read

Alcorn, Randy, *Why Pro-Life: Caring for the Unborn and Their Mothers* (Peabody, MA: Hendrickson Publishers, 2012).

Githens, Marianne and Dorothy McBridge Stetson, *Abortion Politics: Public Policy in Cross-Cultural Perspective* (London: Routledge, 2013).

McBride, Dorothy, *Abortion in the United States: A Reference Handbook* (Santa Barbara, CA: ABC-CLIO, 2007).

Pollitt, Katha, *Pro-Reclaiming Abortion Rights* (London: Picador, 2015).

Segers, Mary and Timothy Bynes, *Abortion Politics in American States* (London: Routledge, 2016).

Notes

1. The Center for Disease Control provides the most accurate data on abortions in the United States. See the data from November 16, 2016 at www.cde.gov.
2. The Guttmacher data on abortion is available at www.guttmacher.org
3. For background on abortion see David Garrou, *Liberty and Sexuality: The Right to Privacy and the Making of Roe v. Wade* (New York: Macmillan, 1994).
4. See Alesa E. Doan, *Opposition and Intimidation: The Abortion Wars and Strategies of Political Harassment* (Ann Arbor, MI: University of Michigan Press, 2007).
5. See Adam Harris, "Everything You Need to Know About the Planned Parenthood Videos," *ProPublica*, January 27, 2016. See also Jackie Calmes, "Shootings at Planned Parenthood Adds to Challenges for Congress," *New York Times*, November 30, 2015.
6. *Planned Parenthood v. Casey* 505 U.S. 883 (1992).
7. Ibid.
8. *Gonzalez v. Carhart* 530 U.S. 914 (2000).
9. Evelyn Nieves, "South Dakota Abortion Bill Takes Aim at Roe," *Washington Post*, February 23, 2006, p. A01.
10. *Roe v. Wade* 410 U.S. 113 (1973).
11. Linda Greenhouse, "Why Bork Is Still a Verb in Politics, Ten Years Later," *New York Times*, October 5, 1997.
12. David Stout, "Alito Is Sworn In as Justice After 58–42 Vote to Confirm Him," *New York Times*, January 31, 2006.
13. See data on race and abortion at www.abortionfacts.com/statistics/race.asp
14. Zoe Dutton, "Abortion's Racial Gap," *The Atlantic*, September 22, 2014.

15. See "State Bans on Insurance Coverage of Abortion Endanger Women's Health and Take Health Benefits Away From Women," National Women's Law Center, December, 2016.
16. Michelle Ye Hee Lee, "Does Obamacare Provide Federal Subsidies for Elective Abortions," *Washington Post*, January 26, 2015.
17. Jaime Fuller, "Here's What You Need to Know About the Hobby Lobby Case," *Washington Post*, March 24, 2014.
18. John Garvey, "Obamacare vs. Little Sisters of the Poor," *Wall Street Journal*, March 20, 2016.
19. William Saletan, "The GOP Argument for Defunding Planned Parenthood Is Incoherent," *Slate*, September 30, 2015. See the Republican position on defunding Planned Parenthood at Barbara Hollingsworth, "GOP Platform Calls for Defunding of Planned Parenthood," *CNS NEWS*, July 13, 2016.
20. Camila Domonoske, "Supreme Court Strikes Down Abortion Restrictions in Texas," NPR, June 27, 2016.
21. "What If Roe Fell," Center for Reproductive Rights, June 1, 2007.
22. Sabrina Tavernise and Sheryl Gay Stolberg, "Trump Win Energizes Abortion Opponents," *New York Times*, December 12, 2016.

11
GUN RIGHTS

Issue Focus

It is safe to say that America is a country of guns and gun owners. Over 300 million guns are in the hands of 55 million American citizens who proudly profess their right to bear arms. But the passionate belief in gun ownership has a huge downside. The United States has developed a reputation around the world as a violent country where liberal gun ownership laws create the opportunity for criminals and ordinary citizens to use handguns and even assault rifles for personal or property protection, to engage in illegal activities, to settle a score, or to commit suicide. Despite over 30,000 gun-related deaths each year, in many cases by individuals with mental disorders, racial hatred, or simply angry outbursts, Congress has been unable and unwilling to put in place measures that would restrict gun purchases or requirements that potential gun owners would be forced to follow. The issue of gun ownership has now shifted to the federal courts and state legislatures where justices and legislators are defining the meaning and scope of the Second Amendment regarding the right to bear arms

Chapter Objectives
This issue chapter will seek to

1. Document the longstanding dispute over the meaning of the Second Amendment right to bear arms.

2. Update the controversy involving gun rights by examining the dispute between the National Rifle Association, the powerful pro-gun lobby, and groups such as the Coalition to Stop Gun Violence, that are seeking reforms to existing laws on guns and gun rights.

3. Discuss the latest issues involving gun rights, particularly in light of a key Supreme Court decision that for the first time addressed the issue of what the Second Amendment means.

SOME BACKGROUND

One of the exasperating characteristics of the Bill of Rights is that it is many times difficult to determine what the Founders were thinking when they wrote these essential building blocks of our personal freedoms. This is certainly the case with the wording of the 2nd Amendment and its definition of gun rights. The 2nd Amendment states that:

> A well-regulated Militia, being necessary to the security of a free State, the right of the people to keep and bear Arms, shall not be infringed.

A reader and interpreter of the 2nd Amendment is likely drawn to the opening phrase about a "well-regulated Militia" and the closing phrase that establishes "the right of the people to keep and bear arms." The question that has befuddled constitutional scholars and set both sides on a collision course in the debate over gun rights in this country is whether the authors of the Bill of Rights were granting the right to bear arms to a well-regulated militia or were extending that right to all citizens of the United States.[1]

Supporters of gun rights in organizations such as the National Rifle Association (NRA) see the 2nd Amendment as granting citizens the right to "keep and bear arms" and that the right "shall not be infringed," meaning that gun ownership should be unrestricted. Opponents of gun rights such as the Coalition to Stop Gun Violence concentrate their position on the opening phrase of "a well-regulated Militia" and state that the Founders never intended gun rights to be universal in the United States but only within the confines of the state Militias, the forerunners of what is now our National Guard.

This critical interpretive divide over what the 2nd Amendment means has created one of many issue battlegrounds in the United States over gun rights. Both sides in this debate about gun ownership not only differ on what the Founders meant in the 2nd Amendment, but whether guns are the causal factor in the high rate of violent crime in the United States, whether a citizen's best defense against a criminal act is the possession of a handgun, whether various forms of automatic weapons should be viewed as protected under the 2nd Amendment, and whether the government has the power to require certain safety features on guns and background checks for potential gun owners. Although all of these issues flow from the central question of whether American citizens possess the right to bear arms under the Constitution, the debate over guns has become multi-faceted and highly divisive.

While the Courts have seen fit to become involved in defining the character and limits of certain rights, such as in the case of abortion, the judicial interpretation of the 2nd Amendment has been rather sparse as justices at both the state and federal levels have sought to stay out of the battlefield of gun rights and let Congress interact with the various interest groups and allow a political rather than constitutional resolution of how to properly apply the 2nd Amendment in the United States. In three cases from the 19th century, the Supreme Court ruled narrowly that the 2nd Amendment restricts only the federal government but not the states. These decisions came during what was termed the pre-incorporation period when the court chose not to expand the Bill of Rights to include state action. As a result of these decisions, the Supreme Court chose not to address the key issue of what the 2nd Amendment means nationally and how it should apply to gun rights for all Americans. In 1939 the Supreme Court took on the first case in which the 2nd Amendment was addressed specifically. In United States v. Miller, the court examined whether a sawed-off shotgun owner (Miller) could be indicted under the National Firearms Act of 1934. The resolution of the constitutional issue was murky as Miller died and the Supreme Court upheld the federal law without a definitive resolution of the key issue of what the 2nd Amendment means and how it should be applied.[2]

The lack of judicial decision-making on the 2nd Amendment has allowed both sides in the debate to form their own positions on what gun rights Americans possess, creating a great deal of constitutional uncertainty and allowing the matter to be played out in the political arena. In the contemporary period, the issue of gun rights rose to national prominence with the assassination of President John F. Kennedy because his killer, Lee Harvey Oswald, purchased the rifle that he used to kill the President from a mail order catalogue. Later, in 1968, when both Dr. Martin Luther King, Jr. and President Kennedy's brother Robert Kennedy were assassinated, Congress passed the Gun Control Act, which banned the interstate sale of firearms, the importation of military surplus, and gun ownership by minors and felons. Then in 1981, when President Reagan was wounded and his press secretary Jim Brady was permanently disabled, there was again a call for further gun restrictions, but it was not until the Clinton administration that the Brady Act was passed, which required a five-day waiting period to purchase handguns and required local law enforcement agents to conduct background checks of gun purchasers. Clinton was also successful, one year later, in getting a crime control bill passed by Congress that prohibited the importation of semi-automatic assault weapons.[3]

These legislative victories for the opponents of gun rights, however, were often matched by laws in states that defended gun ownership and expanded gun rights. In 1986 Congress passed the Gun Owners Protection Act which, in effect, overturned the Gun Control Act of 1968 and permitted the interstate sale of rifles and shotguns. Also, in the 1980s and 1990s, over two-thirds of the states passed laws allowing citizens the right to carry concealed weapons without providing a statement on the application form that that there is a special need for such a privilege.[4] In 1997 the Supreme Court in Printz v. United States struck down the key element of the Brady Act when it found that the requirement that local police officials conduct background checks was a violation of states' rights. In each of these shifts in policy, the National Rifle Association showed its immense lobbying power and legal clout as it fought successfully to turn the tide against gun control legislation.[5]

The battle between gun owners and gun control advocates is relentless as each side marshals data on crime and violence, presents examples from American everyday life that support their position, and targets members of Congress with threats of electoral retribution if they do not support gun rights or gun control. There is perhaps no issue on the American scene that carries with it such dire predictions if laws are passed either restricting gun ownership or expanding the right. But with the FBI estimating that more than 300 million guns are owned by Americans and approximately 93 million people in this country living in households where a gun is present, it is safe to say that we are a nation of guns. The issue thus becomes whether we regulate gun ownership and, if we do regulate guns, how will we regulate those guns? Both of those questions are at the core of the issue of the right to bear arms.

On the Record

President Obama has been a staunch advocate for what he often described as "commonsense" gun regulation, while leaders of the NRA reject any attempts to limit gun ownership. Below are two quotes one from the president on the need for stiffer gun control laws and one from Wayne LaPierre, the Executive Director of the National Rifle Association

President Obama

I respect the Second Amendment; I respect the right to bear arms. All of us can agree that it makes sense to do everything we can to keep guns out of the hands of people who would do other people harm. We need the vast majority of responsible gun owners who grieve with us after every mass shooting, who support common sense gun safety, and who feel that their views are not being properly represented, to stand with us and demand that leaders heed the voices of the people they are supposed to represent.

Mr. LaPierre

I don't know why the NRA or the Second Amendment and lawful gun owners have to somehow end up in a story every time some crazy person goes off and kills children. These people (critics of the NRA) are out to get us and the Second Amendment, and we're not going to let them. The only thing that stops a bad guy with a gun is a good guy with a gun.

Sources: White House and NRA websites

DEBATES, DIFFERENCES, AND DIVISIONS

The two quotes from both sides of the gun rights argument capture the essence of the differences and divisions that mark this controversial issue. To supporters of gun ownership, there is an unwavering belief that Americans have the right to defend themselves and that the constitution provides them with that right. Like Wayne LaPierre, gun owners believe that possessing a firearm provides personal security; taking away that right or compromising it would thus place individuals in danger from the criminal element. When President Obama was in office, he argued that gun ownership is fraught with danger as easy access to firearms fosters their use in the home, the workplace, and in social settings. Gun violence, in President Obama's view, is at epidemic proportions and strict controls thus are essential if Americans are to be truly safe.

It is around these two arguments that both sides in the gun debate present mountains of evidence and personal accounts that support their cases. The

NRA has reams of testimony from supporters of gun ownership who testify that their possession of a firearm foiled a robbery or saved their lives from an attacker, and in its newsletter and other mailings it regularly run stories of how gun ownership was responsible for saving a life or warding off a criminal attack. Opponents of gun rights will counter with an equal number of examples of random violence associated with easy access to guns as deranged individuals kill fellow workers over an employment issue or students seek revenge by killing classmates who bullied them in school. The Columbine High School shootings (1999) and the tragic massacre at Virginia Tech University (2001) are often used by opponents of gun control as examples of the need to control weapons. But these tragic massacres continue as witnessed by the shooting at Sandy Hook Elementary School in Connecticut (2012) where a mentally disturbed teen killed 27 first graders and their teachers.

The gun rights debate is driven by the constant clash of high profile interest group organizations like the National Rifle Association and the Brady Campaign to Prevent Gun Violence (formerly Handgun Control Inc.). There is little question among experts who study interest group politics in the United States that the National Rifle Association is one of the most powerful and effective advocates for its position of broad gun rights. With a national membership of over 5,000,000 gun owners, a staff of 300 lobbyists, researchers, and public relations experts, and an annual budget of $250 million, the NRA has proven its ability to pressure Congress and state legislatures to reject measures that would limit gun ownership. On many occasions the NRA has mounted effective get-out-the-vote campaigns at the grassroots level, relying on its supporters to send postcards, letters, and emails to incumbents and candidates threatening them with electoral retribution should they vote against gun owners' interests. Members of Congress and state legislatures openly admit that the get-out-the-vote efforts of the NRA have had a significant impact on getting pro-gun rights officials into political office.[6]

Compared to the NRA, anti-gun groups, such as the Brady Campaign to Prevent Gun Violence, are akin to the biblical Daniel facing a Goliath. Like the NRA, the Brady Campaign puts out a stream of information on its interpretation of the 2nd Amendment, the links between crime, violence, and guns, and the intransigence of the NRA to even consider moderate regulatory provisions such as background checks, bans on automatic weapons, and the end of trade show gun purchases, which often are the source of easily purchased weapons. Despite the fact that the late James Brady and his wife Sarah have been tireless advocates for gun control and have developed a capable interest group organization with substantial funds and staff to mount an effective counterforce to the NRA, the fact remains that the NRA and other pro-gun rights groups outspend the Brady Campaign to Prevent Gun Violence. A 2006 study by the non-partisan Center for Responsive Politics, which monitors lobbying and spending for lobbying, found that the pro-gun lobby led by the NRA outspent the anti-gun lobby led by the Brady Center by a ratio of 3 to 1.7.

Alongside the supporting testimonials and everyday examples used by the advocates of gun rights and gun control and the lobbying and public relations activities of the NRA and the Brady Campaign to Prevent Gun Violence is a large body of scholarly studies that have also become part of the national debate over the 2nd Amendment and have been used by both sides in this controversy to support their positions. There are two major areas of research and research debate surrounding gun ownership—the relationship between crime and gun ownership and the connection between violence and gun ownership. Dr. Gary Kleck, a noted criminologist from Florida State University, has done work on whether guns have enhanced personal security. Kleck estimated in his study that as many as 2.5 million Americans used a gun in self-defense or to ward off a criminal. Kleck added that, in his study, the mere showing of a gun by the owner helped to enhance personal security as potential criminals were scared off.[7,8] Kleck's research, however, has been challenged by other scholars. David Hemenway, in his work on the impact of guns and public health, questions Kleck's data because the connection between gun use and self-defense came as a result of the testimony of gun owners, not as a result of police investigation or other independent analysis. But Hemenway does admit that there is some valid association between gun ownership and self-protection. In his book *Private Guns, Public Health*, he concludes that the more guns that are available, the more the chance for a range of violent actions.[9]

Also creating scholarly division in the gun control debate is the issue of guns in the home and the incidence of violence. Writing in the *New England Journal of Medicine*, Arthur Kellerman, an emergency room physician, asserted that people who keep a firearm at home increase significantly the chances of a homicide. Kellerman's findings were challenged by a range of critics who stated that the doctor failed to recognize the deterrent effect of guns in homes as residents used the firearm to protect property and save the lives of their loved ones. Kellerman, however, refused to budge on his position that guns in the home can be directly linked to incidents of firearms accidents, spousal killings, and suicide. Suicide, in particular, has been seen as directly related to gun availability. Data from the Center for Disease Control in 2016 showed that 21,175 suicides were the result of firearms.[10]

Data Bank

In recent years, opponents of gun rights have accented the impact of firearms violence on children and have made comparisons with other nations that have tougher gun laws. Below are some data points on gun violence and the safety of children in the United States.

Homicides in the United States are the #2 cause of death in 15–24 year olds.

One child or teen dies from a gun every 3 hours and 28 minutes.

Every day, 48 children and teens are shot in murders, assaults, suicides, suicide attempts, unintentional shootings, and police intervention.

(continued)

Data Bank   (continued)

2,695 students were expelled in 2006–2007 for possession of a gun at school.

The American Medical Association reported that between 36% and 50% of male eleventh graders in the United States stated that they could get a gun with ease, if they wanted one or needed one.

Sources: Children's Defense Fund, American Medical Association, US Department of Education

While the scholarly and medical debates continue on and are used by both sides in the gun rights debate, other concerns regarding gun availability have been raised in recent years. Two issues in particular have become major points of contention between the pro- and anti-gun groups—gun show purchases and background checks of individuals with a history of mental illness. For a number of years, gun control advocates have been pushing state authorities to close the loophole that allows anyone, including those individuals who have been denied a gun license by an authorized gun dealer, to attend a private gun show and purchase a weapon from the trunk of a dealer's car without any background check. Police chiefs and the federal government's Bureau of Alcohol Tobacco and Firearms have for years sought to bring stronger controls to the gun show trade, but without success. Currently, only fifteen states require background checks of gun purchases at gun shows.

In 2008 the Governor of Virginia, Timothy Kaine, introduced legislation to the state's General Assembly to close the loophole and require background checks of individuals purchasing weapons at gun shows. Not surprisingly, advocates of gun ownership shot back at the governor's proposal. Philip Van Cleave of the Virginia Citizens Defense League took a position that has become familiar in the gun debate when he stated, "Criminals don't get guns at gun shows . . . It (the proposed legislation) is not going to do anything about crime." The legislation to close the loophole on gun shows was in response to the Virginia Tech shootings and the lax state laws regarding background checks of the mental history of individuals purchasing firearms. The killer, Virginia Tech student Seung Hui Cho, purchased the automatic weapons used in the massacre at an authorized gun shop, even though he had a past history of mental illness and was ordered by a judge to seek outpatient treatment at a mental health facility. Sueng Hui Cho's condition was never brought to light during the background checks. Opponents of adding the mental health history of potential gun purchasers to the background check was criticized by gun advocates who stated that the answer to avoiding future massacres by mentally ill individuals is in better mental health counseling, not in expanding the background check process.[11]

Also at issue in the gun rights versus gun control debate is the vast difference among state laws and the impact those laws have on gun availability. According to the NRA, there are over 20,000 gun laws on the books in the United States, which from their perspective proves that gun control does exist in this country. However, the issue is not so much the number of laws, but the state to state difference in the laws and the restrictions that emanate from those laws. The intrastate movement of guns is considered by law enforcement officials as one of the most serious challenges faced by communities seeking to limit access to guns, especially to criminals. Massachusetts, for example, has one of the toughest gun control laws in the United States and has passed landmark legislation requiring handgun safety features on all guns purchased in the state. But the City of Boston continues to be faced with gang-related shootings where the guns in question were likely purchased out of state and brought into the city. Public officials in Boston decried the easy access that gang members had to guns in neighboring states, but there was little they could do to counteract laws elsewhere that were not as restrictive as those in Massachusetts.[12]

Where vastly different gun laws among states in this country have caused problems for law enforcement officials, the United States has also been heavily criticized in the international court of public opinion because of its inability and unwillingness to pass strong gun control legislation. Many nations in the industrialized world have strong gun control laws that make it difficult, if not impossible, for their citizens to legally purchase a firearm. Opponents of gun rights often point to England, Japan, and Germany as examples of countries that have strong gun laws and also little violent crime. Americans are often portrayed outside this country as living in a gun culture, which likely developed out of the revolutionary minuteman model and then became further ensconced in the culture as a result of the frontier experience and settlement of the West. Today, Europeans in particular view Americans as obsessed with guns and unconcerned about how the gun culture has become a permanent part of American life in movies, television, video games, and music. With each example of a random killing or a massacre of tragic proportions, the world wonders why the United States does not implement more restrictive gun laws. But when guns are part of a national heritage and have become viewed as an accepted means of self-defense, negative international opinion does not sway national or state legislators to follow the example of other countries. According to data compiled by *The Economist* in 2015, El Salvador led the world with 91.4 homicides per 100,000 people, Honduras was second with 69.9 homicides per 100,000 people, while the murder rate for the United States for 2014 was 4.5 homicides per 100,000 people, a figure that has continued a downward slide in recent years. The lowest rate in recent years for the United States was 4.0 per 100,000 people in 1957.[13] While murder rates in the United States do not match those in Honduras, they nevertheless are extremely high compared to many European countries, Japan, and Australia.

FYI

Gun Laws in Australia

In 1996 an Australian man, Martin Bryant, walked into a café in Port Arthur, Tasmania, and killed 35 people and wounded 23 others. He used a semi-automatic rifle in his killing spree. As a result of that act, Australia instituted a major gun reform effort. Then Prime Minister John Howard led the fight to change Australia's guns laws, especially with respect to semi-automatic rifles. Writing in the *New York Times*, Howard stated, "The fundamental problem was the ready availability of high-powered weapons, which enabled people to convert their murderous impulses into mass killing. Certainly, shortcomings in treating mental illness and the harmful influence of violent video games and movies may have played a role. But nothing trumps easy access to a gun. It is easier to kill 10 people with a gun than with a knife." Howard was successful in passing the National Firearms Agreement that banned certain semi-automatic and self-loading rifles and shotguns and required those seeking a gun license to show "genuine reason" for owning a gun, which could not include self-defense. Howard also instituted a national gun buyback program that allowed the government to purchase 700,000 guns. The buyback program decreased the number of gun-owning households by one-half. Since its implementation of the National Firearms Agreement, the firearm homicide rate has fallen by 59% and the firearm suicide rate by 65%.

Source: Business Insider, October 11, 2015

Both sides got their wish for a Supreme Court showdown over the right to bear arms. In 2007 in a case from Washington D.C., the United States Appeals Court ruled in Parker v. District of Columbia that laws in Washington D.C. that prohibit personal gun ownership were unconstitutional. The D.C. law limited gun ownership to retired police officers only; prohibited the carrying of a firearm, even in one's home; and required that the gun be kept unloaded and disassembled unless used for what was termed by the court as "lawful recreational purposes." The court, in its ruling, stated that the first phrase in the 2nd Amendment referring to the militia was not, in their view, a limiting factor in personal gun ownership for self-protection and that the recognition of the militia and gun ownership should not be the sole basis for determining the right of the people to bear arms.[14] The Parker decision had limited application to the District of Columbia and was appealed to the Supreme Court. In 2008, however, the Supreme Court ruled in a 5–4 decision to strike down the Washington D.C. gun ban and uphold the right of citizens to purchase and keep a gun to protect themselves and their property. Speaking for the majority, Justice Scalia stated that the 2nd Amendment protects an individual's right to possess and use firearms for lawful reasons "unconnected with service in the militia." The decision was hailed by gun owners as the first firm definition of the second amendment and a validation of gun rights. Opponents of the ruling were dismayed with the court's narrow decision and felt that it would only increase gun violence in America.[15]

After a tragic series of mass murders starting with the Sandy Hook Elementary School massacre, President Obama made a concerted effort to take various steps through his executive authority to change gun laws, especially in the area of background checks. In early January 2016, President Obama convened a high-profile town meeting to discuss the issue of background checks and move the political forces both in Congress and the nation toward what he often described as "common sense reform." He promised to expand background checks that would be strengthened by hiring hundreds of federal agents and enforcing existing laws, particularly with respect to the gun show exemption and online firearm exchanges. The president, however, readily admitted that these measures were modest and would not solve the illegal purchase of weapons or weak background check rules. As he stated at the time, "We have to be very clear that this is not going to solve every violent crime in this country . . . It's not going to prevent every mass shooting; it's not going to keep every gun out of the hands of the criminals."[16]

The NRA and gun supporters immediately criticized the president for his use of executive authority and pledged to fight his efforts to control any measure that would limit the purchase of a firearm. Also, the president was criticized by anti-gun groups who felt that the promise of using executive action to make a modest dent in gun purchases was more of a half-hearted attempt to do something with little follow-up or aggressive implementation. Both sides agreed that without Congressional action, there was little the president could do to advance a major reform to gun control in the United States. In the aftermath of the town hall and promulgation of the executive orders, the gun issue faded from view.

While the president was seeking to bring some change to the gun rights issue in this country, much of the activity related to firearms ownership and control was at the state level. Increasingly states, particularly in the South and Midwest, were passing laws permitting the right to carry a concealed weapon or to openly carry a weapon in any public place, including a college campus. Laws to permit concealed weapons were passed in 45 states, with six allowing concealed weapons without a specific permit. It is the open carry option that has created the most controversy as gun advocates have entered restaurants, malls, and major stores with automatic weapons and other guns to show their right by law. These members of what has come to be called the "open carry movement" have caused a high level of distress among citizens and police who are afraid of these individuals and wonder why it is necessary to carry a weapon into a public place. The San Mateo, California, Police Department issued the following statement:

Open carry advocates create a potentially very dangerous situation. When police are called to a 'man with a gun' call they typically are responding to a situation about which they have few details other than that one or more people are present at a location and are armed. Officers may have no idea that these people are simply, "exercising their rights."[17,18]

In some states, however, legislation has been passed that takes on the gun lobby, limits gun ownership, and strengthens existing regulations. Organizations such as States United to Prevent Gun Violence and Americans for Responsible Solutions (founded by former Congresswoman Gabby Giffords, herself seriously injured by a deranged individual with a gun) have been successful in states such as California, Colorado, Washington, and Connecticut to limit purchases of semi-automatic weapons, limit the number of bullets in a clip, and make it tougher to purchase a gun. While these actions at the state level are not supported at the national level in Congress, they suggest a growing movement to develop reforms in the gun laws by working around Congressional opposition. As of 2015 seven states have passed laws banning assault weapons.

The anti-gun lobbying efforts got an unexpected boost when the Supreme Court refused to hear a case from Highland Park, Illinois, which passed an ordinance that banned such weapons as the semi-automatic AR-15 and AK-47 and prohibited possession of these type of weapons with their high-capacity magazines. While Justices Scalia and Thomas dissented in the opinion that let stand an Appeals Court decision in favor of the Highland Park Ordinance, Judge Frank Easterbrook of the Appeals Court stated that "a ban on assault weapons and large capacity magazines might not prevent shootings in Highland Park, but it might reduce the carnage if a mass shooting occurs."[19]

Although gun opponents could be dealt a serious blow to their efforts to control the sale and ownership of guns in this country, public opinion polls consistently show that approximately two-thirds of Americans believe that they possess the right to bear arms and that any decision that would seriously compromise that right would be challenged and lead to an intense political division in this country. Like so many others who work hard for their causes, the proponents of broad gun rights are passionate about the rights they believe are granted them in the 2nd Amendment and would never allow government to engage in any policy that would be interpreted as taking away that right. There are numerous bumper stickers on the road today that champion gun rights and express the fervor with which some gun owners would fight any attempt to limit their gun ownership ("Fight Crime—Shoot Back," "I Love My Country, But I Fear My Government," and "Stop Gun Control Because Freedom is a Terrible Thing to Waste").

But gun control advocates are quick to remind gun owners that their aim is not confiscation and the creation of an all-powerful government that would serve as a kind of Big Brother of gun restrictions. Those from groups like the Brady Center for the Prevention of Gun Violence and certainly President Obama have emphasized what has come to be called "common sense gun control"—stricter controls on gun ownership similar to those that are associated with getting a drivers' license, a ban on automatic weapons and other quick firing weapons whose only purpose is to kill people more efficiently, and an end to the gun show trade that creates a huge underground market for illegally obtained firearms. The fundamental premise of gun control advocates is that groups like the NRA have drawn a broad line in the sand and have refused to accept even modest restrictions that are designed to ensure that guns are in the hands of individuals who would not use them to commit crimes and violent acts.[20]

This line in the sand strategy of the NRA has had remarkable success, and any change in that strategy to achieve some sort of middle road compromise on gun control is highly unlikely. For example, when Republican members of Congress were attacked by a gunman on a baseball field, leaving House Whip Steve Scalise of Louisiana gravely wounded, many conservatives in the House stated that the answer was to arm their members rather than rely on police protection. The NRA knows that its ability to mobilize grassroots supporters has worked effectively to remind legislators that a gun control position would be political suicide. As for the gun control advocates, they have yet been able to match the clout of the NRA, although public opinion polls do show that Americans are in favor of "reasonable" restrictions on gun use and abhor the mass killings that have occurred in this country because of lax gun laws. What this means is that the gun rights versus gun control battle will continue unabated for years to come with each side pressuring national and state legislatures to hold the line or to implement new restrictions. Not only will the debate and divide between gun rights and gun control be around for a long time, but it is safe to state that a resolution that is acceptable to both sides in the debate will remain elusive.

The Great Debate

Although the Supreme Court has defined an expansive interpretation of the right to bear arms, ongoing debates remain about the proper application of the Second Amendment and the so-called "common sense" approach to gun control.

Debate Topic

Should Americans have unlimited gun ownership rights, or if you think limitations on gun ownership are appropriate, what should those limitations be?

Critical Thinking Questions

1. How do you interpret the language of the 2nd Amendment regarding the right to bear arms?
2. What specific regulations do you think are appropriate for gun purchases and gun ownership?
3. Do you believe that violent crime would decrease if there was a ban on guns, or would innocent people be the target of criminals who have obtained guns illegally?
4. What is your view of the Washington, D.C. gun case decision? Did the majority of the Court get it right about the 2nd Amendment?
5. Why don't we follow other industrialized countries and ban the purchase and ownership of guns?

Connections

The National Rifle Association is viewed by many as the most effective lobbying organization in the United States. Its site is at www.nra.org

The NRA is opposed in the gun debate by the Coalition to Stop Gun Violence. Its site is at www.csgv.org

The government agency charged with gun policy on the national level is the Bureau of Alcohol, Tobacco, Firearms and Explosives (ATF). Its site is at http://www.atf.gov

An organization that monitors gun laws and gun initiatives in the states and at the national level is gunpolicy.org. Its site is www.gunpolicy.org

The Center for Gun Policy and Research is an independent think tank at Johns Hopkins University that concentrates on gun violence. Visit its site at www.jhsph.edu/gunpolicy

Some Books to Read

Cook, Philip and Kristin Goss, *The Gun Debate: What Everyone Needs to Know* (New York: Oxford University Press, 2014).

Melzer, Scott, *Gun Crusader: The NRA's Culture War* (New York: NYU Press, 2009).

Klarevas, Louis, *Rampage Nation: Securing America From Mass Shootings* (New York: Prometheus, 2016).

Webster, Daniel, *Reducing Gun Violence in America: Informing Policy With Evidence and Analysis* (Baltimore, MD: Johns Hopkins University Press, 2013).

Younge, Gary, *Another Day in the Death of America: A Chronicle of Ten Short Lives* (New York: Nation Books, 2016).

Notes

1. For background see the discussion of the 2nd Amendment at the website Find-law, http://caselaw.lpfindlaw.com/data/constitution/amendment02
2. A historical guide to the early decisions related to the 2nd Amendment can be found at Nelson Lund and Adam Winkler, "The Second Amendment," www.constitutioncenter.org
3. The essentials of the Brady Law can be seen at the website of the Bureau of Alcohol, Tobacco and Firearms website under the title "Brady Law." View the website at www.atf.gov.
4. See "No Surrender: The Firearm Owners Protection Act of 1986," the NRA-Institute for Legislative Action, January 25, 2011, www.nrail.org
5. *Printz v. United States* 117 S.CT. 2365 (1997).
6. Tom Watkins, "How the NRA Wields Its Influence," *CNN*, January 10, 2013. See also the NRA website, www.nra.org
7. On the issue of spending between the NRA and the Center for the Prevention of Gun Violence see the Center for Responsive Politics, www.opensecrets.org/news/issues/guns/lobbying.php
8. Gary Kleck, "What Are the Risks and the Benefits of Keeping Guns at Home," www.guncite.com/kleckjama01.html
9. Gary Hemenway, *Private Guns, Public Health* (Ann Arbor, MI, University Of Michigan Press, 2006). See also "Evidence Is Growing That Gun Violence in America Is a Product of Weak Gun Laws," *The Economist*, June 18, 2016.
10. "New CDC Report Shows America's Gun Suicide Problem Getting Worse," April, 2016, www.thetrace.org
11. Anita Kumar, "Kaine to Push Background Checks at Gun Shows," *Washington Post*, January 9, 2008.
12. Massachusetts received a grade of A- from the Law Center to Prevent Gun Violence in its gunlawscorecard.org. See www.smartgunlaws.org
13. See *The Economist World in Figures*, 2015.
14. *Parker v. District of Columbia* 478D.3d 370 (D.C. CIR.2007).
15. Robert Barnes, "Justices Reject D.C. Ban on Handgun Ownership," *Washington Post*, June 27, 2008.
16. Michael Shear, "Gun Activists, Obama Debate Views During Town Hall Event," *New York Times*, January 8, 2016.
17. Open Carrying Policy Summary, Law Center to Prevent Gun Violence, August 21, 2015. For background see Ian Urbina, "Fearing Obama Agenda, States Push to Loosen Gun Laws," *New York Times*, February 10, 2010.
18. San Mateo County Sherriff's Office, "Unloaded Open Carry," January 14, 2010.
19. Jess Bravin, "Supreme Court Lets Stand Local Law Banning Semiautomatic Guns," *Wall Street Journal*, December 7, 2015.
20. See "Common Sense Solutions" at the site of the Law Center to Prevent Gun Violence, www.smartgunlaws.org

12 GAY **RIGHTS**

Issue Topic

First there was the civil rights movement, then the women's movement, and now in the 21st century, the gay rights movement. The gay, lesbian, bisexual, and transgender population has become one of the most visible groups seeking to advance their agenda in the American political arena. The key component of this agenda is recognition of gay marriage. Although state laws and a landmark Supreme Court decision have recognized the legality of gay marriage, there remains opposition to allowing homosexual couples to marry and have that marriage sanctioned by civil authorities, in large part because opponents view such unions as contrary to the western traditions of male-female marriage. Proponents argue that the right to marriage, no matter what the sexual orientation of the couple, is a fundamental right of all Americans.

Chapter Objectives

This chapter will seek to:

1. Describe the struggles of the gay and lesbian community to achieve equal rights in the United States.

2. Discuss the contentious issue of gay marriage, which is at the heart of the struggle for gay rights.

3. Examine the current political and legal status of gay rights and gay marriage in the United States.

SOME BACKGROUND

The push for gay rights and the subsequent battles over public policies that establish or extend gay rights is a relatively new issue area in American politics. Although the gay community has long been an active participant in the public arena seeking to break down barriers of discrimination, it is only in the last forty years that individual leaders and organized groups have pressured government at all levels to place their issues on the front burner of national priorities. Although recent data shows that approximately 3.8% of Americans self-identify as being gay, lesbian, or bisexual (with an additional .3% self-identifying as both bisexual and transgender), they have become a force in American politics.[1] The gay community has given generously to political campaigns, primarily on the Democratic side, and they have been determined in their activism to advocate for issues they believe are essential to breaking down barriers of discrimination and hate. But like most minorities in this country who seek recognition and power and work to change the rules of society and politics, gays have encountered obstacles and stiff opposition. From religious groups to conservative organizations, the political agenda of the gay community has been challenged in large part because it diverts from the governing status quo, especially with respect to equal marriage rights, which are seen as a threat to the traditional family and traditional heterosexual relationships. Although the push and pull of gay rights in the United States is still in its formative stages, both sides in this struggle are seeking to define the moral and legal parameters of the debate, point out key policy differences, and assess the political impact of a divisive national issue.[2]

The issue of gay rights entered the political arena first not as a specific policy debate but as a result of violent demonstrations against police intimidation of gays. In 1969 in New York, gays responding to harassment of police at the Stonewall tavern engaged in nightly riots that left scores injured and hundreds arrested. The Stonewall riots were viewed as the beginning of the fight to establish gay rights and develop a movement to advance the cause of gay people in this country.

While the Stonewall riots launched a movement, it was the spread of the deadly HIV/AIDs epidemic that brought the life-threatening challenges faced by gay men into the spotlight. In the early 1980s, when the first signs of the disease were spotted, HIV/AIDS hit hard in the gay community as thousands of men died from this virus that breaks down the body's immune system and leads to a long, horrible death. From 1981 to 2005, over 1.5 million cases of HIV infection were reported in the United States and over 500,000 deaths occurred when the HIV virus led to the onset of AIDS. The AIDS epidemic politicized the gay community as the Reagan administration gave the appearance of unconcern about the spread of the disease and its impact on homosexuals. Numerous protest demonstrations were held in major cities and in Washington to press the Reagan administration to take action against the spread of AIDS. Furthermore, leaders of the gay community criticized the Food and Drug Administration (FDA) for not moving quickly enough to approve new drugs that, in preliminary tests, showed promise in arresting the advance of the AIDS virus. Eventually, promising drugs (often called a "cocktail" because it involves multiple pills that attack the virus) entered the market and slowed the death rate from AIDS, but for members of the gay community it became clear that they needed to become much more vocal and better organized in order to get the attention of the government to fight what they viewed as discrimination against their sexual orientation.[3]

The onset of the Clinton administration thrust the gay issue into the forefront of the American issues arena as one of the first acts of the new president was to issue a "Don't Ask, Don't Tell" policy regarding gays in the United States military (Clinton was fulfilling a campaign pledge made to gays on the matter, who in return gave overwhelming electoral support in the 1992 election). In effect what the presidential order required is that the military not seek out or require public admission of the sexual preference of its soldiers but leave the matter private. The Clinton initiative on gays replaced the long-standing position of the military contained in military policy handbooks that prohibited anyone who, "demonstrates a propensity or intent to engage in homosexual acts" from serving in the armed forces of the United States, since such behavior would "create an unacceptable risk to the high standards of morale, good order and discipline, and unit cohesion that are the essence of military capability." Despite opposition throughout the ranks of the military, the "Don't Ask, Don't Tell" policy of the Clinton administration did show that the new president was sympathetic to the concerns of the homosexual community and that sexual orientation should be considered a private matter and not be used as guidepost for military enlistment or military evaluation purposes.[4]

Gays also gained a key victory in 1996 when the Supreme Court struck down an amendment to the Colorado state constitution that would have prevented gays from bringing civil suits charging discrimination in employment and housing. Conservative groups opposed to gay rights had successfully pushed for the amendment and were victorious in a state referendum that changed the state constitution, but the Supreme Court viewed the amendment as denying a class of people their rights as citizens to be treated equally and protected by the laws in a manner similar to other identifiable groups. The Colorado victory for gay rights was further enhanced in 2003 when the court, in the landmark case Lawrence v. Texas, overturned a previous decision (Bowers v. Hardwick) that upheld a Georgia statute supporting sodomy laws, which were clearly intended to punish gays who engaged in sexual activity, even in the privacy of their homes. In the Lawrence decision, the court stated that the Georgia law violated the fundamental right to privacy and set the stage for many states either ignoring sodomy laws or removing them from the statute books. The decision by the court was a signal to states that sexual orientation should not be the subject of state regulation.[5]

The push for gay rights was not without it roadblocks or disappointments. In 1996 the Republican-dominated Congress passed the Defense of Marriage Act (DOMA) that defined marriage at the federal level as a union between and a man and a woman and advised states to ignore or not implement gay marriages performed in other states, even though at this time there were no states that performed gay marriages. Although many opponents of gay marriage saw DOMA as a powerful statement designed to weaken the position of gays, DOMA has often been overshadowed by state laws and analyzed by legal scholars as requiring Supreme Court review to determine its constitutionality because it sought to deny the opportunity of gay married couples to invoke the Constitution's "full faith and credit clause" and have their marriages valid in all 50 states.[6]

The gay rights movement suffered a setback in 2000 when the Supreme Court supported the policy of the Boy Scouts of America that prohibited gay men from becoming Boy Scout leaders. The court sided with the Boy Scouts, stating that the stated tenets and philosophy of the group, which accented traditional sexual orientation, allowed them under First Amendment grants of free speech to foster a policy of exclusion of gays from leadership positions.

The Boy Scout decision was vilified in the gay community as perpetuating the myth that gays would use their positions as group leaders to engage in homosexual acts and attempt to socialize young boys to change their sexual identity.[7]

Despite the setbacks in Congress and the courts, gay people gained an unprecedented court victory in 2003 when the Massachusetts Supreme Judicial Court narrowly voted to support gay marriage as a civil right. The decision stated that denying gays the right to marry was a violation of the equal protection and due process clauses in the Massachusetts constitution. While the decision was hailed by the gay community and almost immediately led to hundreds of state-validated marriages, it was strenuously opposed throughout the United States by those who saw the decision as destroying the western tradition of male/female marriage and a further example of unwarranted judicial activism. The Massachusetts decision quickly set into motion a wave of antigay marriage groups and initiatives at the state and national level designed to ensure that such decisions or legislative acts would not spread further. President George W. Bush, for example, initially pushed for an amendment to the Constitution barring gay marriage and defending traditional marriage, and numerous states quickly passed laws banning gay marriage.[8]

Because of the Massachusetts Supreme Judicial Court's ruling validating gay marriage, the issue of gay rights in the United States moved to the next level of issue intensity. For example, the California Supreme Court in 2008, in a narrow 4–3 decision, supported the "right of gays to marry," once again setting off a political debate as opponents of same-sex marriage sought to influence a state-wide referendum on the matter.[9] In a highly contentious referendum process, Proposition 8, by a margin of 52% to 47%, overturned the State Supreme Court decision in support of gay marriage. But in 2010, a federal court ruled Proposition 8 unconstitutional, although the decision did not go into effect until 2013, as the result of an appeal process. While in California the movement to approve gay marriage remained contentious, other states such as Connecticut, Vermont, Iowa, Maine, and New Hampshire approved gay marriage laws as a civil right. Advocates of gay marriage, however, faced new setbacks in New York and New Jersey, where the legislatures refused to advance bills that would sanction the right of gays to marry.

On the Record

Chief Justice Margaret Marshall wrote the majority decision in the Massachusetts Supreme Judicial Court ruling (Goodridge v. Department of Public Health) that supported same-sex marriage. Below is the core of her argument in defense of gay marriage.

Marriage is a vital institution, the exclusive commitment of two individuals to each other, it nurtures love and mutual support; it brings

(continued)

On the Record   (continued)

> stability to our society. For those who choose to marry and for their children, marriage provides an abundance of legal, financial and social benefits. In return it imposes weighty legal, financial and social obligations. The questions before us is whether, consistent with the Massachusetts constitution, the Commonwealth may deny the protections, benefits and obligations conferred by civil marriage to two individuals of the same sex who wish to marry. We conclude that it may not. The Massachusetts Constitution affirms the dignity and equality of all individuals. It forbids the creation of second class citizens. In reaching our conclusion we have given full deference to the argument made by the Commonwealth. But it has failed to identify any constitutionally adequate reason for denying civil marriage to same-sex couples.
>
> *Source*: Goodridge v. Department of Public Health

DEBATES, DIFFERENCES, AND DIVISIONS

While the gay rights movement is wide-ranging in scope and designed to eliminate all forms of discrimination against homosexuals, it is the gay marriage component of this movement and the Massachusetts Supreme Judicial Court decision that galvanized public opinion, fostered the formation of numerous interest groups representing both sides in the debate, and developed moral, social, and religious arguments on both sides of the issue. As to the American public, there is no doubt that opposition to same-sex marriage is substantial, but it is trending downward. A Pew Research Center poll in 2015 found that 55% of Americans favored allowing gays and lesbians to marry legally, while 39% were opposed, a significant change from a poll by Pew in 2004 that showed 63% of Americans were opposed to same-sex marriage, and a poll in 2006 that showed opposition at 51%. If the issue is viewed from a generational perspective, older Americans are clearly uneasy with gay marriage and form the largest bloc of the opponents, but younger Americans, those from the so-called Y Generation (or Millennials, young people born between 1980 and 2000) have little concern with gay marriage and provide the bulk of support. A recent study of 17–29-year-olds found that 61% were not opposed to same-sex marriage and supported those gays who sought to have a state-sanctioned marriage.[10]

In the area of interest group activity related to same-sex marriage, both sides have highly aggressive organizations to lobby national and state legislatures and to mobilize grassroots supporters. One of the most prominent gay rights groups heavily involved in political activity is the Human Rights Campaign. It has been especially active in fighting against the various ballot issues that have been introduced in the states to ban same-sex marriage and President Bush's short-lived attempt to introduce a constitutional amendment—The

Marriage Protection Amendment that would have created a national ban on same-sex marriages.[11]

Also prominent in advancing gay rights is the National Lesbian Gay Bisexual Transgender Task Force (LGBTQ), often called "The Task Force." Founded in 1973, The Task Force is committed to enhancing "the grassroots power of the lesbian, gay, bisexual and transgender community." The Task Force has a range of activities from training its membership to providing information and talking points to state and federal officials regarding legislation to protect and expand gay rights. The Task Force has developed an aggressive lobbying effort at all levels of government, and its policy institute has been recognized as one of the few think tanks that is dedicated to providing accurate data and analysis regarding the gay community, including such issues as hate crimes, HIV/AIDs, and discriminatory practices. The Task Force has championed the cause of gay marriage throughout the United States and worked on some of the more narrow issues related to gay marriage such as inheritance, health insurance, and community property.[12] Also prominent in recent years is GLAAD, the Gay and Lesbian Alliance Against Defamation. GLAAD often joins The Task Force in promoting a gay rights agenda.

The Human Rights Campaign, The Task Force, and GLAAD have all been active in pressing Congress to pass anti-discrimination legislation in the workplace and hate crime bills that protect gays and other minorities from violent attacks. The Employment Non-Discrimination Act (ENDA) has been in the legislative pipeline since the late 1990s and targets discrimination that affects bias based on sexual orientation. There has been insufficient support for the legislation and, as a result, it has languished in committee. In the area of anti-hate legislation, the two groups have sought support for the Local Law Enforcement Hate Crimes Prevention Act.[13] The legislation extends federal hate crimes to include sexual orientation, gender identity, and disability to the federal hate crimes statutes. The bill did receive a positive vote in the House of Representatives in 2005 but died in the Senate. The efforts of the two pro-gay-rights groups in pressing Congress to include gender orientation to anti-discrimination and hate crimes in legislation shows the difficulty of moving the political agenda of homosexuals within the American governing system.[14]

There are also a number of activist groups that oppose same-sex marriage, and many of them are linked to the evangelical movement and stress the importance of family values, religious freedom, and marriage between a man and a woman. The most prominent of these groups are the Alliance for Marriage, American Values, the Family Research Council, and Focus on the Family. The official position of the Alliance for Marriage is that "the benefits of marriage for husbands, wives and children derive from the fact that marriage unites the two genders of the human race to share in raising children." The Alliance for Marriage worked closely with the White House on the Marriage Protection Amendment and was an outspoken critic of gay marriage, citing its negative impact on the traditional family and on social stability.[15] American Values is an organization that advocates not just for marriage between a man and a woman but also opposes abortion, stem cell research, and euthanasia.[16]

The Family Research Council (FRC) has strong ties to the evangelical move-ment. The FRC states that it "champions marriage and family as foundations of civilization, the seedbed of virtue and the wellspring of society" and believes that "Government has the duty to promote and protect marriage and family in law and public policy".[17] Finally, James Dobson's Focus on the Family is perhaps the most well-known group opposed to same-sex marriage and has the most visibility. Dobson has been a frequent media presence, and he has taken over as the voice of Christian conservatism after the death of Reverend Jerry Falwell.[18]

Data Bank

At present there are 26 countries (not including the United States) that per-mit gay marriage. Those countries are—Belgium, Brazil, Canada, Colom-bia, Estonia, Spain, South Africa, Norway, Sweden, Argentina, Iceland, Portugal, Denmark, Brazil, Mexico, England, Wales, France, New Zealand, Luxembourg, Malta, Scotland, Slovenia, Uruguay, Finland, and Ireland.

Source: Pew Research Center, "Gay Marriage Around the World"

Also in this mix of groups that are on either side of the debate regard-ing same-sex marriage is the role of organized religion. The Catholic Church, in particular, has taken a very strong position against gay marriage, and in many dioceses across the country, bishops and other church leaders have sought to use the pulpit to encourage their faithful to write state and federal officials in hopes of heading off any future legislation that would endorse or permit same-sex marriage. In Massachusetts, after the court decision permit-ting same-sex marriage, the Catholic Church in the state was very aggressive in pushing for a constitutional amendment that would limit marriage to a union between a man and a woman. In one of the most contentious debates in Massachusetts legislative history, the opponents of same-sex marriage, with considerable support from the Catholic Church (Church property was used to gather signatures for the initiative petition and to hold organization meet-ings), nearly were successful in getting a referendum question on the ballot that would have ended same-sex marriage. After two attempts, the opponents of same-sex marriage failed to get the initiative petition on the ballot.[19]

The issue of the Catholic Church position on same-sex marriage took a new turn when Pope France, in response to a journalist's question about the Pope's views on gays and lesbians asked, "Who am I to judge?" The Pope's apparent willingness not to condemn the homosexual lifestyle was met with surprised support from the gay community and open condemnation from conservative Catholics and those in the Vatican hierarchy who viewed the Pope's statement as moving away from traditional church teaching. Pope Francis continued, however, to state his opposition to same-sex marriage, thereby fostering a middle ground position of showing mercy and love for homosexuals but not supporting marriage between homosexuals.[20]

The evangelical churches, primarily in the south, midwest, and west, were equally active in the same-sex marriage debate. The Southern Baptist Convention, the largest organized evangelical church, along with many of the pastors of mega-churches run by well-known television preachers such as Pat Robertson and Franklin Graham, took firm stances against gay marriage and used their extensive media, Internet, and fund-raising entities in order to drum up support for legislation that would ban any form of same-sex marriage in various states. The role of the evangelical ministers became complicated when many African-American religious leaders came forward also in opposition to gay marriage, despite the pleadings of gay rights leaders that their fight was no different than that of blacks during the Civil Rights era. African-American ministers rejected this idea and held firm to their biblical beliefs that gay relations and gay marriage violated the words and the intent of the Bible. Those Protestant or evangelical ministries that supported gay marriage, such as the Anglican Church, experienced deep fissures in their religious communities. The appointment of a gay minister as bishop of the Anglican Church in the United States caused a major rift and forced some members to break away and form a new more conservative Anglican church with ties to Africa and African bishops.[21]

FYI

In 2011 the FBI reported 1,572 hate crime victims targeted based on a sexual orientation bias, making up 17.7% of the total hate crimes for that year. Of the total victims based on sexual orientation, 56.7% were targeted based on anti-male homosexual bias, 29.6% were targeted based on anti-homosexual and transgender bias, and 11.1% were based on anti-female homosexual bias, with the remainder of the victims targeted being bisexual. After the Supreme Court approved the right of gays and lesbians to marry, there was an uptick in violence against homosexuals, but in 2015 reports from groups like the Gay and Lesbian Task Force reported that hate-motivated violence dropped by 32% compared to 2014. However, violence against members of the transgender community increased by 13% during the same period.

NOTE—Many in the gay community challenge the FBI hate crimes data stating that in their view a large number of hate crimes against gays go unreported or underreported.

Source: FBI Hate Crime Statistics

The movement for gay rights reached a milestone when the Supreme Court in 2015 sanctioned same-sex marriage in a precedent-setting decision. In the case of Obergefell v. Hodges involving the rights of a gay man to be entitled to the inheritance of a deceased partner, despite state opposition, the court, in a 5–4 decision, cited the equal protection clause of the 14th Amendment as grounds for recognizing same-sex marriage. The decision sent shockwaves throughout the country as gays joyfully lined up at courthouses and county clerk offices to get married and receive a marriage license. For those supporting same-sex marriage, the decision of the Supreme Court was a validation of gay rights; to those opposed, it was a bitter pill, but they stated they would not end their efforts to stop gay marriage.[22]

On The Record

Justice Kennedy Writing for the Majority in the Obergefell v. Hodges Case

"The ancient origins of marriage confirm its centrality but is has not stood in isolation from developments in law and society. The history of marriage is one of both continuity and change. That institutions—even as confined to the opposite sex relations—have evolved over time . . . The nature of marriage is that . . . two persons together can find other freedoms, such as expressing intimacy and spirituality. This is true for all persons, whatever their sexual orientation. There is dignity in the bond between two men or two women who seek to marry."

Justice Scalia Writing for the Minority in Obergefell v. Hodges

"What really astounds is the hubris reflected in today's judicial Putsch. Whoever thought that intimacy and spirituality (whatever that means) were freedoms? If intimacy is, one would think that freedom of intimacy is abridged rather than expanded by marriage. Ask the nearest hippie."

One of those opponents was a county clerk in Rowan, Kentucky: Kim Davis. Davis refused to sign the marriage licenses of gays applying for marriage. Davis cited her religious beliefs as the grounds for the refusal. A lower federal court upheld the Supreme Court decision and ordered Davis to comply. When she refused, the judge found her in contempt of court and sentenced her to jail. The jailing of Ms. Davis became a national cause that solidified the opposition to same-sex marriage as conservative politicians and pundits rushed to defend Ms. Davis' right to refuse to sign the marriage licenses of homosexuals.

After five days in jail and a failed effort to appeal to a higher court, Davis remained adamant; nevertheless, she was released since she promised to allow others in her office to sign the marriage licenses of homosexuals seeking to have their marriages sanctioned by the state of Kentucky. Although Kim Davis was the center of gay marriage opposition after the Supreme Court decision, there was little opposition from other local officials to comply with the court decision. Thousands of gays across the country got married, and the issue of same-sex marriage ceased to be a central political issue.[23]

While same-sex marriage was encased as a legal right with the Supreme Court decision, states such as Georgia and North Carolina, in 2016, passed legislation that limited or took away the rights of the lesbian, gay, bisexual, and transgender community (LGBT). The issue this time was the right of transgender individuals to use bathrooms. The governor of North Carolina, Pat McCrory, signed legislation that barred cities from passing anti-discrimination ordinances that protect lesbian, gay, bisexual, and transgender individuals. The legislation in North Carolina immediately caused a response from large corporations, like Dow Chemical, PayPal, and Biogen, who do business in that state. The National Basketball Association and the National Collegiate Athletic Association threatened to remove North Carolina from future events. The corporate response to the legislation had the veiled threat that, if the anti-LGBT law remained on the books, they might be forced to cease business operations or engage in a range of commercial measures designed to show their opposition. The same response from the business community was also recorded in Georgia. The corporate response to anti-LGBT legislation brought attention to the position of corporate America that discriminatory policies at the state level were not part of their business practices and violated their corporate value system.[24] A vote in late 2016 to repeal the legislation was passed by the legislature, although those in the LGBT community remain convinced that the revised legislation is weak and can easily be sidestepped by opponents of gay rights, leaving the issue unresolved.

Every issue in American politics is accompanied by passion, intensity, and activism. The movement for gay rights, and in particular same-sex marriage, however, has generated more passion, intensity, and activism than many of the other issues in the political arena. Because gays are a small minority of the population and form personal relationships that some in this country view as out of the mainstream, that is not part of the mainstream, they face not just the expected obstacles that any minority has encountered in this country in their struggle for rights and acceptance, but also enormous governing roadblocks and deep-seated public antagonism that make their struggle of Herculean proportions. It is thus not an exaggeration to state that the gay rights movement in this country will have to endure many more years of struggle and disappointment before it reaches its goals.

The movement for gay rights and, specifically, same-sex marriage run up against some of the most basic bedrocks of our society and, indeed, western civilization. While there is no doubt that homosexuality has always been part of society, there are critics who claim that it is a "behavioral abnormality" that can be "cured." The fact that gays are seeking societal acceptance and demanding equal rights challenges the views of many Americans who either do not understand homosexuality or are comfortable with their prejudices against homosexuals. The sight of gays showing public affection or seeking to make legal a long-standing relationship is difficult for many Americans to accept, especially when they have been acculturated in a lifestyle and marriage compact that has always been based on one man and one woman.

But as advocates of gay rights and same-sex marriage often emphasize, the movement to expand and guarantee homosexual rights in the United

States is no different than what occurred in the civil rights movement, primarily in the South. Southerners had been acculturated in a social environment that viewed African-Americans as holding a lesser station in life and thus could be treated differently. There was certainly overt prejudice among many in the South and an unwillingness to embrace a new way of thinking about African-Americans and a new way of integrating them fully into society. But a combination of time, generational change, activist pressure, the intervention of the federal government, the leadership of many enlightened Southerners, and the eventual recognition of most in the South that they had treated African-Americans unjustly brought numerous advances in civil rights and a string of laws that tore down the walls of segregation and discrimination.

It is this combination that brought change to the South that the advocates of gay rights are hoping will turn the tide in favor of accepting those that are homosexuals fully into American society and providing them with the kind of equal rights that they have been denied. But just like the civil rights movement, change does not come quickly or without setbacks and conflict. Those in the minority in this country have always had to struggle to make the political system recognize their needs and their rights. Gays in the United States are fully cognizant of the civil rights model with all its challenges and its eventual successes. But gays also realize that their movement is relatively new and is facing stiff opposition. The question thus becomes how long will gays be willing to wait to achieve what they feel are their rights and how willing will those who oppose gay rights be willing to change their positions and accept homosexuals fully into American society?

The Great Debate

With the Supreme Court supporting state-sanctioned gay marriage, it would appear that the debate over homosexuals being allowed to marry is over. But new issues, such as rights for transgender people and new attempts in some states to pass legislation to limit gay rights in hiring and job security based on religious freedom, are now on the policy agenda and causing controversy.

Debate Topic

Should religious freedom be used as the basis for legislation designed to protect those seeking to limit or deny rights to gay and transgender individuals?

Critical Thinking Questions

1. Despite the Supreme Court decision in the Obergefell case, should gay couples be allowed to marry or does such a state-sanctioned union weaken the western tradition of man/woman marriage?

2. How do you explain the generation gap in support of gay marriage with older Americans having larger percentages of opposition compared to younger Americans?
3. There are those who oppose gay rights who claim that the media has actively promoted the gay lifestyle in television and movies. Do you agree?
4. Pope Francis made the controversial statement of "Who am I to judge?" when asked about his views on gays, but came out against gay marriage. Is it possible to reconcile these two views?
5. What is your view of the so-called "bathroom rights" of transgender people?

Connections

The Human Rights Campaign is actively involved in advancing the cause of gays, lesbians, bisexuals, and transgender Americans. See their site at www.hrc.org

One of the more prominent advocates for gay rights is the Gay and Lesbian Alliance Against Discrimination. Visit its site at www.glaad.org

A site that is critical of gay marriage is www.rightwingwatch.org

The status of gay marriage and gay marriage laws can be accessed at www.freedom tomarry.org

The American Civil Liberties Union has often represented homosexuals in local, state, and national court cases. Visit their site at www.aclu.org

A Few Books to Read

Badgett, M.V. Lee, *When Gay People Get Married: What Happens When Societies Legalize Same Sex Marriage* (New York: NYU Press, 2009).

Corvino, John and Maggie Gallagher, *Debating Same Sex Marriage* (New York: Oxford University Press, 2012).

Faderman, Lillian, *The Gay Revolution: The Story of the Struggle* (New York: Simon and Schuster, 2015).

Richards, Lawrence, *The Case for Gay Rights: From Bowers to Lawrence and Beyond* (Lawrence: University of Kansas Press, 2005).

Viefhues-Barleg, Ludger, *Between a Man and a Woman: Why Conservatives Oppose Same Sex Marriage* (New York: Columbia University Press, 2010).

Notes

1. Sandhya Somashekhar, "Health Survey Gives Government Its First Large-Scale Data on Gay, Bisexual Population," *Washington Post*, July 15, 2014.
2. For the history of the gay rights movement see Vern Bullough, ed., *Before Stonewall: Activists for Gay and Lesbian Rights in Historical Context* (New York: Harrington Press, 2002).
3. See Robin Toner and Robert Pear, "A Reagan Legacy Tainted by AIDS, Civil Rights and Union Policies," *New York Times*, June 9, 2004.

4. For a comprehensive discussion of the Don't Ask, Don't Tell policy from the military perspective see Lisa Daniel, "Nine Months After the Repeal, Gay Troops Slowly Come Out," Armed Services Press Service, U.S. Department of Defense, June 20, 2012.

5. *Lawrence v. Texas* 539 US 588 (2003).

6. The DOMA legislation is monitored and analyzed at www.domawatch.org/index.php

7. *Boy Scouts of America et al. v. Dale* 530 U.S. 640 (2000).

8. *Goodridge v. Department of Health* 798 N.E. 2nd 941 (MASS 2003).

9. Laura Dolan, "California Overturns Gay Marriage Law," *Los Angeles Times*, May 16, 2008.

10. Cited in a Pew public opinion poll. See "Changing Attitudes on Gay Marriage," Pew Research Center, July 29, 2015.

11. See the Human Rights Campaign website, www.hrc.org

12. See the National Gay and Lesbian Task Force (now called the National LGBTQ Task Force or The Task Force) website, www.taskforce.org

13. The American Civil Liberties Union monitors the ENDA. See "Fact Sheet: Employment Non-Discrimination Act," 2009, www.aclu.org

14. See The Civil Rights Coalition for the 21st Century at www.civilrights.org/issues/hate

15. See the Alliance for Marriage website at www.allianceformarriage.org

16. See the American Values website at www.americanvalues.org

17. See the Family Research Council website at www.frc.org

18. See the Focus on the Family website at www.focusonthefamily.com

19. See Kristen Lombardi, "The Catholic War Against Gay Marriage," *The Boston Phoenix*, March 26–April 1, 2004.

20. Joshua J. McElwee, "Francis: Christians Must Apologize to Gay People for Marginalizing Them," *National Catholic Reporter*, June 26, 2016.

21. David Masci and Michael Lipka, "Where Christian Churches, Other Religions Stand on Gay Marriage," Pew Research Center, December 21, 2015. For background see Michael Paulson, "Black Clergy Rejection Stirs Gay Marriage Backers," *Boston Globe*, February 10, 2004.

22. Ben Kamisar, "Scalia: Gay Marriage Decision Shows America's 'Ruler' Is Supreme Court," *The Hill*, June 26, 2015.

23. See Corky Siemaszko, "Kentucky Clerk Kim Davis, Who Refused to Issue Marriage Licenses to Gay, Seeks to End Case," *NBC News*, June 21, 2016.

24. "Understanding HB2: North Carolina's Newest Law Solidifies State's Role in Defining Discrimination," *Charlotte Observer*, March 26, 2016.

13 CAPITAL **PUNISHMENT**

Issue Focus

The issue of capital punishment in the United States is undergoing a thorough review. After forty years of state-sanctioned executions, a number of states have declared moratoriums on the use of capital punishment or have been content to let court proceedings drag on, thus delaying the imposition of the death penalty. The decline in capital punishment is the result of new DNA testing that has proven some on death row to be innocent, questions regarding racial discrimination and misidentification, lax legal representation of accused criminals, and recently a number of botched lethal injection executions. Together these concerns have raised the question as to whether innocent individuals may have been put to death. Americans, however, continue to support capital punishment as the ultimate verdict for those who have committed heinous crimes, particularly mass murders and the killing of police officers.

Chapter Objectives
This chapter will seek to:
1. Chronicle the recent history of capital punishment in the United States and the extent of the use of capital punishment by the states.
2. Present the points of contention between the proponents and opponents of capital punishment, particularly those associated with moral, deterrence, and racial issues.
3. Describe the current status of capital punishment in light of new scientific advances in DNA detection and legal challenges based on questions of due process of the law.

SOME BACKGROUND

Just as the 2nd Amendment has posed a challenge for interpretation and application, so has the 8th Amendment, which prohibits "cruel and unusual punishment." The interpretation of exactly what is meant by "cruel and unusual punishment" has served as the basis for the ongoing debate over capital punishment. At issue is whether the state has the constitutional right (and the moral right) to take the life of an individual who has been convicted in a court of law of a capital crime (usually various categories or legally defined degrees of murder). Because the writers of the Bill of Rights did not specify what types of punishments were proper in capital cases, or for that manner in any criminal case, the courts have been required to bring meaning to the words "cruel and unusual punishment."

The 8th Amendment, which also bans excessive bail for prisoners, was included in the Bill of Rights as a response to the harsh treatment of prisoners under British rule both here in the colonies and in England. But once the British were defeated and the Bill of Rights was put into place, states did not shy away from using a wide array of punishments for capital crimes, including hanging and the firing squad. The use of capital punishment was widespread in this country well into the 20th century. Between 1930 and 1968, 3,859 people were executed in the United States. But after World War II, there was a marked decrease in executions. By the 1960s, there was a significant decline in executions as state legislatures banned various procedures, governors commuted sentences to life without parole, or courts intervened to stay executions.[1]

In 1967 Luis Monge became the last individual to be executed (by Colorado's gas chamber) before a 10-year unofficial moratorium began. The issue of capital punishment entered the federal court system and a series of test cases were brought challenging capital punishment as violating the 8th Amendment ban on "cruel and unusual punishment." Opponents to capital punishment, including the Legal Defense Fund, the NAACP, and the American Civil Liberties Union, argued that state laws were not only a violation of the 8th Amendment but were biased against African-Americans in violation of the 14th Amendment guarantee of equal protections of the laws. State governments, especially from southern and western states, responded that they had the right to impose capital punishment and were responding to overwhelming support from voters in referenda.

The Supreme Court took both of these positions into consideration and, in 1972, announced in a landmark case, Furman v. Georgia, that Georgia's capital punishment law was in violation of the 8th Amendment. The case involved the use in Georgia of what was termed a "unitary trial" in which the jurors not only found the individual charged with a capital crime guilty or innocent, but if guilty the jury also decided on the form of punishment. In a 5–4 decision, the justices revealed that they could not arrive at a consensus on capital punishment, although they did agree that the Georgia law was vague in defining what crimes were deserving of capital punishment and that the "unitary trial" procedure leading to a decision on the death penalty was "arbitrary and capricious."[2]

After the Furman decision, many states went back to the legislative drawing board and produced laws that they felt would be approved in future test cases by the Supreme Court. New laws were drafted in 37 states that included more specific language on the crimes worthy of capital punishment and created a bifurcated sentencing system in which jurors were asked to decide on guilt and innocence in one trial and then, at a second trial, determine whether execution was indeed appropriate. In 1976 in Gregg v. Georgia, the Supreme Court upheld the new Georgia law, and those that followed similar procedures, thereby opening up the floodgates of executions in the United States. From 1977 to 2007 there have been 1,099 executions in this country with the state of Texas leading the way with 405 executions through 2007. But in recent years, executions have been down considerably. In 2015 only 28 prisoners were executed, the lowest number since 1991, and in Texas only two convicted criminals were sent to death row, down from 11 in 2014. Nationwide in 2015, 49 people were sentenced to death row, the lowest in modern times.[3]

Although a significant majority of Americans support capital punishment—a 2005 Gallup poll found that 74% of the respondents supported the death penalty for murder—there is at present a reevaluation of state laws and state execution practices, in large part because of new scientific evidence that is used to prove innocence, proof of poor legal representation, bias against minorities, and complications with lethal injections. In a poll taken in 2015 by the Gallup organization, support dropped to 61%, while opposition to the death penalty rose to 37%, the highest in 43 years. Increasingly, Americans are opting for a sentence of life without parole instead of the death penalty. Support for life without parole is now a majority. In 2015 five states declared moratoriums on executions and nineteen repealed the death penalty, leaving only six states that have retained the practice of execution of those convicted of capital crimes. Nebraska repealed the death penalty but placed the final decision on the ballot for a popular referendum in 2016 (the repeal was overturned by the voters).[4]

Because capital punishment is under review, the arguments that have been used to either support the death penalty or to work for its end are also being reexamined. In many respects, the issue of capital punishment is at a crossroads, in much the same way that it was during the time after the Furman case and before the Gregg decision. Government officials at all levels are taking a hard look at capital punishment to determine whether this form of the ultimate sanction against a criminal convicted of a capital offense is not only unconstitutional but also may be seriously flawed. Because public opinion remains supportive of capital punishment and many Americans do not see the death penalty as "cruel and unusual punishment," this issue will remain hotly contested in the coming years even though doubts about the accuracy and fairness of its application are mounting.

On the Record

Governor Tom Wolfe of Pennsylvania issued the following statement as he instituted a moratorium on executions:

> This moratorium is in no way an expression of sympathy for the guilty on death row, all of whom have been convicted of committing heinous crimes. This decision is based on a flawed system that has been proven to be an endless cycle of court proceedings as well as ineffective, unjust, and expensive proceedings. Since the reinstatement of the death penalty, 150 people have been exonerated from death row nationwide, including six men in Pennsylvania. If the Commonwealth of Pennsylvania is going to take the irrevocable

On the Record   (continued)

step of executing a human being, the capital sentencing system must be infallible. Pennsylvania's system is riddled with flaws, making it error prone, expensive, and anything but infallible.

Source: The Death Penalty Information Center, statement recorded on February 13, 2015

DEBATES, DIFFERENCES, AND DIVISIONS

The arguments that have been made for and against capital punishment reveal the complexity of the issue and the intense emotions that are associated with the state sanctioning the taking of the life of a convicted murderer. The debates that have formed around capital punishment in large part involve moral concerns, the deterrent effect, racial and class bias, comparison with other nations, and cost efficiency. Within each of these debate areas there are vast differences of opinion as proponents of capital punishment, especially the family members of a murder victim, approach the execution of the convicted criminal as bringing closure to a traumatic event, while opponents see capital punishment as simply revenge akin to the biblical eye-for-an-eye viewpoint that lessens the value of life and, in the end, allows for no chance of rehabilitation or redemption.

The moral debate surrounding the death penalty is often framed as a matter of whether the state should have the right to take a life and whether that act is indeed cruel and unusual punishment. The questions that are raised when a murder is committed and the murderer is convicted are "What is the proper punishment?" and "Does the punishment fit the crime?" Proponents see capital punishment as removing a violent killer from society's midst and achieving a form of justice that indeed is moral and proper in a civilized culture. Society must retaliate with the highest form of sanction in order to show the gravity of the crime and the revulsion that law-abiding citizens have for such heinous acts. On the other side of the argument is the view that capital punishment brings society down to the level of the killer and cheapens life by engaging in an execution that is, in itself, murder and makes the state an enabler of death. Both moral arguments have merit as one talks about the importance of justice and society registering its abhorrence for murder, while the other places emphasis on the inalienable right to life and the importance of society not being a party to murder.[5]

Also associated with the moral argument is the concern over wrongful death. Opponents of the death penalty point to data that show that, from 1973 to 2005, 123 convicted murderers in 25 states were released from death row as a result of new evidence that proved their innocence. In 2015 alone, 156 convicted murderers on death row were exonerated and released from jail, in large part due to new DNA evidence that proved with certainty that blood or other bodily fluids from the convicted individual did not match evidence brought into testimony during the trial. There was also evidence of individuals being freed from death row as new witnesses came forward or others recanted their testimony. Finally, there have been numerous cases of mistaken identity, especially in cases involving African-Americans where (often white) witnesses have failed to recognize differences in the appearances of black men and have given testimony that, in later years, proved incorrect.[6] All of these examples bring pause into the matter and consideration of whether even one instance of wrongful death is enough of a moral argument to stop the death penalty. There is also evidence that the American people are beginning to recognize that innocent individuals have been executed. A Pew Research Center poll in 2015 found that seven out of ten Americans believe there is a risk of an innocent individual being put to death, a key factor in the decline in support for the death penalty. Opponents of the death penalty are hoping that the combination of DNA-related cases where individuals have been released from death row coupled with the increasing level of doubt among Americans about wrongful death may be the moral spur to end capital punishment in this country.[7]

Although the moral arguments often drive the capital punishment debate and galvanize emotions on both sides, it is the issue of whether the death penalty serves as a deterrent to capital crimes that has received the highest level of expert analysis and quantitative study. Stated simply, the deterrence argument is based on the premise that the threat of execution will serve as the most effective means of stopping capital crimes. While there is a common sense component to this premise, criminologists and other social science researchers have been unable to come to an agreement on whether indeed state-sanctioned executions have an impact on the reduction of capital crimes. Studies have failed to show that states with capital punishment have a lower rate of homicide than those states without such laws. There have been some studies that do show a slight reduction, but no research has been able to prove a direct link between capital punishment and a consistent and comprehensive decline in homicides. Recently, there have been a number of new studies performed by various groups of economists on the deterrent effect of capital punishment with findings that support the connection between the death penalty and the reduction in homicides. The studies showed that in Texas, for example, where punishment is meted out quickly for capital crimes, researchers found that the use of the death penalty prevented anywhere from 3 to 18 murders.[8]

The argument that has been the most effective in supporting capital punishment as a deterrent is the fact that those convicted criminals who are on death row awaiting execution work the judicial system in order to delay their executions, thus counteracting the deterrent effect of swift punishment. Proponents state that the regular stays of execution and delays, while the courts examine new evidence or challenges to the original conviction, only weaken the deterrent impact of capital punishment. The position of those in favor of capital punishment is that if the process of implementing the death sentence moved quickly after the conviction, and those on death row were permitted only one challenge to the decision of the courts, the deterrent effect would be much more visible. At present, most death sentence cases take a minimum of about ten years before the execution of the convicted criminal is carried out, which also means that the number of criminals awaiting execution on death row continues to expand.[9] The average wait on death row is 17.2 years, and 30 people have been awaiting execution for over 25 years. In 2007 a federal appeals judge sparked a controversy when he called for more resources to hire defense lawyers to deal with the backlog of cases and to speed up the appeal process to ensure that execution orders are carried out. What has occurred in California and other states that have capital punishment laws is that governmental leaders who are opposed to the death penalty have fostered a system that, in effect, makes the likelihood of executions slim as court delays are tolerated and budget resources to hire personnel to break the logjam of cases are never approved. In 2016 voters in Oklahoma voted to create special courts that would speed up the process of appeals and move more quickly to the execution stage, a move that would not only save the state money but also perhaps send a signal to criminals that punishment for capital crimes will be swift.[10]

State By State Status of Capital Punishment
States Where Capital Punishment Remains Legal

Alabama
Arizona
Arkansas
California
Colorado
Georgia
Florida
Idaho
Indiana
Kansas
Kentucky
Louisiana
Mississippi
Missouri
Montana
Nebraska
Nevada
New Hampshire
North Carolina
Ohio
Oklahoma
Oregon

Pennsylvania
South Carolina
South Dakota
Tennessee
Texas
Utah
Virginia
Washington
Wyoming

States Where the Death Penalty is Illegal

Alaska
Connecticut
District of Columbia
Hawaii
Illinois
Iowa
Maine
Maryland
Massachusetts
Michigan
Minnesota
New Jersey
New Mexico
New York
North Dakota
Rhode Island
Vermont
West Virginia
Wisconsin

Source: www.deathpenaltyinfo.org

The opponents of linking capital punishment to deterrence cite the fact that most homicides are crimes of passion and are not premeditated acts. Therefore, murderers are not going to be thinking about the death penalty or become influenced by the death penalty as they kill in a jealous rage or act out some deep-seated hatred. Also, opponents of the death penalty rely on those scholars who question the research linking deterrence and a drop in capital crimes. Despite the new findings mentioned above supporting the position that capital punishment deters homicides, critics such as John Donahue III, a law professor at Yale University, question the findings, stating that since the death penalty, "is applied so rarely that the number of homicides it can plausibly have caused or deterred cannot reliably be disentangled from the large year to year changes in the homicide rate caused by other factors."[11]

The most highly charged aspect of the capital punishment debate involves the fact that a large percentage of African-American males are on death row or have already been executed. The most recent data on the racial makeup of those on death row or already executed show that African-American males made up 69% of death row inmates and 34% of those executed since 1976. As stated earlier, African-Americans make up approximately 12% of the population demographic of the United States. Other studies have shown that, although race may be a factor, it is also socio-economic class that must be considered as the poor, whether white or black, do not have the financial resources to hire the best lawyers and thus must rely on public defenders. Critics of the capital punishment laws in various states point to evidence that public defense lawyers have shown a consistent failure to adequately represent their poor clients. Without proper investigative resources and with huge caseload demands, many public defenders do not have the capability to mount the kind of defense that a wealthy defendant, in many instances a white person, can present.[12]

The American Civil Liberties Union, which often represents individuals facing the death penalty, has for years pointed to the connection between faulty defense representation and the prospect of the accused facing capital punishment. As the ACLU states in its position paper on capital punishment, "the quality of legal representation (in the United States) is a better predictor of whether or not someone will be sentenced to death than the facts of the crime." Although the ACLU was talking about the problems of defense representation for all those convicted of a capital offense, it has been especially concerned about the fate of African-Americans who often rely on public defenders. In 1987 the Supreme Court took up the case of McClesky v. Kemp in which the issue of race and the death penalty was presented. Opponents of the death penalty showed that blacks received the death penalty more than whites, but in a 5–4 decision the Court was not convinced that racial bias was a factor in applying the death penalty to capital cases.[13]

Data Bank

According to Amnesty International, a human rights organization that monitors capital punishment laws as part of its mission to end what it considers official abuses of basic human rights, 77 countries impose the death penalty for capital crimes, and those countries are mostly in the Middle East, Africa, and Asia. The United States and Japan are the only industrialized countries that retain capital punishment, although Japan's use of the death penalty is markedly less than that of the United States. In the last 30 years, over 118 countries abolished capital punishment. The most recent countries to do away with capital punishment are the Philippines in 2006, Armenia in 2003, and Cyprus in 2002. Among the 77 countries that retain the death penalty are China, Iran, Saudi Arabia, North Korea, Pakistan, and the Russian Federation.

Source: Amnesty International

The most recent aspect of the capital punishment debate is associated with the constitutionality of lethal injection. Since 1978 each of the 37 states that permit capital punishment employ lethal injection as a means of execution. The so-called three-drug "cocktail" used by prison officials to carry out the death penalty order, however, came under intense scrutiny in 2007 as there was evidence that the procedure is not a painless way to end the life of a convicted murderer but rather masks the pain that the individual experiences before death. Prison officials around the country dispute the allegations that lethal injections cause pain before death sets in. They state that challenging the procedure as a violation of the 8th Amendment prohibition against "cruel and unusual punishment" is just the latest attempt to end capital punishment in the United States.[14]

Despite the position of officials in those states that continue to hold to the position that lethal injection is humane and does not violate the principles of the 8th Amendment, the Supreme Court entered the controversy by stopping the execution of convicted killers in Kentucky, Nevada, and Virginia. Other states, on their own, have stopped executions using lethal injection until the Supreme Court issues a decision on the constitutionality of lethal injection in a case coming out of Kentucky. This temporary moratorium on lethal injections was viewed by opponents of capital punishment as a breakthrough in ending the practice, but state officials and proponents of capital punishment saw it correctly as only a temporary setback: in April 2008, the Supreme Court, in a 7–2 decision, upheld the three-drug protocol used in lethal injection.[15]

The support for lethal injection by the Supreme Court has not stopped opponents of capital punishment, and there does appear to be support within some states for ending the practice. New Jersey, for example, banned capital punishment completely and replaced it with life without parole in 2007. With the new law, New Jersey became the first state in 40 years to reject capital punishment. Then Governor John Corzine, in signing the law, stated, "[T]his is a day of progress for us and for the millions of people across our nation and around the globe who reject the death penalty as a moral or practical response to the grievous, even heinous, crime of murder." The decision by New Jersey took eight individuals off death row and commuted their sentences. But the decision was not without outcries from the families of murder victims. Marilyn Flax, whose husband was murdered in 1989 by death row inmate John Martini, stated, "I will never forget how I've been abused by a state and a governor that was supposed to protect the innocent and enforce the laws." Also, Richard Kanka, who was the driving force behind Megan's Law requiring law enforcement agencies to notify the public about the presence of convicted sex offenders in local communities (his daughter Megan was raped and murdered), said that Corzine's signing of the law was "just another slap in the face to the victims."[16]

The controversy over lethal injection and the definition of "cruel and unusual punishment" continued after a botched execution in Oklahoma where, in 2014, an inmate was injected with a drug called midazolam, which resulted in an extended period of writhing in pain and hours before he was pronounced dead. Three inmates on death row sued the state of Oklahoma, seeking to stop the lethal injection protocol, but in a 5–4 decision the Supreme Court denied their suit and supported the right of Oklahoma to carry out the execution.[17] Despite the decision, the dissent by Justice Stephen Breyer called for a thorough review of the death penalty within the bounds of the 8th Amendment. The controversy over lethal injection and the potential for "botched" executions heightened the debate when the state of Arkansas became involved in a court dispute over the use of midazolam. The pharmaceutical company (McKesson) that makes the drug asked Arkansas officials not to use the drug because it was obtained despite the company's prohibition against its use in executions. But prison officials in the state moved quickly to schedule the executions with the remaining vials of the drug. The issue moved through the federal courts but eventually three executions took place.

Pope Francis also placed himself in the debate when he spoke before a joint house of Congress in 2015 and called for an end to capital punishment.[18] Despite the position of Justice Breyer and the Pope, three states—California, Nebraska, and Oklahoma—passed referenda in 2016 that supported capital punishment and made the process of appeal shorter, thus creating less time from conviction to execution.

FYI

During the use of lethal injection, the inmate is strapped to a gurney and is given a three-step chemical "cocktail." First, sodium thiopental, a barbiturate, is administered, which makes the inmate unconscious. Then pancuronium bromide is injected, which stops breathing and causes paralysis. Lastly, potassium chloride is added, which stops the heart and causes death. It is the injection of pancuronium bromide that has caused the issue as opponents of the death penalty state that, in a number of executions, injection of the drug masks the pain that the inmate endures. As an alternative to the current "cocktail," prison officials are considering using barbiturates to depress the nervous system, followed by certain inhalant anesthetics to terminate breathing and create cardiac arrest. It is thought that taking the pancuronium bromide out of the "cocktail" will do away with the pain that may occur during the execution process.

Source: "What's In a Lethal Injection Cocktail," *New York Times*, April 9, 2011

On another judicial front, the Florida Supreme Court threw out the process used in that state to sentence convicted criminals to death row. The court found that, in Florida, a judge had the power under state law to reach a different decision than juries charged with determining whether to impose the death sentence. As a result of the decision, Florida legislators vowed to change the law to have only juries determine the imposing of the death sentence, not judges. Florida remains a state that continues to have capital punishment and has used executions 23 times since 2011.[19]

There is no doubt that the debate over capital punishment is beginning to be muddled again, as it was during the 1970s, as the courts reexamine lethal injection, New Jersey bans the death penalty, and polls start to show some signs of questioning whether innocent individuals have been put to death. But it is important to point out that the number of Americans who remain supportive of capital punishment continues to be in the 70% range. Some hold to the "eye-for-an-eye" biblical position where capital punishment is seen as a matter of simple justice; others are convinced that the death penalty is a deterrent to future crimes; while others, especially the families of victims, see the executions as a form of closure, as the person who took their loved one's life also loses his/her life. As with the support for gun rights, a sizeable majority of Americans believe that capital punishment is what the Founders intended and that it is a policy that should not be tinkered with, much less abandoned.

Since capital punishment laws are centered in the states and changes in the laws will come from state action, the decision of the Supreme Court on lethal injection, or any other future challenge to the death penalty, will likely spur states to make adjustments to their procedures or to the legal process that leads to an execution. It will not be until a time when the American people make a significant shift away from supporting capital punishment that other states will join New Jersey and ban publicly sanctioned executions. In the meantime, those convicted murderers on death row will seek to use the legal system to delay their executions, while state officials and the supportive courts will seek to speed up the time between conviction and execution. While these maneuvers are going on, the proponents and opponents of capital punishment will continue their lobbying efforts and court challenges, all in an effort to define more precisely what "cruel and unusual punishment" means and how it should be applied in 21st-century America.

The Great Debate

Supporters of capital punishment often point to the killing of children by sex offenders, the murder of police officers, mass murders, and serial killings as examples in which capital punishment is justified.

Debate Topic
Under what circumstances, if any, should capital punishment be permitted?

Critical Thinking Questions

1. Is the death penalty inherently immoral?
2. Is lethal injection a "more humane" form of capital punishment?
3. Should the punishment for a capital crime be life without parole rather than some form of life-ending punishment?
4. There is substantial data that shows that African-Americans are not properly defended in murder trials and thus are more likely to be found guilty. How can this problem be avoided, and is this a sufficient reason to end the death penalty?
5. Do you believe that capital punishment will eventually be stopped by most states?

Connections

For accurate and timely data on capital punishment see the Department of Justice, Bureau of Statistics at http://www/ojp.usdoj.gov/bjs/cp.htm

A website that supports the death penalty is www.prodeathpenalty.com

The foremost critic of capital punishment is the American Civil Liberties Union. Its position on capital punishment can be seen at www.aclu.org/capital/general/35665res20080530.html

An organization that is prominent in the fight against the death penalty is the National Coalition to Abolish the Death Penalty: www.ncadp.org

For the most accurate account of individual deaths through capital punishment in the United States see the site of the Death Penalty Information Center, www.deathpenalty.org

Some Books to Read

Banner, Stuart, *The Death Penalty: An American History* (Cambridge, MA: Harvard University Press, 2003).

Bedau, Hugo Adam and Paul Gassell, *Debating the Death Penalty* (New York: Oxford University Press, 2004).

Blecker, Robert, *The Death of Punishment: Searching for Justice Among the Worst of the Worst* (New York: St. Martin's Press, 2013).

Breyer, Stephen, *Against the Death Penalty* (Washington, DC: Brookings Institution Press, 2016).

Prejean, Helen, *Dead Man Walking, an Eyewitness Account of the Death Penalty in the United States* (New York: Vintage, 1994).

Notes

1. For background and historical data see the US Bureau of Justice Statistics, "Capital Punishment," 2013, www.bjs.org
2. *Furman v. Georgia* 408 U.S. 238 (1972).
3. "Who Killed the Death Penalty," *The Economist*, December 19, 2015.
4. See Baxter Oliphant, "Support for the Death Penalty Lowest in More than Four Decades," Pew Research Center, September 29, 2016. See also Frank R. Baumgartner, Suzanna L. DeBoef, and Amber Boydstun, *The Decline of the Death Penalty and the Discovery of Innocence* (New York: Cambridge University Press, 2008).
5. Still considered the seminal book on the morality of capital punishment, see Walter Berns, *For Capital Punishment: Crime and Morality of the Death Penalty* (New York: Basic Books, 1979).
6. See the arguments put forth by the Innocence Project, "The Death Penalty," February 2, 2009. Also see Harry Weinstein, "Death Penalty Overturned in Most Cases," *Los Angeles Times*, June 20, 2000.
7. Baxter Oliphant, Pew Research Center, op. cit. See also Barry Scheck, Peter Neufeld, and Jim Dwyer, *Actual Innocence: Five Days to Execution and Other Dispatches From the Wrongly Convicted* (New York: Doubleday, 2000).
8. See Adam Liptak, "Studies Spark New Execution Debate," *Boston Globe*, November 18, 2007.
9. See "Federal Death Row Prisoners," Death Penalty Information Center, March, 24, 2016. The NAACP has taken an active role in criticizing the fact that large numbers of African-Americans are on death row.
10. Aliyah Fruman, "Election 2016: Nebraska, Oklahoma Vote in Favor of Death Penalty," *NBC News*, November 9, 2016.
11. John Donahue and Justin Wolfers, "The Death Penalty: No Evidence for Deterrence," 2006, www.deathpenaltyinfo.org
12. See "Death Row U.S.A.: A Quarterly Report" by the Criminal Justice Project and the NAACP Legal Defense and Educational Fund, Inc., Winter, 2016.
13. *McClesky v. Kemp* 481 U.S. 279 (1987).
14. Tracy Connor and NBC News, "Like Being 'Burned Alive'? Execution Case Fires Up Supreme Court," *NBC News*, April 29, 2015.
15. *Baze v. Rees* 533 U.S. 35. 2008.
16. Tom Hester, "New Jersey Become First State in 42 Years to Ban Death Penalty," *StarNewsOnline*, December 17, 2007, www.starnewsonline.com
17. Robert Barnes, "Supreme Court Upholds Lethal Injection Procedure," *Washington Post*, June 29, 2015.
18. Mark Berman, "Pope Francis Tells Congress 'Every Life Is Sacred' Says the Death Penalty Should Be Abolished," *Washington Post*, September 24, 2015.
19. Mark Berman, "Florida Supreme Court Says State's New Death Penalty Law Is Unconstitutional," *Washington Post*, October 14, 2016.

14 MONEY AND POLITICS

Issue Focus

Running a democracy is not supposed to be a matter of dollars and cents, but indeed American democracy has become a costly venture. Billions and billions of dollars are spent every election period to pay for the campaigns of those running for office, whether at the local, state, or national level. Injecting money into the democratic process has led to numerous problems, from corruption of public officials to influence peddling by lobbyists seeking to sway the votes of politicians to access to government officials by those with money. The influence of money in American politics has become so problematic that questions are often raised about who really matters in the United States—the American people or those who use money to advance their special interests.

Chapter Objectives
This issue chapter will seek to:
1. Explain the impact of campaign contributions and fundraising on the practice of contemporary American politics.
2. Describe the attempts to define and control the limits of campaign fundraising and spending in American politics.
3. Discuss the issues of public financing of campaigns and other reforms suggested as remedies to the abuses associated with money and politics.

SOME BACKGROUND

As the old saying goes, money is the mother's milk of politics. Although a bit graphic, money can indeed be linked to that which nourishes and sustains politics and politicians. Without huge infusions of money, American election campaigns would not be able to function to pay for an army of organizational workers, numerous specialized consultants, constant polling, endless media advertising, coast-to-coast travel, and all those necessary miscellaneous costs from funny hats and t-shirts to envelopes and stamps. In the 2000 election for the presidency, the bill for capturing the White House was, according to Federal Election Commission data, approximately $450 million; in 2004 the amount increased to $650 million, and the 2008 election surpassed the $1 billion mark. In 2012 the amount spent was approximately $ 2.6 billion, and in 2016 the two major candidates, Donald Trump and Hillary Clinton, spent $689 million. By adding the money spent by all the other Democratic and Republican candidates, the total amount surpassed $5 billion. It must be added that the final total spent did not include so-called "Dark Money" contributions, but more on that later.[1]

These dollar figures do not include races for the House of Representatives and the Senate. In 2004 and 2006, the cost of all Congressional races reached $4 billion with the average cost of winning a House seat at over $1 million and a Senate seat around $8 million. In 2012 the cost of national elections for House was over $1 million and a Senate seat at approximately $10.2 million, although some Senate races in key states and with party competition high, the amount spent far exceeded $8 million. In 2016, for example, the race for the Senate seat in Florida eventually won by Marco Rubio was $44 million ($52 million was actually raised). Remember that members of the House and Senate receive an annual salary that, varying on their seniority and position within the hierarchy of power, is still less than $200,000 a year. By any measure, that's a great deal of money to spend in order to win a job that pays a handsome, but not exorbitant salary.[2]

The connection between money and American politics has a long history going back to the days of Andrew Jackson and his "Spoils System," where potential office seekers paid handsomely to get a government job. In the more modern era, campaign contributions to candidates for public office were largely unregulated leading to stories of bags full of money being given to candidates and a variety of expensive perks (vacations, gifts, homes) being offered to politicians with the clear understanding that something was expected in return. The triggering event for campaign financing reform came after the Watergate scandal when an organization associated with Nixon reelection campaign of 1972 (Committee to Reelect the President—CREEP) was found to have engaged in illegal activities. In the wake of the Watergate and CREEP scandals, Congress passed the Federal Election Campaign Act of 1972, which required disclosure of all contributions to federal candidates over $100 and allowed citizens to check off a $1 deduction that would be used to finance presidential elections. A companion Federal Election Campaign law in 1974 established the Federal Elections Commission, provided for public financing of presidential elections, and set specific limits on campaign contributions to federal candidates.[3]

But with each step forward for campaign finance reform, there was often a step backward as either court decisions or loopholes in the existing laws allowed money to remain a critical ingredient in the electoral process. In 1976 in a landmark decision on campaign finance (Buckley v. Valeo), the Supreme Court struck down the section of the 1972 Federal Election Campaign Law that sought to place a limit on the personal contributions that individuals running for office could spend on their campaign. The Court also struck down sections of the 1972 law that set limits on overall spending and on contributions by private groups. In the decision, the Court invoked the First Amendment stating, "The candidate, no less than any other person, has a First Amendment right to engage in the discussion of public issues and vigorously and tirelessly to advocate his own election." The use of the First Amendment free speech argument as a basis for campaign contributions gave Congress the opportunity to avoid sweeping financial reform or moving to comprehensive public financing of elections. Spending one's own money or permitting individuals, corporations, or other entities to write campaign checks was seen as part of the constitutional protection of free speech, since providing money to candidates was another form of political expression.[4]

While the Buckley decision weakened the 1972 law considerably, for a time it did place some limits on individual contributions, especially from major donors. Quickly, though, loopholes in the law were found that allowed money to be given to political parties, rather than to candidates. This so-called "soft money" became the avenue for huge contributions from wealthy donors and continued the process of unrelenting spending on federal campaigns. The use of "soft money" became so important to fundraising for political parties and for the candidates, who became the beneficiaries of the loophole windfall, that the reform effort again gathered steam as more and more Americans became convinced that money had corrupted the political system and made incumbents and candidates for office beholden to donors, whether individual, corporate, or interest group.[5]

In 2002 Republican Senator John McCain of Arizona and Democrat Russ Feingold of Wisconsin pushed campaign reform legislation through Congress. The Bipartisan Campaign Reform Act (BCRA) did away with "soft money," which was viewed as closing a key funnel for campaign funding. But in a compromise measure, the legislation also raised the individual contribution limit to $2,300 and allowed contributions up to $28,500 to the national party committee. In total, under the BCRA, an individual could contribute up to $108,200 in one biennial period. Not surprisingly, the BCRA faced new constitutional questions and efforts to find ways to move around the "soft money" restrictions.[6]

In order to avoid the rules of BCRA, some party-linked groups formed 527 organizations. Named after Section 527 of the IRS Code, these groups, which were formally not aligned with a political party, exploded onto the political scene as they advocated for a particular cause and, in the process, the candidates who are supportive of the cause by mobilizing voters through direct mail, television advertising, and other media outlets. As a result of the IRS Code, 527 organizations were not limited in the amount of money they could spend on advocacy campaigns and were very successful in getting out their message and that of the candidate who was aligned with their cause. The most notable of the 527 organizations was the Swift Boat Veterans who, in the 2004 presidential campaign, cast doubt on the veracity of John Kerry's war record and the medals for bravery that he received. Most observers of the campaign believed that the Swift Boat ads on television painted Kerry in a bad light and contributed in part to his electoral loss.[7]

Campaign finance changed dramatically when, in 2010, the Supreme Court handed down a ruling called Citizens United v. Federal Election Commission. The ruling, in effect, opened up campaign contributions and placed no real limit on spending private money to support a candidate. In the decision, the justices said that political spending on candidates is a form of free speech and thus protected by the First Amendment. What that ruling translated into is that corporations, unions, and Super PACs (Political Action Committees) could spend unlimited amounts of money on all sorts of political activities. The ruling also spawned the formation of so-called Dark Money organizations—campaign entities that are formed to make donations without having to reveal the donors.[8]

In Citizens United, the majority of the justices were of the opinion that groups spending huge amounts of money in a campaign would be independent of the candidate when, in effect, campaign finance had been taken over by Super PACs, corporations, and unions, with billionaire contributors playing a huge role in supporting a candidate. Critics of the post-Citizens United campaign finance system say that what the ruling has done is foster a climate of influence peddling and access buying that borders on corruption and puts democracy up for sale.[9] In 2010 the Brennan Center for Justice found that of the $1 billion spent by Super PACs on the federal level, 60% came from just 165 individuals and their spouses. Although under the current law the legal maximum limit is $5200, what most wealthy contributors do is make the contribution of $5200 and then follow that with an unlimited contribution of perhaps in the millions to a candidate through a Super PAC or a Dark Money entity.[10]

The history of campaign finance and campaign finance reform is thus one of fits and starts, progress and failure, but always a search for new loopholes and new opportunities to skirt the law and raise money for candidates. The result of all the effort to reform and evade the way this country finances federal elections has led to numerous incidents of political corruption and an occasional wave of political scandals. Just as important, the relentless pursuit of ways to continue funneling huge amounts of money into the political process has led to a weakening of public confidence in the electoral and legislative systems. The United States has become a nation where money talks in politics, and efforts to control money have been difficult, if not impossible.

On the Record

The official judgment or holding of the Supreme Court in the Citizens United case, which reversed a district court finding, is as follows:

> The Freedom of the Speech Clause of the First Amendment to the United States Constitution prohibits the government from restricting independent political expenditures by a nonprofit organization. And the provision of the Bipartisan Campaign Reform Act prohibiting unions, corporations and not-for-profit organizations from broadcasting electioneering communications within 60 days of a general election or 30 days of a primary election violates the clause of the First Amendment to the United States Constitution. United States District Court for the District of Columbia reversed.

Source: Citizens United v. Federal Election Commission

DEBATES, DIFFERENCES, AND DIVISIONS

When Americans give money to candidates, either individually or through a corporate, union, or trade association, they are not doing so for altruistic or high-minded purposes. The name of the political game in Washington is access and with access comes the hope of influencing public policy. There is nothing innately wrong or illegal about using contributions to gain favor with candidates for political office or, more likely, incumbents seeking reelection. The First Amendment to the Constitution encourages petitioning government, which in this case does not mean signing a long letter but rather a check. The problem with campaign contributions is that most Americans do not have the resources to give money to candidates for public office, and if they do, it is usually a modest amount. The result is that most Americans are not likely to enjoy access to government officials and the prospect of influencing public policy because they cannot match the contributions of the major economic players in the Washington political process.

As evidence, the Federal Elections Commission published the list of the top campaign contributors in the 2016 presidential election. The list is a who's who of the major interest groups that seek access to the White House and members of Congress and certainly have the opportunity to make their case on specific public policy issues, which might sway votes in the favor of their organization and its membership. The donor list and the contributions are copied below (amounts are rounded off).

> Fahr LLC—$66 million
> Renaissance Technologies—$50 million
> Paloma Partners—$38 million
> Newsweb Corporation—$34 million
> Las Vegas Sands—$26 million
> Elliott Management—$24 million
> Carpenters and Joiners Union—$23 million
> Soros Fund—$23 million
> Priorities USA—$23 million
> National Educational Association—$21 million
>
> *Source*: Federal Elections Commission

Another way to look at campaign contributions is to examine individual donors. The Center for Responsive Politics, using Federal Election Commission data, published a list of those individual donors who gave $50,000 or more to federal candidates and parties during the 2016 presidential election cycle.

Top Five Trump Donors

Donald Trump—$56.1 million
Sheldon Adelson—$10.5 million
Bernard Marcus—$7.0 million
Linda McMahon—$6.2 million
Robert Mercer—$5.8 million

Top Five Clinton Donors

S. Donald Sussman—$21.8 million
JR and Mary Pritzker—$17.5 million
Haim and Cheryl Saban—$12.5 million
George Soros—$11.8 million
Fred Eychan—$10.9 million

Source: Center for Responsive Politics, www.openscrets.org/orgs/index.asp

A third way of looking at campaign financing of national elections is by examining various economic sectors and the total of their contributions during the 2016 election cycle.

Finance and Insurance—$912 million
Single Issue organizations—$411 million
Communications and Electronics—$254 million
Health Care and Pharmaceuticals—$222 million
Lawyers and Lobbyists—$198 million
Energy—$149 million
Labor—$142 million

Source: Federal Elections Commission

The above list of sector donors is a crosssection of finance, pharmaceuticals, energy, high tech, labor, and special interests that see their contributions as assisting their organizations in interactions with government over a range of legislative, regulatory, and public relations issues. In short, all of these economic sectors want something from government and see campaign contributions to key legislators or candidates running for the presidency as smart business practice. These contributions are within the law and the contributors are not seeking to "buy" a legislator or get ironclad assurance of a vote in their favor. What they want is access and influence, both of which can be achieved with campaign contributions. The only problem with these lists is that they are made up of powerful individuals and businesses, unions, and trade associations. The difficult democratic question can thus be asked, if the average American cannot play this campaign contribution game of politics, how can their interests be protected? How do everyday Americans, who can't afford major contributions, get access to government? What can everyday Americans do to influence government officials like the powerful groups and wealthy individuals?

Data Bank

The *National Journal,* using data from the Federal Elections Commission and the Center for Responsive Politics, documented the manner in which Barack Obama's campaign utilized some of his campaign donations. In their findings, the *National Journal* found that a huge chunk of the campaign funds went to advertising. Of the $736.9 million in expenditures by Obama's campaign, 65% went to advertising, especially television and radio airtime, digital marketing, and print advertising. Such expenditures provide a financial boon to those agencies and organizations that offer advertising services. For example, the advertising firm GMMB was paid $389.5 million by the Obama campaign; AD Data, a direct marketing consulting, made $29.8 million. Travel also provides a boon to vendors. United Airlines made $1.1. million during the campaign, and Holiday Inn earned $163,000. Finally, the pizza vendor Domino's made $9,300 in feeding staffers. In the 2016 presidential election cycle, Hillary Clinton spent $897 million and Donald Trump spent $429 million. Clinton spent the largest amount of her campaign funds on media buys—$30.3 million spent to Trump's $19.3 million. Trump spent $2.0 million on t-shirts, hats, and mugs—those emblazoned with the slogan "Make America Great Again."

Source: *National Journal,* "How Do Presidential Candidates Spend $1 Billion?" June 8, 2015

But if money can be described as the "mother's milk of American politics," then money can also be seen as "the root of all evil." Whether it is campaign contributions given by "fat cats" to candidates for public office in order to gain access to powerful leaders or "influence peddling" by shady lobbyists anxious to achieve an advantage for their clients in the halls of Congress or the executive establishment, money can have a corrupting effect on the political process. Although each case of public corruption is different, there are some common denominators about the corrupting effects of money and politics. It is safe to state that the longer a political party remains in power, the greater the chances are that money will have a corrupting effect and eventually lead to damaging scandal. Furthermore, the participants in the money scandal usually are individuals who have years of seniority and have risen to positions of power where their decisions and actions can impact the direction of a particular public policy. But what is most important is that, with every act of public corruption, the level of public trust takes a hit as the fears of the American people that political decisions can be influenced by spreading money around to willing members of Congress or the executive branch are born out to be true.

Take for example the corrupting effects of money and politics on Representative Randy "Duke" Cunningham of California. In 2005 Cunningham resigned from Congress after pleading guilty to charges that he received $2 million in bribes from defense contractors in his San Diego congressional district. Government prosecutors stated that Cunningham sold his home to a defense contractor for an inflated price and that he used the "profit" to purchase a Rolls Royce, a yacht, antiques, and other valuables that he used to decorate his $2.5 million mansion. After Cunningham pleaded guilty, federal prosecutor Carol Lam summed up the damage that was done to the American political system and to the faith in government officials that is the bedrock of a democratic society: "The citizens who elected Cunningham assumed that he would do his best for them. Instead, he did the worst thing an elected official can do—he enriched himself through his position and violated the trust of those who put him there."[11]

Of even larger proportions was the so-called Abramoff scandal of 2006, which had a damaging effect on the Republican leadership in the House of Representatives and most likely had an impact on their loss of control in the mid-term elections that year. Jack Abramoff was what is often termed in Washington as a super lobbyist: he had a long list of clients, access to the key players in government, and numerous success stories of influencing the policy process for those who pay for his services. Abramoff was the chief lobbyist for the Choctaw Indians who were seeking numerous federal permissions for their gaming and casino enterprises. Abramoff was placed under suspicion for favors that members of Congress and their staffs were provided so as to benefit the legislative agenda of the Choctaw Indians.[12]

Abramoff provided members of Congress and their staffs with football tickets, golf trips, vacations, and free meals at expensive restaurants, as well as campaign contributions, all in violation of federal laws regarding lobbying. Abramoff was indicted and, in a plea agreement with the federal prosecutor, he named names including Congressman Bob Ney of Ohio, who eventually resigned. House Majority leader Tom Delay was also indicted on unrelated charges, as were staff members who were found to have benefited from Abramoff's favors. By the time the scandal had run its course, up to 60 members of Congress and staff members were under a cloud of suspicion, including the Speaker of the House, Dennis Hastert. Many of these members of Congress survived the scandal, but they often returned the campaign contributions that came from Abramoff and apologized to their constituents.[13]

FYI

Congress has very specific regulations regarding gifts that members and their staffs may accept. The general provisions regarding the acceptance of gifts are as follows:

* A Member or employee of Congress may accept a gift only if it is unsolicited and the gift is valued at less than $50.
* Aggregate value of gifts from one source in a calendar year is less than $100, though no gifts with a value below $10 count toward the $100 annual limit.
* Gift cannot be cash or a cash equivalent (such as stocks and bonds). The only exceptions are gifts made by relatives as parts of an inheritance.
* Favors and benefits are not to be offered under circumstances that might be construed by reasonable persons as influencing the performance of their governmental duties.

Note: There are 23 exceptions to these General Provisions.

Source: US Congressional Budget Office

The growing role that money plays in election campaigns and the concerns over the influence of campaign contributions on policymaking in Washington and in state government has often caused critics to point to financing systems and practices in foreign countries. For example, in Great Britain, a political party running to control the House of Commons can spend only $29.7 million in a general election. Should individual party candidates relying on the general fund be found to have spent more than the amount allocated to them, they are disqualified from running for the seat. Furthermore, each candidate is given the same amount of airtime on television for free and is permitted to send out only one free election brochure to voters in the representative district. In Canada, the public financing laws are more relaxed but still severely limit expenditures. Candidates for seats in the House of Commons can spend only $8 million for the election campaign. Television and radio stations are required to provide some free airtime, and like the British campaign system, the Canadian electoral process takes weeks, not months or years. In 2004 total spending in the Canadian parliamentary elections was $212 million, considerably less than the billions spent in the US congressional elections.[14] Although the British and Canadian public financing of elections system may seem attractive and certainly cheaper, such systems do not appear to be supported in the United States. Polling data show that the American public is in no mood to move to a public financing system. A 2013 Gallup poll found that 50% of the American public supported public financing of elections with 44% opposed.[15]

While there are regular calls for the United States to move to a completely publicly financed system of elections at the federal level, there is research that shows that campaign contributions and the enormous cost of elections may not be harmful and not necessarily the breeding ground for corruption. University of Wisconsin professor John Coleman, an expert on money and politics, stated in a study that "campaign spending makes an important contribution to key aspects of democratic life, such as knowledge and accuracy about the candidates, and does not damage the public's trust or involvement." Furthermore, a study done by John Samples of the Cato Institute found that rather than sway voters with campaign contributions, politicians at all levels of government receive money from donors with the understanding that they share a common belief in a particular public policy or government initiative. Money and politics are certainly connected, and there are numerous examples of money being the source of corruption and unethical behavior on the part of public officials. But money and politics does not automatically create an unsavory atmosphere in the political arena that leads politicians to make policy decisions based on the amount of the contribution. Contributions, in effect, are used as a means of showing support and seeking that all-important opportunity to gain access to the politician to pitch an idea or advance a policy proposal through the labyrinth of the governing process.[16]

In many respects, politicians are captives of the money machine in that they grow weary of all the effort that goes into raising and spending mountains of cash, but at the same time recognize that placing stiff restrictions in the law or moving to a European-style public financing system might jeopardize their incumbency or completely overhaul the traditional method of using cash contributions as a means of influencing public policy. Many members of Congress and candidates for the presidency have complained openly in recent years about the amount of time they spend on the phone or at fundraisers begging for money from deep pocket "fat cats." Newly elected in 2006 as a Senator from Pennsylvania, Bob Casey commented on the grueling race for cash when he said, "I am sick and tired of fund-raising . . . when you sit in a room for four hours making calls, it kind of has a deadening effect on you. Anything that reduces the amount of time that you are spending fund-raising is good for the country, and it definitely is good for me."[17]

The comments of Senator Casey notwithstanding, when reform groups push for new campaign finance regulations, or when elected officials are publicly taken to task for receiving contributions from corporate, union, or any number of special interest groups, many Senators and members of the House continue to cast votes against legislation that would reduce the amount of time used for fundraising or place stiff limitations on expenditures. Instead, they push for free air time to get their message to the voters. Most members of Congress remain silent on the matter of campaign finance reform and continue to collect contributions from wealthy contributors or Political Action Committees. When they do make a public comment, they often say they are not beholden to these contributors or fall back on the First Amendment argument about free speech and the right of Americans to use their checkbook as a vehicle of political speech.

It is probably a safe bet that comprehensive campaign finance reform and publicly financed federal elections will not become a reality in American politics; there is just too much at stake, too much money involved, and too many people making a living off the billions currently spent to achieve meaningful reform. The 2016 campaign for the presidency was, to say the least, unusual in terms of the role of money and politics. Republican Jeb Bush, seeking to continue the family dynasty in the White House, raised over $100 million from deep-pocket donors but was never able to mount a viable campaign. Donors were quietly outraged that their contributions went to naught. On the other hand, Donald Trump spent relatively little on the campaign, relying instead on free media coverage and personal loans to his campaign. Trump, in a sense, created a new model of campaign financing by using public rallies to show support for his candidacy and then making controversial statements or personal attacks that created a news buzz, all for free. Because of the failure of Bush to become the front runner and the Republican establishment's disdain for Trump, major conservative donors such as Sheldon Adelson and the Koch Brothers held back on their contributions until after the convention and instead put their substantial financial resources into preserving the Republican majorities in the House and Senate.[18]

On the Democratic side, Hillary Clinton faced substantial criticism for raising money in the more traditional manner by seeking contributions from major donors, banks, corporations, and Super PACs. In particular, she was taken to task by her primary challenger Senator Bernie Sanders for accepting hundreds of thousands of dollars in speaking fees from major Wall Street firms such as Goldman Sachs, suggesting that she was beholden to the top financial institutions in the country that played a role in the near collapse of the American economy in 2009. Sanders, on the other hand, took a different tack as he relied on small donations from thousands of his supporters and throughout most of the campaign raised more money than Clinton, thus again upsetting the established method of connecting money to politics.[19]

Both the Trump and Sanders's strategies will certainly become important in future elections as they call into question whether private contributions are essential to running a campaign. Also, Super PACs continued to play a major role in television advertising as these groups, technically not connected to a particular candidate, ran endless ads touting either the positives of their candidate or relying on negative commentaries on the faults of those competing with their candidate. Television and Super Pacs were, in a real sense, made for each other as this tactic provided a visual image in support of a candidate without the candidate making a personal appeal or, for that matter, paying for the personal appeal.

It is important to stress that, despite the problems associated with the abuse of campaign contributions and influence peddling, the vast majority of members of Congress and candidates for office do not end up indicted by federal prosecutors or sent off to jail for their misdeeds. Most follow the rules established by the Federal Elections Commission and have strict internal monitoring processes to ensure compliance with those rules. But the real problem with the connection between money and politics in the United States is that the system, as presently constituted, is the breeding ground for public mistrust and public cynicism. The level of trust of national political leaders by the American public remains embarrassingly low as many citizens complain that, rather than solve nagging national problems, those leaders continue the hunt for dollars in a manner that casts doubt on whether they are voting in the national interest or to satisfy a special interest.[20] But it is important to remember that the billions spent on election campaigns in the United States is the price we pay for our democratic way of life. It would probably be better if the price was less and that it came without the excess baggage of scandal, but this is how we elect our leaders. Sadly, this model of money driving politics will undoubtedly continue to create issues of trust in the electoral process and our elected officials.[21]

The Great Debate

Because of the controversial Supreme Court decision in the Citizens United case, the debate continues over the wisdom of defining campaign contributions as a form of free speech protected by the First Amendment.

Debate Topic

Are campaign contributions a form of free speech protected by the First Amendment?

Critical Thinking Questions

1. Do you think that total public financing of federal campaigns is a violation of the First Amendment freedom of speech?
2. What do you see as the key reasons that public financing has not taken hold in the United States when it is found in many other industrialized countries?
3. Politicians say that campaign contributions do not influence their vote or performance in office. Is that a credible position?
4. How do we "clean up" American politics and lessen the influence of money and lobbyists with money?
5. Why is campaign finance reform so difficult to achieve in American politics?

Connections

The Federal Elections Commission is the financial watchdog of national elections. Visit its site at http://www/fec.gov

A non-partisan site that monitors campaign spending is www.FollowTheMoney.org

Common Cause is one of the most prominent public interest and reform groups active in the area of money and politics. See www.commoncause.org

The Center for Responsive Politics has a website called Open Secrets that examines campaign spending primarily at the national level. See www.opensecrets.org

The Clean Elections Institute is concerned with a range of issues related to elections, finance, and electoral reform. See www.azclean.org

A Few Books to Read

Corrado, Anthony, Thomas E. Mann, and Trevor Potter, *Inside the Campaign Finance Battle: Court Testimony on New Reforms* (Washington, DC: Brookings Institution Press, 2004).

La Raja, Raymond, *Small Change: Money, Political Parties and Campaign Finance Reform* (Ann Arbor, MI: University of Michigan Press, 2008).

Mutch, Robert, *Campaign Finance: What Everyone Needs to Know* (New York: Oxford University Press, 2016).

Smith, Melissa and Larry Powell, *Dark Money, Super PACs and the 2012 Election* (Lexington, MA: Lexington Publishers, 2014).

Smith, Rodney, *Money, Power and Elections: How Campaign Finance Reform Subverts American Democracy* (Baton Rouge, LA: LSU Press, 2014).

Notes

1. "Tracking the 2016 Presidential Money Race," *Bloomberg Politics*, December 9, 2016.
2. See the Center for Responsive Politics for data on election spending from 1998–2012, "The Money Behind the Elections," at the site www.opensecrets.org/bigpicture/
3. The Federal Elections Commission provides a description of recent campaign financing laws and regulations. See www.fec.gov/info/appfour.htm
4. *Buckley v. Valeo* 424 U.S. (1976).
5. See David Mutch, *Buying the Vote: A History of Campaign Finance Reform* (New York: Oxford University Press, 2014).
6. See Bipartisan Campaign Reform Act of 2002 at the Federal Election Commission site, www.fec.gov
7. Kate Zernike, "Kerry Pressing Swift Boat Case Long After Loss," *New York Times*, May 28, 2006, p. A1.
8. *Citizens United v. Federal Election Commission* 588 U.S. 310.
9. See Ellen L. Weintraub, "Taking On Citizens United," *New York Times*, March 30, 2016.
10. Daniel I. Weiner, "Citizens United Five Years Later," *Brennan Center for Justice*, January 15, 2015.
11. "Congressman Resigns After Bribery Plea," www.cnn.com/2005/POLITICS/11/28/cunningham
12. Susan Schmidt and James V. Grimaldi, "The Rise and Steep Fall of Jack Abramoff," *Washington Post*, December 29, 2005.

13. Gail Russell Chaddock, "How Far Will Abramoff Scandal Reach," *Christian Science Monitor*, June 5, 2006.
14. See David B. Mableby, Paul C. Light, and Christina Nemacheck Pearson, "Campaign Financing in Britain and Canada," in *Government By the People*, 16th edition (2013).
15. Lydia Saad, "Half of U.S. Support Publicly Financed Federal Campaigns," *Gallup*, June 24, 2013.
16. John Coleman, "Comments for Public Election Funding Conference," University of Wisconsin, January 28–29, 2006.
17. See John Samples, *The Fallacy of Campaign Finance Reform* (Chicago: University of Chicago Press, 2006).
18. David Kirkpatrick, "Senate Measures Puts Spotlight on Fund-Raising," *New York Times*, January 20, 2007.
19. See Jim O'Sullivan, "Money's Influence Not a Given: Mountains of Super PAC Cash Have Not Exactly Paid Off," *Boston Globe*, March 24, 2016. See also "The Biggest, Most Influential Political Donors on the 2015 Forbes 400," *Forbes*, September 30, 2015.
20. See https://www.opensecrets.org/politicians/summary/
21. See Jeff Milyo, "Do State Campaign Finance Reforms Increase Trust and Confidence in State Government," presented at the Midwest Political Association, Chicago, April 2012.

RELIGION **AND** POLITICS

Issue Focus

It is often said that people should not talk about two topics—politics and religion. However, in today's political climate, politics and religion are not only becoming topics of everyday conversation but also creating contentious national debates about the proper relationship between the two. Politics and religion have fused into a powerful mix that has a major impact on the governing process. Supporters from many faiths seek to bring their views on moral issues into the political arena and influence policy decisions on difficult issues from abortion to gay marriage. Those who define themselves as more secular than religious seek to limit the influence of religion on politics and policy decisions. As a result, politics and religion are engaged in a difficult battle of ideas and beliefs that has divided the United States.

Chapter Objectives

This issue chapter will seek to:
1. Explore the tension between those who want a strict separation of church and state and those who want to foster a closer link between religion and governing.
2. Describe the points of controversy over the role of religion in public life.
3. Discuss the current developments in church-state relations and the prospects for defusing the tensions.

SOME BACKGROUND

The United States is a nation steeped in religion and religious beliefs, a condition of national life that brings both a sense of common values and the prospect of deep political divisions. While many European countries are moving further and further away from mixing religion and politics to establish a firmly grounded secular society, the United States is moving in the opposite direction as religion and religious beliefs are becoming defining characteristics of our way of life and of our politics. In a Pew Research poll in 2014, 89% of adult Americans polled said that they have a belief in God, a huge level of support but a slight decline from a high of 92% in 2007.[1] Nevertheless, a small decline in belief in a supreme being is much more significant when compared to Europe where only 60% of the French, British, and Germans have such a belief. But the strong belief factor present among Americans is only part of the picture of a uniquely religious country. A recent poll from the Pew Forum on Religion and Public Life found that 72% of those Americans polled agreed with the statement, "The president should have strong religious beliefs" and 51% said that "churches should express views on political matters."[2] Perhaps most relevant to the status of religious belief in the United States is a study done by the website Crux in 2014 that showed that 21% of Americans surveyed have no religious preference, a record high; moreover, Millennials are increasingly showing little interest in organized religion as under 35% declare themselves as having expressed no religious attachment. Also in the study, the number of Americans who defined themselves as atheists increased from 5% to 9%.[3]

The relationship between religion and politics has a long history in the United States. The first immigrants to this country, the Pilgrims, left England to escape religious persecution, thus establishing toleration of religious beliefs as one of the founding principles of this new land. Furthermore, many of the Founders and societal leaders at the time of independence and the formation of the constitution were deeply religious individuals. For example, the opening and closing lines of the Declaration of the Independence refer to the "Creator" and "Divine Providence." The traditions of religious toleration and religious belief were joined in the First Amendment, which directed Congress to "make no law respecting the establishment of religion, or prohibiting the free exercise thereof." But at the core of the relationship between religion and politics is the position taken by Thomas Jefferson who advocated for a "wall of separation" between religion and the state as he feared that religious influence would be a divisive force in the formation and implementation of public policy decisions. It is important to point out that despite the strong religious beliefs held by many of the early Founders of this country, nowhere in the Constitution is the word God mentioned. When asked at the time why God and religion were not included in the Constitution, Alexander Hamilton answered that the matter of religion "never came up."[4]

Since those early days, religion has played a part in many of the social and political battles for change such as the push for women's suffrage and the civil rights movement. Moreover, this country has seen our presidents take the oath of office ending with "So help me God" and finish their State of the Union address by saying "God Bless the United States of America." Many presidents have often invoked the name of God during wartime as a means of rallying public support and providing a dose of heavenly legitimacy on a controversial policy decision. George W. Bush, in his speech to Congress after 9/11, for example, stated, "Freedom and fear, justice and cruelty, have always been at war; and we know that God is not neutral between them." After the arrest of Saddam Hussein, President Bush again invoked God when he said, "freedom is the Almighty God's gift to every person, every man and woman who lives in this world. That's what I believe. And the arrest of Saddam Hussein changed the equation in Iraq. Justice was being delivered to a man who defied that gift from the Almighty to the people of Iraq."[5] President Barack Obama, whose religious affiliation and support for religious belief was regularly under attack (some conservatives maintained that the president was a Muslim not a Christian), did express his deep religious conviction and his reliance on prayer during difficult times.[6] As he said at one point in his presidency, "My faith is a great source of comfort to me. I've said before that my faith has grown as president. This office tends to make a person pray more; and as President Lincoln once said, 'I have been driven to my knees many times by the overwhelming conviction that I had no place to go.'" As for President Donald Trump, his religious affiliation is defined as Presbyterian, although there hasn't been much evidence of a strong commitment to religious beliefs or practice.[7]

Despite the fact that organized religion and God are embedded in our culture and our governing values and system, clarifying the exact boundaries between religion and the state have been the subject of numerous constitutional challenges and legislative debates. Although the First Amendment would seem to clearly state that Congress could not establish an official religion or prohibit the free exercise of religious belief, the Supreme Court has been called upon to interpret the meaning of the "establishment" clause and "the free exercise "clause as they relate to issues such as saluting the American flag, providing public financial assistance to religious schools, conscientious objection to military service, the role of religion in the workplace, and the protection of religious practices.

In many of these landmark cases, the rights of minority religious groups have been the focus of the constitutional challenges as these groups advocated to practice their faith, which in most cases were untraditional and not in the mainstream of American life. For example, the court found that the children of Jehovah's Witnesses should be not be forced to salute the flag during classroom exercises, thereby upholding their view that adoring images not of their God was a violation of their faith. The court also overturned a Wisconsin law that required children to attend school up to age sixteen, which was a violation of the Amish people's practice of not allowing their children to attend school beyond the eighth grade. Finally, the court permitted a small Cuban-American religious group to engage in animal sacrifice as part of their religious ceremonies, despite local health and safety rules in Florida. The decisions rendered in these cases proved that the justices in the Supreme Court viewed the "free exercise" clause of the First Amendment as immutable, despite the unique circumstances involved in the cases.[8]

However, there have been areas of interpretation of the First Amendment freedom of religion where the court has placed a wall of separation between church and state such as in attempts by various religious organizations to use public funding for a church-related school, or curtailing the practice of erecting nativity scenes on public property during the Christmas season, or prohibiting morning prayer in public schools where "God" was referred to in the state-sanctioned prayer. Although, in the last twenty years, challenges to the meaning and application of the First Amendment freedom of religion have declined significantly, that has not meant the issue has disappeared in regards to exactly how the walls of separation between church and state should be constructed or whether there should be breeches in that wall in order to permit religion to play a larger role in national politics and governmental decision-making.

In fact, in 2007, there was a highly publicized challenge to the saying of the Pledge of Allegiance in California as an atheist father, on behalf of his daughter, challenged the pledge as a violation of religious freedom and separation of church and state because it includes "under God." He eventually lost the legal challenge, but his suit reminded Americans that the tension between religion and politics continues.[9]

Prayers and religious symbols before football games, especially in the South, also created controversy. One school system in Fort Ogelthorpe, Georgia, banned high school cheerleaders from painting banners with biblical sayings on them that the players would then run through at the start of the game. The decision caused such an uproar among the townspeople that parents and fans in the stands started to bring posters with biblical sayings on them in protest. Also in the area of religious symbols, former Fox News commentator Bill O'Reilly started a campaign to stop what he called the "assault on Christmas." O'Reilly and other conservatives were upset when public officials changed some of the language of the Christmas season by calling the Christmas tree a "holiday tree," using the greeting "Happy Holidays" rather than "Merry Christmas," and castigating school districts that did not permit religious Christmas carols from being sung or other displays of Christian-based practices of the season.[10]

The connection between religion and politics is not just restricted to constitutional interpretations of the First Amendment. Rather, religion plays an important role in the self-definition of the American people, which carries over into political self-definition and electoral participation. In terms of general religious categories, Protestants currently make up 51% of Americans who self-identify their religious affiliation. Among Protestants, Baptists are the largest denomination, and they are based largely in the South and Midwest. Increasingly, the mainline Protestant organizations such as the Methodists, Presbyterians, Congregationalists, and Episcopalians are in a period of membership decline, but evangelical groups like the Baptists are expanding dramatically and becoming more visible and politically active. Catholics, who make up about 25% of the nation's religious population, are found in major industrial cities in the Northeast and Midwest and in western border states where Hispanics are dominant. Jewish people, who make up a small but influential religious group, are concentrated in eastern cities such as New York and in certain regions of Florida. Mormons, the fastest growing religious denomination in the United States, dominates the population of Utah, and they are spreading their influence to other western states. Finally, there are an estimated three million Americans of the Muslim faith in a number of communities such as Dearborn, Michigan, and Minneapolis-St. Paul, Minnesota.[11]

The presence of these religious groups in various locations and regions in the United States also carries over into the political arena as religious identity is linked to political identity and eventually to political activity. Baptists and other evangelical groups are solidly Republican and provide a strong base of support for the Republican Party; Catholics have historically been steadfast in their support of the Democratic Party, but their alliance with that party may be changing. Jews, however, identify and vote consistently Democrat, while

Mormons, like the Baptists, have deep ties to the Republican camp. It is important to point out that these religious affiliations and their connection to political
parties are not etched in stone but are tendencies that can and do change over
time. For many years after the Depression of the 1930s, southern white Protestants voted consistently for the Democratic Party, only to shift allegiance
to the Republican Party when Ronald Reagan ran for the presidency because
of dissatisfaction with the liberal views of the Democratic Party. In the 2004
presidential election, George W. Bush surprised many by receiving a majority
of the Catholic vote, even though John Kerry was a practicing Catholic and
Catholics had for years been major supporters of Democratic candidates. In
the 2008 and 2012 presidential elections, Barack Obama gained voter support
from Hispanic Catholics while white Catholics moved increasingly over to the
Republican Party in large part due to Obama's position on abortion and his
support for stem cell research using fetal tissue.[12]

Because the religious affiliation of Americans is not isolated in churches
around the country but spreads out into the political arena, politicians,
whether in office or seeking office, cannot ignore the evangelical vote, or Catholic policy positions, or Jewish views. Because there exist cracks in Jefferson's
walls of separation, it is impossible to examine the electoral and government
processes without considering the influence that organized religions and religious believers may have on election and policy outcomes. More importantly,
the cracks in the walls of separation appear to be widening as churches and
members of churches see the need to bring their beliefs into the political arena,
whether it is endorsing candidates for office, asking members to sign petitions
or attend rallies, or placing pressure on public officials to support specific
policy positions that are part of their religious agenda. Churches and church
members have become major players in American politics and no longer see
their role as only quiet communion with their God.

On the Record

In a letter to the Danbury Connecticut Baptist Association in 1802, Thomas
Jefferson said the following:

> I contemplate with sovereign reverence that act of the whole Ameri-
> can people which declared that their legislature should 'make no law
> respecting an establishment of religion, or prohibiting the free exercise
> thereof' thus building a wall of separation between Church and State.

DEBATES, DIFFERENCES, AND DIVISIONS

The contemporary tension between religion and politics developed with the
Roe v. Wade decision legalizing abortion and the strong response, largely from
the Catholic Church. Church leaders from the Pope to the American cardinals

to the parish priests sought to challenge the decision with a range of lobbying efforts, demonstrations, and pleas to the faithful at Mass. Each year on January 22nd, the anniversary of the Roe decision, Catholic dioceses in the United States stage rallies and marches to show their unwavering opposition to abortion on demand. Right to Life organizations with strong Catholic influence and funding have been formed throughout the country, and although prohibited from endorsing specific candidates, pastors sometimes use the pulpit to remind parishioners of their responsibilities as members of the church to fight abortion and those who support abortion, even to the point of questioning the right of Catholic legislators and executives to remain in the Church while publicly supporting abortion rights. In recent years Catholic Church leaders have expanded their political agenda to include opposition to gay marriage as they support laws in many states that limit marriage to a union between a man and a woman. While public opinion polls show that Catholics are not unified in their opposition to either abortion or to gay marriage, there has been sufficient support for the church position that Democratic incumbents and candidates (who for the most part support both issues) cannot ignore.

The intersection of religion and politics was most pronounced, however, during the administration of George W. Bush. As a born-again Christian, President Bush developed a close alliance with the evangelical movement and relied on its support not only to win two elections but also to support various policy initiatives and values-based positions. Early in his first administration, President Bush established the Office of Faith-Based Initiatives, which was charged with encouraging churches and other religious organizations to work with government agencies to address a range of social ills and societal concerns. President Bush felt strongly that accenting the role of people of faith in responding to poverty, homelessness, hunger, and family dysfunction would be more effective and successful than dealing with these problems through a large and impersonal federal bureaucracy. Critics of the initiative stated that they feared funneling federal dollars into faith-based groups would be a violation of the separation of church and state doctrine and be merely a new way of interjecting religion into the policy sphere. The establishment of the White House Office of Faith-Based Initiatives was followed in 2004 with the formation in Congress of a "faith-based caucus" made up largely of Republicans who openly stated that their objective was to make it easier for federal money to reach church groups and other religious organizations in order to respond to social welfare needs.[13]

FYI

When it comes to the intersection of religion and politics, Pope Francis cannot be ignored; in fact, his strong defense of migrants and their settlement in wealthy countries, his open acceptance of global warming and its effects

(continued)

FYI   (continued)

on humankind, and his outspoken condemnation of income inequality have endeared him to the poor, the environmental movement, and progressives active in creating a more equitable minimum wage regime and other policies to close the income gap. Pope Francis incurred the wrath of Donald Trump over the pledge to build a wall between Mexico and the United States; the Pope made a well-publicized trip to the border with Mexico and talked about building bridges rather than a wall. The Democratic candidate for the presidency Bernie Sanders made a hastily arranged trip to the Vatican before the key New York primary in April 2016, in what many pundits felt was a tactical maneuver to capture the Catholic vote in a key delegate-rich state. Despite his positions on social justice issues, the Pope continued to oppose same-sex marriage and contraception and berated the culture of extravagant consumerism and hedonistic lifestyles often portrayed in the press and movies. He also created news when, in November 2016, he authorized that priests can forgive women who have had an abortion.

Source: Various news service reports

President Bush's strong religious beliefs and his close ties to the evangelical movement led to stinging criticism of his war policies in Iraq and his views toward the Islamic world. President Bush was heavily criticized early on in his post–9/11 speeches when he talked about a "crusade" to liberate Afghanistan and those countries in the Middle East that were controlled by authoritarian governments. The use of the word "crusade" brought back images in the Middle East of the religious wars of Catholic Europe in the 8th and 9th centuries to regain the Holy Land. Also many of the president's public pronouncements were analyzed by his liberal critics to find a pattern of religious zealotry. David Domke, writing for the *Seattle Post Intelligencer*, compiled a study of Bush statements and found that many of the statements were filled with religiously associated terms such as presenting policy options as "good vs. evil" or as "a calling," linking God to concepts of freedom and liberty, and numerous suggestions that God was on our side. Bush, along with his religious allies such as Attorney General John Ashcroft (who started each day with a prayer group in his office), Kansas senator Sam Brownback (a Catholic conservative who started his campaign speeches with the call "All for Jesus, All for Jesus, All for Jesus"), and former House majority leader Tom Delay (who once said, "The enemies of virtue may be on the march, but they have not won, and if we put out trust in Christ, they never will.") faced criticism by some as efforts to move the United States to a theocratic-state where religion and religious values play a prominent role in government decision-making.[14]

The growing involvement of religion in public life is in large part a response to what many evangelicals and other mainline religious leaders feel is the secularization of American society and the formation of policy decisions without concern for religious principles and traditional moral practices. With growing evidence that a number of Americans have "no religious preference," the potential to impact the secularization of American society and ultimately American politics is significant. The increase in secularism among the 18–25-year-old group (where 20% described themselves as having "no religious preference") is especially important. This rise in secularism has benefited the Democratic Party, which has seen its support among those who define themselves as not church-goers increased from 55% in 2002 to 67% in 2006. Democratic candidates are reluctant to stress that a solid portion of their voter support comes from the "no preference" group since they seek to make inroads among churchgoers and attract some of the evangelical vote. But it is clear that the secularization of American politics has benefited the Democratic Party.[15]

Conservative Republicans are constantly emphasizing that the connection between seculars and the Democratic Party is dangerous for American society and will eventually lead to a weakening of our traditional values. The code term for the religious fight against secularization is the need to embrace "family values," which often translates into opposition against abortion, gay marriage, and homosexuality in general, and what is viewed as the despoiling of our popular culture in movies, music, the Internet, and the behavior of celebrities. Conservative church leaders, particularly the evangelical preachers, along with family values advocates, have stated openly that it is essential that religious principles and religious values become part of the political debate and that established rights, such as in the case of abortion and homosexuality, that run counter to those principles and values be revoked. The religious agenda thus includes overturning the Roe v. Wade abortion decision, stopping any efforts to sanction gay marriage, and limiting, if not ending, school curriculums that emphasize evolution over the biblical interpretation of creation.[16]

Although the Democrats are ambivalent about support from seculars and seek to remake their image as committed churchgoers, the evangelicals pose their own problems for the Republican Party. Republican party leaders are afraid that the support of evangelicals may be viewed by mainstream church members and voters in general as a sign that the party has been captured by narrow-minded religious conservatives who advocate a policy agenda that would be unattractive to the majority of the American electorate and paint the GOP as being pushed off the center of the political spectrum. In the 2008 Republican primaries, for example, the candidacy of former Arkansas governor Mike Huckabee, an ordained Baptist Minister who does not believe in evolution, was popular among evangelicals, which led to a series of primary victories in southern states. But Republican leaders quietly worried that a Huckabee candidacy would send the wrong message to the American voters and create the impression that the Republicans had become the party solely of the evangelical right.[17]

Dissension also arose within the Christian right movement over whether it should stick with its family values agenda or extend its message to include issues that it heretofore had not been interested in such as global warming and efforts to reduce poverty. In 2007 the National Association of Evangelicals criticized leaders of the Christian right who had called for the firing of its Washington policy director, Rev. Richard Cizik, for his involvement in efforts to address global warming. Two prominent leaders of the Christian right, James Dobson of the Focus on Family organization and Tony Perkins, President of the Family Research Council, demanded the resignation of Cizik for "using the global warming controversy to shift the emphasis away from the great moral issues of our time." Cizik was defended by many leaders in the National Association of Evangelicals, including the Reverend Paul de Vries, the president of the New York Divinity School, who said that "I am as much against abortion as Jim Dobson, but I want that baby to live in a healthful environment, inside the womb as outside the womb."[18]

The dispute within the evangelical movement over holding true to the family values agenda or expanding to an environmental and economic agenda points to the fluid nature of how religion impacts national politics. Evangelical leaders such as Cizik, de Vries, and the mega church minister Rick Warren, who wrote the national bestseller *The Purpose Driven Life*, recognize that, if their movement is to increase its membership and have an influence on public policy debates, it must not be perceived as rigid, mean-spirited, and out of the mainstream of the key issues facing most Americans. The new group of evangelicals is keenly aware that young evangelicals and young people in general have shown that their priorities are not just family values driven, but more global and economic in nature. Moreover, nationally conservative positions on abortion, gay marriage, and the teaching of evolution are not resonating with the American public as are issues such as global warming and the growing economic gap between the rich and the poor. The positions thus taken by Cizik, de Vries, and Warren are being embraced by an increasing number of Republican activists and leaders who see their influence not only expanding the base of the evangelicals but making the evangelical movement more mainstream.[19]

Data Bank

According to exit polls reported by the Pew Research Center linking religious affiliation with voting for Donald Trump or Hillary Clinton, the following results show the role of religion in the 2016 election.

	Trump	Clinton
Protestant (all)	58%	39%
Catholic (all)	52%	45%
White, Non-Hispanic Catholic	60%	37%
Hispanic Catholic	26%	67%
Jewish	24%	71%

Other religion	29%	62%
Secular	26%	68%
White evangelical/born again	81%	16%
Mormon	61%	25%

Source: The Pew Research Center, "How the Faithful Voted," November 9, 2016

In the 2008 presidential election, the connection between religion and politics played a major role, particularly in the campaign contests on the Republican side. The early leader, Mitt Romney (the former governor of Massachusetts), was questioned repeatedly about his Mormon faith and his allegiance to the government over his faith. In a manner much like John Kennedy, who in the 1960 campaign responded to questions about his allegiance to the Vatican over the constitution, Romney pledged that his personal religious beliefs would not influence his public decisions. Nevertheless, Romney had a difficult time with many evangelicals, who viewed Mormonism as not a Christian religion and therefore were suspicious of his candidacy. When Romney dropped out of the race, Mike Huckabee took up the standard of the evangelicals at the expense of a surging John McCain, who was viewed by many conservative religious Republicans as not only too moderate in terms of his policy positions but not closely tied to the religious right. When McCain eventually won the Republican nomination, he sought to mend fences with the evangelical movement by accepting the endorsement of religious leaders such as Texas pastor John Hagee, a prominent member of the religious right.[20]

On the Democratic side, the issue centered around Barack Obama's Muslim roots (his father was an African Muslim, and Obama attended Muslim schools as a young boy). Although Obama had for years been a member of a black Protestant Church in Chicago and defined himself as a Christian, there remained a residue of concern among some voters that he was not in the mainstream of American religious life. Conservative critics such as Ann Coulter, Sean Hannity, and Rush Limbaugh repeatedly mentioned that Obama's middle name was Hussein, sending a not-too-subtle signal that the African-American candidate for president was perhaps a closet Muslim.

Once elected, Obama entered a maelstrom of controversy when he accepted an invitation to speak at Notre Dame University and receive an honorary degree. Conservative Catholics launched a vigorous nation-wide campaign to stop the Catholic university from giving the degree to a president who was pro-choice. Obama did attend the graduation ceremony and sought to sooth the opposition by talking about finding common ground and keeping open minds and open hearts. Obama talked about the influence of the Catholic Church on his community activism and the importance of the Catholic Church in the civil rights movement. However, despite the attempt at lowering the voices of opposition, the Catholic right and their bishops were energized to fight on against the pro-choice position of the president.[21]

President Obama faced new levels of criticism from Catholic Church leaders and from other denominations over portions of the Affordable Care Act, which offered free contraceptives as part of health care plans available to the uninsured. This support for open access to contraceptives opened the door for a wave of legal challenges by conservative religious groups and religious leaders. In a landmark case, Burwell v. Hobby Lobby, the Supreme Court by a 5–4 margin agreed that a for-profit, family-owned company, in this case the national craft chain Hobby Lobby, cannot lose or have their religious beliefs taken away or compromised by an act of government. As characterized by Lori Windham, a counsel for the owners of Hobby Lobby (the Green family), "The Supreme Court recognized that Americans do not lose their religious freedom when they run a family business." Also, as Justice Kennedy, writing for the majority stated, "Among the reasons the United States is so open, so tolerant, and so free is that no person may be restricted or demeaned by government in exercising his or her religion." The Hobby Lobby decision was seen by main constitutional experts as opening up the floodgates of challenges to government policies that are viewed as conflicting with personal religious beliefs.[22]

Those floodgates did indeed open up as those opposed to the Affordable Care Act and its support for providing insurance coverage for contraception and other drugs that could cause sterilization and abortion-inducing conditions took their views to the courts. This time the plaintiffs were the Little Sisters of the Poor in Washington, D.C., a non-profit religious group, not a for-profit company like Hobby Lobby. Although the Obama administration sought to "accommodate" the Little Sisters (by allowing them to sign a waiver that would exempt the sisters from participation in the plan) the Catholic nuns refused to abide by the "contraception mandate" that would cover their employees and those under their care, citing the fact that signing such a waiver would still make them complicit in this process of providing contraception. The sisters instead moved to have their case heard by the Supreme Court and had their day in court in March 2016. In May 2016, the Supreme Court sent the Little Sisters case back to a lower court and didn't rule on the merits of the case. But court experts agreed that by sending the case back to the lower court the Supreme Court showed a proclivity to endorse the sisters' position on contraception and their challenge to the regulations put in place by Obama's Affordable Care Act.[23]

With the Hobby Lobby victory and the case of the Little Sisters of the Poor settled in a way that supported their position, conservatives are growing more confident that they can advance a religious agenda into the policy arena whether it be anti-gay measures, pro-life legislation, opposition to the teaching of evolution and textbook choices that espouse evolution, and the general despoiling of popular culture in movies, music, the Internet, and the behavior of celebrities.

During the 2016 presidential election, religion played a key role, especially among evangelicals. Texas Senator Ted Cruz made no effort to hide his strong evangelical beliefs to the point where he often quoted Bible scripture and brought his strong religious beliefs into the public policy arena. Cruz was also joined by Mike Huckabee and Ben Carson in promoting religious values and policies, especially in the area of abortion. As for Hillary Clinton and Bernie Sanders, they rarely brought religion into their campaigns. Both Clinton and Sanders were vying for the votes of secular progressives and the millennial generation who show a diminishing interest in linking politics and religion.

After Donald Trump emerged as the nominee of the Republican Party, the religion and politics linkage focused on the billionaire's behavior toward women and split the evangelical movement into two camps. Some evangelical leaders such as Jim Wallis criticized Trump for his misogynistic comments about women and a tape that emerged showing Trump using vile language to describe his sexual approach to some women, especially celebrities. Wallis and other evangelical preachers reminded their faithful about the obligation to hold to their family values and not support a candidate who talked so offensively about women. Other evangelical leaders, such as Franklin Graham, praised Trump because of his stand against abortion and his pledge to clean up the corruption in Washington, as evidenced by the charges leveled against Hillary Clinton. Eventually, the evangelical vote broke for Trump as his conservative, pro-market promises won over the religious right.[24]

With Trump in the White House and a Republican majority in both the House and the Senate, liberals worried that the choice of Neil Gorsuch as a replacement for Justice Scalia would likely support a rejection of Roe v. Wade and advance the religious freedom position that many on the left believe is discriminatory to minorities and women. It is clear that the election of Donald Trump will usher in a period in which religion and religious beliefs will have a marked impact on the separation of church and state and bring religion further into the policy process of government. For example, Trump's cabinet picks for Secretary of Housing and Urban Development, Dr. Ben Carson, and Secretary of Education Betsy DeVos are openly supportive of bringing their religious views into the governing arena.

Despite Mr. Jefferson's belief in the importance of maintaining that wall of separation between church and state, it is now a reality of American politics that religion and religious organizations are firmly involved in national political debates and seek to influence national policy. Because Americans remain a nation of believers and churchgoers, it was inevitable that the role of religion in politics would move beyond the proclamation of "In God We Trust" on our currency to a more critical involvement in the governing process. The leadership and membership of major religious denominations in this country are now so well organized and so politically focused that it will be difficult to go back to a time when religion was a purely private matter and Americans saw religion as having little if any relationship to government decision-making.

But in all this discussion of the role of religion in the political realm there seems to be an emerging consensus about how to properly balance these two powerful forces. Andrew Sullivan, one of the leading conservative thinkers in the United States and a frequent critic of the religious right, states that what is important in the political process is to move beyond religious values to what is morally correct. As he states, "The essential civic discipline in a pluralist democracy is to translate your religious convictions into moral arguments— arguments that can persuade and engage people of all faiths or none."[25] What Sullivan is saying is that public policy should be guided by shared principles and values that are deeply held in our American culture. Religion and religious organizations can help policymakers move toward those shared principles and values; in fact, they have a responsibility to help them move toward those shared principles and values. But there is a difference between showing the way and interfering in the policy process by setting out a forceful agenda, demanding compliance with that agenda, and then entering the political fray to achieve those objectives in a manner that is designed to move this country toward a theocracy. Sullivan and others like him are saying that it is the constitution that should guides us as we make public decisions, not the Bible or the Book of Mormon or the Q'uran.

It will be important for the future of American politics to see to what extent religion and religious organizations strike a balance between making demands and just guiding political leaders toward shared principles and values as they make decisions. The American political system has always worked best when it has been based on compromise, consensus, and cooperation, and when policy prescriptions were developed and approved that were moderate, centrist, and backed by the majority of public opinion. Breeching Jefferson's walls of separation occasionally when the national interest merits it may be a positive development, but tearing down the wall in order to remake the country along religious lines would clearly violate the intent of the Founders and the political traditions that have guided this nation since its inception.

The Great Debate

The development of a strong religious component in American politics has increasingly created a national culture that accents the importance of infusing government decisions and policies with religious values and principles in ways that are at odds with the separation of church and state doctrine advocated by Thomas Jefferson. In such a national culture, could we be headed for a national religion, or at least, a publicly established limitation on certain religions?

Debate Topic

Should there be a strict separation of church and state in the United States or should public policy be guided by religious-based values and principles?

Critical Thinking Questions

1. Do you believe that religious leaders are involving themselves too much in matters of politics and public policy?
2. Do religious leaders have a moral obligation to speak out on controversial policy issues, even if that means taking partisan political positions and supporting specific candidates?
3. What dangers, if any, does partisan political activity by religious leaders pose to our democratic political system?
4. In today's political arena, how would you set the proper balance between church and state?
5. When political leaders face a conflict between their personal religious beliefs and a Supreme Court decision that runs against those beliefs, how should they respond?

Connections

A useful blog that presents a wide range of views on religion in American life is US Religion. See http://usreligion.blogspot.com

The Pew Forum has regular studies on the role of religion in American life and politics under the general title of Religious Landscape. See http://pewforum.org/religion-america/

A scholarly website that addresses religion in American society is the American Academy of Religions. See www.aarweb.org

The Christian Coalition, perhaps the most influential evangelical organization in the United States, provides a comprehensive examination of its positions toward political issues. See www.cc.org

The United States Conference of Catholic Bishops is the primary source of Catholic Church positions on politics and public policy. Visit its site at www.usccb.org

A Few Books to Read

Corrigan, John and Winthrop Hudson, *Religion in America*, 8th edition (London: Routledge, 2010).

Duncan, Ann W. and Steven Jones, eds., *Church-State Issues in America Today* (Westport, CT: Praeger, 2007).

Haidt, Jonathan, *The Righteous Mind: Why Good People Are Divided By Politics and Religion* (New York: Vintage, 2012).

Meacham, Jon, *American Gospel: God, the Founding Fathers and the Making of a Nation* (New York: Random House, 2007).

Wilcox, Clyde and Carin Larson, *Onward Christian Soldiers: The Religious Right in American Politics* (Boulder, CO: Westview Press, 2006).

Notes

1. Frank Newport, "Americans' Views Related to Religiousness, Age, Education," *Gallup Poll*, June 2, 2014.
2. Michael Lipka, "Americans Are Somewhat More Open to the Idea of an Atheist President," Pew Research Center, May 29, 2014.
3. Emily Swanson, "General Social Survey," *Crux*, March 23, 2015.
4. See Martin Marty, "Religion and the Constitution: The Triumph of Practical Politics," *The Christian Century*, March 23, 1994.
5. www.whitehouse.gov/news/releases/2001/09/200109208.html
6. Jennifer Agiesta, "Misconceptions Persist About Obama's Faith, But Aren't So Widespread," *CNN Politics*, September 14, 2015.
7. John Fea, "The Echoes of Abraham Lincoln in President Obama's Prayer Breakfast Speech," Religious New Service, February 11, 2015.
8. For a list of key cases related to religious freedom see "Religious Liberty: Landmark Supreme Court Cases," Bill of Rights Institute, 1998, www.billofrightsinstitute.org
9. *Elkgrove Unified School District v. Newdow* 542 U.S. 1 (2004).
10. See Catherin Taibi, "Bill O'Reilly Launches First Counter-Offensive in the 'War on Christmas,'" *Huffington Post*, December 14, 2014.
11. "America's Changing Religious Landscape," Pew Research Center—Religious and Public Life, May 12, 2015.
12. "How the Faithful Voted: 2012 Preliminary Analysis," Pew Research Center—Religion and Public Life, November 7, 2012.
13. David Domke, "Bush Weds Religion, Politics to Form World View," *Seattle Post Intelligencer*, August 22, 2004.
14. Ross Douthat, "Crisis of Faith," *The Atlantic*, July 2007, www.theatlantic.com/doc/200707/religion. See also "Brand Disloyalty," *The Economist*, March 1, 2008, pp. 34–35.
15. Michael Lipka, "U.S. Religious Groups and Their Political Leanings," Pew Research Center, February 23, 2016. See also Douglas Main, "Study: America Becoming Less Christian, More Secular," *Newsweek*, May 12, 2015.
16. Ibid., Michael Lipka, op. cit.
17. Andrew Sullivan, "The Right and Religion," *The Atlantic*, December 14, 2007.
18. Laurie Goldstein, "Evangelical Group Rebuffs Critics on the Right," *New York Times*, March 14, 2007.
19. Rick Warren, *The Purpose Driven Life* (New York: Zondervan, Harper Collins Christian, 2002).
20. Andrew Sullivan, op. cit. See also E.J. Dionne, "Souled Out: Reclaiming Faith and Politics After the Religious Right," *Washington Post*, January 22, 2008.
21. See "Transcript: Obama's Notre Dame Speech," *Chicago Tribune*, May 17, 2009.
22. See "Supreme Court Rules in Favor of Hobby Lobby," 2014, http://hobbylobbycase.com/the-case-/the-decision
23. Ashley McGuire, "Obama's War on the Little Sisters of the Poor," Real Clear Politics, November 11, 2016. See www.realclearpolitics.com/articles/2015/11/11/
24. Laurie Goodstein, "Religious Right Believes Donald Trump Will Deliver on His Promises," *New York Times*, November 11, 2016.
25. See Andrew Sullivan, *The Conservative Soul* (New York: Harper Perennial, 2007).

16
SCIENCE AND POLITICS

Issue Focus

Just like religion, many Americans do not normally like to mix science with politics. Yet it is clear that science and politics are connected, particularly as science influences a wide range of public policy issues such as global warming, stem cell research, and evolution. Moreover, much of scientific research in the United States is supported through government appropriations. Congress funds huge scientific institutions such as the National Institutes of Health and the National Aeronautics and Space Administration, which face regular oversight by committees to ensure compliance with the law. However, as with many of the issues, and the fact that scientific inquiry and scientific problem-solving lead to conclusions or recommendations that require governmental action, it is inevitable that controversy and disagreement will arise. Many in the scientific community would prefer to stay above the political fray, but their work often leads to debate, differences, and divisions.

Chapter Objectives
This issue chapter will seek to:

1. Describe the intersection between science and politics in contemporary American governing.

2. Examine the key issues that are at the core of the public disputes involving science policy and scientific discovery.

3. Discuss the changes in the relationship between science and government from the George W. Bush administration to the Obama administration and the prospect for change in the Trump administration.

SOME BACKGROUND

Science and politics are from two different worlds. Science is about exploring the unknown, proving hypotheses, and finding answers to age-old problems. Politics, on the other hand, is about responding to citizen or special interest demands, using the power of government, and making public decisions. On the surface there would seem to be little similarity between science and politics—one is precise and disciplined, the other is messy and unpredictable.

Yet despite their inherent differences, the scientific world and the political world are increasingly interconnected. Scientific discoveries or scientific initiatives, especially in recent years, have led to major public controversies—moral, intellectual, and ultimately political.

Furthermore, scientific research has a long history of reliance on governmental funding and governmental oversight. The National Science Foundation, the National Aeronautics and Space Administration, the National Institutes of Health, and the Center for Disease Control, to name the most visible examples of federal government involvement in scientific and medical research, inevitably bring the political world into the work of the scientific community. This link of science to the public sector has often created tensions within the political process as specific initiatives, such as the use of stem cells from human embryos for medical research has led to partisan disagreements and acrimonious policy debates. We have already examined the challenges faced by scientists who have warned the American people and their elected representatives about the dangers of global warming, only to be ignored by some as making conclusions without adequate proof or seeking to impose their own economic value system as a way of dealing with what they see as a global threat of epic proportions.

So even though science and politics are from different worlds, they often intersect and, when they do intersect, it is because the work or discoveries of scientists and other researchers alert the nation to a dangerous new strain of virus that requires quick national action, or points to the potential of a new field of study that should be supported by public funds, or offers an exciting opportunity that governmental leaders should not ignore because it may change the way we live. But with these often beneficial results from the scientific community, there are also discoveries and experiments that lead to intense political disputes and vocal opposition that ultimately enter the political arena as the push and pull of public opinion and interest group activity elevate the discoveries and experiments into national issues. The scientific community relishes the independence of thought and the need to be free of intervention as they seek the truth, but that process of scientific investigation and discovery can and has led to heated debates, political differences, and societal divisions.[1]

In recent years, there has been increased tension between the scientific community and government over a range of issues from climate change to drilling for natural resources to wetlands protections. There have also been controversies related to the cloning of animals, genetically modified food, the use of animals in scientific experiments, alternative medicine, and the teaching of evolution in public schools. What scientists are finding out is that their research and, more importantly, their recommendations are running into either stiff opposition or a refusal to even acknowledge the validity of the research or the value of their recommendations. Moreover, for the first time in recent memory, competing countries, particularly China, South Korea, and India, are placing huge amounts of government resources in areas such as health, technology, and space, thus challenging the United States for leadership in the world of science.

Scientists have learned a difficult lesson about how interest groups and public opinion can unite with the political establishment to block or ignore the warnings of those who have been studying a problem for years. Part of the problem, according to MIT professor Lawrence Susskind, is that complex science has not translated well into the political sphere and scientists are novices when it comes to working the political and governmental systems in order to transform their findings and warnings into public policies that will address critical environmental, biological, and medical challenges. To remedy this tension, Susskind has been advocating for programs that seek to harmonize science and politics through mediation and other consensus-building strategies.[2]

Yet despite these tensions between science and politics, the quest for scientific discoveries and scientific advances continues unabated. The explosion of knowledge in the contemporary era has been so dramatic that the scientific community is moving with lightning speed to address a whole host of areas that for years remained a mystery, especially in the area of genetics, disease control, and microbiology. With increasing frequency, laboratories and research institutes across this country are engaged in cutting-edge work that will lengthen life, cure deadly illnesses, expand food production, develop new energy sources, and explain, not just our world, but the universe. In many respects, this is the most exciting time for science, but at the same time it is also the most frustrating time as the scientific community interacts with the political community, not only over the findings of science but also their application and implementation in American society.

DEBATES, DIFFERENCES, AND DIVISIONS

It is important to point out at the outset that the United States has long been a leader in science with many distinguished men and women making significant contributions in a wide range of fields of study. From the earliest days of the republic, from Benjamin Franklin and his experiments with electricity to James Watson's discovery of DNA, Jonas Salk's cure for polio, Werner von Braun's rocket technology, and, of course, the unlimited brilliance of Albert Einstein's theories of space and time, Americans, either by birth or by adopted citizenship, have made medical breakthroughs that have saved countless lives, discovered new ways of understanding life, explained the universe we live in, and pushed the boundaries knowledge beyond anything ever imaginable. Our excellence in the field of science has been recognized by the largest share of Nobel Prizes in science and medical research. From 1950 to 2006, Americans won 206 of the 357 Nobel Prizes in Medicine, Physics, and Chemistry, which is 58% of the awards given out during this period. As of 2014, 260 Americans have been awarded Nobel Prizes in Medicine (100), Physics (89), and Chemistry (71).[3]

On the Record

One of America's most celebrated yet controversial scientists, J. Robert Oppenheimer (often termed the "father of the atomic bomb"), writing after the explosion of the atomic bomb over Hiroshima, Japan, in 1945, said the following:

> The atomic bomb made the prospect of future war unendurable. It has led us to those last few steps to the mountain pass; and beyond there is a different country.

Source: *American Prometheus: The Triumph and Tragedy of J. Robert Oppenheimer*

The worldwide notoriety and leadership that the United States scientific community achieved in the 20th and 21st centuries has thrust it into uncharted ethical and moral territory. This has certainly been the case with the efforts by many scientists and medical professionals to advocate for the expansion of and federal grant support for embryonic stem cell research. Stem cells can be found in most multi-cellular organisms. Stem cells offer the opportunity for scientists to transform them into muscle or nerve tissues that can then be used as medical therapies. Scientists engaged in stem cell research are convinced that they can use stem cells to achieve major breakthroughs in medicine as these cells can be targeted to treat a range of diseases such as leukemia, spinal cord injuries, and cancer.[4]

The controversy over stem cell research involves the use of embryonic cells, taken from a human embryo. Initially, research involving embryonic stem cells required the development of what is termed a "line" of these cells and, as a result, necessitating the destruction of a human embryo. Scientists at the center of stem cell research stated that the benefits of destroying the human embryo in order to create the "lines" could provide enormous breakthroughs in medicine and lead to cures of some of the most serious diseases and conditions facing humankind. Although there has been some recent research that supports procedures in which the embryo is not destroyed, which may offer a less controversial pathway to stem cell development, many scientists continue to value the embryonic stem cells as having the greatest potential. Opponents of embryonic stem cell research, however, vehemently disagreed with the procedures supported by many medical researchers as they viewed the destruction of the embryo as, in fact, destroying life, a life entitled to constitutional and legal protection. Even those who saw the value of stem cell research admit that it creates an ethical "slippery slope" as such experiments can then lead to other controversies such as cloning of humans in a manner that has been experimented with in sheep and cattle.[5]

The controversy over embryonic stem cells and stem cell research entered the American governing process when President George W. Bush in 2001 stated categorically that he was opposed to this avenue of research, largely on pro-life grounds. In a compromise, Bush did support federal funding for the use of currently available "lines" of embryonic stem cells for research purposes but not for federal grant support of any new lines. Then in 2006 and 2007, Bush, in direct opposition to Congress, vetoed the Stem Cell Research Enhancement Acts, which supported additional funding for new lines of embryonic stem cells and for the research conducted at the National Institutes of Health and other research facilities around the country. Bush's position permitted federal funding for an existing 60 stem cell "lines" but not further funding for additional lines. His position did not apply to privately supported funding of embryonic stem cell research.[6]

Despite his recognition that embryonic stem cells held the potential for major advances against cancer and spinal cord injuries, Bush said, "I worry about a culture that devalues life, and believe as your President I have an important obligation to foster and encourage respect for life in America and throughout the world."[7] The president was not without his critics. Besides many prominent scientists and medical researchers who pointed to the vast potential of stem cells, Bush also had to face the pleas of former First Lady Nancy Reagan, who said on numerous occasions that stem cell research could have helped find a cure for Alzheimer's disease, which debilitated and eventually ended the life of her husband.

One of the unique characteristics of science is that it is not static and those in the scientific community are forever moving forward with new experiments and new discoveries. Already there are signs that new techniques using adult skin cells may be able to harvest stem cells from sources other than embryos, thus lessening the chances of a continuing ethical, moral, and political battle. These new techniques have lessened the intensity of the political battles over stem cell research. Meanwhile, laboratories around the world are working closely with their governments to move forward on embryonic stem cell research, which has left scientists in the United States dismayed that their own government has not allowed them to take the lead in this area of medical research.

The funding controversy over embryonic stem cell research brings up a larger issue that has come to the fore in Washington and, indeed, within the most prestigious centers of scientific and medical research. The Bush administration was the target of growing complaints that funding for science had not kept pace with other countries and, as a result, the United States lost its lead as the center of scientific experimentation and discovery. In his 2008 State of the Union address, President Bush stated that "To keep America competitive into the future, we must trust in the skill of our scientists and engineers and empower them to pursue the breakthroughs of tomorrow."[8] But this positive endorsement by the president was immediately responded to by leading scientists who saw the government as participating in a "retardation of research" by regular cutbacks in funding. A particle physicist at Northeastern University in Boston bemoaned the lack of funding and the decline in the dominant position that the United States had developed in this field. Pran Nath stated that "the Bush administration was unable to arrest this decline, leaving Europe and Japan to assume the leadership role in this area."[9]

The disagreements with the Bush administration's lack of support for science were not only limited to funding, but also surfaced in the area of presidential appointments and disputes over data. Scientists were especially disturbed by what they considered to be numerous examples where scientific data had been suppressed or publicly criticized by Bush administration officials, Republican members of Congress, or conservative allies associated with advocacy groups or think tanks. Charges were leveled at the Bush administration that it questioned findings related to harmful chemicals, climate change, evolution, and sex education. Roger Launius, a former chairman of the Division of Space History at the Smithsonian Institution's National Air and Space Museum, took the lead in criticizing the Bush administration on its attack on scientific research stating, "some in industry and on the religious right have disliked the use of scientific studies by government officials as justification for actions that they viewed as counterproductive to their best interests . . . the Bush administration has been at the forefront of this effort in the first part of the 21st century."[10]

As could be expected, the issue of declining government support for science, the politicization of scientific research, and the loss of world leadership in science and technology eventually entered the partisan arena. In 2003 Henry Waxman, Democratic Congressman from California, issued a scathing report criticizing what he and other minority members of the House Committee on Government Reform viewed as serious deficiencies in the Bush administration's approach to science. In the report, Waxman identified over twenty issue areas where the Bush administration had sought to undermine science and medicine from abstinence education and substance abuse to global warming and missile defense. Waxman also charged that the Bush administration used three major tactics in order to weaken the influence of scientific research—"manipulating scientific advisory committees, distorting and suppressing scientific information, and interfering with scientific research and analysis." In his conclusion of the study, Waxman stated, "The Bush Administration has repeatedly suppressed, distorted, or obstructed science to suit political and ideological goals. These actions go far beyond the traditional influence that Presidents are permitted to wield at federal agencies and compromise the integrity of scientific policymaking."[11]

Moreover, scientists and other researchers point to the fact that when research dollars have increased, they have often been related to defense and national security initiatives (such as missile defense), not to disease control, particle physics, biomedicine, or neuroscience. The National Institutes of Health was especially hard hit during the Bush years as budgets that would fund a wide range of scientific and medical research were kept at the same funding level. The Democratic Congress in 2007, for the first time in years, approved a significant increase in the NIH budget and gained the president's approval, despite his initial decision to cut the budget by $279 million. Researchers at the NIH were encouraged by the budget increase and the greater attention that was given by Congress and a president who in his last year in office began to support the work of the premier government-supported research institute.[12]

President Obama, taking a position quite different from his predecessor, made it clear that his administration would substantially increase scientific research and help restore scientific integrity to government. He also promised that scientists would be "free from manipulation or coercion and that the government would listen to what they tell us, even when it is inconvenient." The Obama administration's position was quickly greeted with support from scientific and medical researchers who saw a new era of funding and public support for their work. In particular, the NIH was encouraged that it would receive the funding it needed to take its research on a wide range of medical issues to a new level.[13]

Despite the encouraging words of President Obama, funding for scientific research was caught in the budget cutting sequestration battles with Congress in 2013 and 2014, which had a devastating impact on not only research but also researchers. For example, National Institutes of Health Director Francis Collins said at the time, "While the scientific opportunities have never been more exciting than right now, the stress on the biomedical community in the United States has never been more severe . . . many young investigators are on the brink of giving up because of the difficulty of getting support." The NIH budget peaked in 2010 at $31.2 billion but fell to $30.1 billion in 2014.[14]

With the election of Donald Trump to the presidency, the scientific community became alarmed over the apparent lack of support for scientific research and science in general by the new president and key members of his cabinet. Global warming deniers filled key positions in the Trump cabinet and the president often ridiculed scientific research on climate change in his social media tweets. There was also fear that federal government support for research in agencies such as NASA, NIH, and NSF would be cut by conservatives in the House and Senate who often devalued the work of scientists.[15]

Leading scientists have weighed in on the future of science under a Trump administration. Michael Lubell, Director of Public Affairs for the American Physical Society said, "Trump will be the first anti-science president we have ever had . . . the consequences are going to be very, very severe."[16] Robin Bell of the Lamont-Doherty Earth Observatory at Columbia University stressed the negative impact of the Trump presidency on scientific funding. As he stated, "There is a fear that the scientific infrastructure in the United States is going to be on its knees . . . Everything from funding to being able to attract the global leaders we need to do science research."[17] Time will only tell if the fears of many in the scientific community toward the Trump administration will be accurate.

FYI

The American space program has long been recognized as one of the great scientific achievements of humankind. Since President John F. Kennedy challenged the nation to reach the moon by 1970 (Neil Armstrong landed on the moon in 1969), presidential administrations have made the space program run by the National Aeronautics and Space Administration (NASA) a

(continued)

FYI   (continued)

major priority. President Bush continued this support of the space program when in 2004 he announced plans to send astronauts back to the Moon by 2020 and later to Mars. Called the "Vision for Space Exploration" program, the president proposed spending $12 billion by 2009 to change the mission of NASA to one of future exploration using the moon as a launching pad. Bush's new vision was based on the completion of the international space station and the likely end of the space shuttle program, thus allowing for the United States to take a new direction in space. But within a year of the announcement, NASA announced that it was facing a serious shortfall in its funding (estimated to be $6 billion between 2006 and 2010) because of extraordinary expenses in the shuttle program, placing the president's plans for a new vision of space exploration in jeopardy. If there is a note of optimism in United States space flight and exploration, despite the cuts to NASA, the private sector has moved in to replace government funding to develop commercial space vehicles and human transport ships. In the near future, it is hoped that innovators such as Elon Musk and other private space entrepreneurs will recapture the lead the United States lost to Russia and its international space station.

Source: Various News Services

Perhaps the most passionate battleground in science in the Bush and Obama years was the dispute between the scientific community and religious conservatives over the teaching of evolution in the public schools. Not since the famous Scopes Trial in Tennessee in 1925 has the issue of evolution been debated with such intensity. The Scopes Trial in many respects mirrors the social and religious conditions that have made the teaching of evolution based on Charles Darwin's theory of natural selection a major national issue today. At the time of the so-called "Monkey Trial," fundamentalist Christianity was on the rise in the state of Tennessee, and religious leaders were exercising growing influence within the state legislature. As a result, the Butler Act was passed in 1925 prohibiting the teaching of Darwin's theory and requiring that the Bible version of creation be at the center of the curriculum. The famous trial that pitted William Jennings Bryan (supporting what came to be called creationism) versus Clarence Darrow, who advocated on behalf of the teaching of evolution, has been fictionalized in literature and in the movie *Inherit the Wind*. But both in the trial and on appeal to the Tennessee Supreme Court, the prohibition against the teaching of evolution was upheld. It was not until the Tennessee law was challenged in 1967 that the US Supreme Court overturned a similar law in Arkansas (Epperson v. Arkansas) as an infringement of the First Amendment establishment clause banning public laws whose major focus was religious in nature.[18]

Today, with again an active and politically involved evangelical movement, supporters have advanced the theory of intelligent design, which is a more elaborate defense of creationism. Creationists view their belief as a worthy challenge to Darwin's theories and a necessary addition to existing science curriculums in public schools. Intelligent design, as defined by its major advocacy group the Discovery Institute, takes the position that "certain features of the universe and of living things are best explained by an intelligent cause, not an undirected process such as natural selection." In short, the advocates of intelligent design believe that the complexity of all living matter could have been designed only by an intelligent creator, not by the randomness suggested by Darwin. Intelligent design is presented as an alternative scientific approach to evolution and is supported by a small but vocal group of scientists and researchers, many of them associated with the Discovery Institute. President Bush endorsed intelligent design stating that "both sides ought to be properly taught . . . so people can understand what the debate is about." However, an overwhelming number of scientists and groups such as the National Center for Science Education and the National Science Teachers' Association have condemned intelligent design as pseudo-science and without merit.[19]

Data Bank

In a Gallup Poll from 2014, 42% of the respondents in the United States believe that God created humans in their present form 10,000 years ago. The majority of Americans believe humans evolved, but of that number, a majority believe that God guided the evolutionary process. Further polling from 2014 showed that 65% of Americans believe that creationism and evolution should be taught side by side, while 35% responded that creationism should be taught instead of evolution.

Source: "In US 42% Believe Creationist View of Human Origins," Gallup Poll, June 2, 2014.

Despite the criticisms of mainline scientists, intelligent design and the general movement to replace the teaching of evolution with creationism (or at least have them taught side by side) became a national issue when school committees and boards of education in some states became dominated by conservative evangelicals who sought successfully to include the teaching of creationism in the science curriculum. In Dover, Pennsylvania, the school committee in that small town passed a policy change in the science curriculum that mandated the teaching of creationism alongside evolution. The decision immediately touched off a firestorm of controversy as the scientific community came to realize that evolution was under attack and that the actions of the school committee in Dover could spread elsewhere. The decision of the school committee was challenged in the Pennsylvania court system and went to trial in 2005 (Kitzmiller v. Dover Area School District). Representatives from the intelligent design argument and the supporters of evolution took the stand

and made their case not only in terms of the traditional arguments supporting each side but also in terms of whether the actions of the school committee were in violation of the First Amendment establishment clause. In a stinging rebuke of intelligent design, the judge in the case stated that intelligent design was a religious doctrine, not science, and therefore its teaching was prohibited by the First Amendment. The scientific community hailed the decision as a vindication of evolution and a public denial of intelligent design as pseudo-science.[20]

The Dover trial was conducted at the same time that the Kansas Board of Education, again dominated by conservative evangelicals, voted to adopt the Discovery Institute's "Critical Analysis of Evolution" curriculum as part of the overall science curriculum for Kansas public schools. The Kansas scientific community, especially the State Board of Science Hearing Committee, blasted the decision as including a religious doctrine into the public school curriculum. Many in Kansas were torn by the dispute between intelligent design and evolution, but at election time, six of the members of the Board of Education lost their seats and their decision was overturned by the State Science Hearing Board. In their reinstatement of evolution as the sole source of explaining the development of humans within the curriculum, the Board stated that science would once again be limited "to the search for natural explanations for what is observed in the universe."[21] Recently in Texas, the battle over textbooks became embroiled in a controversy about allowing scientific experts from academia to fact check the content of science textbooks that the State Board of Education approves for 5.1 million high school students. At issue was how the science texts dealt with climate change and the role that biblical figures had on the Founders.[22]

As the Data Bank survey shows, the vast majority of Americans believe in a God-centered creation and have little support for the evolutionary argument of Darwin and modern-day scientists. While the teaching of evolution remains firmly in place in public school curriculums, the Dover and Kansas controversies over intelligent design pointed out the work that the scientific community has before it as it seeks to convince Americans that the evolutionary explanation of human development is indeed accurate and provable. Many in the scientific community have for too long been reluctant to engage in a defense of their research results or to become involved in public educational programs that explain their views on evolution. But because Americans are deeply religious people, and many are firm believers in the Bible story of creation, it is not surprising that the poll results would show such a significant difference between a God-centered creation and an evolutionary explanation for human development. It is difficult for many Americans to accept that their ancestors were apes and that over hundreds of thousands of years these apes evolved into modern humans. Furthermore, the randomness of natural selection as presented by Charles Darwin is difficult for most Americans to understand. It is more logical to assume that the intricacy of human life must have been the result of an intelligent designer or a powerful force or God.

Many scientists, however, have not been prepared for the debates, differences, and divisions that have developed in the political arena as a result of their analysis and discoveries. The result has been an extended period of tension between the government and the scientific community that is a new development in American politics. Many American scientists benefit from government outlays and expect that their research and recommendations will serve as the basis of government action. But both in terms of support and status, scientists entered a new world in recent years where government leaders and bureaucratic agencies fashioned their own policy agenda that on numerous occasions clashed with that of the scientists.[23] It will be up to President Trump to determine what level of support and influence scientists have in the coming years and whether their findings and recommendations will be accepted without being politicized or whether they will face a continued level of governmental antagonism and endure frequent partisan criticism. Whatever the outcome, it is certain that American scientists now recognize more clearly the connection between science and politics.

The Great Debate

The United States is a country of both extraordinary scientific and medical achievements and strong beliefs about the role of God in the creation and evolution of humankind.

Debate Topic

What should be the proper balance between science and religion in guiding public policy in the United States?

Critical Thinking Questions

1. Do you believe that intelligent design views on creation should be taught side by side with evolution in high school?
2. In matters of science and medicine, what role should religion play in making public policy?
3. Where do you stand on the embryonic stem cell debate? Does the importance of using human embryos to harvest stem cells overshadow the possibility of bringing a cure for many of today's diseases?
4. Should scientists play a larger public role in defending their research findings and their views on public policy debates?
5. Are we becoming anti-science in the United States?

Connections

The National Science Teachers Association is the lead organization challenging intelligent design and other efforts to question the teaching of evolution in schools. Visit their site at www.nsta.org

The Center for Science and the Public Interest presents science and public policy issues. See https://cspinet.org

The Coalition of Americans for Research Ethics takes positions on a range of controversial scientific and medical research, including embryonic stem cell research. See www.stemcellresearch.org

The National Science Foundation is the primary government agency responsible for science policy. See www.nsf.gov

The Center for Science and Public Policy is a non-partisan organization that examines issues related to science policy. See their site at www.sourcewatch.org

A Few Books to Read

Boisvert, Kate Grayson, *Religion and the Physical Sciences* (Westport, CT: Greenwood Press, 2008).

Lane, Julia, *The Science of Science Policy: A Handbook* (Palo Alto, CA: Stanford Business Books, 2011).

Marburger III, John H., *Science Policy Up Close* (Cambridge, MA: Harvard University Press, 2015).

Neal, Homer and Tobin Smith, *Beyond Sputnik: US Science Policy in the 21st Century* (Ann Arbor, MI: University of Michigan Press, 2008).

Pielke, Roger, *The Honest Broker* (New York: Cambridge University Press, 2007).

Notes

1. See Cary Funk and Lee Rainie, "Americans, Politics and Science Issues," Pew Research Center—Internet, Science and Tech, July 1, 2015. See also Adam Frank, "A Problem Like No Other: Science and Politics," National Public Radio (NPR), June 10, 2014.
2. As quoted in Alex Madrigal, "Synthesizing Science and Politics," *Wired Science*, February 17, 2008.
3. "Nobel Prize Winners: Which Country Has the Most Nobel," 2014, www.telegraph.co.uk
4. For a thorough discussion of the stem cell issue, see "The Stem Cell Debates," *The New Atlantis*, Winter, 2012.
5. Rich Weiss, "Catch-22," *Washington Post National Weekly Edition*, August 6–12, 2007.
6. www.whitehouse.gov/news/releases/2001/08/20010809-2.html
7. Ibid.
8. www.whitehouse.gov/news/releases/stateoftheunion/2008/index.html
9. As quoted in Live Science; See www.livescience.com/technology/080130-Bush-legacy.html
10. Steven Sulzberg, "Disappointing Science Funding," www.genome.fieldofscience.com

11. "Politics and Science in the Bush Administration," US House of Representatives Committee on Government Reform—Minority Staff, August, 2003.
12. Amy Goldstein, "2007 Budget Favors Defense," *Washington Post*, February 5, 2006.
13. See "The President's Plan for Science and Innovation," Office of Science and Technology Policy, May 7, 2009, www.ostp.gov
14. As quoted in Liz, Szabo, "NIH Director: Budget Cuts Put U.S. Science at Risk," *USA Today*, April 23, 2014. See also Paul Alivisatos, Eric D. Issacs, and Thom Mason, "The Sequester Is Going to Devastate U.S. Science Research for Decades," *The Atlantic*, March 12, 2013.
15. See Sarah Kaplan, "What Will President Trump Mean for Science," *Washington Post*, November 9, 2016.
16. As quoted in Jeff Tolleson, Lauren Morello, and Sara Reardon, "Donald Trump's Election Win Stuns Scientists," *Nature*, November 9, 2016.
17. Sara Kaplan, "What Will President Trump Mean For Science," op. cit.
18. *Susan Epperson et al. v. Arkansas* 393 U.S. 97.
19. See Peter Baker and Peter Slevin, "Bush Remarks on Intelligent Design Theory Fuel Debate," *Washington Post*, August 3, 2005.
20. *Tammy Kitzmiller et al v. Dover Area School District et al.* 05 CV 2688 (2005).
21. Peter Steven, "In Kansas A Bitter Debate on Evolution," *Washington Post*, May 6, 2005, p. A01.
22. Philipa Stewart, "The Great Texas Textbook Debate," *Al Jazeera English*, March 11, 2014.
23. For background see Jessica Wang, *American Science in an Age of Anxiety* (Chapel Hill, NC: University of North Carolina Press, 1999).

17 THE **DRUG** WAR

Issue Focus

One of the more intractable problems facing the United States today is drug use. Whether marijuana, cocaine, heroin, or so-called party drugs, illegal narcotics have become part of American life and a huge multi-billion dollar "industry" that enriches drug barons but sadly creates enormous personal, family, and societal problems. For years, governments at all levels have been seeking ways to stop drug use, especially among the young, but many of these efforts have had only mixed results. Police and drug enforcement officials have waged a constant war against drug cartels and street dealers, yet their efforts have had little impact on drug use in the United States. As a result of the failure of the war on drugs, there have been calls for a relaxation of punishment for use of certain narcotics such as marijuana. These calls for a change in some of the drug laws have not quieted those who want to continue stopping the transport and sale of illegal drugs, and so the war go on.

Chapter Objectives
This issue chapter will seek to
1. Describe the ongoing efforts by federal, state, and local authorities to stem the tide of illegal drugs entering the United States.
2. Discuss the different approaches to combating drug use in the United States and the debates that have ensued over the issue of how best to conduct the drug war.
3. Examine the growing threat from Mexican and other foreign-based drug cartels as they increase their presence in the United States and engage in mounting violence over control of the lucrative trade in drugs.

SOME BACKGROUND

In 1972 President Richard Nixon, in a major national pronouncement, declared a war on drugs. This was not a declaration of war in the sense that the United States would engage its military in pitched battles against another country, but rather the war on drugs was a comprehensive governmental attack on both the suppliers of a range of narcotics, largely from Latin America and Asia, and the distributors of the narcotics. Although the war on drugs is a more recent policy direction, Nixon's initiative was part of a long line of government policies dating back to the days of alcohol prohibition, from 1920–1933, that sought to control, if not eliminate, drug use because of its impact on crime, social stability, and moral decline.[1]

Since the declaration of a war on drugs the United States has developed a bureaucratic/enforcement system designed to stop the supply and distribution of narcotics and allocated billions of dollars to end the illegal drug trade. President Nixon established the Drug Enforcement Agency in 1973 to enforce drug laws and work with foreign governments to stem the tide of illegal narcotics entering the United States.[2] In 1988 President Reagan established the Office of National Drug Control Policy as part of the Anti-Drug Abuse Act with a so-called Drug Czar as the head of the White House unit.[3] Following suit, states and localities developed anti-drug programs and specialized police for the express purpose of waging the war on drugs on the streets, in schools, and in neighborhoods.

As with most wars, the war on drugs has been expensive. In 2005 a federal government report stated that $12 billion had been spent on all administrative efforts to control the drug supply, pay those involved in anti-narcotics efforts, and rehabilitation costs. A separate study, done at the same time, added to these costs the amount spent on incarcerating drug offenders, which included policing, the full range of legal adjudication, and local and federal prison costs. These costs totaled an estimated $45 billion. Not included in these figures were the personal or societal costs related to drug dealing and drug imprisonment, such as the loss of employment, and the impact of violence, family hardship, and health care costs.[4] Recent data show that since the beginning of the war on drugs, governments at all levels have spent over $1 trillion, with increasing levels of spending at the state and local levels for enforcement, prevention, and rehabilitation. But more important than the cost factor is the devastating impact on those using drugs. For example, the opioid crisis—driven by use of heroin—has claimed thousands of lives, with 23,000 deaths in 2013 and 47,000 in 2014.[5]

The war has also led to a huge spike in those Americans jailed for drug possession, drug dealing, and drug use. An estimated 1 million Americans are arrested and/or jailed each year for violating drug laws, and the majority of the prison population is made up of individuals who have been convicted of a drug crime. Since the mid-1990s, the prison population in the United States tripled, with most of the increase due to drug convictions.[6] Currently, 1 in every 99 adults incarcerated is in jail for drug-related crimes, a number that is the highest in the world, and in 2015, 643,121 people were arrested in the United States for marijuana-related offenses.[7]

The war on drugs has not been confined to the United States. Administrations since Nixon have advocated for an aggressive interdiction program to stop the supply of drugs from Latin America and Asia. In particular, the United States Drug Enforcement Agency, the Coast Guard, the Bureau of Customs, and the Border Patrol have worked with governments in Bolivia, Colombia, Mexico, Peru, and many of the mini-states in the Caribbean to destroy cocaine and marijuana fields, capture drug cartel kingpins, and dismantle the money-laundering apparatus that has allowed the drug gangs to hide billions of dollars in ill-gotten gains. The most ambitious of such overseas drug war programs was the $5 billion Plan Colombia instituted by the George W. Bush administration to assist Colombia along with Bolivia, Brazil, Ecuador, Panama, and Venezuela in combating drug trafficking and guerrilla activity that was financed by the drug trade.[8]

The reason for the interest in expanding the drug war to countries like Colombia was that, for many years in the 70s, 80s, and 90s, it was the major supplier of narcotics to the United States. According to US government data, between 56% and 80% of the world's supply of cocaine and heroin came from Colombia, and the drug trade provided the drug cartels of Colombia with an annual income of $4 billion in non-taxed and money-laundered profits. Although Colombia was the premier source of illegal drugs coming into the United States (until new governments successfully cracked down on the trade), Mexico, Bolivia, and Peru were also major suppliers. The burgeoning drug trade from Mexico prompted the government to station hundreds of drug enforcement agents along the border and use Navy ships to patrol the waters in the Caribbean and the Pacific to seize contraband narcotics. The Bush administration worked closely with the government of then Mexican president Felipe Calderon in his expanded program to destroy the drug cartels, which were responsible for over 2600 killings in 2006 alone.[9] Much of the support was in the form of an increased presence of Drug Enforcement agents and greater border and sea patrols. For Drug Enforcement agents and others involved in anti-narcotics interdiction, the work of stopping the supply of drugs from this region remains extremely dangerous as violent gangs are well-equipped with weapons, speedboats (even submarines), and aircraft, which makes them a formidable and violent force. Most importantly, these gangs have the cash to buy off local authorities, who often signal the drug kingpins when an interdiction operation is underway.

The Obama administration continued the policies of the Bush administration, while also sending over 450 law enforcement agents to the border and cracking down on the illegal gun trade that allowed the drug cartels to challenge the Mexican military and police. The cooperation of the Obama administration with Mexican authorities was also viewed as a matter of domestic security as over 250 cities and towns in the United States are estimated to have a Mexican drug presence, including major drug hubs such as Atlanta, Georgia, and Chicago, Illinois. Chicago, in particular, became a violent drug hub with hundreds of killings each year starting in 2013 as gangs with ties to Mexico fought for turf and drug sales.[10] With 80% of the methamphetamines, 90% of the cocaine, and 1,110 metric tons of marijuana estimated to be entering the United States from Mexico, the Obama administration recognized the importance of joining with Mexico in vigorously pursuing the drug war, but it also placed increased emphasis on the rehabilitation of drug users and directed more budget resources toward programs that assisted communities dealing with the drug epidemic.[11] As for President Trump, his controversial statement during the campaign accusing Mexicans of being "rapists and drug dealers" and his pledge to build a wall along the border to keep out drug dealers soured relations with Mexico but was viewed positively by many Americans as a key step in stopping the flow of drugs into the United States.[12]

The United States has been in the war on drugs for over forty years and in that time there have been some notable successes in terms of drug seizures, the capture of key drug lords, and the imprisonment of thousands of dealers and members of drug gangs. Despite the successes in the war, drug use remains prevalent in the United States, especially among the young. New, more powerful and more dangerous drugs enter the marketplace with disturbing regularity and evidence of drug abuse and drug-related deaths continue to fill the news. The resilience of the drug culture in the United States has on occasion sparked a discussion about legalizing certain drugs, especially marijuana, but such talk often leads to a stern rebuke from government officials who insist on continuing the war and punishing those who have broken the law. The reality of widespread drug use colliding with the support for the war on drugs has created a huge divide in this country over what the next steps should be in dealing with this national and international issue.[13]

On the Record

Michael Bottacelli, White House drug official during the Obama administration, often reminded those who favored a tough stance on drug dependency and substance abuse that they should rethink their opposition to new approaches to finding ways to treat the illness rather than incarceration or spending millions for enforcement. As Botticelli stated in an interview from 2015:

> Locking people up for minor drug offenses, especially people with substance abuse disorders, is not the answer; it is cruel, it's costly and it doesn't make the public any safer.

DEBATES, DIFFERENCES, AND DIVISIONS

The issue of drug use and drug enforcement in the United States is one of the most complex and difficult challenges facing public officials and, indeed, the public in general. One of the key problems of drugs in America is the matter of legality and the question of why certain drugs are legal, while others are illegal. It is often heard in debates about drug policy that alcohol and cigarettes, along with certain prescription medications such as OxyContin, are legal drugs that can lead to addiction and other harmful physical and psychological problems, but possession of even small amounts of marijuana is a punishable offense, even though marijuana has been shown to have medicinal benefits and is no more dangerous than alcohol. Then there is also the issue of punishment for possession and distribution of illegal drugs, which has been the primary cause of our overcrowded jails. Many of those in jail, especially minorities, have been incarcerated for extended periods of time for minor drug dealing. Finally, there is the matter of whether it is cost effective and smart policy to continue a war on drugs that, by most accounts, is not making major headway and may actually be a huge failure. Most drug enforcement officials openly admit that barely 5% of the narcotics coming into the United States are confiscated and that, for most drugs, the supply is so plentiful that the price is affordable, if not cheap.[14]

Each of these issues of legality, incarceration, and policy effectiveness stem from the prevailing position among many government officials that any loosening of the position on drug use in this country would pose a distinct danger to social order and personal responsibility. Decriminalization of small amounts of marijuana, for example, would open up the floodgates of drug use and lead to experimentation with more dangerous drugs. Lessening the sentences of small time drug dealers in the inner cities is often viewed as a certain path toward deepening crime by not punishing lawbreakers. Also, admitting that a forty-year war on drug trafficking and drug use has not been won and may have been ill-advised is difficult to face, especially when so much money has been spent with such meager results. But moving toward new approaches to drug use and drug enforcement has been extremely difficult in this country as the public fear of relaxing laws, changing incarceration policies, and developing different methods of responding to the problems linked to drugs has faced stiff opposition in government and in society.

Data Bank

The annual death rate for Americans from various drugs:

Tobacco—400,000
Alcohol—100,000
All legal drugs—20,000
All illegal drugs—15,000
Caffeine—2,000
Aspirin—500
Marijuana—0

Source: National Institutes on Drug Abuse and the Bureau of Mortality

The policy debate over the legalization or decriminalization of marijuana has perhaps led to the sharpest differences and social divisions of any of the issues related to drug use and drug enforcement. Many in government associated with the war on drugs have consistently viewed marijuana as a "gateway" narcotic, which if used regularly may lead to the use of other drugs. In 1995 the Partnership for a Drug-Free America, along with White House Office of Drug Control Policy, issued a report that stated that marijuana users were 85 times more likely to try cocaine than those who did not use marijuana.[15] Other

Americans, especially those under thirty, view marijuana as a "safer" drug, causing fewer harmful effects on the user. The position of marijuana supporters that the drug is not dangerous or a "gateway" to other drug use was supported by the 2006 study done by the American Psychiatric Association that found that there was no connection between marijuana use and subsequent other drug usage. Both sides in this debate have marshaled arguments and data that support their point of view in a battle over the potential harmful effects of marijuana use.[16]

But because marijuana has a level of public support and a body of evidence showing that it may not be a "gateway" narcotic, its possession and use have been the subject of intense lobbying in order to either make it completely legal or to decriminalize it by mandating fines rather than arrest and possible jail time for possession or use. The debate over the legal status of marijuana has become even more complicated as the narcotic has been shown to have medicinal benefits for those individuals involved in chemotherapy and other cancer treatments where nausea is a side effect. In fact it is the debate over the medicinal value of marijuana that has taken center stage in the policy arena as state officials have struggled with the issue, especially as medical professionals validated the benefits that are associated with marijuana use as an anti-nausea treatment.[17]

Because of public pressure for medical marijuana, there has been some success in the area of decriminalization for possessing small amounts of the drug. Since the 1970s, a number of states, including Oregon, Alaska, California, Colorado, New York, Nebraska, North Carolina, and Ohio have passed various forms of decriminalization legislation with most of the sanctions in the form of a small fine. But in the area of legalization, marijuana supporters have faced stiff opposition. In the meantime, 23 states have approved the use of medical marijuana. As to the question of legalization of recreational use, Colorado was the first state to permit the use of marijuana for purely recreational purposes, while also allowing the creation of a commercial sector that permits the sale of the drug over the counter in hundreds of "pot stores." Six other states and the District of Columbia have also passed expansive laws legalizing marijuana for recreational use. Currently, 26 states and the District of Columbia have passed laws legalizing marijuana in some form, either for medical or recreational purposes. In Massachusetts, which in 2016 legalized marijuana use for recreational purposes through a referendum, the legislature quickly moved to delay implementation until 2018 after it sorted out all the tax, regulation, and distribution issues. It is important to state that marijuana remains illegal at the federal level.[18] The importance of the federal ban on marijuana was given more weight when the new Attorney General under the Trump administration, Jeff Sessions, declared that he would support legislation and government action to end state support for recreational marijuana, thus setting up what would likely be an ongoing battle between Washington and the states over legalized marijuana.

While many questions remain about the law enforcement, abuse, tax benefits, and regulation of legalizing marijuana for purely recreational purposes, numerous public opinion polls consistently show that Americans are in favor of moving toward permitting the use of marijuana above and beyond its use for medical purposes. In Colorado, Governor John Hickenlooper stated the following as he signed the bill legalizing marijuana for recreational use, "Certainly this industry will create jobs. Whether it's good for the brand of our state is still up in the air. But the voters passed Amendment 64 by a clear majority; that is why we are going to implement it as effectively as we can."[19]

FYI

Some preliminary numbers are in regarding the financial impact of the marijuana industry in Colorado. In 2015 the sale of marijuana brought in $2.39 billion in tax revenue and employed 18,005 people. The sale of cannabis products on the open market is now the fastest-growing economic sector in Colorado, surpassing the gold ore mining industry. By 2020 it is estimated that the revenue from marijuana will surpass tobacco in terms of excise taxes raised. The financial success of marijuana in Colorado has even created in Congress a cannabis caucus among US Representatives from states either with laws on the books or anticipating the legalization of marijuana for recreational purposes.

Source: Denver Post, October 26, 2016

Besides the issue of whether marijuana use should be legalized or decriminalized, there has also been a debate surrounding the financial benefits that would be created if marijuana would have the same status as alcohol and cigarettes. Studies have shown that enforcement costs related to marijuana are estimated to be over $7 billion and that if the government was to legalize its use and tax its sale, over $6 billion could be raised in revenue—money that currently often ends up in the hands of either petty criminals or organized crime syndicates. Moreover, there is an agricultural angle to marijuana in that it is a cash crop that is vital to the informal (and currently illegal) economy in at least twelve states. One study shows that marijuana production may add over $35 billion in value to the economy of those states where it is grown.[20]

One of the most hotly debated questions concerning the war on drugs is whether it has been worth it. Certainly a case can be made that an illegal "industry" that makes an estimated $60 billion a year and is patronized by an estimated 16 million people over the age of 12 needs to be addressed, especially since it has fostered a criminal element, led to devastating personal crises of abuse, and created a national culture where Americans have come to rely on some form of drug use, whether legal or illegal. But increasingly the issue of whether the expenditures for the drug war on the federal, state, and local levels, combined with the dramatic expansion of the prison population, has come front and center into the policy debate with both advocates of reform and supporters of maintaining an aggressive war posture facing off over the question of whether a war that started in 1973 should continue to be waged.

If a measure of the success of the war on drugs is the movement toward a "drug free America," then without question the effort has been a complete failure. It is unreasonable to assume that a nation of 320 million people living in an open society with standards of privacy and permissiveness would be able to establish a "drug free" environment. The formation of drug-free zones around public schools, zero tolerance of drug use in schools and the business world, and drug testing by many large and small businesses has not had an appreciable impact on drug use. What has occurred that is disturbing in terms of the war on drugs is that narcotics such as heroin and methamphetamines and illegally obtained prescription drugs like OxyContin have increased in usage. If alcohol use were included in the discussion of drug usage, even though it is legal, the results would show a continued high level of reliance on drug use by Americans.[21]

One measure of the drug war that has changed significantly is the public's view of the issue as a critical priority. For much of the 1970s and 1980s, surveys that asked Americans to name the issues that required a high level of attention found that drug use was usually in the top ten. But since 2001, national concerns over drugs and drug usage has virtually disappeared from survey responses and is rarely discussed in policy debates or in campaign discussions at the national level. There continues to be an active discussion about drugs and drug policy at the state and, particularly, the local level, but even at the grassroots of American society the drug war is but one of many concerns facing the public and governmental officials. There has been almost a kind of grudging acceptance that drugs are part of the local landscape along with a growing realization that marijuana use may not be as dangerous as alcohol abuse, especially among the young.

But the epidemic of heroin use and deaths related to heroin use have sparked renewed interest in drug policy, especially at the state and local levels.[22] As heroin use moved from the cities to suburban and rural areas and deaths spiked, governmental leaders and community activists renewed calls for drastic measures, accenting a mix of policing, prevention, education, and rehabilitation. In the final days of the 2016 Congress, the 21st Century Cures Act was passed, which allocated $1 billion to respond to the opioid crisis in this country.[23] Yet this new interest in dealing with heroin-related deaths by no means assures a battle won in the war on drugs. Nearly every day in some of the wealthiest communities in our country and in iconic rural American towns, obituaries chronicle the death of a young person—a mother, son, or brother, usually with the code phrase "died unexpectedly."

For many who are critical of the war on drugs, the issue that often rises to the surface of discussion is whether there should have been a "war" in the first place. Taking a kind of military approach to drug use and drug enforcement, in the view of critics, placed too much emphasis on interdiction, confiscation, and incarceration rather than promoting a whole host of preventative methods and rehabilitation. Stated simply, the war on drugs concentrated on the supply routes and dealers rather than on the reasons for drug demand and strategies to diminish that demand. Although federal, state, and local budgets have allocated money for prevention and rehabilitation, and many privately funded programs have made enormous positive strides in dealing with the adverse effects of drug use and drug abuse, at the federal level, in particular, the focus continues to remain on a war strategy.[24]

There has often been a comparison of the drug war to the Prohibition era when the government, in an attempt to influence personal behavior—in this case the use of alcohol—passed a constitutional amendment and spent millions of dollars and extensive personnel in order to stop what became a highly lucrative underground business enterprise dealing in illegal alcohol. Americans responded to Prohibition by frequenting "speakeasy" bars, making their own moonshine, and accepting the crime and corruption that was linked to the illegal trade. In the end, Prohibition was viewed as a huge public policy failure, and the nation rejoiced in 1933 when the Twenty-First Amendment negated the Eighteenth Amendment and brought the nation back to a time when alcohol was legal.

Today critics point to the failures of the war on drugs as another example of Prohibition as the government, since 1973, has sought to control the private behavior of American citizens with only limited success. In some respects the push to relax drug laws and drug punishments, especially for marijuana, has been driven by the admissions of major political figures. President Bill Clinton, in a highly controversial admission during his run for the White House that he smoked, but did not inhale, a marijuana cigarette, became the stuff of jokes, but did awaken many Americans to the realities of drug use by a younger generation. During the 2008 campaign, Democratic candidate Barack Obama admitted that he used cocaine as a teenager, and Cindy McCain, the wife of Republican candidate John McCain, did not shy away from her past drug dependency on barbiturates. Although not illegal, President Bush admitted early on in his candidacy that he was a recovered alcoholic who on at least one occasion was arrested for driving under the influence.

The drug and alcohol use of key political figures in recent years has further fostered a more tolerant attitude toward the use of some narcotics and more public campaigns to remind people about the dangers of alcohol abuse. The accent now is more on overcoming addiction and developing prevention programs rather than stressing the need for a stiff crackdown in a manner akin to war. As President Obama stated in 2010, "By boosting community-based prevention, expanding treatment, strengthening law enforcement and working collaboratively with our global partners, we will reduce drug use and the great danger it causes in our communities."[25]

To say that the war on drugs is winding down would be an exaggeration; for example, Attorney General Jeff Sessions has made statements that he will fight state policies that have legalized the recreational use of marijuana and will continue to emphasize the value of taking a hard line on drug use with little mention of prevention and rehabilitation. Nevertheless it is safe to state that support for what was a high government priority and a near passion of past administrations has undergone a transformation in recent years. There is a growing recognition that some drugs are more dangerous than others, that legalization and decriminalization of marijuana would not create a full scale rush to harder drugs, that the incarceration of hundreds of thousands of African-American males has had a devastating effect on the black community, and that the money spent on the war could be much better spent on other more pressing domestic priorities. It is impossible to predict with any certainty whether there will be significant changes in the drug laws under a new presidential administration or whether funding for the war on drugs will be cut back or redirected to prevention and rehabilitation. There remains a strong divide between those Americans who want reform of the drug laws and drug enforcement policies and those who fear that opening the door to reform will only lead to a society that is even more immersed in the drug culture. It may take a generation of continued differences and divisions before any change occurs in the war on drugs.

The Great Debate

The drug policies of the United States are beginning to soften, at least toward marijuana. However, government officials continue to stress the connection between drugs, addiction, and violence. These officials remain adamant about continuing the war on drugs as new threats such as those from heroin use escalate.

Debate Topic

Should the United States continue an aggressive war on drugs both domestically and internationally or concentrate its efforts on prevention and decriminalization of drug use and rehabilitation of drug users?

Critical Thinking Questions

1. Is the drug war lost? If so, how did we lose it?
2. Should federal, state, and local officials move toward complete legalization of some drugs like marijuana?
3. Do you fear that a relaxation of current drug laws will have a harming effect on our society and lead to increased crime and addiction?
4. What role should militarization and policing play in drug policy and enforcement at the national, state, and local levels?
5. How would you advise government officials on the best way to deal with the drug issue in our country?

Connections

The Drug Enforcement Agency (DEA) is the frontline agency responsible for the war on drugs. Visit its site at http://www/usdoj.gov/dea/index.htm

The White House Office of National Drug Control Policy presents the administration's point of view on drug policy. See www.whitehousedrugpolicy.gov

All facets of the war on drugs are documented at http://www/drugwarfacts.org

A critical website devoted to the negative impacts of the war on drugs is StoptheDrugWar. See www.stopthedrugwar.org

A site that examines all facets of drug policy and the drug war is the Drug Policy Alliance. Its site can be found at www.drugpolicy.org

Some Books to Read

Boggs, Carl, *Drugs, Power and Politics: Narco Wars, Big Pharma and the Subversion of Democracy* (London: Routledge, 2015).

Branson, Richard, *Ending the War on Drugs* (New York: Random House, 2016).

Campbell, Howard, *Drug War Zone: Frontline Dispatches From the Streets of El Paso and Juarez* (Austin, TX: University of Texas Press, 2010).

Quinones, Sam, *Dreamland: The True Tale of America's Opiate Epidemic* (New York: Bloomsbury Publishers, 2015).

Slater, Dan, *Wolf Boys; Two American Teenagers and Mexico's Most Dangerous Drug Cartel* (New York: Simon and Schuster, 2016).

Notes

1. For background on US policy toward drugs and drug use see Erich Goode, *Drugs in American Society*, 6th edition (New York: McGraw Hill, 2004), Chapter 4.
2. http://www.usdoj.gov/dea
3. http://www/whitehousedrugpolicy.gov
4. See "National Drug Control Strategy—Budget Summary," White House, February, 2005.
5. See Haeyoun Park and Matthew Bloch, "Epidemic of Drug Overdose Deaths Ripples Across America," *New York Times*, January 20, 2016.
6. See "Criminal Justice Fact Sheet," of the NAACP. The site is at www.naacp.org
7. See Christopher Ingraham, "Police Arrest More People for Marijuana Use Than for All Violent Crimes-Combined," *Washington Post*, October 12, 2016.
8. See Michael Brown, "Counternarcotics Strategies in Latin American," Testimony Before the House Committee on International Relations, Sub-Committee on Hemispheric Affairs, March 3, 2006. Also see Joanne Kawell, "Drug Economies of the Americas," NACLA Report on the Americas, September/October, 2002.
9. See Sam Enriquez, "Mexican Leader Joins War on Drugs as U.S. Turns Its Back," *Baltimore Sun*, February 4, 2007.
10. Jason McGahan, "Why Mexico's Sinaloa Cartel Loves Selling Drugs in Chicago," *Chicago Magazine*, September 17, 2013.
11. Christopher Ingraham, "The Radical Way Obama Wants to Change the Drug War," *Washington Post*, February 10, 2016.

12. Tal Kopan, "What Donald Trump Said About Mexico and Vice Versa," *CNN Politics*, August 31, 2016.
13. Peter J. Reilly, "White House Blows Smoke at Pot Petitions," Forbes Magazine, January 9, 2013.
14. Eduado Porter, "Numbers Tell of Failure in Drug War," *New York Times*, July 3, 2012.
15. See "Partnership for a Drug-Free America Reports on Teens and Parents' Attitudes About Drugs," April, 1996.
16. For a commentary on marijuana as a gateway drug see Robert Dupont, "Marijuana Has Proven to Be a Gateway Drug," *New York Times*, April 26, 2016. For a commentary on marijuana as not a gateway drug see Maia Szalavitz, "Marijuana as a Gateway Drug: The Myth That Will Not Die," *Time*, October 29, 2010.
17. See Gerald McKenna, "The Current Status of Medical Marijuana in the United States, Hawaii," *Journal of Medicine and Public Health*, 2014, Vol. 73(4), pp. 105–108.
18. See "State Marijuana Laws in 2016 Map," *Governing*, November, 2016.
19. David Kelly, "Governor Who Called Legalization 'Reckless' Now Says Colorado's Pot Industry Is Working," *Los Angeles Times*, May 17, 2016.
20. "Marijuana Production: Comparison With Other Cash Crops," *Drug Science*, 2006, www.drugscience.org
21. Elijah Wolfson, "Prescription Drugs Have Pushed Heroin Into the Suburbs," *Newsweek*, May 5, 2014.
22. Katherine Q. Seelye, "In Heroin Crisis, White Families Seek Gentler War on Drugs," *New York Times*, October 30, 2015.
23. Jessica Davis, "Obama Signs 21st Century Cures Act Into law, Funding Precision Medicine, Cancer Moonshot, HER Improvements," *Healthcare IT News*, December 14, 2016. $1 billion of the bill was targeted for dealing with the drug crisis.
24. Rep. Hank Johnson, "The Failed 'War on Drugs' Is Militarizing Law Enforcement, Fueling Police Violence," *Huffington Post*, December 24, 2014.
25. See "President Obama Releases National Strategy to Reduce Drug Use and Its Consequences," The White House, May 11, 2010. For a more recent discussion by President Obama on drug policy see "President Obama Is Taking More Steps to Address the Prescription Drug Abuse and Heroin Epidemic," as reported in the *New York Times*, March 30, 2016.

18

ENERGY USE AND
ENERGY CONSERVATION

Issue Focus

Traditional energy sources (oil, coal, and natural gas) and economic development are so closely intertwined that should the supply of these natural resources be cut off or depleted, the United States and, indeed, the entire world would experience serious challenges. Because the link between energy and growth is so critical, the issues of how best to develop new energy sources, how to protect existing sources, and deciding how to properly prioritize the use of a range of energy resources have prompted major debates in the political arena and among the American people. At the same time that the debate over energy is causing division in the nation, another area of debate is occurring over conservation measures and their impact on economic growth. We now live in a "green era" in which many Americans are stressing the importance of moving from oil, gas, coal, and nuclear power to solar, wind, geothermal, and biofuel and are joining these new "green" sources of energy with strict conservation measures. Not surprisingly, the advocates of green alternatives are clashing with the proponents of traditional sources of energy and, in the process, creating a deep divide in Washington and throughout the country.

Chapter Objectives
This issue chapter will seek to:

1. Explain the challenges the United States faces in this age of energy exploration, dependency on foreign sources of energy, and the emergence of alternative energy sources.

2. Discuss the political differences that exist over energy exploration, energy use, and energy conservation as they relate to the impact on the national economy and the environment.

3. Explore the public policy options that are currently being discussed to address energy exploration, energy use, and energy conservation.

SOME BACKGROUND

The United States is the largest user of energy in the world as its people consume about 26% of the energy resources available. The major source of this energy use is fossil fuels, in particular petroleum, which provide approximately 40% of the total followed by coal (23%) and natural gas (another 23%);

the remaining 14% is made up of a mix of nuclear and hydroelectric power and other renewable sources.[1] As the United States moved from a rural and agricultural society where wood and later coal were the energy mainstays to an urban and industrial society where petroleum was king, the level of energy consumption increased significantly. Added to this demographic and economic shift was the rise of an ever-growing consumer society with the accent on the acquisition of more and more products that were petroleum-based, especially the automobile.

At present, the primary consumer of energy in the United States is the industrial sector with transportation second (residential users and commercial enterprises make up the remainder of the energy sectors). American economic development over the years has been "fueled" by heavy usage of available energy sources as our manufacturing sector, or smokestack industries, relied heavily on oil and coal. Besides the industrial sector, the critical source of energy use, mainly gasoline products, has been in transportation. Americans love their cars, especially big cars, and show little interest in mass transit. In terms of comparison, American cars average about 20 miles per gallon while European cars, which are much smaller, average about 40 miles per gallon. In the United States, taking the train or subway to work is not popular, while Europeans take pride in their extensive and heavily used train systems. As a result, the combination of a vibrant industrial sector and a nation in love with the automobile has created heavy energy use and an unquenchable reliance on petroleum products.

Translating this reliance on petroleum products into numbers, US oil consumption has been import-based, reaching a high of 65% in 2004. The current level of importation of oil, however, is at the lowest mark since 1985. To show how the oil market has changed in recent years, data reveal that the United States is increasingly becoming less dependent on foreign oil. In 2014 the United States spent $333 billion on imported oil, down from $388 billion in 2013 and considerably down from the $700 billion spent in the mid-2000s.[2] Much of the decrease in oil consumption and importation costs is due to American consumers and businesses moving to alternative energy sources—solar, wind, geothermal, ethanol—combined with increased conservation measures as consumers "tighten up" their homes during high use seasons and businesses implement cost-reducing measures in their factories and offices. Moreover, in recent years, domestic production of oil and natural gas has increased significantly as a result of new techniques such fracking—a process of drilling deep into the earth and with high pressure water opening up new sources of oil and gas—and expansion of existing oil fields in the Gulf of Mexico, Texas, Oklahoma, and Alaska.

The major benefactors of US imported oil use are largely, but not exclusively, Middle Eastern countries. Fifty-five percent of the imported oil Americans use comes from foreign sources, especially Saudi Arabia, the world's largest producer of oil. Saudi Arabia, along with other countries such as Nigeria, Venezuela, and the United Arab Emirates are members of the oil cartel known as OPEC, the Organization of Oil Exporting Countries. The OPEC members have, over the years, sought to control the world's supply of oil, thus driving up the cost per barrel and, as a result, amassing huge public and private fortunes. In recent years, there have been stark disagreements among the members over production levels as world prices for petroleum declined significantly.[3]

In 1973 Americans got a hint of the impact that foreign oil production and price controls can have as OPEC staged an embargo on the sale of oil to the United States in retaliation for our foreign policy support of Israel. For months, the oil embargo created long lines at gas stations and short tempers as Americans waited to fill up their cars with expensive gas. I have (MK) vivid memories of sitting in a gas line to get my three-gallon allotment from the gas station manager who stood with the gas pump in one hand and a tire iron in the other for protection. The oil embargo came to an end, but OPEC and Middle Eastern countries made their point about the connection between foreign policy positions in the West and the availability and price of gasoline.[4]

As gas returned to acceptable pricing after the embargo was lifted, Americans bought big SUVs and trucks, drove 70 to 80 miles an hour, and took long automobile or recreational vehicle vacations. The automobile industry did little to dissuade Americans from buying big cars and trucks and even fostered the driving culture that created the huge Hummer SUVs that took pride in getting less than 12 miles per gallon. Besides the push for bigger gas-guzzlers, there was little concern about moving away from oil as a source of home heating and no compunction to embrace new sources of energy such as solar or even programs to make homes more energy efficient. Americans often could not bring themselves to place huge solar panels on their roofs and support wind farms in some areas of the country. Alternative energy sources and energy conservation programs faced the Not In My Backyard (NIMBY) syndrome as it became just too easy and cheap to pay for gas or home heating oil.

The rollercoaster ride of oil prices went upward again in 2007 and 2008, forcing the American people and government officials to begin taking action to respond to $4.00 a gallon gasoline and home heating oil. Inflation began to rear its ugly head and workers, desperate to make ends meet in the new energy environment, struggled to find ways to cut back on gasoline. In a matter of months during 2008, the subway and the train became instant options as Americans left their cars at home. The energy cost crunch was not expected to be a temporary problem for Americans, but with countries such as China and India becoming major users of petroleum products, demand for oil increased, further affecting not just the price of gasoline and heating products, but all sorts of food and commercial products that relied on oil in some form of the production stage. Americans reluctantly came to realize that not only had the price of gasoline changed but that the world had changed and that they were no longer going to be the privileged minority in the world that benefited from cheap energy. Americans might continue to use energy more than other countries, but they would now have to pay for that energy at levels never anticipated.[5]

In recent years, with less demand for oil as alternative energy sources came into play and the United States moved to oil independence, the price of oil on international trading markets dropped precipitously from $100 a barrel to a low of $40 in 2015 and 2016. The drop in the price per barrel of oil created serious economic and financial problems for OPEC member countries and weakened its clout and that of other non-members, such as Russia. After decades of oil dependence and periodic price fluctuations, the United States entered a new era of energy dominance.

On the Record

As early as 1999, leading figures in the oil industry were predicting significant changes in energy sources and energy usage. Mike Bowlin, Chairman and CEO of ARCO and Chairman, at that time, of the American Petroleum Institute said the following:

> We've embarked on the beginning of the Last Days of the Age of Oil. Nations of the world that are striving to modernize will make choices different from the ones we have made. They will have to. And even today's industrial powers will shift energy use patterns . . . The market share for carbon-rich fuels will diminish, as the demand for other forms of energy grows. And energy companies have a choice: to embrace the future and recognize the growing demand for a wide array of fuels; or ignore reality, and slowly—but surely—be left behind.

As an update to Mr. Bowlin's prediction, the three largest integrated oil companies—Chevron, Exxon Mobil, and Occidental Petroleum—reported a quarterly profit in 2015 of $4.9 billion, the lowest quarterly profit since 2005. While profits for major oil companies have inched upward since this low point, the bottom line for the Big Three integrated companies has been nowhere near the glory days of oil profits recorded in 2012 and 2013 when quarterly profits ranged from $17 billion to a high of $24 billion.

Source: Winning the Oil Endgame, www.oilendgame.com

DEBATES, DIFFERENCE AND DIVISIONS

The energy use culture in the United States has changed dramatically from the days of paying little attention to the costs of gas and home heating. Following in large part the models of energy conservation used during the Arab oil embargo of the 1970s, the American consumer has harkened back to the tried and true conservation measures such as purchasing hybrid cars that increase miles per gallon, winterizing their homes, using highly efficient light bulbs and appliances, and driving less or taking public transportation. Public opinion surveys support the move by Americans to change their lifestyle and move toward conservation. A Gallup poll in 2013 found that more than 76% of Americans supported government efforts to develop solar and wind power and 71% supported government spending to develop alternate sources of fuel for automobiles.[6] Furthermore, although many Americans believe that, ultimately, technological advances will ease the energy crisis, they have little confidence that a magic solution to the energy crisis will come anytime soon and have decided to take whatever small measures they can in order to bring down fuel costs.

While Americans are seeking to move away from the traditional reliance on fossil fuels and accenting energy conservation measures, the national government is locked in a fierce fight over just how best to set national energy policy. Those from the conservative side are convinced that the answer lies with tax incentives to develop traditional energy sources, a lessening of regulations to drill for oil in regions that have a protected status, and fighting efforts to advance so-called carbon taxes as a way or reducing dependence on fossil fuels. Those of the liberal persuasion stress that government must take a more active role in using the tax system to discourage the purchase of gas-guzzlers, increase the tax burden on oil companies' profits, and limit efforts to open up new areas for drilling. Because the conservative model is largely based on technological advances and market-based incentives and the liberal view relies on government tax sanctions, energy conservation, and energy independence, national energy policy has become embroiled in an intense debate over how best to solve a national problem.

In President Bush's last State of the Union address in 2008, and at a later major conference on renewable energy, the administration went on record as committed to aggressively pursuing measures that will make the United States energy independent.[7] The president, at the International Renewable Energy Conference, stated that his administration had spent $12 billion on research to develop alternative energy sources and was working with the private sector to encourage, through tax incentives, further research on alternative energy sources. At the top of the president's list of alternative energy sources were biodiesel and ethanol. Biodiesel fuel (produced through biological processes in agriculture) had for a time during the Bush presidency grown dramatically with over 650 biodiesel fueling stations in the United States. But it was ethanol that the president was most excited about and viewed as a key answer to energy independence. Ethanol, which is largely derived from corn, experienced a significant expansion program under Bush. The Energy Department spent over $1 billion in research to make the fuel more cost-efficient and cost-competitive. Also, President Bush emphasized the need to renew our national commitment to nuclear power. Because of citizen and environment concerns over nuclear power, nuclear waste, and nuclear accidents, this country has not built a new nuclear plant in decades. The president was committed to changing that situation and pressing to ease permitting and regulatory limits on new nuclear power plant construction. Together all these new and old alternatives were viewed by the Bush administration as creating new industries, new technologies, and, most of all, new jobs.[8]

While President Bush was touting the enormous possibilities of new technologies and new sources of energy, he was not willing to support any policy initiatives that placed immediate and strict controls on CO_2 emissions in the form of a carbon tax on automobiles and industries and other tax measures that would in his view be "anti-economic growth." As he said on numerous occasions, his administration would not support the Kyoto Accord, which was designed to limit CO_2 emissions through a carbon tax and more aggressive target dates for a reduction in emissions. The president remained adamant that agreeing to the positions in the Kyoto Accord would have a detrimental impact on the national economy as our industrial and automotive sectors became less competitive and less profitable.

Instead of supporting the Kyoto Accord and any proposals from Democrats that would affect the economic development and corporate viability, Bush praised the essential elements of the Energy Independence and Security Act of 2007 that supported research on alternative energy sources and required gas mileage targets to increase energy efficiency.[9] Bush, however, was not content to just advocate for changes in our use of oil and the need to move to new energy sources. He also continued his support for drilling at the Arctic National Wildlife Refuge, which was opposed by environmentalists and liberal Democrats in Congress, and for a relaxation of regulations on further drilling in the Gulf of Mexico, off the coast of California, and in the Southwest.[10] Bush and the oil and gas industry, using government estimates, reminded Americans that these areas could contain as much as 25–30 billion barrels of oil and 80 trillion cubic feet of natural gas. Critics remained concerned that drilling in these areas posed a major threat to the environment, both in terms of animal and fish life and the prospects of oil leaks and other threats posed by drilling.

Data Bank

The Ten Most Polluted Metropolitan Areas in the United States

Fresno, California
Bakersfield, California
Visalia-Porterville, California
Modesto, California
Los Angeles, California
El Centro, California
San Jose, California
Cincinnati, Ohio
Pittsburgh, Pennsylvania
Cleveland, Ohio

Source: www.stateoffair.org/2015/city-ranking/most-polluted-cities.html

(continued)

Data Bank   (continued)

The Ten Cleanest Cities in the United States

Bellingham, Washington
Bend/Redmont/Pineville, Oregon
Bismarck, North Dakota
Blacksburg, Virginia
Brownsville/Harlingen, Texas
Brunswick, Georgia
Burlington, Vermont
Cape Coral, Florida
Charleston, South Carolina

Source: www.stateofair.org/2015/city-ranking/cleanest-cities.html

Democrats in Congress and candidates running for the Presidency in 2008 agreed with President Bush on the need for alternative energy sources, conservation, and so-called "green" incentives to promote environmentally sound technologies. During the 2008 campaign, Barack Obama, for example, set his goals for energy policy as "support for the next generation of biofuels, setting America on a path to oil independence, and improve energy efficiency by 50% by 2030." While there was some commonality with the Bush administration on energy policy, the Democrats did differ with the White House on numerous other policies and policy initiatives. Democratic leaders like Speaker of the House Nancy Pelosi and numerous Congressional leaders targeted the oil companies for their excess profits and, in particular, for their staunch defense of government subsidies that reached $18 billion in 2008. The oil company executives who were brought regularly to House and Senate hearings faced angry Democrats who wanted to know why the subsidies were necessary and, of course, why gas prices were so high. The executives defended the subsidies as a way of assisting them in the very costly process of finding new oil fields and in developing new refining capacity. They defended the price of gasoline as the result of heightened world-wide demand (from emerging economic powers like China and India) and regular supply dislocations as instability in some oil-producing countries like Nigeria posed serious problems that elevated the cost of oil per barrel.[11]

Democrats also took on the SUV and the pickup truck, which benefitted from less stringent fuel efficiency standards, and continued to pressure the Bush administration over what they felt was too slow a push to achieve high fuel efficiency goals. The Democrats berated Bush for making 2020 the target date for enhanced fuel efficiency standards, stating that this was a concession to the automotive industry, which many members of Congress felt was dragging its feet on making American-made cars attain higher levels of fuel efficiency. The Democrats and the Democratic nominee Barack Obama, however, were criticized by the Bush administration and others in the corporate community for making bold statements that they would reduce oil consumption by 35%, or 10 million barrels per day, by 2030 by increasing fuels standards and setting tough energy efficiency goals without sufficient and specific plans to achieve that objective. Despite the criticism of vague promises of energy efficiency, the Democratic position on energy efficiency was to pressure Detroit car-makers to move quickly to produce energy-efficient cars. As Barack Obama stated to an audience in Detroit in 2007, "I went to Detroit, I stood in front of a group of automakers, and I told them that when I am president, there will be no more excuses—we will help them retool their factories, but they will have to make cars that use less oil."[12]

Also the Democrats pressured the Bush Administration to dip into the United States Strategic Petroleum Reserve, an oil depository system of 640–700 billions of gallons of oil that the United States keeps in reserve for crisis periods or shortages (the Reserve would likely provide about 50 days of oil should an emergency arise). The Democrats wanted the Bush Administration to open up the reserve and pump billions of gallons of gas into the consumer system as a way of lessening the impact of price increases. The Bush Administration refused this request. But Congress persisted in trying to loosen up the administration's reluctance to make changes in the status of the Strategic Petroleum Reserve. The Democrats in Congress passed legislation in 2008 demanding that the Energy Department discontinue purchasing oil to place in the reserve. The Energy Department did comply and ended contracts with OPEC that placed 70,000 barrels of oil a day in the reserve. Most experts, however, saw the end of the purchase orders and the 70,000 barrels a day as having little impact on the daily price of oil.[13]

With the arrival of the Obama administration, energy policy entered a new era as the president vowed support and financing to help foster the development of green technologies and, perhaps most importantly, pressure Detroit automakers to produce cars with high mileage ratings and low carbon emissions. By bringing new appointees into the Environmental Protection Agency and the Department of Energy, Obama moved quickly to reverse Bush policies that placed the United States in opposition to international agreements such as the Kyoto Accord, placed new emissions regulations on the coal and electric power industries, and included billions of dollars in his first budget to promote energy-saving projects along with tax credits for working families to bring greater energy efficiency to their homes.

Early on in his administration, Obama angered environmentalists when, in 2010, he announced that he would support offshore drilling in the Gulf of Mexico, in Alaska, and off the east coast as one part of his overall energy policy. But Obama's support for offshore drilling took a turn later in 2010 as an oil-drilling platform in the Gulf of Mexico caught fire and eventually collapsed, killing eleven men. At first, British Petroleum (BP), which leased the platform, downplayed the environmental impact from the escaping oil, but within a few days the assessment of the expanse of the oil spill created by the platform fire increased significantly. An oil spill the size of Connecticut affected the coastline from Louisiana to Florida and endangered animal and plant life throughout the region, along with some of the nation's most plentiful shrimp-fishing grounds. As the oil spill spread and BP was initially unable to stop the leak, critics began to describe the environmental disaster (the worst in US history) as "Obama's Katrina" as they accused the government of not acting quickly enough and with a level of bureaucratic coordination necessary to deal with the oil spill. Environmentalists, on the other hand, reminded Americans and the proponents of offshore drilling that this catastrophe proved their point, not only about the dangers of such resource extractions close to American shores, but also about the need to move away from dependence on oil.[14]

In 2016 Obama heeded the warnings of environmentalists when he, in cooperation with Canada, ordered that millions of acres of federally owned land in the Arctic and the Atlantic Ocean be withdrawn from oil and gas drilling. As Obama said at the time, "These actions . . . protect a sensitive and unique ecosystem that is unlike any other region on earth. They reflect the scientific assessment that even with the high safety standards that both our countries have put in place, the risks of an oil spill in this region are significant and our ability to clean up from a spill in the region's harsh conditions is limited."[15]

But the most controversial and contentious debate over energy policy during the Obama presidency was over the construction of the Keystone XL pipeline. The pipeline is a proposed 1,179 mile line that would take oil from the sandy soil in Alberta, Canada, to Steele City, Nebraska. If constructed, the Keystone pipeline would bring 830,000 barrels of oil to the United States each day. The construction of what was then called the Keystone line was completed during the George W. Bush administration, but a new reconfigured line was proposed (Keystone XL) to shorten the route to its destination in Nebraska and then on to Cushing, Oklahoma, using the existing pipeline.

The arguments in favor of Keystone XL were that it would mean less dependence on Middle East oil and create an estimated 42,000 jobs over a two-year construction period, with as many as 35,000 permanent jobs for maintaining the pipeline. Although Republicans in Congress enthusiastically supported the construction, the Environmental Protection Agency advised President Obama not to lend his support, citing adverse effects to the environment in those areas where the pipeline would be built, especially the possibility of spillage from the line. After considerable political debate over the benefits and drawbacks to the project that lasted seven years, President Obama rejected the application from TransCanada (the company building the proposed pipeline), and the company asked to have its proposal put on hold.[16] The debate quieted down considerably as the price of oil dropped in 2015, and the Obama administration moved in the direction of supporting alternative energy sources, particularly solar, as the future of energy production.

FYI

Support for alternative energy sources was born out in a 2015 Gallup Poll in which Americans were asked how much emphasis this country should place on a range of alternative energy sources. The result are presented below:

	% More emphasis	% Some emphasis	% Less emphasis
Solar power	79	12	9
Wind	70	14	14
Natural gas	55	32	12
Oil	41	27	30
Nuclear power	35	28	33
Coal	28	27	43

Source: Gallup Annual Environmental Poll, March 5–8, 2015

The oil pipeline controversy did not end with the Keystone XL debate. The movement of oil from North Dakota to an energy hub in Illinois mirrored the Keystone XL controversy as Native Americans sought to block the building of a 1,170 mile pipeline that crossed the Missouri River in North Dakota. At the Standing Rock Sioux Reservation, over 5000 Native American protesters claimed that the $1.8 billion Dakota Access oil pipeline would cross sacred waters and any oil leak along the river would damage their drinking water. In late 2016, a tense standoff between local, state, and federal police, the US Army Corp of Engineers, and the Native Americans ensued with periods of conflict and numerous injuries. Over 500 protesters were arrested and police used water cannons and rubber bullets to try to disperse the crowds. The Native Americans pledged not to budge from their positions and the standoff became a microcosm of the debate over energy production, environmental safety, and claimed land rights. In late 2016, after days of tense standoffs between the protesters and federal and local police, the US Army Corp of Engineers denied the easement for the pipeline and the Native Americans declared victory. As for officials from the Dakota Access pipeline group building the pipeline, they pledged to return to court and seek a court judgment allowing them to continue with the project.[17] But in January 2017, President Trump gave a renewed boost to both the Keystone Pipeline and the Dakota Access Pipeline by signing an executive order that gave the green light to renewed construction, a decision sure to spark renewed protests. Also, Trump's appointment of Scott Pruitt as head of the Environmental Protection Agency created a firestorm of controversy since Pruitt, during his time as Attorney General of Oklahoma, was a fierce supporter of the oil and gas industry and took the EPA to court numerous times to limit their regulatory powers.

Developing a workable energy alternative to oil, coal, and natural gas has caused controversy and conflict, but there are examples of initiatives that have been less confrontational. One of the most promising areas of energy development is wind power. Texas has taken the lead in wind power, followed by California. Both states have developed wind farms with the Horse Hollow Wind Energy Center in Texas taking the lead as the nation's largest wind farm. Also, solar energy is moving forward again, after an initial start in the 1970s and then a steep drop-off in support. States such as Nevada have built major solar power centers as part of its Solar Energy Generating Systems. Nine solar plants have been constructed in the desolate Mojave Desert, making the entire system the largest solar plant in the world. Finally, there is geothermal energy with 75 projects either completed or underway. Currently, the United States leads the world in geothermal energy.

But support for alternative energy sources like wind power are not always welcomed. Massachusetts has been involved in a long debate over placing a wind farm off the coast in Nantucket Sound. There has been extensive opposition from residents in the area as they claimed a negative impact on the ocean and on marine and bird life.[18] Nevertheless, despite the opposition in the fall of 2016, the first offshore wind farm opened up off the waters of Rhode Island. Many feel that it is only a matter of time before a wind farm opens in Nantucket Sound.

Despite the initiatives to introduce energy alternatives and advance conservation efforts in the United States, there are many experts who believe that this country will never become energy independent and that market forces rather than government programs remain the most effective way to provide Americans with the oil that they need. Despite all the promise shown by alternative technologies, the advance of these sources of energy will not be sufficient to provide the United States with that $1.4 billion a day craving for oil. Justin Fox, the editor-at-large of the business magazine *Fortune,* advocated for market forces and a continued flow of oil from the Middle East when he stated, "right now it costs less to pump oil from the sands of the Arabian peninsula than from pretty much anywhere else on earth. Why would we want to punish ourselves by cutting ourselves off from the cheapest oil?"[19] While Fox's position may not resonate with Americans paying ever-rising prices for gas at the pump, the argument made by Fox is that "going green" will not automatically make the United States energy independent, at least not in the next 30 to 40 years. Despite the promises of politicians, we will likely remain energy dependent and must accept the harsh reality of a long-term process of change and sacrifice that may bring us closer to energy independence. Fox's position is echoed by highly respected energy expert Daniel Yergin, who stated in *Foreign Policy* that "global energy use will increase almost 50% from 2006–2030 and that oil will continue to provide 30% or more of the world's energy in 2030."[20]

The energy challenges that currently face the United States will be dealt with on a number of fronts. There will be incentives and encouragement to develop new energy technologies, there will be a transition to new fuel sources, there will be a push to build more fuel-efficient automobiles and trucks, there will be new efforts to find new fields of oil and natural gas, and there will be pressure placed on the oil producers to keep the price of "liquid gold" as low as possible. In the coming years, there also will be considerable pressure placed on automakers, oil and gas companies, and industrial users to take aggressive and costly measures to address the energy needs. Many Americans are convinced that there are solutions to our energy dependence, especially in the auto industry, that have languished for years without action being taken. Moreover, Americans believe that oil and gas companies have been making windfall profits without care and concern for the impact on the American consumer, the American economy, and the American environment. Americans will demand action of their national political leaders and will hold them accountable if significant changes in our energy system are not forthcoming.[21]

The Great Debate

The key to the energy challenges faced by the United States appears to be a transition from the traditional sources of energy such as oil, coal, and natural gas to a range of alternative sources such as solar, wind, and geothermal. For this transition to occur, there will also have to be a change in the thinking and habits of the American consumer.

Debate Topic

Is it possible to move to alternative energy sources in the near future and lessen our dependence on fossil fuels? What steps will have to be taken in order to achieve this goal?

Critical Thinking Questions

1. Why has the United States taken so long to move toward energy independence?
2. Do you believe that the American people and American business can make the adjustments and the sacrifices necessary to bring an end to our energy challenges?
3. Are wind, solar, geothermal, and biofuel the answers to our energy challenges?
4. Do you agree with the policy of offshore drilling and pipelines through the heartland of this country even though there could be environmental dangers?
5. What suggestions would you make in order to deal with the energy challenges in this country?

Connections

The United States Department of Energy is responsible in large part for our energy policy. Visit its site at www.doe.gov

The Environmental Protection Agency is a critical bureaucracy also developing and implementing environmental policy in the United States. See www.epa.gov

The Energy Collective is a non-partisan organization made up of energy experts that comments on and evaluates energy policy. Visit the site at www.energycollective.com

The Energy Information Administration provides valuable data on the status of energy initiatives and energy projections. See www.eia.gov

The Sierra Club has long been one of the most visible organizations advocating for environmental protection and alternative energy sources. See www.sierraclub.org

A Few Books to Read

Jacobs, Meg, *Panic at the Pump: The Energy Crisis and the Transformation of American Politics in the 1970s* (New York: Hill and Wang, 2016).

Gold, Russell, *The Boom: How Fracking Ignited the American Energy Revolution and Changed the World* (New York: Simon and Schuster, 2014).

Hakes, Jay, *A Declaration of Energy Independence: How Freedom From Foreign Oil Can Improve National Security, Our Economy and the Environment* (New York: John Wiley, 2008).

Skipka, Kenneth and Louis Theodore, *Energy Resources: Availability, Management and Environmental Impacts* (London: CRC, Taylor Francis Group, 2014).

Yergin, Daniel, *The Prize: The Epic Quest for Oil, Money and Power* (New York: Free Press, 2008).

Notes

1. US Department of Energy, Annual Energy Report, July, 2016.
2. The data is from the US Energy Information Administration, March 17, 2016.
3. Ibid.
4. See Oil Embargo, 1973–1974, Office of the Historian, US State Department.
5. Ashley J. Tellis, "India and China Rise: Competition and Cooperation?" Carnegie Endowment for Peace, January 15, 2008.
6. Dennis Jacobe, "Americans Want More Emphasis on Solar, Wind," *Gallup Poll*, March 27, 2013.
7. http://whitehouse.gov/news/releases/2008/03/20080305.html
8. http://www/whitehouse.gov/news/releases/2008/03/20080305-2html
9. "The Energy Independence and Security Act of 2007: A Summary," Congressional Research Service, December 21, 2007.
10. See Keith Laing, "Governor-Elect Rick Scott Blasts Obama's Offshore Oil Drilling Ban," *The News Service of Florida*, December 2, 2010.
11. See Seth Hanlon, "Big Oil's Misbegotten Tax Gusher," *Center for American Progress*, May 5, 2011.

12. Nick Bunkley and Michelene Magrod, "Obama Criticizes Automakers on Fuel Economy," *New York Times*, May 7, 2007, www.nytimes.com/2007/05/07/us/politics/07cnd.obama.html

13. "House Proposal to Tap Strategic Oil Reserves Fails," *MSNBC*, www.msnbc.com/id/25839620

14. John M. Broder, "Report Slams Administration for Underestimating Gulf Spill," *New York Times*, October 6, 2010.

15. See Darryl Fears and Juliet Eilperin, "Obama Limits Ocean Drilling," *Washington Post*, December 21, 2016.

16. See "Keystone, XL Pipeline: Why Is It So Disputed," *BBC News*, 2015, www.bbc.com/news/world-u-canada-30103078. See also "What the Keystone Pipeline's Death Really Means," *Fortune*, November 8, 2015.

17. Jack Healy, "Tensions Rising Over Pipeline, Tribes Dig In: We're Staying," *New York Times*, October 10, 2016.

18. See Tatiana Schlossberg, "America's First Offshore Wind Farm Spins to Life," *New York Times*, December 14, 2016.

19. Justin Fox, "Energy Independence Is a Disaster in the Making," *Fortune*, March 1, 2006.

20. Daniel Yergin, "It's Still the One," *Foreign Policy*, September/October, 2009.

21. Brendan Moore and Stafford Nichols, "Americans Still Favor Energy Conservation Over Production," *Gallup Poll*, April 2, 2014. See also Michael Levi, "America's Energy Opportunity: How to Harness the New Sources of U.S. Power," *Foreign Affairs*, May/June, 2013.

19

POVERTY, **INEQUALITY,** AND **SOCIAL** WELFARE

Issue Focus

One of the functions of the US government that has expanded over time is responding to the needs of those Americans who are poor and require some level of assistance. Since the Depression of the 1930s and during the recent Great Recession, government has become increasingly involved in developing policies and programs that seek to alleviate poverty and provide opportunities for those who are poor to move out of poverty. Despite the growth in government's social welfare responsibility, there has been widespread opposition from those who believe that the expenditures related to poverty reduction are excessive and not properly monitored. Moreover, an additional criticism is that governmental leaders, especially Democrats, have not been vigorous in demanding that those in poverty help themselves and not become dependent on assistance programs. As a result of these criticisms, there have been significant changes made in social welfare policy in the United States and more are expected in the coming years by the Trump administration. But whatever changes are introduced, it is certain to create heated debates over how much the government should support those in need and at what cost.

Chapter Objectives

This issue chapter will seek to:

1. Present the policy evolution of public-supported welfare in the United States, with particular emphasis on the welfare reform achieved during the Clinton administration and future changes during the Trump administration.

2. Examine the points of division both in the United States and in policymaking circles over whether government at all levels should provide assistance to those in need or should instead rely more on private support and focus on personal responsibility.

3. Describe the current challenges faced by those in poverty or those facing economic, health, or personal problems and the role of government in dealing with those challenges.

SOME BACKGROUND

Despite the enormous wealth in the United States, there are approximately 47 million Americans, or about 15% of the population, who have been designated as living in poverty. In a country of 320 million people, that means that one in eight Americans is defined as poor, with almost 13 million children growing up in poverty. When compared with other advanced industrial democracies, the United States has not been successful, despite numerous programs, at reducing poverty and moving the poor into the mainstream of American economic life. As Isabel Sawhill, a noted poverty expert at the Brookings Institution has stated, "Despite our wealth . . . poverty is more prevalent in the United States than in most of the rest of the industrialized world. It is also more prevalent now than it was in the early seventies, when the incidence of poverty in America reached a post-war low."[1]

The profile of a poor person in the United States is an individual or a family who is defined by the government as falling beneath the poverty line, an income level that is used to determine who is eligible for the various programs designed to assist the poor. A 2014 calculation set the poverty line at an annual income of $24,300 for a family of four. In many cases that family of four is headed by a single female who is likely to be an African-American or a Hispanic who lives in a rural area (one in seven residents) or urban center (one in nine residents).[2] Whites make up approximately 10% of those who are poor in the United States; African-Americans, 26%; Hispanics, 24%; Asians, 12%; and Native Americans, 26%. As to the geographic region with the largest percentage of poor people, the South, according to census data compiled in 2003, had 14% of the population who were defined as poor, with the Midwest coming in with the lowest level of poverty with 10.7% poor.[3] The states with the highest incidence of poverty are New Mexico, Mississippi, and Louisiana; those states with the lowest incidence of poverty are Maryland and New Hampshire.[4]

The key demographic relative to poverty in America are young, single women. Much has been written about what is termed the "feminization" of poverty in the United States as young women who have children out of wedlock, or whose husbands or boyfriends have divorced them, abandoned them, or have been incarcerated, fall into poverty. Divorce, especially, creates serious poverty challenges for women. Studies have shown that, when a woman is divorced with young children, her standard of living decreases by 73%, while the standard of living for the man actually increases by 42%. The young women who make up the bulk of those Americans on welfare typically have little education, young children, irregular child support payments, and few marketable skills.[5] According to US Census data from 2013, the poverty rate among single male heads of households was 15%, while the poverty rate among single female heads of households was a staggering 39.8%.[6]

Although there has been much emphasis placed on the "feminization" of poverty in the United States, being poor in America can touch just about anyone and can be found just around the corner. The loss of a job or some sort of disability can easily contribute to a person or family falling below the government standard. Even those Americans who are working often can qualify for government assistance as minimum wage jobs ($7.25 at the federal level, although 30 states exceed that amount) do not provide enough income to lift a working family above the poverty line. The government estimates that about 10% of those families who qualify for assistance do so even though they are employed full-time. There is also growing evidence that America is now a country where there are millions of working homeless people as high rents and energy costs combined with low wages make it difficult for working poor to maintain a residence, forcing them into shelters or some type of congregate housing.[7] There is also mounting evidence that the United States has a high incidence of income inequality as the gap between the rich and the poor grows and the numbers of Americans in the middle classes are struggling to maintain a modicum of income stability. As mentioned earlier, a study from the Federal Reserve Board in 2013 that surveyed American consumers found that 47% of the respondents could not meet a $400 emergency unless they borrowed the money, sold a possession, or did not address the emergency.[8]

Data Bank

Inequality and Poverty in the United States

The poorest half of the United States owns 2.5% of the country's wealth, the top 1% owns 35% of the wealth.

The top 1% of Americans own 50% of investment assets (stocks, bonds, mutual funds); the poorest half own just .5% of the investments.

The bottom 90% of America owns 73% of the debt.

Young people in the United States are getting poorer. The median wealth of people under 35 has dropped 68% since 1984. The median wealth of older Americans has increased 42%.

In 1946 a child born into poverty had about a 50% chance of scaling up the income ladder into the middle class. In 1980 the chances were about 40%; in 2015 the chances are 33%.

Source: US Census and Pew Research

To respond to the presence of poverty in America, over the years federal and state governments have developed a wide range of public assistance or welfare programs that are designed to address the many causes and challenges faced by those who are poor. It is often said that the United States has a two-tiered social welfare system. The top tier of social insurance is for members of the middle class who benefit from programs such as Social Security, Medicare, and unemployment compensation. In each of these programs the employee or the employer or both will make a contribution through a payroll deduction toward the payment of the insurance and then receive the benefit upon retirement, if hospitalized, or unemployed. These social insurance programs are popular among Americans since they help fund retirements, hospital stays, and periods of unemployment.

Then there is the second or lower tier of the social welfare system, which is designed to address the economic problems brought on by poverty or disability. Such programs are usually made up of direct payments to single parents with children, food stamps, housing subsidies or public housing placements, job training, and free or reduced medical care. At the core of the second tier social welfare system are programs well known to American such as food stamps (subsidies to purchase food), Medicaid (medical care for the poor), Supplementary Security Income (SSI) to assist seniors with additional income, the US Department of Labor's Employment and Training Administration, and Temporary Assistance for Needy Families (TANF), which in 1996 replaced the Aid To Families with Dependent Children (AFDC) program. These programs are in large part based on a means test, which requires those seeking assistance to prove that they fall below the government poverty standards and are indeed eligible for assistance. The government has also developed a tax credit program called the Earned Income Tax Credit (EITC), which provides rebates for poor Americans who file their income tax and show a level of income that merits a tax rebate through the EITC program. Finally, the Affordable Care Act has addressed the lack of health insurance for many American at or below the poverty level through its subsidized program and the Children's Health Insurance Program (CHIP), a joint federal and state program that provides health insurance to children whose families earn too much to receive Medicaid assistance but not enough to purchase private insurance.[9]

Programs such as Social Security, Medicare, and unemployment compensation are viewed positively as social insurance in which citizens or their employers or both make contributions to the funds. The second tier programs, which provide a safety net for those who are less fortunate or need some temporary assistance to get them through a tough period, do not, however, receive the same level of citizen or political support and, as a result, have often been the target of government belt-tightening, partisan bickering, and citizen criticism. A series of polls by CBS and *The New York Times*, taken in the mid-1990s before substantial welfare reform was initiated, showed overwhelmingly negative views toward those on welfare. Responses such as "people are so dependent on welfare that they will never get off" were common. An updated poll in 2014 poll showed, however, that there was less blame put on the poor for creating their own circumstances of poverty and more sensitivity to the reality that poverty is the result of forces out of their control (for example, the Great Recession of 2009 with its subsequent high unemployment, loss of homes, and difficulty in finding new job opportunities).[10]

Poverty, disability, and growing income inequality in America have been the driving forces behind numerous social welfare programs that were developed dating far back in the early 20th century. An example is the so-called "mother's pensions" given to single mothers who had no means of support and had a number of children to care for. These public assistance programs were expanded significantly during the Great Depression era in the 1930s when President Franklin Delano Roosevelt introduced the New Deal with its "alphabet soup" of lettered programs (such as the Civilian Conservation Corp—CCC—and the Works Progress Administration—WPA) that were designed to put unemployed Americans to work on public projects. After World War II, and certainly during the heyday of liberal Democratic control of the presidency and the Congress, welfare programs expanded, specifically during the Johnson administration's Great Society initiatives such as the food stamp program, Head Start (early childhood education), and housing subsidies.

It was not until the Reagan administration in 1981 that public assistance or welfare programs came under greater scrutiny and criticism as the emphasis of government shifted toward personal responsibility, church and community assistance, and job training. Although the welfare programs that had been in place since the New Deal and the Great Society continued to receive government support, budget increases were more modest and eligibility requirements were tightened. Moreover, there was greater reliance placed on state solutions for those on welfare rather than large-scale government programs. The key transition in the fight to change welfare policy in the United States came in 1994 when the Republicans took control of the House and Senate and pushed the Clinton administration to support new approaches to poverty reduction. After decades of liberal Democratic solutions to poverty that accented heavy government involvement and huge outlays of federal funds, the conservative revolution started by Ronald Reagan placed its mark on the welfare system.[11]

DEBATES, DIFFERENCES, AND DIVISIONS

It is often said that Americans are the most generous and caring people on earth, but that designation has not stopped them from engaging in spirited public policy debates over the extent to which government should come to their assistance with a range of programs from cash handouts, tax rebates, food and housing subsidies, and other forms of redistributive programs. Many Americans continue to hold true to the work ethic, self-reliance, and the principle of individual responsibility as the keys to economic success rather than government programs. Large government outlays for welfare and a redistributive policy of moving assistance from taxpayers to the poor are viewed as paternalistic, fostering dependency, and creating a "nanny state" where government spends huge portions of the national budget on taking care of the poor. Because of widespread support for this anti-welfare position, frequent efforts have been made in the political arena to either cut back many of the second tier programs, make eligibility more difficult, or move those eligible into work or training programs. Conservatives in policymaking circles have often targeted income transfer programs to the poor such as Transitional Assistance For Needy Families (TANF), food stamps, and Medicaid as creating a cycle of dependency, claiming the poor rely on these assistance programs and, as a result, feel no pressure to remove themselves from the welfare rolls.

Supporters of government intervention in poverty reduction, however, stress the humanitarian nature of government poverty reduction programs and the obligation of government to provide a safety net of support for those most vulnerable. These supporters of government activism cite the failures of the market system to address poverty, the income inequality that is growing in this country, and the inability of religious, community, and charitable organizations to fully respond to the growing level of poverty in this country. Moreover, the supporters of government poverty reduction programs show that there have been many welfare programs that have had a positive impact on the poor such as the Head Start program that places young poor children in pre-school environments as a way of providing them with an early educational experience. Also, many government-sponsored job training programs have helped to lift the poor out of poverty by providing them with the skills necessary to become financially independent.

In recent years, the trend in policy circles has been to move away from these income transfer programs and begin experiments with what has come to be called workfare, which are programs that set limits on the time an individual can receive welfare benefits and thus must find work or be trained for work in order to eventually move out of the public assistance system. As a result of a waiver from the Reagan administration regarding rules associated with the AFDC program, the state of Wisconsin began the experimentation process as it developed its own workfare program that eventually became a model for other states and for pushing the federal government to take measures that completely revamped the long-running Aid To Families with Dependent Children (AFDC). In a ten-year period ending in 1997, the AFDC caseload statewide in Wisconsin dropped by 50%, and in the inner city, the drop was 25%. The success achieved in Wisconsin in dramatically reducing the AFDC recipients spread to a whole host of states during the administration of George H.W. Bush as states took the lead in forming reform policies that accented work and set time limits for participation in AFDC programs.[12]

The welfare reform movement that started in Wisconsin eventually led to the national debate over federal involvement in poverty reduction. This debate centered around the landmark legislation formally called the Personal Responsibility and Work Opportunity Reconciliation Act, which came to be called the Welfare Reform Act of 1996. After two versions of the bill were vetoed by President Clinton because of his concern that Republicans were merely seeking to end welfare without proper safeguards for work training and work opportunities, the president signed a third version of the bill in large part because, in his 1992 election campaign, he promised to "end welfare as we know it" and Republicans pressured him to keep that promise.[13] Clinton paid a heavy price for his agreement to sign the legislation as liberals said that Clinton was trapped by his own rhetoric and Republican demands that he keep his promise about ending welfare.

On the Record

Franklin Delano Roosevelt, who was president during the Great Depression, said the following about poverty in America:

> We cannot be content, no matter how high that general standard of living may be, if some fraction of our people—whether it be one-third

(continued)

On the Record   (continued)

> or one-fifth or one-tenth—is ill fed, ill clothed, ill housed, and inse-
> cure. The test of our progress is not whether we add more to the abun-
> dance of those who have much, it is whether we provide enough for
> those who have too little.
>
> It seems to me to be equally plain that no business which
> depends for existence on paying less than living wages to its work-
> ers has any right to continue in this country. By "business" I mean
> the whole of commerce as well as the whole of industry, by workers
> I mean all workers, the white collar class as well as the men in over-
> alls, and by living wage I mean more than a bare subsistence level.
> I mean the wages of a decent living.

The Welfare Reform Act had as its core the concepts of welfare to work
and time limits for receiving benefits. The legislation required that, after six
years, at least 50% of those on the state welfare rolls would be required to
work. If those targets were not met, federal funding would be reduced. The
key to the welfare reform initiative was state control through block grants,
large appropriations of federal money used to fund the new programs and
provide job training, and other assistance to those seeking to get off welfare.
The legislation, for example, dismantled AFDC and replaced it with a scaled-
down federal program, TANF. Most importantly, the legislation allowed each
of the 50 states to set rules for how long welfare recipients could remain on
the assistance rolls while they sought work or trained for work. After a certain
period, those on the welfare rolls would be removed from receiving assistance.
The 1996 Welfare Reform Act thus made poverty reduction and government
programs a largely state responsibility.

The most controversial part of the Welfare Reform Act was the over
$54 billion that was saved by steep cuts in the food stamp program and the
decision to refuse welfare benefits to legal immigrants. The food stamp program had been a regular target of Republicans, who saw it as filled with fraud
and abuse. But supporters of the program feared that the cuts from 80 cents
per person per meal to 66 cents per person per meal would translate into a
reduction for a family of four of $435 by 1998, with some of the poorest fam-
ilies losing over $600 in food stamp subsidies.[14] The other decision to deny
benefits to legal immigrants was also controversial and contested. With over
600,000 legal immigrants losing Medicaid benefits and over 1 million losing
food stamp subsidies, the personal and financial impact was devastating. The
position of those supporting the cuts to legal immigrants claimed that the benefits were a magnet to family members of immigrants already in the United
States and that federal or state programs should not be offered to those individuals who are not citizens.[15] Opponents of the cuts claimed that these legal
immigrants paid taxes, held jobs, and were law-abiding residents of this country who would be seriously impacted. Because of the shift to state control of

welfare reform, some governors pledged that they would provide assistance to legal immigrants despite the intent of the law.[16]

The Welfare Reform Act set off a chain reaction of state welfare programs designed to meet the federal legislation and to implement rules and regulations on time in assistance programs, job training requirements, and benefit levels. Almost immediately it became apparent that some states with more resources would be able to offer more training and benefit alternatives. Vermont, for example, was viewed as a state that would be able to invest more generously in welfare reform programs, while Texas and many southern states would not have the capability to provide a range of alternative employment options. Wisconsin, the initial leader in welfare reform, offered four employment options—regular employment, trial jobs with state subsidies, community service jobs, and transitional skill development for those with few marketable skills.

But what became clear in the days after the law was passed was that there would be extensive state experimentation in implementing the law and a range of uses for the federal block grants designed to speed the movement from welfare to work. Some states like Arkansas decided to provide incentives that would provide bonuses to welfare recipients who found jobs, while New York developed a large public works programs much like the New Deal "alphabet" programs. The states, however, did have a common approach to the new law: welfare officials would help recipients train and find work and, more importantly, assistance was temporary.

In February 2006, Congress reauthorized the TANF program and mandated that states increase the amount of work participation among those receiving welfare benefits. Currently, 50% of welfare recipients must work at least 30 hours per week to receive benefits, but there are differences among the states as to what qualifies as work, how to calculate the level of state work participation, and the manner in which states will be credited for caseload reductions. Despite these areas of disagreement over the rules, nine states have already toughened the work requirements with Iowa, Michigan, Tennessee, and Wisconsin demanding that welfare recipients work 40 hours a week. There is agreement among state and federal officials that those states that have not strengthened their work requirements will have to do so in the coming years.[17] In 2016 low-income residents in 21 states were notified that they would lose their food stamp supplements if they failed to meet more stringent work requirements. This notification affected over 1 million poor Americans in states like Florida, Tennessee, and North Carolina. A rule change in the Federal Supplemental Nutrition Assistance Program was triggered by an improving national economy, but advocates for the poor state that many of those who receive food stamps will not easily find work, especially in states with lingering unemployment rates.[18] Currently, as a result of the 1996 Welfare Reform Act and the rules that were implemented, states require able-bodied adults between the ages of 18–49 who have no children or other dependents to work, volunteer, or attend education/training classes for at least 80 hours a month in order to receive the food aid.

During the heady days of economic prosperity during Clinton's second term, the Welfare Reform Act achieved significant success, at least in terms of substantial reductions of those receiving governmental assistance. From 1994–2002 there was a 57% reduction in the welfare case load in the United States as those on assistance moved into the world of work. In many states, government officials pressed hard to get people off the welfare rolls, even though single mothers, for example, had difficulty with daycare needs, and men often could not find work that paid a sufficient salary to move them above the poverty line. While many political leaders praised the Welfare Reform Act and its implementation by the states, there is another side to this success story.

The substantial drop in the welfare rolls benefitted from a strong economy, low unemployment, and states with the capacity to provide worker training programs. Conservatives touted the success rate in the new welfare environment as not only reducing the number of people receiving government assistance, but fostering a new culture of work and responsibility. Michael Tanner of the Cato Institute, citing a study done by the Manpower Demonstration Research Corporation, stated that "the majority of former welfare recipients believe that their lives will be better in one to five years. Many of these recipients actually praise welfare reform for encouraging them to look for work, for giving them a fresh start and for giving them a chance to make things better for themselves and their children."[19]

But as the country entered difficult economic times in 2008 and 2009, the number of people seeking welfare assistance increased dramatically, and political leaders, particularly Democrats who initially supported the legislation, began to have second thoughts. Peter Edelman, a former assistant secretary in the Department of Health and Human Services during the Clinton administration and a critic of the Welfare Reform Act, blasted the legislation as an attack on the poor, and single mothers in particular, and that it was an unrealistic experiment in moving people from poverty into work.[20]

FYI

The Great Recession devastated the American economy and exacerbated the challenges of homelessness and hunger. An estimated $16.4 trillion of household wealth was lost during the recession, with the poor being hardest hit. This loss of wealth contributed to chronic homelessness, which in 2009 was estimated at 643,000 individuals and 649,000 individuals in 2010. Once the national economy began to improve and the federal government, states, and non-profits began to aggressively address homelessness with financial resources and housing development, the number of chronic homeless began to show faint signs of improvement. In 2015 the chronic homeless count dropped to 564,708. But much work needs to be done to build new homes, improve shelter services, and in many states, get homeless individuals and homeless families out of hotels and motels that are cramped and often not near vital services. An even greater challenge is hunger. In 2014 there were an estimated 48.1 million Americans who were defined as food insecure, which means that according to the US Department of Agriculture the poor "lack access at times to enough food for all household members." Currently, one in six Americans is categorized as food insecure. To address this problem, many communities in the country have opened up food pantries with donated food to assist those who are food insecure. These pantries are only expanding and serving more adults and children.

Source: US Department of Housing and Urban Development and Department of Agriculture

The 1996 Welfare Reform Act has fostered numerous ten-, fifteen-, and twenty-year studies to determine just how successful the legislation was and whether improvements in poverty reduction have indeed been achieved. What researchers found was that, initially, welfare rolls shrank as people found jobs and poverty rates declined, as did hunger. But when the national economy deteriorated, especially as a result of the Great Recession, job opportunities evaporated, wages stagnated, and training programs were scaled back. The safety net began to shred and poverty rebounded. Poverty experts did conclude that "the entire package of reforms had little effect on income and poverty" but that "certain policies—including more lenient eligibility requirements for welfare recipients and more generous financial incentives to work—did seem to make a difference, at least during the good economic times." Of greatest concern for the welfare reform researchers was the continued high level of child poverty in the United States and the problems associated with sufficient funding of childcare subsidies and health care coverage for children. Childhood poverty continues to be a disturbing condition in the United States, and the weakened national economy combined with insufficient support at the federal and state level has done little to address the growing numbers of young people who are poor.[21]

Since the signing of the Welfare Reform Act of 1996, there is no doubt that the concepts of welfare to work, time limits for receiving benefits, block grants from the federal government to the states, and state control of welfare requirements are now firmly in place in the United States. Proponents of the changes will tout the declining caseloads and the thousands of success stories of former welfare recipients now leading independent and successful lives. Critics of the new system, while acknowledging the decline in caseloads and evidence of successful transitions from welfare to work, point out that much of the positive results came during strong economic times and that, as a result of the softer economy since 2007, there are new signs that those in poverty are growing in numbers and the demands for a deeper safety net are increasing. If the national economy continues to remain weak, while federal and state support for those in need remains inadequate, the gains achieved in welfare reform since 1996 will be nullified and the policy prescriptions placed into question.[22]

The record of the Obama administration on poverty reduction has been mixed. In raw numbers, those in poverty increased by six million during President Obama's administration. Officially as of 2013, the number of people in poverty was 45.3 million, some 5.5 million more than in 2008 when Obama took office. In 2008 there were 13.2% Americans in poverty; in 2013 there were 14.5% Americans in poverty. Critics such as Mitt Romney, who ran against Obama in 2012, often used this data to slam Obama for a failed poverty policy as the Republican candidate accented the importance of building jobs, not expanding costly government programs. As for Obama, his administration cited data that showed the overall number of those in poverty was the result of the impact of the Great Recession and that the percentage of those in poverty actually decreased from 15.1% in 2010 to the 14.5% in 2013. Nevertheless, the Obama administration's record on relieving a serious poverty problem was not successful.[23]

It is fair to state, however, that the Obama administration made a major effort in the wake of the Great Recession to respond to the devastating impact on the poor.[24] The American Recovery and Reinvestment Act, the stimulus legislation that Obama was successful in implementing in the early days of his first term, was in part an anti-poverty bill. For example, $20 billion was earmarked for the Supplemental Nutrition Assistance Program (SNAP), designed to expand food programs for the poor; $2 billion for the Neighborhood Stabilization Fund, a program to build community institutions and service agencies; $1.5 billion for homelessness initiatives; $5 billion for weatherization of urban homes, and $3.9 billion for job training. All these programs plus increases and extensions of unemployment compensation were designed to have an immediate impact on those hit hard by the Great Recession.[25]

In his second term, President Obama stressed the growing economy and the drop in the unemployment rate as the keys to addressing poverty; there was evidence that those in poverty were beginning to lift themselves up. But again the move upward out of poverty was slow and often wrapped in the debate over how best to reduce the numbers of those in need—government programs or job expansion. During the 2016 presidential campaign, little was said about poverty in America as the middle class became the focus of attention, and what commentary did surface was often criticism alleging that Obama's policies and federal expenditures had little impact on the overall number in poverty. President Obama did emphasize in the closing months of his presidency that recent economic data pointed to a 5% increase in personal income and a significant decline in those in poverty. The increase in personal income and the drop in poverty were viewed by Obama as proof that his economic policies had revitalized the country from the depths of the Great Recession and, combined with low unemployment rates, were signs of a vibrant economy and a sign that poverty was diminishing. Despite the good news presented by the president, the debate over how best to deal with the millions in poverty remains unresolved.[26] Donald Trump, during the campaign, regularly castigated the president for the high level of poverty during his eight years in office. Trump promised to use job creation as the key to ending poverty in America. The Republican-controlled Congress echoed Trump but went further as Republican members pushed to make cuts in the safety net in areas such as food stamps and housing subsidies, and they made efforts to weaken Medicaid.

Because the welfare system in this country has, in large part, moved from a government spending/income transfer approach to a welfare-to-work model with time limits, poverty reduction programs in this country are now part of a larger ideological debate between liberals and conservatives. Liberals remain convinced that support for key programs like food stamps, Medicaid, health insurance for children, daycare subsidies, and housing support is insufficient to meet the needs of the poor, while conservatives hold true to their belief that poverty will not be reduced by large government programs but rather by individual responsibility, job training, and work. As can be expected when two differing ideologies ram heads, there are elements of truth and effectiveness in both approaches. If poverty reduction were an easy policy challenge, then moving poor people toward a more prosperous life would have been solved decades ago. If there is an answer with some degree of certainty regarding persistent poverty, it is that a government safety net (one that does not foster lifelong dependency, combined with solid incentives and opportunities to move off welfare into the world of work) and independence are the pathways to poverty reduction and welfare reform. One thing is certain, however, and that is that a strong economy often is the critical ingredient for moving people from welfare to financial independence.

The Great Debate

Because poverty remains a serious problem in the United States, there continue to be differences in policy approaches for dealing with those that are poor. Liberals embrace government support and assistance programs, conservatives stress jobs and assistance from private sources.

Debate Topic

What model of poverty reduction is best in dealing with poverty, the government-sponsored safety net approach or the work and personal responsibility approach?

Critical Thinking Questions

1. Why do you believe there are over 47 million Americans officially classified at poor?
2. The United States has one of the highest levels of income inequality between the rich and the poor. Why do such inequalities exist in one of the richest countries in the world?

3. Where do you stand on the personal responsibility and workfare approach to welfare reform?
4. Do you believe that the United States government has been too generous with financial support for poor people, or is it necessary to provide a substantial safety net for those who fall into poverty?
5. What are our obligations as US citizens to help those who are poor?

Connections

The Welfare Rights Organizing Coalition is one of the more prominent advocates for those on welfare. See http://wroc.org

For critiques on welfare and welfare policy see the Republican Party positions at www.republicanviews.org

The Voices of Poverty is a site that chronicles the hardships of those in poverty in the 21st century. See www.thevoicesofpoverty.org

The National Center for Children in Poverty advocates for those young people mired in poverty and hunger. See www.nccp.org

The US Interagency Council on Homelessness is the federal government's advocate for the homeless. Visit its site at www.ich.gov

A Few Books to Read

Edelman, Peter, *So Rich, So Poor: Why It's So Hard to End Poverty in America* (New York: New Press, 2012).

Hatcher, Daniel, *The Poverty Industry: The Exploitation of America's Most Vulnerable Citizens* (New York: NYU Press, 2016).

Novak, Michael, *Social Justice Isn't What You Think It Is* (New York: Encounter Books, 2015).

Schaefer, H. Luke and Kathryn Edin, *$2.00 a Day: Living on Almost Nothing in America* (New York: Mariner Books, 2016).

Tirando, Linda, *Hand to Mouth: Living in Bootstrap America* (New York: G.P. Putnam and Sons, 2014).

Notes

1. See Isabel Sawhill, "Poverty in the United States," *The Concise Encyclopedia of Economics*, 1988, www.econlib.org
2. See "Income and Poverty," United States Census Bureau, September 13, 2016.
3. See Drew DeSilver, "Who's Poor in America? 50 Years Into the 'War on Poverty,' a Data Portrait," Pew Research Center, January 13, 2014.
4. See Erika Rawes, "6 States and D.C. With the Most Poverty," *USA Today Money*, February 16, 2015.

5. See Carman Rios, "These 5 Statistics Prove That We're Feminizing Poverty (And Keeping Women Down in the Process)," *Everyday Feminism*, June 20, 2015.
6. "Income and Poverty," op. cit.
7. Julia Vitello-Martin, "Homeless in America," *Wall Street Journal*, January 18, 2007.
8. See Neal Gabler, "The Secret Shame of Middle Class Americans," *The Atlantic*, April 18, 2016.
9. Arloc Sherman, Danilo Trisi, and Sharon Parrott, "Various Supports for Low-Income Families Reduce Poverty and Have Long-Term Positive Effects on Families and Children," *Center on Budget and Policy Priorities*, July 30, 2013.
10. See Patrick O'Connor, "Attitudes Toward Poverty Show Dramatic Change," *Wall Street Journal*, June 20, 2014.
11. See a discussion of the Reagan policy toward social welfare policy in D. Lee Baldwin, *The Social Contract Revisited: Aims and Outcomes of President Reagan's Social Welfare Policy* (New York: Urban Institute, 1984).
12. Robert Rector, "Wisconsin's Welfare Miracle," Hoover Institution, March and April, 1997.
13. See Remarks on Signing of Act, Bill Clinton Transcripts, http://findarticles.com/p/articles/me_m2889/is_n34_v.32/ai_18819256
14. Dan Froomkin, "Welfare's Changing Face," *Washington Post*, July 23, 1998.
15. Chris Jenkins, "Food Stamps Must Stretch Even Further," *Washington Post National Weekly Edition*, June 28, 2008.
16. Steven Camarota, "Welfare Use By Legal and Illegal Immigrant Households," *Center for Immigration Studies*, September, 2015.
17. See Jennifer Medina, "California Weighs Protections for Immigrants Threatened by Trump Policies," *New York Times*, December 4, 2016.
18. Andrew M. Grossman, "Welfare Reform's Work Requirements Cannot Be Waived," Heritage Foundation, August 8, 2012.
19. "Many My Lose Food Stamps Under Federal Rule Changes," As reported in the Boston *Globe*, January 31, 2016.
20. Michael Tanner, "The Critics Were Wrong: Welfare Reform Turns 10," 2016, www.cato.org/pub_display.php?pub_id=6629
21. Peter Edelman and Barbara Ehrenreich, "Why Welfare Reform Has Failed," *Washington Post*, December 6, 2009.
22. See Clyde Haberman, "20 Years Later, Welfare Overhaul Resonates for Families and Candidates," *New York Times*, May 1, 2016.
23. Erik Eckholm, "Recession Raises Poverty Rate to a 15 Year High," *New York Times*, September 16, 2010.
24. Jonathan Capehart, "Obama's Call to Action on Poverty," *Washington Post*, February 13, 2013.
25. See the discussion of the American Recovery and Reinvestment Act at www.whitehouse.gov/issues/poverty
26. See Binyamin Appelbaum, "U.S. Household Income Grew 5.2% in 2015, Breaking Pattern of Stagnation," *New York Times*, September 13, 2016.

20 NATIONAL DEFENSE

Issue Focus

Defending the United States from attack and protecting our interests abroad is not only the highest priority of the American government but it is also big business. Thousands of companies are tied into the defense establishment, making billions of dollars in profits and employing hundreds of thousands of workers. Because of its importance to the nation, defense spending is one of the key stimulants of the American economy. However, defending the United States, despite its high priority, is not without its detractors and competitors for scarce government resources. Although the defense establishment has historically been adept at convincing Congress and the American people of the need for increased spending, the contentious issue of setting the proper balance between national security spending and domestic programs remains. This competition for the attention of government and the budgetary resources decisions made by the government has created a lively debate over national priorities.

Chapter Objectives

This issue chapter will seek to:

1. Explain the influence of what President Dwight Eisenhower called the military-industrial complex on defense spending and federal budget priorities.

2. Discuss the issues and concerns surrounding weapons procurement and defense contracting and the impact of defense spending on the national economy.

3. Describe the approach to defense spending of recent presidents and the relationship of that spending to our foreign policy objectives and international involvement.

SOME BACKGROUND

It is generally accepted in this country and most others that the primary purpose of government is the protection of the nation and its people from attack or the threat of attack. In the United States, the Preamble to the Constitution validates this purpose when it states that one of the chief responsibilities of government is to "Provide for the Common Defense." In order to achieve this objective, the United States government has, since its inception, formed a military and provided that military with the weapons, equipment, training, and support necessary to complete its stated mission. Over time, the United States military has grown not just in numbers and weapons, but in its role both as defender of the nation and as peacemaker, liberator, and occupying force in foreign theaters of operation.

Ronald Reagan, who was most responsible for a major buildup in national defense with his efforts to build a 600-ship Navy and spent trillions on a space-based nuclear weapons shield (better known as Star Wars), best summed up the importance of maintaining a strong defense when he gave a memorable national security speech in 1983 and said:

> Since the dawn of the atomic age, we've sought to reduce the risk of war by maintaining a strong deterrent and by seeking genuine arms control. "Deterrence" means simply this: making sure any adversary who thinks about attacking the United States, our allies, or our vital interests, concludes that the risks to him outweigh any potential gains. Once he understands that, he won't attack. We maintain the peace through our strength; weakness only invites aggression.[1]

Since the end of the Cold War and the demise of the Soviet Union, the United States military has become the #1 military force in the world with the best trained and best equipped armed forces. Because of its size and superiority, the American military often has been viewed as the logical choice for responding to the challenges in the world from small brush fire wars and humanitarian relief efforts to major invasions and occupations. Furthermore, after the tragedy of 9/11, the United States has been in a national security mode, thereby heightening the importance of the military. This is indeed a heady responsibility, but one that the Defense Department, the Joints Chiefs of Staff, and the men and women on the ground have responded to when called upon by the president and Congress.

The United States military has indeed come a long way from the early days of the revolution. From Washington's valiant efforts to keep his army intact during those dark days at Valley Forge and the overwhelming odds of facing the experienced British forces to the current Department of Defense residing in one of the world's largest buildings and controlling huge levels of government spending, the armed forces of the United States have historically been the leading institution within the government. Today, the United States Defense Department, by far the nation's largest bureaucracy, is made up of 2.7 million people, 1.5 million of whom are on active duty. After China, the United States has the largest armed forces in the world.[2]

The cost of running this large bureaucracy is staggering. In 2015 the defense budget was $612 billion, about 37% of total government spending and 54% of all discretionary spending (discretionary spending is spending that is not mandated payments to individuals such as Social Security and Medicare). The budget outlays in recent years are lower than in past years because the United States has removed most of its troops from Iraq and Afghanistan and Congress has put in place cost reduction requirements related to sequestration spending limits. In 2008, for example, at the height of the Iraq war, the United States defense budget was $750 billion. At the current level of spending, the United States allocates 3.5% of its GDP to the military, which is relatively low when compared to spending during World War II (37%) and the Vietnam War (9.4% in 1968). Spending for defense is concentrated in areas such as overseas operations, maintenance of bases and soldiers, and procurement of new weapons systems. It is important to point out that US military spending is larger than 168 other nations and is larger than the combined expenditures of the next nine countries such as China, Russia, France, Germany, and the United Kingdom.[3] To bring some perspective to the defense budget, the cost of running the State Department, our diplomatic bureaucracy, was $50 billion in 2015, and there are more members of all the military bands than there are Foreign Service officers.

With so many employees and such a significant budget, the Defense Department dominates the public policy scene in Washington. Presidents have often won the highest office because of their unqualified support for the armed forces and their willingness to use the military in order to achieve a national security interest. Congress has also played a key role in enhancing the power and influence of the Pentagon as members regularly jockey to win support for new weapons systems in their home district as well as protecting military bases that may be situated in their state. Further, the American public can almost always be counted on to show its patriotic spirit by supporting the men and women in uniform and viewing the military establishment and the enormity of its spending in a positive light.

The sheer size and cost of the military establishment in this country and its influence within the corridors of power in Washington often raises key questions such as "How much military spending is enough?" and "What about other competing national priorities?" As many critics of defense spending and Pentagon influence often remind the president and members of Congress, the constitution also mandates that the government should "Establish Justice, Ensure Domestic Tranquility, and Promote the General Welfare". President Eisenhower, in a memorable speech upon leaving the presidency in 1960, warned the nation about the power of what he termed the "military-industrial complex." In Eisenhower's view, the military and its partners in industry, who vie for lucrative weapons, equipment, and supply contracts, have such influence on the policy process and setting national priorities that, combined, they pose a threat to the fair and balanced budget setting and, indeed, the national interest. Eisenhower's admonition to the American people to be wary of the military-industrial complex has not diminished in relevance as there are constant debates in policy circles about the cost of maintaining our military establishment and what those costs mean in terms of their impact on other social and domestic programs.[4]

Besides the issue of the budget/spending power of the military and its allies in the industrial and technological sectors of the national economy, there is also the critical concern about the capability and readiness of the modern United States military. Since the Vietnam War, when the Johnson Administration imposed a military draft, the armed forces have been completely volunteer in nature, both in the regular service components of Army, Navy, Air Force, and Marines, and the state national guards and reserves. But in recent years, as a result of the commitments of ground troops in Afghanistan and Iraq, there have been major questions raised about whether the military is suffering from "over stretch" as troops serving in the Middle East have been forced to endure long periods of duty and being brought back into service despite returning to the reserves.[5] There was much talk by military commanders and critics of the Bush policy in Afghanistan and Iraq about whether the military has been severely weakened and its war-fighting capacity compromised. As a result of these issues of capability and readiness, there have been calls for new recruitment efforts and the creation of whole new battalions, and there have been even some legislative efforts to move to a return to the military draft.

Because the United States military occupies such a prominent and essential position in the government and in American society, it has enjoyed a high level of national trust and respect. But when examined from the perspectives of competing for scarce budgetary resources, defining its role in an ever changing and demanding international arena, and justifying its commitment to serve the national security interests, the military has, in recent years, faced increasing scrutiny and criticism. There is no doubt that the Iraq and Afghanistan wars have cast a light on the military and military leadership and forced a review of spending, mission, and readiness. The outcome of this review in the coming years will play an important part in defining the military of the future and may lead to a transformation of the armed forces.

On the Record

Upon leaving office in 1961, Dwight Eisenhower gave what is now considered his most famous speech on the dangers of the military-industrial complex. Below are the key sections of that speech:

This conjunction of an immense military establishment and a large arms industry is new in the American experience. The total influence—economic, political, even spiritual—is felt in every city, every state house, every office of the federal government. We recognize the imperative need for this development. Yet we must not fail to comprehend its grave implications. Our toil, resources and livelihood are all involved; so is the very structure of our society. In the councils of government, we must guard against the acquisition of unwarranted influence, whether sought or unsought, by the military-industrial complex. The potential for the disastrous rise of misplaced power exists and will persist.

DEBATES, DIFFERENCES, AND DIVISIONS

Because of its responsibility for national security and its high standing among the American public, debates, differences, and divisions involving the defense establishment have for decades centered not on the importance of the military or personnel issues, but rather on issues such as the cost of weapons systems, the cozy relationship with business interests providing those weapons systems, and the value and effectiveness of modernizing the armed forces. In recent years, the Defense Department has placed increased emphasis on more sophisticated and, ultimately, more costly weapons systems in order to match new war strategies. For example, the F-22A Raptor fighter program, the Air Force's most advanced combat aircraft, originally had a price tag of $62 billion. The cost for the F-22A exploded to the point where the Air Force had to reduce its purchases of the aircraft from 648 to 183. But even with that reduction in number and cost, one F-22A still will cost the American taxpayer $339 million per plane.[6] Recently there have been attempts by some in Congress to revive production of the F-22A to meet the original number, but the costs associated with developing new software and avionics equipment, plus the fact that, when completed, the jet would be outdated, has worked against a revival of the popular but flawed front line fighter jet.

The F-22 A is not the only high tech weapon to be swept up in cost overruns that have regularly embarrassed the Pentagon and fed the critics of military spending with new ammunition. The Government Accountability Office in 2008 did a study of weapons systems purchased by the Pentagon and found that, in 72 of these weapons purchases costing a total of $1.6 trillion, there was evidence of $295 million in cost-overruns. One particular program, the Army's Future Combat System, the next generation of computer-driven weaponry for the battlefield, cost $200 billion, which was $40 billion over the initial 2003 estimate. These cost overruns are joined by numerous examples of corruption and misspending, especially in Iraq and Afghanistan. Senator Bernie Sanders of Vermont, a long-time critic of the Pentagon and defense spending, documented a long list of waste and fraud such as the Air Force paying a private contractor $32 million to construct an air base in Iraq that was never built and a $300 million contract with the Afghan military where old and defective ammunition was sold through the Army Sustainment Command. Even more troublesome was the fact that the faulty ammunition was shipped through China, which was an apparent violation of United States statutes. As Sanders stated in his criticism of defense-related waste, "At a time when this country has a $9.3 trillion national debt, a declining economy, and enormous unmet needs, the time is long overdue for Congress to stop rubber-stamping White House requests for military spending and to address the Pentagon's needs within the context of our overall national priorities."[7]

FYI

The Pentagon continues to develop new weaponry not only to replace outdated weapons systems but also to respond to modernization efforts from its international competitors and rivals like China and Russia. In recent years, the United States has developed four major new weapons and weapons systems that are viewed as continuing this country's dominance as the world's strongest and most advanced military. Those weapons and weapons systems are:

The Ford class aircraft carrier—a new generation of aircraft carrier that has superior technological advances and is capable of anti-submarine, anti-ship, and land attacks along with providing air superiority.

The Virginia class submarine—the most advanced nuclear submarine in the world with advanced technology that neither China nor Russia has yet developed.

The B-2 Spirit bomber—capable of traveling 6,000 miles to deliver its bomb and missile payload, with stealth capabilities that are undetectable.

The F-35 Lightning Joint Strike Fighter—despite development cost overruns, this next generation of fighter jet is far superior than any in the arsenal of China or Russia.

Source: Department of Defense

The enormous costs of four new weapons systems has, in recent years, led the Defense Department to keep a closer eye on expenditures and to take action against contractors that have either delayed in finishing the project or have engaged in questionable billing and construction practices. In 2007 Navy Secretary Donald Winter canceled the construction of the second Littoral Combat ship with Lockheed Martin. The cancellation was based on Lockheed Martin's decision to increase the cost of the Littoral Combat ship from $220 million to $410 million. The Littoral Combat ship was supposed to be the next generation of the Navy's fleet and eventually make up one sixth of the 313-ship United States fleet, but cost overruns and tensions between the Pentagon and Lockheed Martin reduced the number developed.[8] In test runs in 2015 and 2016, the Littoral Combat ship had numerous problems, including an embarrassing complete shutdown as it traveled through the Panama Canal.

Another side to the military-industrial complex is the foreign military sales program that has been aggressively pursued by the Defense Department and the various major defense contractors. Between 2005 and 2006, $21 billion in contracts for US-made weapons and weapons systems were sold abroad. The Bush administration increased its foreign military sales as a means of currying favor with its allies and making new friends, particularly in the new 9/11 world of anti-terror initiatives. Countries that previously were banned from receiving United States arms sales such as Pakistan, India, and Indonesia were allowed to purchase weapons. Pakistan, a key ally in the war on terrorism, purchased $5 billion in sophisticated F-16 fighter jets in 2005 from Lockheed Martin Corporation, and Saudi Arabia placed an order worth $3 billion for Black Hawk helicopters and the Bradley armored land vehicles. Even smaller countries like the tiny sheikdom of Bahrain purchased $1 billion in military equipment from 2001–2006.[9]

For defense contractors, foreign military sales are a hedge against cuts in regular military procurement and, of course, are enormously profitable. Critics of this arms trade emphasize that the United States is the number one supplier of weapons to countries around the world, thus contributing to an ever growing arsenal of deadly weapons, often times to support autocratic regimes.[10] Moreover, such enormous sales of sophisticated weapons shift resources in many countries away from domestic needs to national defense. Military sales did not drop off during the Obama administration. The United States under Obama remained the world's largest seller of armaments. In fact, 50% of the global market in weapons and weapons systems is now controlled by the United States. In 2015 the sale of arms to foreign governments was $40 billion, up from $26 billion in 2014. The top purchasers of weapons in recent years were South Korea and Iraq.[11]

It is important also, when talking about major defense contractors, that mention be made of their impact on state and local economies as their manufacturing and research and development facilities are job generators that contribute significantly to economic development. During the Vietnam war and then the Reagan era of modernization, it was estimated that one out of ten working Americans was employed in a defense-related industry, either directly or in an industry that received some government contracts. That ratio diminished during the Clinton and also Bush years, but it does point out the importance that defense contractors bring to state and local economies.[12] So too with military bases, which house thousands of soldiers and their families. In states with major military installations like Ft. Hood (Texas), Ft. Campbell (Kentucky), Ft. Benning (Georgia), Newport News Naval Base (Virginia), 29 Palms Marine Base (California), and Offutt Air Force Base (Nebraska), surrounding towns have benefitted from the presence of the military personnel in terms of off-base housing, retail stores, banking, and numerous small businesses.

Since 1989, the Department of Defense and Congress initiated a series of base closures and realignments that were hotly contested in communities and states that recognized the economic impact of such actions. In four rounds of closures—1989, 1991, 1993, and 1999—over 350 military bases and installations were closed by the Base Realignment and Closure Commission (BRAC). The largest number of closings occurred during the Clinton administration, which did not have a good relationship with the military community and, as a result, faced a huge outcry of criticism by local officials and state and national representatives who knew that the closings would force businesses to close and housing prices to decline, creating near ghost towns that were once booming communities. But the Clinton administration accepted the BRAC recommendations and went ahead with the closures and realignments. A fifth round of closures in 2005 was part of Secretary of Defense Donald Rumsfeld's effort to streamline the military, making it more mobile and ready for quick responses to threats around the world.[13] Although the closure program has largely ended, the aforementioned sequestration cutbacks in military appropriations and labor and the Obama-directed end to major deployments overseas has left the key military bases with not only fewer soldiers, but also lessened the need for support services such as housing, PX shopping facilities, and medical centers.

Data Bank

There are thousands of military contractors large and small that provide the Pentagon with a range of equipment and armaments totaling billions of dollars and employing hundreds of thousands of employees. The top ten military contractors with revenue from 2012, number of employees, and primary area of weapons and equipment production are listed below (in reverse order):

10. Computer Services Corporation—$6 billion, 91,000 employees, aircraft simulation services.
9. Oshkosh—$7 billion, 12,400 employees, trucks and armored personnel carriers.
8. SAC—$8.2 billion, 43,000 employees, anti-terror technology.
7. United Technologies—$11.4 billion, 208,000 employees, Black Hawk helicopters.
6. L-3 Communications—$13 billion, 63,000 employees, command and control and surveillance equipment.
5. Raytheon—$23 billion, 46,000 employees, missiles and electronics.
4. General Dynamics—$24 billion, 90,000 employees, main battle tank.
3. BAE Systems—$25.4 billion, 83,000 employees, electronic systems and cyber security.
2. Boeing—$29 billion, 160,000 employees, aircraft.
1. Lockheed Martin—$40.1 billion, 126,000 employees, aircraft.

Source: Defense Systems and Business Insider

There are mixed signs regarding the views of the American public toward the fiscal impact of military spending on the overall federal budget and on critical national priorities. A Gallup poll in 2008 found that 44% of those Americans polled said that the government was spending "too much" on defense, while 22% said that the government was spending "too little."[14] Part of this negative view of defense spending is that Americans were growing more conscious of the costs associated with the Iraq and Afghanistan wars. Some analysts, such as Nobel economist Joseph Stiglitz, stated that the war in Iraq cost as much as $3 trillion. But in a Gallup poll in 2015, of those Americans questioned about military spending, one in three (34%) said the United States was spending "too little," while another third stated that the United States was spending "too much," and 29% said spending was "about right."[15] The support for more spending was the highest since 2001. President Trump has tapped into this greater support for military spending and, as a result, promised to increase military spending dramatically over the next 10 years as a way of enhancing our military and sending a message of American military power to our adversaries.[16]

Currently, two critical issues are facing the United States military and the Pentagon. One is the budgetary uncertainty caused by the cutbacks in appropriations associated with the sequestration. Obama's Secretary of Defense, Ashton Carter, lamented that what the Pentagon needs is some certainty about what level of appropriations can be expected in the coming years. At present, Carter stated, the military is not able to plan effectively in terms of weapons development and overall expenditures on overseas operations. Michael O'Hanlon of the Brookings Institution and former CIA Director General David Petraeus echoed Carter's concern in a *Foreign Affairs* article in 2016,

> 15 years of war and five years of budget cuts and Washington dysfunction has taken their toll. The military is certainly neither broken nor unready for combat, but its size and resource levels are less than is advisable given the range of contemporary threat and the mission for which it has to prepare . . . Yet there are also areas of concern. The navy's fleet and the army are too small, and current budget trajectories imply further cuts rather than increases. And the scale of some hugely expensive weapons programs in the pipeline or on the drawing boards, such as the F-35 fighter jet and some new nuclear weapons needs to be reassessed. The challenge for the next president will thus be how to build on the strengths, address the problems, and chart a course for continuing to maintain US military dominance in a strategic environment that never stops evolving.[17]

Also facing the military and military planners is the level of involvement in responding to wars and terrorist threats abroad. President Obama refused to challenge President Assad from Syria when he used the full force of his military to attack his own people who had rebelled against his rule. Obama did not want to be caught in another Iraq-like military commitment, and despite threats of action against Assad, Obama chose to stay out of any military engagement. Yet in terms of destroying the Islamic state that had gained control of parts of Iraq, the Obama administration, after much deliberation, decided to send over 500 military trainers to assist the Iraqi army and their Kurdish allies to crush the Islamic state and regain the ground lost and major cities like Mosul that were lost during 2013 and 2014.[18] As for President Trump, he made numerous comments during the campaign about bombing the Islamic State and criticized the American generals for not knowing how to properly fight the war against terrorists. This kind of criticism of military leaders by Trump did point to a more aggressive use of military force by the United States in areas of conflict such as in Iraq and Syria.[19] Moreover, once in the presidency, Trump promised to make major budget increases for the military and was joined by the Republican Congress. Early estimates showed that spending in 2017–2018 would increase by $38 billion. To make these cuts work in a tight budget, Trump and the Republican Congress moved to make cuts in social welfare programs and other domestic initiatives.

The ongoing national debate over how much military spending is enough, whether budget resources should be shifted to domestic needs, and how involved the military should become in areas of conflict around the world is not new to American politics and will certainly continue. Even if there is a reduction in our presence in the Middle East, there are new threats in the world from China, Iran, and North Korea. Members of both parties in Congress can be expected to support an expansion of the American military at what will likely require huge budgetary resources that will again compete with domestic needs. Unlike the fall of the Soviet Union, which allowed the Clinton administration to benefit from the "peace dividend" as it cut military spending, the post-9/11 world has numerous threats or potential threats to United States security interests requiring enhanced military spending. The complexity of the dangers in this new world of multiple threats will do little to diminish the power and influence of the military-industrial complex.

President Dwight Eisenhower provided a glimpse of his concern over military spending when he stated, "Every gun that is made, every warship launched, every rocket fired signifies, in the final sense, a theft from those who hunger and are not fed, those who are cold and not clothed. This world in arms is not spending money alone. It is spending the seat of its laborers, the genius of its scientists, the hopes of its children."[20] It may be surprising to many that an American president whose whole career before he entered the White House was in the military would be so worried about the military-industrial complex and the impact of military spending on domestic programs and domestic needs. But because Eisenhower was a military man, he understood the power of the military and its allies in industry to dominate the budget process and drive national priority setting. Eisenhower was not soft on the use of military force, but he did recognize that valuable and essential programs that deal with education, health, and welfare can be marginalized if not eliminated in the race to defend this country or extend our influence abroad by military means. What Eisenhower was likely seeking is a proper balance between military spending and domestic spending and a commitment on the part of future presidents to ensure that this nation not only "Provide for the Common Defense but also Promote the General Welfare".[21]

The Great Debate

Military spending is necessary to ensure the protection of the United States and the United States' interests abroad. New threats, whether in the form of terrorist threats, civil wars, cyberattacks, or challenges from aggressive adversaries, have all contributed to the argument made by the Trump administration that heightened military spending is essential.

(continued)

The Great Debate   (continued)

Debate Topic

Should the United States continue, if not increase, its level of military spending to meet these challenges, scale back its spending during this time of budget deficits and national debt, or shift budgetary resources to pressing domestic needs?

Critical Thinking Questions

1. What is your impression of President Eisenhower's warning about the undue influence of the military-industrial complex?
2. How do you respond to the critics of military spending who say that such spending takes valuable budget resources away from social programs and other areas of national life?
3. Do you agree with President Trump's plan to increase military spending and use US military power in a more aggressive manner?
4. What role if any should the United States military take as a peacekeeper or police force in the world?
5. Do you foresee a period of military conflict involving the United States in the near future? Where might this conflict occur?

Connections

The first stop in gaining a better understanding of US military policy is the Defense Department website. See www.defenselink.mil

The Senate Armed Services Committee has a valuable website on military policy and programs. See http://armed-services.senate.gov

For a compendium of recent defense related news and trends, see the Defense News site at www.defensenews.com

The independent voice of the military is Military Times. The site is at www.military times.com

Policies and procedures of the military along with pertinent articles on the current military can be found at www.militarysource.mil

A Few Books to Read

Bacevich, Andrew J., *America's War for the Greater Middle East: A Military History* (New York: Random House, 2016).

Mattis, James and Kari Schake, eds. *Warriors and Citizens: America's View of Our Military* (Stanford, CA: Stanford University, Hoover Institution Press, 2016).

Millett, Alan and Peter Maslowski, *For the Common Defense: A Military History of the United States From 1670–2012* (New York: Simon and Schuster, 2012).

Reveron, Derek, Nikolas K. Gvosdev, and Mackubin Thomas Owen, *U.S. Foreign Policy and Defense Strategy: The Evolution of an Incidental Superpower* (Washington, DC: Georgetown University Press, 2014).

Vine, David, *Base Nation: How U.S. Military Bases Abroad Harm America and the World* (New York: Metropolitan Books, 2015).

Notes

1. www.famousquotes.me.uk/speeches/Ronald_Reagan/3.htm
2. See "How Much Stronger Is the U.S. Military Compared with the Next Strongest Power," January 30, 2014, www.military1.com
3. See "The United States Spends More on Defense than the Next Seven Countries Combined," Peter G. Peterson Foundation, April 18, 2016.
4. Public Papers of President Dwight D. Eisenhower, 1960, pp. 1035–1040.
5. See Justin Fox, "America's in Danger of Imperial Overstretch," *Bloomberg View*, July 13, 2016.
6. James Hazlik, "The Real Reason the U.S Air Force Won't Build New F-22 Raptors," *The National Interest*, April 25, 2016.
7. Bernie Sanders, "An Expanding Military Budget Taxpayers Can't Afford," *Boston Globe*, May 20, 2008.
8. Noah Schahtman, "Navy Chief Smacks Lockheed, Cancels LCS," *Wired*, April, 2007, http://blog.wired.com/defense/2007/04/last_week_when_.html
9. Allan Smith and Skye Gold, "This Map of US and Russian Arms Sales Says It All," *Business Insider*, August 13, 2014.
10. Zach Toombs and R. Jeffrey Smith, "Why Is the U.S Selling Billions in Weapons to Autocrats?" *Foreign Policy*, June 21, 2012.
11. See Denver Nicks, "The U.S. Is Still No.1 at Selling Arms to the World," *Time*, December 26, 2015. For background see also Thom Shanker, "U.S. Sold $40 Billion in Weapons in 2015," *New York Times*, December 27, 2016.
12. Jennifer, Schultz, "Military's Impact on State Economies," *National Conference of State Legislatures*, September 19, 2016.
13. Defense Base Closure and Realignment Commission, 1993 Report to the President (PDF), U.S Department of Defense (1993-07-01).
14. "Military and National Defense: Gallup Historical Trends."
15. See Justin McCarthy, "Americans Split on Defense Spending," *Gallup Poll*, February 20, 2015.
16. See Charles Tiefer, "President Trump Is Likely to Boost U.S Military Spending by $500 Billion to $1 Trillion," *Forbes*, November 9, 2016.
17. Michael O'Hanlon and David Patraeus, "America's Awesome Military and How to Make It Even Better," *Foreign Affairs*, September/October, 2016.
18. See Arshad Mohammed and Jonathan Landay, "Report: Obama Is Weighing Military Action in Syria to Counter Russia and Assad," *Business Insider*, October 13, 2016. See also Greg Jaffe, "Washington's Foreign Policy Elite Breaks With Obama Over Syrian Bloodshed," *Washington Post*, October 20, 2016.

19. See Michael O'Hanlon, "Trump and the Generals," *Brookings*, September 14, 2016.

20. Public Papers of President Dwight D. Eisenhower, op. cit.

21. The issue of balancing military and domestic spending is addressed in a study from *The Center for Budget and Policy Priorities*. See "Policy Basics: Non-Defense Discretionary Programs," February 18, 2016.

21 CHINA

Issue Focus

When conversations among international affairs experts turn to the issue of power projection and global influence in the 21st century, China is often the first nation discussed. China is clearly an emerging power, an economic juggernaut that is growing each year by leaps and bounds. China has become the factory to the world, exporting its goods and reaping the wealth associated with its export sector. China's growth has contributed to an expanding middle class anxious for consumer goods and a political and military class that seeks to play a wider role in Asia and long-term in the world. In the next twenty years, China will be a country that cannot be ignored, but its growing power has concerned many in the West, particularly in the United States, worried about its expansionist desires, its militarization, and its continued economic challenge to the West. Some hope that China and its leaders will move to a more democratic form of government and use diplomatic measures to solve critical international problems, especially in the South China Sea region. Currently, however, the Communist leadership is refusing to open up the country's political system; in fact, it is becoming more repressive. How the United States and the Trump administration will deal with the power of China and its efforts to spread its influence throughout Asia has led to serious debates in the United States over just how the American government and its allies should deal with China.

Chapter Objectives
This issue chapter will seek to:
1. Describe the enormous economic growth of modern-day China and its impact on trade, investment, and other ties to the United States.
2. Explain the points of disagreement between China and the United States in the areas of human rights, currency valuation, military expansion, and product safety issues.
3. Present the future challenges for the United States as it interacts with China, an economic powerhouse and potential military competitor.

SOME BACKGROUND

In 1949 the People's Republic of China (PRC) was established under the leadership of communist revolutionary Mao Zedong. The communists had defeated Chiang Kai-Shek and his Nationalist camp, forcing them to retreat to the island of Taiwan. Mao would spend the next three decades designing a nation that would fulfill the contours of his Marxist-Leninist ideology. In the

1950s, he unfolded his Great Leap Forward, a series of five-year plans that would underwrite the industrial development of China by transforming its immense agrarian countryside into units of industrial production. The collectivization of agriculture in China became an unmitigated disaster as policy errors created massive shortfalls in the production of food, an ensuing famine, and the deaths of millions of Chinese. Mao was also responsible for the highly controversial Cultural Revolution in which fanatical Red Guard youths were mobilized to eliminate impediments to Mao's collectivist initiatives by destroying any vestiges of Western culture, capitalism, tradition, or religion. The guards assisted in relocating millions of members of the middle and intellectual class into reeducation camps and imprisoning those who challenged the existing doctrine of the Communist Party elite, all in the name of reviving China's revolutionary spirit. Mao's China became one gigantic experiment in orthodox communism and a cruel totalitarian state.

After the death of Chairman Mao in 1976, China entered a two-year period of struggle as moderates in the Communist Party sought to strip the ideologues of power (in particular the so-called Gang of Four, which included Mao's wife). By 1978 the old guard was pushed out, and a new group led by Deng Xiaoping took power. Under the leadership of Deng, China shed its ideological orthodoxy and put in place an economic system that would not only modernize China, but also set it on a path toward capitalist production. In the 1980s, Deng established his "Open Door Policy," which removed barriers for foreign investment in China and encouraged marketization and the development of a private sector. These policy changes—along with China's low wages and absence of environmental and labor safety regulations—led to an economic boom in China. Despite economic liberalization, political liberties continued to be suppressed in China. In 1989 students and workers in Beijing staged a massive protest in Tiananmen Square that glorified western democracy and criticized the political restrictions of their government. Deng and his supporters in the party sent in the People's Liberation Army to crush the demonstration and jail or execute thousands of the protesters. To the rest of the world, the Chinese Communist Party had sent a clear signal that it would maintain its repressive grip on power, even as it had liberalized its economy.

Since the crackdown at Tiananmen Square, the Chinese leadership has continued the melding of economic liberalization with authoritarian rule. However, China's dismal human rights record and its refusal to open up the political system have not diminished its continuing "off the charts" economic growth rate. Since opening its economy to foreign investment, China's GDP has grown exponentially, from less than 150 billion US dollars in 1978 to 8,227 billion US dollars in 2012.[1] It has maintained yearly growth rates of 8–10%, widened its huge trade surplus with western countries, and amassed trillions of dollars in foreign reserves. Chinese goods now flood the market of most western countries, making it the unquestioned "factory to the world." China has also taken steps to integrate more fully into the global trading system, gaining entry into the World Trade Organization in 2001. They broadcasted their growing influence on the international stage when they hosted the 2008 Summer Olympics in Beijing.

In many ways, however, China remains a developing country. While 600 million Chinese have escaped poverty since the Mao era, per capita income in China remains far below levels in the West. In 2015 China's GDP per capita was $7,924 compared to $55,836 in the United States.[2] Even as Beijing, Shanghai, and Hong Kong have become modern, world-class cities, deep pockets of poverty still exist in rural areas where schools, hospitals, and adequate housing are in short supply. Despite its uneven development, there is no doubt that China has experienced an economic miracle in the last thirty years.

While China's growth has remained steady, its relationship with the United States has, over the years, ebbed and flowed. The United States has continuously viewed China as both an opportunity and a threat, and this perception has structured the contours of its relationship with China from the very beginning. In the 1950s and 1960s, the United States maintained a cold distance from communist China as fears about the spread of communism had reached fever pitch. Washington perceived China as an aggressive and expansionist power that threatened the security of its allies in the region and pursued a strategy of containment to deal with this threat. The Americans cut off all trade to China, orchestrated a larger international embargo, prohibited Americans from travelling to China, and encouraged countries in the region to cut off diplomatic ties with China

US strategy toward China changed, however, with the ascension of Richard Nixon to the presidency in 1970. Nixon sought to normalize relations between the United States and China in order to gain leverage over the Soviet Union. If relations between Washington and Beijing thawed, he argued, the Sino-skeptic Soviets may soon show an interest in improving relations with the United States as well. Moreover, Nixon thought that an opening to China might help resolve the conflict in Vietnam, since the war had become a political liability for the Nixon administration. Nixon presumed that Hanoi would be pressured to negotiate seriously if its two largest patrons, China and the Soviets, began communicating with the United States. With the steadfast assistance of his Secretary of State Henry Kissinger, Nixon embarked on an historic trip to China in February 1972. During the visit, the United States and China signed the famous Shanghai Communique, a treaty that declared a mutual wish to normalize relations between Washington and Beijing—although diplomatic ties would not be officially restored until 1979.

Since that fateful opening, the United States has gradually, and cautiously, drawn closer to China. The Clinton administration worked to create a "constructive strategic partnership" with China, overseeing first the granting of most-favored-nation status to China, and subsequently, its ascension into the WTO. Despite harsh rhetoric during his 2000 campaign, President Bush continued Clinton's pragmatic policies. While neo-conservatives in the administration favored a hardline approach to China, viewing it as a "strategic competitor" antagonistic to US interests, President Bush was able to manage the more hawkish elements in his governing circle and avoid confrontation with the rising Asian power. When President Obama moved into the Oval Office in 2009, US–China relations entered a new era. Anxious to leave behind the Bush era quagmire in the Middle East, the Obama administration decided to "Pivot to Asia," rebalancing its military resources in Pacific countries and strengthening its diplomatic ties to China's neighbors. Many policymakers, including Chinese officials, perceived Obama's pivot as a strategy to counterbalance China's inevitable rise. However, Obama was quick to underscore the vast opportunities that China holds for American companies looking to capitalize on its growing domestic consumer base.

Nonetheless, the line between partner and competitor remains blurry, and Washington continues to remain skeptical of Chinese intentions. Many perceive a rising China as a threat to the security of the United States. As proof, they point to China's military buildup and its aggressive land reclamation projects in the South China Sea. Moreover, many in the United States are concerned about Chinese economic dominance in Asia, fearing that China is attempting to wrestle economic leadership of the region from the hands of the United States. For those that have benefitted from US predominance in the international economic system, China's rise is worrisome. Other thorny issues have shaken relations between the United States and China, most of which are related to seemingly bad behavior on the part of the Chinese regime. Issues over the suspected devaluation of China's currency, accusations of cyber espionage, concerns about intellectual property theft on the part of Chinese corporations, and ongoing opposition to the China's repressive tactics have prevented the United States from getting too close to China.

DEBATES, DIFFERENCES, DIVISIONS

The rise of China has sparked contentious debate across America. Policymakers, pundits, intellectuals, and citizens differ in their opinions about the direction of US–China policy as some favor confrontation and others favor engagement. In many respects, Americans' perceptions of China's behavior and intentions shape the policies they wish to see implemented. Some view China as an aggressive power that seeks to challenge the Unites States, both economically and militarily. To counter such a threat, they argue, a dynamic strategy of containment should be pursued, one that presents a challenge to China's growing ambitions. Others perceive the Chinese differently, arguing that while China is a powerful nation, neither its actions nor aspirations present a danger to the interests of the United States. They are a nation that seeks wealth and grandeur, they contend, and their burgeoning domestic markets could be a boon for American companies. As such, the United States should engage with China for the mutual benefit of both nations.

There is little doubt that the economies of the United States and China are intimately intertwined. China is, unquestionably, America's largest goods trading partner, having surpassed Mexico in 2006. In 2015, trade with China amounted to 659 billion US dollars, up from 521 billion US dollars in 2013.[3] Most Chinese exports to the United States include computers, computer accessories, household appliances, furniture, home decor, apparel, and footwear, while their imports from the United States include agricultural products, industrial machinery, vehicles, and plastic materials. Investments between the United States and China is similarly substantial. In 2014 US Foreign Direct Investment (FDI) in China amounted to 65.8 billion US dollars (a 9% increase from the previous year), while Chinese FDI in the United States was 9.5 billion US dollars (a 12% increase from the previous year). But the market relationship between these two economic giants is imbalanced as China exports far more to the United States than we export to them. While the United States exported 161 billion dollars worth of goods to China in 2015, it imported nearly 500 billion dollars in Chinese factory-made wares, leaving a trade deficit of approximately 339 billion dollars.[4] Moreover, in 2008, China surpassed Japan to become the largest holder of US debt, in the form of government treasury bonds. For many Americans, these Chinese-held treasuries, coupled with an ever-increasing trade deficit, signal our growing dependence on China.

Data Bank

Economic growth in China has accelerated in the modern era to spectacular heights. China has become the "factory to the world" as it opened its economy to international investment and provided suppliers and consumers with the widest range of goods from steel to sneakers to toys. This march to economic development is best seen in terms of real GDP growth over time.

Real GDP growth by year

1990–3.8%
1995–6.4%
2000–8.5%
2005–11.4%
2010–10.6%
2011–9.5%
2012–7.9%
2013–7.8%
2014–7.3%
2015–6.9%

Source: International Monetary Fund, 1990–2015

These economic imbalances have remained the central bone of contention in the debate among policymakers over the US–China policy. Many Congressional leaders decry the trade policies of the Chinese, arguing that they persistently break the rules of the World Trade Organization by unfairly subsidizing their industries. The Chinese have also been accused of artificially undervaluing their currency, the renminbi (or the yuan). Both of these policies make Chinese goods more competitive on the international market, boosting their export capacity (thus, helping to keep unemployment at bay) and under-cutting the profitability of American firms. The loss of manufacturing jobs in the United States, they argue, is directly related to Chinese policies and requires the United States to take a firm stance against unfair competition.

For many in Congress, standing up to China means erecting trade barri-ers on its imports in order to make American-made goods more competitive, thus shoring up dying manufacturing industries across the country. President Obama received considerable pressure from members of Congress—especially those in manufacturing states throughout the "Rust Belt"—to counter Chinese policies with our own protectionist trade measures. Criticizing the passivity of current and former administrations, Senator Sherrod Brown, a Democrat from Ohio, exclaimed in a statement, "Since China joined the WTO, Ameri-can workers have not been assured that the government would defend them against unfair trade."[5] Likewise, in lamenting the loss of blue-collar Amer-ican jobs to Chinese competitors, Alabama Republican Jeff Sessions added, "I don't believe you have a middle class in America without a vibrant manu-facturing base. We'll stand up and take our lumps and take our gains in a fair competition."[6]

The ire against Chinese policies appears to increase cyclically, reaching its height during election seasons, as presidential and congressional hope-fuls try to win support through China-baiting tactics. The "China problem" was a common talking point on the 2012 campaign trail, where Mitt Romney was highly critical of President Obama's inaction on unfair Chinese practices. "Did you know they even have an Apple Store?" Governor Romney asked the crowd at a 2012 campaign rally, "It's a fake Apple Store. They sell counterfeit Apple products. This is wrong. We're gonna crack down on China . . . when they steal our goods, when they don't respect our intellectual property. We're gonna make sure that China understands we mean business. Trade is gonna work for us, not just them."[7] But even as politicians recognize the electoral advantages they may gain by engaging in anti-China rhetoric, many have been forthcoming about the potential dangers in confronting China's prac-tices through protectionist measures. For one, erecting trade barriers against Chinese imports may force Beijing to pursue retaliatory measures, and such tit-for-tat tactics could spiral into a trade war between the world's two largest economies. The economic consequences of such a conflict could be devastat-ing for the American consumer, who has become accustomed to the low prices of Chinese imports, and American exporters—as well as their wage earning employees—who have gained from the lucrative Chinese markets for aircraft parts, automobiles, and other manufactured goods. As Connecticut Senator Joe Lieberman explained, "During times of economic recession such as the one we are in now, over history nations have repeatedly become protectionist. But history also shows that protectionist policy makes the economic problems worse, not better."[8] Others have argued that increasing trade tariffs on Chinese goods could potentially alarm other nations and provoke them to erect their own barriers. Likewise, it would weaken the legitimacy of the United States as the leader of an international economic system built on the premise of free trade. Others have been more pragmatic, recognizing that the trade deficit with China could not possibly be reversed since Chinese goods are deeply integrated into the supply chains of US retailers.[9] Protectionist policies, therefore, would be counter-productive and foolhardy, and escalating tensions with such an integral trade partner would not be worth the risk.

While these arguments have been persuasive, many believe China should be held accountable for its practices, especially the "egregious and prevalent" currency manipulation of which it has been accused.[10] Besides, the political stakes were high. At the height of the Great Recession, unemployment figures topped 10% in the United States. On Capitol Hill, there had been a pressing political need to act to assure Americans that their congressional representatives were addressing the problems that plagued the economy. Scolding the Chinese seemed to be a way to accomplish this. In October 2011, the Senate passed a bipartisan bill that solicited the Treasury Department to conduct an investigation into currency manipulation in the international financial system. Based on those findings, the bill would order the Commerce Department to impose tariffs on those found to be undervaluing their currency to gain an advantage in trade. The drafters of the legislation were careful to avoid explicitly naming China as a culprit, but the intention was clear. Prominent economists praised the move, arguing that China's currency devaluation had weakened US export growth, which was the key to America's economic recovery from the recession.[11]

President Obama—receiving considerable pressure from Beijing—was hesitant to support the bill, suggesting that it may, itself, violate WTO regulations. Some congressional leaders were also skeptical of the move, including John Boehner who called the bill "dangerous" and warned that such legislation could provoke a trade war with China. Others argued that the bill was simply "populist" diversion. As the Cato Institute's Dan Ikenson explained, "The majority of Americans fear China's economic rise. Then you have a Congress that isn't well regarded, that can't seem to deal with all of our real economic problems, so why not look for a scapegoat."[12] The American business community was split on the issue; small manufacturing firms that face tough import competition from China supported the measure, while large multinational corporations with considerable investment in China opposed it. As of yet, Chinese officials have been unwilling to make wholesale changes on the value of the yuan, in large part because its current inflexibility has been the primary reason for trade dominance and the growth in its foreign reserves.

While Obama resisted sparring with Beijing over currency manipulation, the administration did choose to take action, where appropriate, to counteract the negative effects of other Chinese economic policies. In 2009, Obama imposed tariffs on tires imported from China in order to boost the ailing tire industry in the United States (a move that was in accordance with WTO laws). More recently, the Unite States imposed tariffs on some Chinese steel imports after it accused China of dumping its excess steel production on the US market in order to gain market share. In response to these measures, Beijing has often responded in kind. In 2010 China imposed tariffs on American chicken feet exports, arguing that the United States had unfairly subsidized the poultry industry and then dumped its chicken feet products (a delicacy in China and an unused by-product in the United States) on the Chinese market, undercutting local poultry producers. In general, the Chinese have shown a willingness to strategically retaliate against US policies with protectionist measures of their own, adding legitimacy to the claims of those Americans wary of an impending trade war with China.

Problems with the trading relationship between China and the United States go beyond the complexities of import taxes or international currencies and have often centered on the concerns of the American consumer. In 2007 there were a series of product problems with goods made in China as tests showed high levels of lead paint in toys, contaminated dog food, and toothpaste and cough syrup that contained chemicals used in anti-freeze. Numerous deaths were reported both in the United States and around the world, along with hundreds of cases of illness as young children came in contact with the lead-contaminated toys. The Consumer Product Safety Commission, which monitors non-food goods, stated that in recent years 60% of all its recalls were related to Chinese-produced items. The main source of the problem is that China has lax regulatory and environmental rules and high levels of corruption in its factories and bureaucratic ministries (the head of the Chinese bureaucracy responsible for food safety was executed for corruption in 2007). US companies that contracted with Chinese firms to manufacture these consumer products were also criticized for lax oversight, and the Food and Drug Administration (FDA) was taken to task by Congress for not being aggressive enough in monitoring Chinese food products entering the United States.

Disputes between the United States and China are not just associated with economic concerns; a number of key foreign and military policy disputes have caused serious differences and have the potential to create a troubling division between these two trading partners. In recent years, the Obama administration attempted to engage China in order to increase trust and diffuse icy tensions between East and West, and China's leadership transition opened up an opportunity for the United States to improve relations with China. Current President Xi Jinping appears to have a more casual manner and a tighter grip on power than his predecessor, Hu Jintao, which Obama's administration believed could lead to more "wide-ranging, frank discussions" between the two nations.[13] To this end, President Obama invited President Xi to the Sunnylands Estate in Rancho Mirage, California, for an historic meeting in 2013. Obama sought to build a more comfortable relationship between himself and Xi so that, moving forward, discussions between the United States and China could be as productive as possible. The meeting was a success in that both parties pledged to form a "new model" of US–Chinese relations. But it was also clear that a number of disagreements would continue to hamper efforts at building a more solid partnership.

The most significant issue of concern for the United States has been China's increasingly aggressive behavior in the South China Sea, an area that serves as an essential gateway for international commercial shipping. In recent years,

China has made assertive territorial claims over the waters, proclaiming a nine-dash line that demarcates their historic rights to areas of the sea, including the Spratley and Paracel Islands as well as other reefs and atolls. Their claims of sovereignty in the South China Sea have angered many of their neighbors, including the Philippines and Vietnam, who themselves claim rights to portions of these waters. The Chinese have also undertaken a series of ambitious land reclamation projects in the sea, which involve dredging large amounts of sand from the seafloor onto reefs. These projects have created seven new islets in the South China Sea, which are mainly used by Chinese naval forces.

The manufacturing of these lands have worsened geo-political tensions in the area because China has used the islands as storing houses for fighter jets, cruise missiles, and radar systems. China claims that its actions in the region involve nothing more than natural resource discovery as prospectors allege that the sea contains 11 billion barrels of untapped oil and 190 trillion cubic feet of natural gas.[14] But others perceive China's militarization of the South China Sea as nationalistic and hostile, including Japan, which views Chinese aggression in the region as its main foreign policy concern. In response to the actions of China, the Japanese have sold military equipment to the Philippines and Vietnam to assist these nations in enhancing their military capabilities. The United States—which counts the Philippines among its allies—has also been highly critical of China's behavior in the South China Sea, claiming that their presence has impeded the free navigation of ships along this vital trading route. The international community at large has also condemned China's sovereignty claims there. In a July 2016 ruling on an arbitration case brought forward by the Philippines, an international tribunal in The Hague ruled that China's claims to sovereignty over the disputed territory had no legal basis and that their land reclamation efforts had not only violated the sovereign rights of the Philippines but had done "irreparable harm" to the marine environment from over-fishing and oil spills in the area.[15] Many suspect that China—which soundly rejected the decision—will react defensively to the decision by creating an Air Defense Identification Zone over the South China Sea, which would allow them to monitor and regulate foreign aircraft entering the airspace.[16]

Washington has fiercely debated potential policy responses to China's behavior in these waters. Some argue that Beijing's conspicuous militarization of the South China Sea dispels any claims that China's rise is a peaceful one. China—armed with a "new confidence in its wealth and power"[17]—is carving out a maritime sphere of influence; therefore, the United States, they say, should respond with military pressure. Others suggest that such a move would provoke a defensive China, giving them, "justification to regularly send naval units to the surrounding waters."[18] But many are concerned about appearing to accommodate China's "bullying" behavior. Writing in the *National Interest*, Patrick Cronin argued, "[I]f we are not prepared to back our principles with strength, then we should not be surprised when an opportunistic and increasingly capable China takes full advantage of a vacuum of power."[19] Despite these debates, the United States has shown some willingness to flex its muscles in the South China Sea. In October 2015, the United States deployed a guided-missile destroyer to the waters off the coast of the Spratley Islands, sailing within 12 nautical miles of the disputed territory and, thereby, directly challenging China's claim to the atoll.

On the Record

Chinese President Xi Jingping has had differences with the United States and neighboring countries in the South China Sea over its expansion into uninhabited reefs and small islands where it has claimed sovereignty and has built military bases and airstrips. Although an international court has rendered a decision that China cannot claim sovereignty over these tiny land masses, Xi Jingping continues to move forward with the expansion and, in the process, has had sharp words for both President Obama and now President Trump. There have also been incidents of military confrontations. Xi Jingping in *China Today* commented on the issue and the tensions that the expansion has created:

"The vast Pacific Ocean has ample space for China and the United States. We welcome a constructive role by the United States in promoting peace, stability and prosperity in the region. We also hope that the United States will fully respect and accommodate the major interests and legitimate concerns of Asia-Pacific countries".

Source: China Today, 2016

Another area of dispute between Washington and Beijing involves China's alleged cyberattacks on American corporations, government offices, and military contractors. In recent years, Chinese hackers linked to the People's Liberation Army have been accused of penetrating the networks of such companies as Google, Yahoo, Northrup Grumman, and Lockheed Martin in order to obtain information about political dissidents and to access product blueprints, manufacturing plans, and other intellectual property from industries in which the Chinese appear to lag (such as defense and technology). Also, in December 2014, Chinese hackers breached the systems of the US Office of Personnel Management, gaining access to the personal information of millions of current and former federal employees. Security experts claimed that the strings of attacks were part of a "concerted political and corporate espionage effort that exploited flaws in e-mail attachments to sneak into the networks of major financial, defense and technology companies and research institutions in the US."[20] The Chinese chided the United States for what they perceived to be "groundless" accusations of cyber espionage, claiming that it is the United States that "wields absolute advantage and control" of the Internet.[21]

Many in the United States feel that China is attempting to write new rules for global Internet governance, rules that will contain fewer penalties for the theft of intellectual property and condone government censorship. China is known for its "Great Firewall," a system of instruments that prevent ordinary Chinese citizens from accessing a number of selected websites, including politically sensitive sites. But many Americans disagree on how to confront the Chinese about their unlawful actions without jeopardizing the already fragile relations between Washington and Beijing. In a March 2013 speech, Obama's National Security Advisor, Tom Donilon, suggested that China's breach of cyber security had "moved to the forefront of our agenda." But Obama treaded lightly, refraining from directly naming the Chinese Army as the culprit of cyberattacks, so as not to embarrass the Chinese. The administration was concerned that strongly pushing China on this issue would only harden nationalistic elements within the Communist party, escalating tensions and, perhaps, prompting further cyberattacks. They preferred to negotiate with the Chinese, reminding Beijing that their actions would impede economic growth since Americans companies are less likely to invest where their cyber security is at risk. Others in Washington castigated Obama for his inaction on the issue. Former US Ambassador to China Jon Huntsman explained, "China is two-thirds of the intellectual property theft problem, and we are at a point where it is robbing us of innovation to bolster their own industry, at a cost of millions of jobs. We need some realistic policy options that create a real cost for this activity because the Chinese leadership is sensitive to those costs."[22] Advocates of a more direct and confrontational approach suggest that the United States should deny visas to suspected hackers, levy tariffs to get back losses from the Chinese theft of intellectual property, and impose economic sanctions on China for its actions. Some have even recommended that the US military cyber command launch counterattacks against the Chinese.

But the accusations of cyber warfare are only the latest in a number of actions taken by the United States that the Chinese perceive as hostile and that threaten to undo progress made on creating a more cooperative partnership with this rising power. For one, President Obama took a keen, in some ways unprecedented, interest in the Pacific region, a move that put Chinese leadership on alert. Along with his Secretary of State Hillary Clinton, Obama spearheaded a the aforementioned "Pivot to Asia," which was intended to be a defining foreign policy initiative of his presidency. As part of his pivot, the president shifted 2,500 Marine troops to Australia and actively sought stronger diplomatic, economic, and military ties with other Asian countries. He also began dialogue with the 12 Pacific Rim nations (excluding China) that would later sign onto the Trans-Pacific Partnership (TPP), the largest regional trade accord in history. The Obama administration was eager to underline the economic logic behind the pivot and was careful to avoid portraying it as a containment policy meant to curb the ambitions of a rising China. In attempting to assuage Chinese fears, Secretary Clinton explained, "The fact is that a thriving America is good for China and a thriving China is good for America. We both have much more to gain from cooperation than conflict." But the Chinese leadership—especially the ostensibly nationalistic Xi Jinping—has perceived the US pivot as a move that directly challenges its leadership of the region and curbs their inevitable rise to global power player. Of particular concern to the Chinese has been the strengthening of military ties between the United States and other countries in the region (both its enemies and its allies) as a result of the pivot; in particular, the selling of arms to Taiwan and the lifting of the arms embargo on Vietnam.

The signature policy of Obama's "Pivot to Asia" has been the Trans-Pacific Partnership. This ambitious trade agreement was aimed at uniting the economies of the Pacific Rim into a single trading community, creating a more coherent regulatory system and more efficient supply chains. But it also excludes China, thereby reducing its economic predominance in the region and strengthening the economic alliance between South Korea, Vietnam, and the United States. The TPP has had its fair share of vocal critics within the United States who have decried the secrecy of the negotiations and the threat it poses to American manufacturing jobs. Others see the trade accord as potentially problematic for Sino–US relations, arguing that it will establish an economic rivalry between Beijing and Washington in the region. The Chinese themselves perceive the TPP as a "No China Club" and another instance of the United States attempting to retard its economic growth. Moreover, Beijing believes it will impede the internationalization of the renminbi, which the Chinese wish to see as a global reserve currency alternative to the predominant US dollar. President Obama only amplified Chinese suspicions of the TPP when he explained, "If we don't write the rules [on Pacific trade], China will." Opposition to the TPP reached a hight point when President Trump pulled the United States out of the agreement citing its negative impact on American workers and the American economy. More on this later.

In response to American attempts to challenge China's economic sphere of influence, Beijing has established its own multilateral economic organizations, including the Asian Infrastructure Investment Bank. The AIIB supports the building of critical infrastructure—like roads, bridges, and hydroelectric dams—in the Asia-Pacific region and is largely set up as a rival to the World Bank and International Monetary Fund (both dominated by Western countries).

FYI

Chinese students love to come to the United States to study at our colleges and universities. In 2017 an estimated 375,000 students will leave their homes and their supportive parents and head to the United States for either one term or to achieve an undergraduate or graduate degree. In 2011 the number of Chinese students heading to the United States was approximately 180,000; by 2020 the student population will be an estimated 450,000. In recent years the number of high school students coming to the United States has also increased—from 2005–2014 the number of Chinese high school students sky-rocketed sixty-fold to 40,000, and there is no sign of a let up. All this educational exodus has the blessing of Chinese parents as a study by the Shanghai Academy of Social Sciences found that 57% of the parents were supportive of their children going abroad, if the family could afford the cost. Perhaps most interesting is that, of the 4 million Chinese who have left their country to study abroad, over half have not returned.

Source: International Studies Abroad

Differences between China and the United States have also risen in recent years over Chinese control of Tibet. Since 1959 Tibet has been under the control of the Chinese government, after an uprising of the Tibetan people triggered an intervention by the People's Liberation Army and stripped the nation of its independence. The leader of the Tibetan opposition is the Dalai Lama, a religious monk who went into exile in 1959 and has worked since then to reestablish independence for his country and its people. After taking control of Tibet, the Chinese crushed dissent, imprisoned opposition leaders, and refused to consider any type of autonomy for what was once an independent nation. In recent years, the Chinese have built a railroad to the capital city of Lhasa, which has allowed the migration of the Han ethnic group (the dominant Chinese ethnic group) into Tibet as a means of extending China's control. They have not hesitated to put down uprisings against their rule by using deadly force against protestors.

Since 2002, the Dalai Lama has engaged in intermittent and informal talks with the Chinese government about the future of Tibet and the status of his own exile. While some suggest that moderate elements in the Communist Party seek rapprochement with the Dalai Lama, Beijing has made it strikingly clear that Tibetan autonomy is "not up for discussion."[23] President Obama was supportive of the Dalai Lama's efforts, met with him in 2010, 2011, 2014, and 2016, and encouraged direct dialogue between the Tibetan leader and China. These actions angered the Chinese, who consider the Dalai Lama to be an "anti-China separatist"[24] who condones and foments violence against China. While the White House has been careful to reiterate that the United States does not support Tibet's claims to independence, the Chinese perceived the Obama administration's repeated reception of the Dalai Lama to be a "gross interference in China's internal affairs."[25]

If there is a distinct common theme in China–United States relations, it is convincing the Chinese leadership to follow policies that respect human rights, democracy, and international standards regarding freedom of movement, access to information, and the rule of law. Despite China's close trade and investment ties to the United States and its expanding middle-class consumer society yearning for western goods, the government remains firmly authoritarian. There are some small signs of nascent democratic movements—particularly at the village level and in the city-state of Hong Kong—and a general national desire to be like western nations, but too often the communist party leadership clamps down on dissidents, blocks Internet access, supports rogue regimes (like Sudan) for economic gain, and drags its feet on seeking diplomatic solutions to difficult national and international problems.

The United States has been on the record seeking to push China into the mainstream of western democratic practice and international standards of behavior. Most of these efforts to change China can be categorized as "quiet diplomacy," as Washington officials have not sought to pressure China or engage in public denouncements of its regime and the manner in which it operates. Naturally, the significant trade and investment ties with China are part of the reluctance to pressure its governing leaders in ways that jeopardize American economic and financial interests. But many supporters of human rights in China are counting on the next US administration to be much more forceful with the Chinese over their handling of public protest groups and the general climate of authoritarian control.

For now the United States appears to be willing to allow the forces of capitalism to push China away from its authoritarian roots and begin the formation of democratic values and practices. The future of US–Chinese relations depends on whether President Trump will choose to pressure and isolate China or whether he will choose to deepen our engagement with China. During the early days of his administration, President Trump sought to work with China regarding North Korea's nuclear program, hoping that pressure from China would stop North Korea's nuclear testing and threats of developing a ballistic missile with a range that could reach the United States. Trump also lessened his strong words about Chinese trade imbalance, currency manipulation, and designs on the South China Sea. However, it also depends on whether China seeks to move beyond becoming an international economic powerhouse to begin to play a military and strategic role in Asia or use its enormous foreign reserves to gain even larger control of US corporate and financial interests. Should that happen, quiet diplomacy and cooperation could easily lead to public displays of tension and, perhaps, even confrontation.

The Great Debate

The debate about China's rise in economic and political power centers around the question of whether the United States should seek to engage Beijing—both economically and politically—or take more aggressive action to constrain China with respect to both trade and military disputes.

Debate Topic

Should the United States punish China for its trade restrictions by imposing tariffs on lucrative Chinese exports?

Critical Thinking Questions

1. What is the best approach for the United States to take in confronting China over alleged intellectual property theft, cyberattacks, and WTO violations?
2. Has the United States become too dependent on Chinese consumer goods just like it has become too dependent on Middle Eastern oil? If so, what should the United States do about this dependency?
3. Is China destined to become the next military threat to the United States?
4. Should the US government become more aggressive in supporting the Tibetan people in their struggle against Chinese domination?

5. Should the United States apply political pressure to the Chinese Communist Party to improve its human rights record?

Connections

The United States–China Economic and Security Review Commission is one of the US government's key agencies with specific responsibility for monitoring the US relationship with China. Visit its site at www.uscc.gov

The US–China Business Council is a trade organization that seeks to advance economic and financial ties with China. See www.uschina.org

The Chinese Embassy in the United States is a valuable source for examining the latest in US–China relations. See www.china-embassy.org/eng

The University of Southern California has one of the foremost institutes devoted to China. See http://china.usc.edu/

The Korbel School at the University of Denver has a research center devoted to US–China cooperation. See www.du.edu/korbel/china/

Some Books to Read

Chan, Steve, *Looking for Balance: China, the United States, and Power Balancing in East Asia* (Redwood City, CA: Stanford University Press, 2012).

Christensen, Thomas J. *The China Challenge: Shaping the Choices of a Rising Power* (New York: W.W. Norton, 2015).

Dickson, Bruce J., *The Dictator's Dilemma: The Chinese Communist Party's Strategy for Survival* (Oxford: Oxford University Press, 2016).

Gifford, Rob, *China Road: A Journey Into the Future of a Rising Power* (New York: Random House Trade Paperbacks, 2008).

Goldstein, Lyle, *Meeting China Halfway: How to Defuse the Emerging US-China Rivalry* (Washington, DC: Georgetown University Press, 2015).

Notes

1. Mark Purdy, "China's Economy, in Six Charts," *Harvard Business Review*, November 29, 2013, https://hbr.org/2013/11/chinas-economy-in-six-charts
2. "GDP per capita (current US $)," World Bank and OECD National Accounts Data, 2015, http://data.worldbank.org/indicator/NY.GDP.PCAP.CD
3. "Top 10 Trading Partners of the Chinese Mainland," *ChinaDaily.com.cn*, 2015, www.chinadaily.com.cn/bizchina/2014-02/19/content_17290565.htm
4. Office of the United States Trade Representative "U.S-China Trade Facts," 2015, https://ustr.gov/countries-regions/china-mongolia-taiwan/peoples-republic-china
5. Peter Whorisky and Anne Kornblut, "U.S. to Impose Tariff on Tires From China," *Washington Post*, September 12, 2009, www.washingtonpost.com/wp-dyn/content/article/2009/09/11/AR2009091103957.html

6. Jennifer Steinhauer, "Senate Jabs China Over Its Currency," *New York Times*, October 11, 2011.
7. Ari Shapiro, "Obama, Romney in Tug of War Over China Trade," *NPR*, September 17, 2012.
8. Steinhauer, "Senate Jabs China Over Its Currency."
9. Howard Schneider, "Obama Urged to Act on Currency Manipulation," *Washington Post*, March 26, 2010.
10. Steven Mufson, "Senate Passes Bill Targeting Currency Manipulators," *Washington Post*, May 14, 2015.
11. Schneider, "Obama Urged to Act on Currency Manipulation."
12. Amy Bingham, "Will Currency Manipulation Bill Ignite Trade War With China?" *ABC News*, October 11, 2011, http://abcnews.go.com/blogs/politics/2011/10/will-currency-manipulation-bill-ignite-trade-war-with-china/
13. Zeke J. Miller, "Obama-Xi Sunnylands Summit: What to Expect," *Time*, June 7, 2013.
14. "Territorial Disputes in the South China Sea."
15. Jane Perlez, "Tribunal Rejects Beijing's Claims in South China Sea," *New York Times*, July 12, 2016.
16. "Kerry Warns Beijing Over Air Defense Zone for South China Sea," *Reuters*, June 4, 2016, www.reuters.com/article/us-southchinasea-usa-china-idUSKCN0YR01D
17. Orville Schell, "For China, a Plunge and a Reckoning," *The Wall Street Journal*, August 28, 2015.
18. Feng Zhang, "Provoking Beijing in the South China Sea Will Only Backfire on Washington," *Foreign Policy*, May 21, 2015.
19. Patrick Cronin, "America Must Take a Stand in the South China Sea," *The National Interest*, September 5, 2015.
20. Ariana Eunjung Cha and Ellen Nakashima, "Google China Cyberattack Part of Vast Espionage Campaign, Experts Say," *The Washington Post*, January 14, 2010.
21. Keith Bradsher, "China Blasts Hacking Claim by Pentagon," *New York Times*, May 7, 2013.
22. David E. Sanger, "As Chinese Leader's Visit Nears, U.S. Is Urged to Allow Counterattacks on Hackers," *New York Times*, May 21, 2013.
23. Simon Denyer, "Rapproachment With the Dalai Lama? No Way, Says China," April 16, 2015.
24. Colleen McCain Nelson, "Obama Sees Dalai Lama at White House," *The Wall Street Journal*, June 15, 2015.
25. Ben Blanchard and Jeff Mason, "China Slams U.S. 'Interference' After Obama Meets Dalai Lama," *Reuters*, July 17, 2011.

22 IRAN

Issue Focus

Through much of the Cold War era, the United States and the Soviet Union competed in a nuclear arms race in which both countries increased their arsenals of nuclear weapons and delivery systems. Since the Reagan administration, the United States and the Soviet Union (now Russia) signed a series of agreements to cut back their nuclear arsenals. However, while the tensions over nuclear weapons between these two superpowers waned, other countries sought to build their missile capacity, thus beginning an era of nuclear proliferation. Iran is one of those countries. For the last decade, despite objections from the United States and the international community and stiff economic sanctions, Iran moved forward with the development of a nuclear capacity, which their leaders said was to be used for peaceful purposes only such as energy enhancement. Western nations were unconvinced about the intentions of the Iranian government and saw the nuclear buildup as a means of national power and regional dominance. During the Obama administration, Secretary of State John Kerry was able to negotiate a controversial agreement with the Iranian government that postponed for a period of years the development of a nuclear capacity in return for a relaxation of economic sanctions. Opposition to the deal from Republicans and conservatives was immediate, but the deal went into effect as Kerry and President Obama hoped that the agreement would soften the radical positions of the Iranian government and lead to a normalization of relations. Despite the deal, there remain serious concerns about the intentions of the Iranian government and a fear that Iran remains a security threat to the region and the world.

Chapter Objectives
This issue chapter will seek to:
1. Describe the emergence of Iran as a potential nuclear threat and dominant strategic force in the Middle East.
2. Explain the approaches to dealing with the Iranian government by the Obama and now the Trump administration.
3. Examine the short-term and long-term implications of a nuclear Iran.

SOME BACKGROUND

US–Iran relations in the 20th and 21st centuries can best be described as a complex web of distrust and hostility. The United States has a long history of involvement in Iran, dating back to the 1950s when it formed a close diplomatic and economic relationship with the majority-Shia country. Iran became the center of American influence in the Middle East and a key provider of oil for the US economy, while the United States supported the regime of the authoritarian monarch, Shah Mohammed Reza Pahlavi.

But the relationship between the United States and Iran changed dramatically in 1978. The administration of Jimmy Carter had weakened its support of the Shah's regime, allowing radical Islamic elements in Iran, led by the high-ranking cleric Ayatollah Khomeini, to gain political strength. In January 1979, Islamists ousted the Shah from power, forcing him into exile. The anti-monarchist revolution ushered in a new, theocratic government in Iran, one that held openly hostile views toward the United States. Khomeini had referred to America as the "Great Satan"—an imperial power that sponsors corruption and meddles in the affairs of sovereign nations. Iranian disdain for the United States was compounded by the memories of an American-led coup of Mohammad Mosaddegh—a democratically elected leader—in 1953. Under Mosaddegh, Iran had nationalized its oil fields, threatening both British and American interests in the region; the coup replaced Mosaddegh with the staunchly anti-Communist Shah. Iranians detested the Shah's corrupt regime and directed their ire at America, which funded his repressive grip on power.

Tensions between the United States and Iran came to a head in November 1979 when Khomeini permitted a group of Islamist students to storm the US embassy in Tehran and take 52 Americans hostage. They would be released, they were told, when the Shah was extradited to Iran to stand trial for his crimes against the Iranian people. The hostage crisis infuriated US officials and the American people. In response, the United States broke diplomatic relations with Iran, imposed sanctions on the nation, and placed a ban on its oil imports. The crisis lasted for 444 days, finally coming to an end on the day of President Ronald Reagan's inauguration in January 1981. But it marked the beginning of an enduring animosity between America and Iran.

Iran's hostility toward the United States grew stronger during the 1980s when they fought a bitter and destructive eight-year war with Iraq, its Sunni-majority neighbor. The Iran-Iraq war commenced in September 1980 after Saddam Hussein's army invaded Iran over concerns that the Iranian revolution would inspire Iraq's Shia minority to rebel against his secular regime. Because the United States was interested in blocking the expansion of Soviet influence in the region, it took sides in this local, sectarian conflict, offering political, financial, and military support to the Iraqi regime and tacitly condoning Hussein's use of chemical weapons on the Iranians. The war, then, only furthered Iranian suspicion of the West as they came to believe America had orchestrated the conflict.[1]

During the administrations of George H.W. Bush and Bill Clinton, the rivalry between Washington and Tehran continued unabated. The United States was increasingly angered by the hostile actions of the Iranian Revolutionary Guard Corps (IRGC), a branch of the Iranian Armed Forces known for funding and training radical organizations like Hezbollah in Lebanon. The IRGC was responsible for a wave of kidnappings, bombings, and assassinations of Western targets, dating back to the 1983 bombing of US and French army barracks in Beirut. Because of such activities, the Clinton administration designated Iran as a state-sponsor of terrorism and signed the Iranian and Libyan Sanctions Act in 1996—legislation that approved sanctions for foreign companies investing in Iran.

Relations between the United States and Iran thawed in 1997, however, when Iran elected a reformist President to its executive post. Mohammad Khatami signaled that he wished to begin a dialogue with the United States so that the two countries could move forward into a "new century of humanity, understanding, and durable peace."[2] In response, President Clinton relaxed the sanctions in an attempt to engage Iran. But the warming between old enemies did not last as tensions between the two nations reached new heights during the administration of George W. Bush. The United States grew ever more suspicious of Iranian intentions, especially after documents shared with US intelligence sources in 2002 revealed a clandestine nuclear program in Iran. Two years later, satellite pictures confirmed the existence of a uranium enrichment plant at Natanz and a heavy water plant in Arak.

The Bush administration began to view Iran as a rogue state, bent on producing weapons of mass destruction, and resolved to create instability in the Middle East through its support of terrorist groups. These views were dramatized during Bush's 2002 State of the Union address in which he named Iran, Iraq, and North Korea as a new "Axis of Evil." Concerned about the combined threats of terrorism and nuclear proliferation, the Bush administration singled out these regimes as potential facilitators of nuclear terrorism. The speech was perceived by many as war-mongering; it infuriated the Iranian government and squashed any hope of a diplomatic dialogue between these nations on the nuclear issue.

The fissure between Iran and the United States grew wider with the election of Iranian president Mahmoud Ahmadinejad, a former mayor of Tehran and a religious conservative with hardline views. Throughout his tenure Ahmadinejad expressed extremist views, repeatedly calling for the destruction of Israel—and the "uncivilized Zionists" who dominate it—and even questioning the historical record of the Holocaust.[3] Much of his ire was directed at the United States, which he perceived as a "bullying power" that was nearing collapse.[4] Ahmadinejad was also responsible for advancing Iran's nuclear program, moving quickly and openly to resume uranium enrichment after it had been voluntarily suspended under the European-negotiated "Paris Agreement" in 2004. Despite US and European admonishments and the repeated complaints of the International Atomic Energy Agency that Iran was not complying with the Nuclear Nonproliferation Treaty, Ahmadinejad continued to press forward with the nuclear program, insisting it was to be used for peaceful purposes.

In response, the Bush administration imposed unilateral sanctions on the government of Iran, state-owned banks, and the IRGC in an attempt to isolate the regime. It also won international support for a series of United Nations resolutions that directed UN members to "prevent the supply, sale or transfer

. . . of all items, materials, equipment, goods and technology which could contribute to Iran's . . . development of nuclear weapon delivery systems."[5] But U.N., United States, and European sanctions failed to curb the production of enriched uranium or the development of ballistic missile systems in Iran. Moreover, Iran's activities in Iraq, Afghanistan, and Lebanon were threatening the security of the entire Middle East. The Bush administration felt the United States was headed for an inevitable confrontation with Iran in order to prevent the spread of radical Islam in the region.

The election of Barack Obama to the presidency in 2009 did little to soothe the hostility between the United States and Iran. However, a new strategy was pursued. The Obama administration stepped up the campaign to devastate Iran's economy and isolate them from the international community as a means to compel the Islamic Republic to the negotiating table. The approach ultimately resulted in the historic Joint Comprehensive Plan of Action—known as the Iran Deal—that negotiated a significant reduction in the enrichment capabilities of the Islamic Republic in exchange for the termination of nuclear-related sanctions.

DEBATES, DIFFERENCES, DIVISIONS

The emergence of Iran as a radical Islamic state with potential nuclear capacity has sparked debate among policymakers about the best way to respond to this threat. Some have favored greater diplomatic engagement with Iran. Isolating Iran, they reason, would only strengthen their nuclear ambitions. Others remain distrustful of the intentions of the Islamic Republic, suggesting that engagement would be foolhardy. Some have advocated that the United States engage in covert activities to invoke regime change in Iran. Others, worried about Iran's belligerence toward Israel, have advocated for military action.

While an armed intervention never materialized under George W. Bush, his administration took a tough stance with its Iranian rivals. During his tenure as president, Bush pursued an active policy of containment with respect to Iran. In much the same way it dealt with the Soviet threat throughout the Cold War, the Unites States aimed to check the growing influence of Tehran in the greater Middle East and contain its expansionist objectives. Bush pursued this strategy in two ways. First, the United States projected its own power in the region by building up its military presence in the Persian Gulf. In 2007 the United States dispatched two aircraft carriers to the gulf—the USS Stennis and the USS Eisenhower—in order to conduct a major naval exercise meant to send a "strong signal" of warning to the regime.[6] Secondly, the United States attempted to build a "broad-based alliance" against Iran with other regional actors that were wary of growing Iranian influence.[7] By negotiating arms packages with Gulf states like Saudi Arabia—whom the administration considered to be moderate Arab regimes—the United States believed that it would be able to check Iran's growing regional hegemony.

The Bush administration was also quick to suggest that military intervention in Iran remained a possibility. In response to the deployment of the

USS Stennis, Vice President Dick Cheney proclaimed that "[W]e haven't taken any options off the table."[8] The effects of the administration's increasingly bellicose language were amplified by actions taken in Congress. Concerned that Iran was arming Hezbollah, Hamas, and insurgent groups in Iraq and Afghanistan with heavy weaponry and training, the Senate passed a non-binding resolution (known as the Kyl-Lieberman amendment), declaring the IRGC—and its elite Quds Force—a terrorist organization. After considerable debate in the White House, the Bush administration made a similar designation. Although there was substantial support for taking such action, it was the first time that a nation-state declared an armed unit of a sovereign country a terrorist organization.

Although President Bush vigorously pursued a policy of containment, Iran's nuclear ambitions threatened to derail its effectiveness. Brookings Institution Fellow Kenneth Pollack noted that, if Tehran were to augment its military capabilities with weapons of mass destruction, "it could eliminate the ultimate deterrent of an American conventional military attack as a restraint on aggressive Iranian efforts to destabilize the Middle East."[9] The balance of power in the region would surely shift to Tehran. In order to prevent this scenario and boost its own containment strategy, the Bush administration offered the Iranians political and economic incentives to persuade the regime to suspend its nuclear agenda. But with each offer, Ahmadinejad balked, remaining resolute in his decision to continue uranium enrichment. Facing Iranian recalcitrance, President Bush imposed a series of economic sanctions targeting the assets of foreign individuals, private entities, and any governments that contributed to the development of Iran's nuclear and missile capability. These sanctions were extended and enhanced in 2006 under the Iran, North Korea, and Syria Nonproliferation Act (INKSA). President Bush also improved the enforcement of sanctions by creating two new offices: one in the Department of Justice charged with helping to prosecute entities charged with selling technology, materials, or arms to Iran and another in the Department of the Treasury charged with leading the effort to "cut the lines of financial support to international terrorists and . . . enforce economic sanctions against rogue states."[10]

In addition, the administration also covertly supported groups inside the country that were inimical to the regime, a strategy favored by the more hawkish elements in the Bush administration. In fact, the United States funded a 75 million dollar democracy program that was designed to undercut clerical rule in Iran. Bush's support for regime change in Tehran illustrates what has been called his "Two-Clock Strategy." That is, the Bush administration aimed to use sanctions in order to stretch out the time it would take Iran to reach nuclear capability all while "accelerating the demise of an Iranian government bent on proliferation" with covert activities.[11]

Bush's tough—at times bellicose—actions toward Iran drew fierce criticism from a number of domestic and international actors. Among Bush's critics were the European countries that attempted to negotiate a settlement with the Ahmadinejad government that would reduce economic sanctions and provide a series of trade-and-aid incentives. Throughout these talks, the Bush administration was a reluctant partner and often objected to portions of the incentive package, especially guarantees of security for Iran and a respected role in the Gulf region. The Bush administration refused to sign on to any agreement that, in effect, legitimatized the Ahmadinejad regime and gave Iran the potential for free rein in the Gulf. As for the Europeans, they were convinced that the Bush administration missed an opportunity to negotiate with the Iranians and achieve a "grand bargain" that would lessen, if not eliminate, the potential nuclear threat from Iran and provide it with assurances that the United States would not engage in a military strike in the future.

Some Congressional Democrats were also critical of Bush's hardline approach. For one, many criticized Bush's regime change strategy. Senator Joe Biden saw an administration that was fixated on taking down the Iranian regime, instead of focusing on the greater threat of a nuclear Iran triggering an arms race throughout the Middle East. Such a strategy, he argued, would only amplify Tehran's nuclear ambitions, alienate our allies, and undermine our efforts to create a unified, multilateral approach to the Iranian threat. Biden tended to favor a diplomatic strategy instead, insisting that the United States reach out to moderate reformers in Iran and engage in "hard-headed" diplomacy in order to diffuse dangerous tensions between Washington and Tehran.[12] Some congressional Democrats were also adamant in opposing the president's move to designate the IRGC a terrorist organization, suggesting that it would only hamper efforts to achieve a diplomatic breakthrough. Moreover, many felt the designation—and the accompanying Senate resolution—contained language that could be used to pursue war. The prospect of another war in the Middle East was unnerving. It would destabilize the entire region, they argued, and wreak havoc on our long-term interests in the Middle East. Besides, US troops were already conspicuously overstretched in Iraq and Afghanistan.

The most significant blow to Bush's Iran policy came in November 2007 when a National Intelligence Estimate found that Iran had halted its nuclear weapons program in 2003. The estimate concluded that while Iran had increased its enrichment of uranium, there was no substantial evidence suggesting the enriched uranium has been "diverted to an illicit weapons program."[13] The NIE's analysis weakened the arguments of the Bush administration, which all along had claimed that Iran posed a serious nuclear threat. The estimate caused uproar within the White House and emboldened congressional Democrats, who had increasingly felt that the administration was, yet again, using unsubstantiated claims about weapons of mass destruction as a pretext for military confrontation. President Bush was quick to downplay the relevancy of the report, remaining steadfast in his belief that the regime was pursuing nuclear power, even if they didn't yet have the capability to make a plutonium bomb. The president explained that the estimate "doesn't do anything to change my mind about the danger Iran poses to the world—quite the contrary."[14] Nonetheless, the National Intelligence Estimate diminished the ability of the Bush administration to push for a more aggressive policy toward Iran and gave the Iranian government a public relations victory.

Questions over Iran's nuclear capabilities did little to halt the Bush administration's policies toward the regime. In 2007, US military units entered the Iranian consulate in Erbil, Iraq, and arrested five members of the staff who were viewed by US intelligence as security threats. The Iranian government responded to the Bush administration with its own threatening actions. In 2007, the Iranians captured and briefly detained 15 British sailors on the high seas for allegedly invading Iranian territorial waters, an allegation that the British government firmly denied. Then in 2008, Iranian speedboats engaged American warships in what US Navy commanders described as provocative actions as they moved close to American warships in the Strait of Hormuz. In the waning days of the Bush presidency, the fissure between Tehran and Washington seemed as wide as ever.

President Obama's election ushered in a new era of US–Iranian relations, one based on finding common ground between these two hardened adversaries. In his first inaugural address, Obama signaled to the Ahmadinejad regime that he wished to create dialogue between Washington and Tehran on Iran's nuclear program by proclaiming, "We will extend a hand if you are willing to unclench your fist." But Obama's initiative to engage Iran was quickly met with Iranian hostility when, in May 2009, the Ahmadinejad regime launched a Sejil-2 missile that had the capability to reach Israel and parts of Western Europe. The test launch unnerved the Obama administration because the missile used was powerful, fast, and could be easily moved or hidden. It also emboldened Obama's critics who had called into question the feasibility of direct engagement with Tehran. The launch, they argued, was an act of defiance by an Iranian regime that was incapable of finding a diplomatic solution. Ahmadinejad was said to have told a crowd of supporters that Iran's intention was to send a message to the West that "the Islamic Republic of Iran is running the show" (according to translations on Iranian television).[15]

But Obama maintained his position that a diplomatic solution with Iran was within reach. For one, the Ahmadinejad regime began to show signs of weakness. In June 2009, thousands of protestors took to the streets to protest Ahmadinejad's re-election, which they perceived as fraudulent. Although the protests began with a group of angry voters chanting such slogans as "Where is my vote?" it quickly grew into an organized movement that demanded the rights that had been promised in the 1979 revolution. Members of the Green Movement, as it was called, even demanded the resignation of Iran's Supreme Leader, Ayatollah Khamenei, which many saw as a fundamental rejection of the clerical regime. However, by early 2010, the leadership had stamped out public displays of opposition, using tools of repression in order to remain in power. For the Americans, the suppression of the Green Movement seemed to suggest that regime change in Iran was a mere fantasy.

FYI

Change is coming slowly to Iran and its theocracy. But a new generation of Iranians are beginning to turn the country away from the belief system of the now deceased Ayatollah Khomeini that "Islam is the solution." College educated bloggers, human rights activists, and opponents of strict rules against women are active in Iranian society, despite the fact that the regime cracked down hard on the Green Movement that sought change during the 2009 election. Although some of the leaders of this movement such as Mir Hossein Mousavi and Mehdi Karroubi remain under house arrest, others have taken up the cause, but in less confrontational ways and without openly challenging Islam. Instead, this new generation is seeking to bring to Iran an era of what some call an enlightenment—new ideas, new writings, new solutions—that are stimulating quiet, but sustained, change to the system. This enlightenment remains a fringe movement, but with a new generation comes inevitable change.

Source: From *Children of Paradise: The Struggle for the Soul of Iran* by Laura Secor

In the face of Iran's persistent hostility and continued uranium enrichment, President Obama chose to extend and expand the sanctions placed on Iran during the Bush administration in order to goad Tehran to the negotiating table. In 2010, Congress passed the Comprehensive Iran Sanctions, Accountability and Divestment Act (CISADA), which enacted the toughest sanctions to date against Iran for failure to comply with its NPT obligations. The sanctions effectively cut them off from the global banking system and specifically targeted their oil and natural gas sectors. While Iran is one of the world's largest oil exporters, at the time of CISADA's passing, it imported nearly 30% of its oil from abroad because the poor condition of its refineries did not allow Iran to produce enough refined oil to meet its domestic demand. Sanctions made it difficult for Iran to import oil as several international oil corporations—facing punishment from the CISADA provision—halted the sale of refined petroleum products to the regime. With this approach, Obama explained, the United States was "striking at the heart of the Iranian government's ability to fund and develop its nuclear program."[16]

Data Bank

The economic sanctions imposed on Iran by both the United States and other countries have had a serious impact on the national economy. Below are comparisons of crude oil exports, pre- and post-sanctions, from Iran to its trading partners. Many of the countries listed dropped their imports of crude oil from Iran by a considerable amount.

Buyer	Average pre-sanction amount	Average post-sanction amount
European Union	600,000 barrels	Negligible amount
China	550,000 barrels	410,000
Japan	325,000 barrels	190,000
India	320,000 barrels	190,000
South Korea	230,000 barrels	130,000
Turkey	200,000 barrels	120,000
South Africa	80,000 barrels	0
Malaysia	55,000 barrels	0
Sri Lanka	35,000 barrels	Negligible amount
Taiwan	35,000 barrels	10,000
Singapore	20,000 barrels	0

Some were critical of Obama's sanctions strategy, arguing that sanctions have a poor track record in achieving desired foreign policy goals. Critics cited the long-standing sanctions against Iraq that were designed to force Saddam Hussein's regime to abolish its weapons of mass destruction. Those sanctions amounted to a near total trade and financial embargo, but the Iraqis "found ways around the financial controls" and the nearly 13-year-long sanctions did little to change the behavior of the Hussein regime.[17] Sanctions against Iran, they argued, would yield similar results. Besides, as Kenneth Pollack suggested, Iran may be "strong enough to withstand and outlast any sanctions that might be imposed on it."[18] Moreover, critics of the sanctions approach were keenly aware of the humanitarian implications of these actions as comprehensive sanctions would exert hardships on ordinary Iranians. Finally, European countries continued to believe that they would be able to strike a deal with the Iranian regime without imposing further sanctions. But when it became clear that efforts at negotiating with the Ahmadinejad regime had stalled indefinitely, the European Union ultimately joined the United States in executing its own sanctions on Iranian banks and financial institutions, as well as their energy sector. Australian and Canadian sanctions soon followed. Even Russian and Chinese companies—which had considerable stakes in Iran's oil market—bowed to US pressure and joined the effort to isolate Tehran. Obama had successfully built a robust, multilateral coalition that aimed to make the nuclear ambitious Iran a "pariah state."[19]

Even as the Islamic Republic faced isolation from the global economy, it continued to expand its influence in the region through its support of insurgent groups in Iraq, Afghanistan, Yemen, and Lebanon and remained steadfast in its pursuit of nuclear power. In the tug-of-war between moderate Iranian policymakers, who advocated for reform, and hard-liners with strident nuclear ambitions, the latter seemed to be gaining the upper hand. Iran continued to claim that, under the provisions of the Nonproliferation Treaty, of which it was a signatory, it had every right to pursue nuclear power, and its intentions were peaceful. But fears mounted in the West as intelligence revealed that levels of enriched uranium in Iran were nearing nuclear capacity and Iran was diversifying its route to a nuclear bomb by producing increased levels of plutonium in its Arak complex.[20] Moreover, the IAEA began to express "serious concern" about the potential military uses of Iran's uranium enrichment program.[21]

In response to the seemingly imminent threat of a nuclear Iran, the United States amplified its covert actions against the Islamic Republic. In order to undermine Iran's nuclear program, Obama chose to accelerate cyberattacks on their enrichment facility at the Natanz plant; one computer worm temporarily destroyed a fifth of Natanz's running centrifuges.[22] Iran also accused the United States of assisting Israeli operatives in carrying out a wave of assassinations of high-level nuclear scientists in Tehran. But many in the United States claimed that covert actions alone could not eliminate the nuclear threat. Some congressional Republicans and neo-conservative policy wonks pushed the Obama administration to conduct airstrikes against Iran's nuclear facilities in the belief that military action was the only remaining option.[23] Others warned that airstrikes would be costly for the United States. In addition to draining resources, it would create a public opinion backlash against America and could possibly increase domestic support for the clerical regime, even legitimate the nuclear weapons program in the eyes of the Iranian people. Israeli Prime Minister Benjamin Netanyahu complicated the debate over airstrikes when he warned that Israel had the capacity to carry out lone attacks on Iran's nuclear facilities. With pressure mounting, the Obama administration was eager to find a solution to the Iranian challenge.

On the Record

Ali Khameni, the supreme religious leader of Iran, has been a strident critic of the United States and has stood in the way of many efforts to build diplomatic ties with America. A sample of his vitriolic hatred of the United States is below:

Today, America poses a threat to peace and security in the world. Therefore the slogan "Death to America" is no longer used by our people. Today, you see throughout the world people setting fire to the effigy of the American president and chanting the slogan "Death to America." This is because of American regime's exaggerated demands, its arrogance, its vanity, and its desire to control, and because it is a pawn in the hands of the Zionists.

Source: Iranian News Service

The election of a moderate Iranian cleric, Hassan Rhouhani, in 2013 seemed to offer the desired solution. A former nuclear negotiator, President Rhouhani adopted a more conciliatory tone than his predecessor and signaled that he was interested in finding a resolution to the Cold War between the Islamic Republic and the West in order to reduce international pressure on Iran. The sanctions had begun to take their toll on the country as inflation led to a decrease in the value of Iran's currency (the rial) and persistent shortages of food and medicine. By September, Presidents Obama and Rouhani had engaged in the first direct contact—a phone call—between the United States and the Islamic Republic since 1979. Then in October 2013, Iran joined a group of six world powers in "substantive" and "forward-looking" discussions on the future of Iran's nuclear program.[24] Negotiations between Tehran and Washington—led by foreign minister Mohammad Javad Zarif and Secretary of State John Kerry—continued for two years, repeatedly stalling over fundamental disagreements between Western powers and Iran. On July 14, 2015, an international agreement between Iran, the P5+1 (the five permanent members of the U.N. Security Council—China, France, Russia, the United Kingdom, the United States—plus Germany), and the European Union was reached.

The architecture of the Joint Comprehensive Plan of Action (JCPOA)—known as the Iran Deal—was as sweeping as it was specific. Iran agreed to limit its enrichment of uranium to 3.7 percent and reduce its stockpile of enriched uranium by 98 percent for 15 years. It would scale back its Natanz facility by reducing the number of active centrifuges by half and rebuild its reactor at Arak in such a way as to prohibit the manufacture of weapons-grade plutonium. Iran agreed to ship its spent fuel out of the country and convert the plant at Fordo into a center for scientific research. Finally, Iran would permit the IAA greater access to its nuclear facilities for inspection, including its mines, mills, and storage facilities. In exchange, international sanctions on Iran would be lifted.

For President Obama, the Iran Deal was the greatest diplomatic achievement of his presidency. He praised the agreement, claiming that now "every pathway to a nuclear weapon is cut off" for Iran.[25] In drumming up support for the Iran Deal, Obama expressed a sense of urgency. Without an agreement, he argued, the multilateral sanctions regime would soon crumble, giving Iran the financial and material resources needed to reach nuclear capacity and triggering a nuclear arms race in the Middle East. The accord would alleviate this immediate threat and extend Iran's "breakout time"; that is, the time it would take Iran to produce enough material to build a bomb should it abandon the agreement.

But the deal had its fair share of fierce critics. Many expressed concern about the timetable of the 15-year agreement, suggesting that it only delays and defers Iran's nuclear ambitions. After the JCPOA reaches its conclusion, no legally binding document prevents Iran from picking up where it left off. Moreover, critics felt that Western countries had capitulated to too many of Iran's demands, including the eventual lifting of an embargo on conventional arms and ballistic missiles sales. The accord also preserved Iran's ability to conduct research on advanced centrifuges after eight years. Such research, critics suggested, could reduce Iran's breakout time to zero once the agreement ends. In this way, the deal simply "sets Iran as a nuclear power and finances its aggression abroad."[26]

Others doubted that the Islamic Republic would adhere to the terms of the agreement, given their recent history of clandestine nuclear facilities and illicit procurement. These critics were distrustful of Iranian intentions, suspecting that Tehran had merely accepted the deal to remove international sanctions without abandoning its nuclear ambitions. As Leon Wieseltier writes in the *Atlantic*, "[T]here is no evidence that the Iranian regime has made a strategic decision to turn away from the possibility of the militarization of nuclear power."[27] Similarly, Senator Bob Menendez, a New Jersey Democrat, explained, "With little known about Iran's true intent, we find ourselves today opening a floodgate of frozen assets to a regime that is bent on opposing our interests." But Obama was quick to assure critics that the agreement is "not built on trust—it is built on verification."[28] The deal included rigorous mechanisms designed to detect cheating and a so-called "snapback mechanism" that would reimpose sanctions on Iran if it fails to comply with the agreement's provisions. Obama admitted that Iran may continue its menacing behavior in Lebanon, Syria, and other Mideast hotspots, but that the agreement would achieve what it intended—to prevent Iran from obtaining a nuclear weapon. "It is a practical, common-sense position," Obama explained, "It's not naïve."

The deal's fiercest critic was Israeli Prime Minister Benjamin Netanyahu, who called the agreement an "historic mistake" that will create a "sure path to nuclear weapons" for Iran.[29] Because of Iran's continued belligerence toward Israel—even under the leadership of a less vitriolic Rouhani—Israelis view Iran as an existential threat. As such, Netanyahu preferred an approach that would fully eliminate Iran's nuclear infrastructure rather than an agreement that partially preserved their nuclear capacity and freed material resources that could be used to fund terrorism in Israel. Netanyahu even took his case to Capitol Hill after House Republicans, in an unprecedented move, invited him to speak to a joint session of Congress. Obama retorted, reminding the Israelis—and their Republican allies—that nuclear "know-how" could never be eliminated, and airstrikes would simply force Iran's nuclear program underground. Nonetheless, the deal rocked the boat in the region, and the Obama administration was forced to offer additional security guarantees to Israel and other Gulf allies that were wary of the effects of the removal of sanctions on Iran's already aggressive foreign policy.

Once the accord was signed, Congress was given 60 days to review the agreement, after which they could choose to reject it. While President Obama had the power to reject a congressional veto of the Iran Deal, he very much wanted Capitol Hill's endorsement. This proved to be difficult, however, as Senate and House Republicans slammed the agreement as soon as it was reached Congress. Speaker of the House John Boehner exclaimed, "This is a bad deal with decades-long consequences for the security of the American people and our allies, and we'll use every tool at our disposal to stop, slow and delay this agreement from being fully implemented." The Senate moved to block the deal. Majority Leader Mitch McConnell first attempted to bring a resolution of disapproval to the floor and, in a last ditch effort, put forth an amendment that would prohibit the lifting of Iranian sanctions until the

Islamic Republic had released American prisoners in Iran and recognized Israel's right to exist. Eager to hand President Obama a victory, Senate Democrats blocked both maneuvers. A faction of House Republicans also led an effort to block the Iran Deal but was ultimately unsuccessful. Overall, the American people seemed as skeptical of the Iran Deal as Republicans. A Gallup poll conducted in February 2016 found that nearly 60% of American disapproved of the Iran Deal, while a CNN poll conducted in September 2015 found that 37% of Americans believed that Iran was likely to violate the obligations of the agreement. This seems to stand in sharp contrast to the view from Tehran, where jubilant Iranians danced in the street and brandished victory signs thanking Rouhani when the nuclear accord was signed.

In many respects, the future of US–Iranian relations is intimately tied to the future of the Iran Deal. The future of the agreement is cloudy, however. On the 2016 campaign trail, then-candidate Donald Trump explained that his "number one priority is to dismantle the disastrous deal with Iran," while Supreme Leader Ayatollah Khameini responded that, if the United States turned its back on the Iran Deal, the Islamic Republic too would "set fire" to the agreement. Since taking office, President Trump has continued to express hostility toward Iran, while the Islamic Republic has begun to test the limits of the new administration by launching a missile test in January 2017. Despite these issues, the Iran Deal has given the Islamic Republic a chance to become a prosperous member of the international economy and a productive partner in the global community. Whether it chooses to embrace this opportunity depends on decisions made by the stalwart clerical regime, but it also depends on whether the United States continues to show its commitment to bridging the divide between these two nations or turns its back on a potential reconciliation.

The Great Debate

The Iran Deal is critical to the future of US–Iranian relations, but has been rejected by conservative lawmakers, the Trump administration, and one of America's closest allies—Israel. The controversial deal provides a perfect theme for a debate.

Debate Topic

Should the United States abandon the Iran Deal and reimpose sanctions on the Islamic Republic?

Critical Thinking Questions

1. Is the Iran Deal "good" for US national security interests?
2. How should the United States respond to Iran's covert support for terrorist groups across the Middle East?

3. Should the United States engage in covert operations to encourage regime change in Iran?
4. How should the United States respond to Israeli critics of the Iran Deal? Can America keep its commitment to the Iran Deal without alienating Israel?
5. How should the United States respond if Iran were found to have violated the terms of the Iran Deal?

Connections

View the 2007 National Intelligence Estimate on Iran's nuclear capability at http://www.dni.gov/press_releases/20071203_release.pdf

See the full text of the Iran Deal (Joint Comprehensive Plan of Action) at www.state.gov/e/eb/tfs/spi/iran/jcpoa/

The House of Representatives Committee on Foreign Affairs held a hearing on the Iran Deal. Read the proceedings here: http://docs.house.gov/meetings/FA/FA00/20160525/104985/HHRG-114-FA00-Transcript-20160525.pdf

The Council on Foreign Relations houses opinion pieces from across the web on their website. View the collection here: www.cfr.org/region/iran/ri357

An informative resource for information on Iran can be found at the United States Institute of Peace's "Iran Primer" page. Find it here: http://iranprimer.usip.org

Some Books to Read

Axworthy, Michael, *A History of Iran: Empire of the Mind* (New York: Basic Books, 2008).

Crist, David, *The Twilight War: The Secret History of America's Thirty-Year Conflict With Iran* (New York: Penguin Books, 2013).

Evans, Michael D., *Showdown With Nuclear Iran: Radical Islam's Messianic Mission to Destroy Israel and Cripple the United States* (New York: Thomas Nelson, 2006).

Pollack, Kenneth, *Unthinkable: Iran, the Bomb, and American Strategy* (New York: Simon and Schuster, 2013).

Solomon, Jay, *The Iran Wars: Spy Games, Bank Battles, and the Secret Deals That Reshaped the Middle East* (New York: Penguin Random House, 2016).

Takeyh, Ray, *Hidden Iran: Paradox and Power in the Islamic Republic* (New York: Holt, 2007).

Notes

1. James G. Blight, Janet Long, Hussein Banai, Malcolm Byrne, and John Tirman, *Becoming Enemies: U.S.-Iran Relations and the Iran-Iraq War, 1979–1988* (Lanham, MD: Rowman and Littlefield, 2012), p. 77.

2. Amir Soltani Sheikholeslami and Rita Nakashima Brock, "Iran Will Rise Above the Ashes," *Boston Globe*, July 30, 2009.
3. Mahmoud Ahmadinejad, "Statement by H.E. Dr. Mahmoud Ahmadinejad, President of the Republic of Iran Before United Nations General Assembly Sixty-Seventh Session, General Debate," Speech, New York, September 26, 2012, http://gadebate.un.org/sites/default/files/gastatements/67/IR_en.pdf
4. Mahmoud Ahmadinejad, "Statement by H.E. Dr. Mahmoud Ahmadinejad, President of the Republic of Iran Before United Nations General Assembly Sixty-Third Session, General Debate," Speech, New York, September 23, 2008, www.un.org/ga/63/generaldebate/pdf/iran_en.pdf
5. United Nations Security Council Resolution 1737, S/Res/1737, December 23, 2006, www.iaea.org/sites/default/files/unsc_res1737-2006.pdf
6. Michael Abramowitz, "Cheney Says U.S. Is Sending 'Strong Signal' to Iran," *Washington Post*, January 29, 2007.
7. Vali Nasr and Ray Takeyh, "The Costs of Containing Iran: Washington's Misguided New Middle East Policy," *Foreign Affairs*, January/February, 2008.
8. Abramowitz, "Cheney Says U.S. Is Sending 'Strong Signal' to Iran."
9. Kenneth M. Pollack, "Containing Iran," The United States Institute of Peace's Iran Primer, 2010, http://iranprimer.usip.org/resource/containing-iran
10. Office of Public Affairs, "Bush Administration Announces Creation of New Office in Ramped Up Effort to Fight the Financial War on Terror," U.S. Department of the Treasury Press Center, March 8, 2004, www.treasury.gov/press-center/press-releases/Pages/js1219.aspx
11. Jacob Weisberg, "The Two Clocks," *Slate*, January 31, 2007, www.slate.com/articles/news_and_politics/the_big_idea/2007/01/the_two_clocks.html
12. Joe Biden, "Statement by Senator Joe Biden on Iran's Release of British Hostages," April 4, 2007 Online by Gerhard Peters and John T. Woolley, *The American Presidency Project*, www.presidency.ucsb.edu/ws/?pid=116186.
13. Seymour M. Hersh, "Iran and the Bomb," *The New Yorker*, June 6, 2011.
14. "Democrats Incredulous over Bush's Account of Iran Report," *CNN*, December 5, 2007, www.cnn.com/2007/POLITICS/12/04/bush.iran/
15. David Sanger and Nazila Fathi, "Iran Test-Fires Missile With 1,200-Mile Range," *New York Times*, May 20, 2009.
16. Barack Obama, "Remarks by the President at the Signing of the Iran Sanctions Act," The White House Office of the Press Secretary, July 1, 2010, www.whitehouse.gov/the-press-office/remarks-president-signing-iran-sanctions-act
17. Kenneth M. Pollack, "Pariahs in Tehran," *The National Interest*, November/December, 2010.
18. Ibid.
19. Ibid.
20. Michael D. Shear and David E. Sanger, "Iran Nuclear Weapon to Take Year or More," *New York Times*, March 14, 2013 and David E. Sanger and William J. Broad, "Iran Is Seen Advancing Nuclear Bid," *New York Times*, May 22, 2014.
21. Ambassador Kenneth C. Brill, "Statement on the Implementation of Safeguards in the Islamic Republic of Iran," October 27, 2014, www.iaea.org/newscenter/statements/statement-implementation-safeguards-islamic-republic-iran
22. David E. Sanger, "Obama Order Sped Up Wave of Cyberattacks Against Iran," *New York Times*, June 1, 2012.
23. David Kenner, "Who Wants to Bomb Iran?" *Foreign Policy*, February 8, 2010.

24. Michael R. Gordon, "After Talks on Iran's Nuclear Program, Officials Highlight the Positive," *New York Times*, October 16, 2013.

25. The Historic Deal that Will Prevent Iran from Acquiring a Nuclear Weapon, www.obamawhitehouse.archives.gov

26. "Hiyatollah," *The Economist*, July 18, 2015.

27. Leon Wieseltier, "The Iran Deal and the Rut of History," *The Atlantic*, July 27, 2015.

28. Barack Obama, "Statement by the President on Iran," The White House Office of the Press Secretary, July 14, 2015, www.whitehouse.gov/the-press-office/2015/07/14/statement-president-iran

29. William Booth and Ruth Eglash, "Israeli Leaders Condemn Iran Deal, 'One of the Darkest Days in World History,'" *The Washington Post*, July 14, 2015.

23 RUSSIA

Issue Focus

The Cold War era, with its tensions between Moscow and Washington, ended with the collapse of communism and the rise of a struggling democratic governing system and an evolving private sector economy. But the Russia that was viewed with hope by the West and many officials inside policymaking centers in the United States was short-lived. Vladimir Putin, formerly the head of the KGB, a mix of the CIA, the FBI, and a Gestapo-like secret police, rose to power and began dismantling the democratic institutions and bringing economic decisions within his circles of cronies. Moreover, Putin began a series of expansionist actions that rattled the West: going to war with neighboring Georgia, taking control of Crimea from the Ukraine, fomenting civil war in eastern Ukraine, threatening the Baltic states and Eastern European nations for moving closer to the West, and violating long-standing nuclear agreements with the United States. Putin even took his international meddling one step further by allegedly authorizing the hacking of the presidential campaign of Hillary Clinton in an attempt to weaken the democratic process in this country. It has become increasingly clear that Putin is determined to rekindle the Russian state and appeal to his people by challenging the West in a manner akin to the old Soviet Union. Despite the fact that Russia's domestic economy is weak, depending on oil and gas for revenue, Putin has played the "Russia will be great again card" as he is determined to challenge the West and foment democratic instability in Europe and even the United States. There is perhaps no greater debate in American politics than how best to handle Putin and his authoritarian-expansionist ambitions.

Chapter Objectives
This issue chapter will seek to:
1. Examine the evolution of Putin's Russia and the current state of his regime.
2. Describe the various issue areas, domestic, foreign, and clandestine, that Putin has advanced in his attempt to create a new, powerful Russia.
3. Explore the "threat scenarios" that could play out as Putin continues to test the West and the United States.

SOME BACKGROUND

The rivalry between the United States and Russia has dominated international politics for much of the twentieth and twenty-first centuries. After cooperating with the Soviet Union and other Allied powers to defeat Nazi Germany in World War II, the United States began to pursue a policy of containment in order to limit the spread of Soviet geopolitical influence throughout the globe. The policy was outlined in the 1947 Truman Doctrine, which articulated the need to provide political and financial support to governments—both those in Europe that were rebuilding after the war and newly decolonized nations in the Third World—in order to prevent the spread of communism to these regions. US containment strategy would ultimately lead to massive increases in defense and military spending, a nuclear arms race, and proxy wars fought on distant shores.

The first two decades of the Cold War were marked by high tensions that, at times, escalated into direct confrontation. The first crisis came in 1948 when Soviet forces blocked railway, road, and canal access to the western (and Allied controlled) section of Berlin. In response, Western powers, led by the United States, organized a counter-blockade, airlifting food, clothing, and medical supplies to the people of West Berlin for 15 months. While US ingenuity helped to resolve the crisis peacefully, the Berlin Blockade only served to harden US perceptions of the Soviet Union as an international bully.[1] Relations between Washington and Moscow reached a nadir in October 1962 when US intelligence received information that the Soviet Union was placing middle-range ballistic missiles on the island nation of Cuba. Disaster was averted after 13 days of tense negotiations between President John F. Kennedy and his Soviet counter-part, Nikita Khrushchev, after which the Soviets agreed to dismantle their missiles in exchange for a US promise to refrain from taking offensive action in Cuba. Nonetheless, the Cuban Missile Crisis had brought these two powers to the brink of nuclear war. While these events were significant in the timeline of US–Soviet relations in the 1950s and 1960s, much of the rivalry between Washington and Moscow revolved around science and technology—and in particular, spaceflight capabilities—as Americans felt they would be endangered should the Soviets reach technological superiority.

After engaging in a nearly ten-year proxy war in Vietnam that pitted the US-backed South Vietnamese government against the Soviet-backed North Vietnamese forces, US–Soviet relations entered a period of détente in the 1970s. During this time, the easing of geopolitical tensions allowed the two powers to negotiate significant international treaties on armament control and territorial integrity, including the Strategic Arms Limitation Talks Agreement (SALT I) and the Helsinki Accords. As Robert Kaiser, former editor of the *Washington Post*, explained, the United States had been in a "position of strength" in the decades following World War II and so had "decided to grant the Soviets at least the symbolic status of equal superpower."[2]

The détente period, however, was short-lived as the Soviets moved to usurp the US global position. In December 1979, the Soviet Union invaded Afghanistan, setting back the improvements they had made in relations with Washington in the previous decade. At the same time, the newly elected President Reagan had promised to take a more aggressive, muscular approach to challenging Soviet power. Reagan's strategy involved considerable military armament aimed at compelling the Soviets—whose crumbling economy could not withstand an intensified arms race—to the negotiating table. The ballooning military budget was accompanied by fierce anti-Soviet rhetoric and saber-rattling speeches in which President Reagan promised Americans that he would "stand up to the Russians."[3] Mutual suspicion was ripe, threatening to escalate the Cold War into a nuclear confrontation. Reagan's Strategic Defense Initiative (nicknamed "Star Wars") led the Soviets to believe that the United States intended to develop space weapons, while US-led joint military exercises—such as 1983's Able Archer missile system—sent the Politburo into a panic that could have resulted in a nuclear first strike.

Tensions between the two superpowers eased, however, when Mikhail Gorbachev assumed the Soviet's top leadership position. Gorbachev was a reformist leader whose policies of glasnost and perestroika aimed to restructure and buttress the floundering Soviet economy and allow limited political liberalization. His reforms opened the door to "realistic engagement" with Washington, and by June 1988, President Reagan had made an historic visit to Moscow in which he signified an end to the Cold War with a symbolic walk through Red Square. The collapse of the Soviet Union proceeded swiftly in the following years as the Berlin Wall fell and Soviet Republics began to declare independence. Before the final dissolution of the Soviet Union, Gorbachev and President George H.W. Bush brokered a peaceful resolution of the Cold War, culminating in a joint agreement in which the Soviet Union and the United States consented to broadly decreasing their nuclear arsenal.

During the 1990s, President Bill Clinton maintained a close and amicable relationship with his Russian counterpart, Boris Yeltsin, meeting with him 18 times during his time in the Oval Office. The United States supported political and market reform in the former Soviet Union with financial assistance and oversaw Russia's accession into the G-8 in order to ensure that Russia's interests would be included within the group of the world's most powerful countries. Although Moscow and Washington maintained good relations during the Clinton administration, diplomatic challenges persisted, especially with regard to matters of European security and the management of the nuclear arsenal.

Once former KGB officer Vladimir Putin took the reins of leadership—first as Russia's Prime Minister in 1999 and then as President after 2000—the relationship between Russia and the United States began to change. While Moscow was both cooperative and supportive of President George W. Bush's counterterrorism efforts across the globe after the September 11th attacks, relations between the two countries soured after the Russian invasion of Georgia in 2008. The former Soviet constituent republics sparred over the Georgian breakaway region of South Ossetia, with Russian land, air, and sea forces launching a full-scale assault on their neighbor to the south. The United States was quick to throw its support behind Georgia with a congressional resolution, sponsored by Senators Joe Biden, Richard Lugar, and Mel Martinez, condemning Russia for violating international law and gravely undermining Georgia's territorial integrity.[4] Once President Bush had left office and the tensions of the Russo-Georgian war had subsided, President Obama sought to "reset" relations with Moscow. However, Obama's reset faltered, due to the increasingly aggressive behavior of Russia in Eastern Europe, mutual accusations of nefarious cyber activity, and their positions on opposite sides of the Syrian Civil War.

DEBATES, DIFFERENCES, DIVISIONS

While US–Russian relations have improved considerably since the Cold War, the marks of old wounds are still very much present. Today, the relationship between Washington and Moscow involves, on the one hand, lukewarm engagement on pressing global matters and, on the other, mutual mistrust. Under the direction of President Vladimir Putin and guided by a resurgent nationalism, Russia has taken an interest in expanding its global sphere of influence. Putin's desire to restore Russia to the status of a great power has been manifested in dramatically increased military spending as well as aggressive foreign policy behaviors. Policymakers in Washington are divided over how to appropriately respond to Russian saber-rattling, with some suggesting the United States take a hardline approach that would isolate Russia and others advocating cautious engagement. As Putin expands his influence in the geopolitical theaters of both Europe and the Middle East, the debates have become increasingly relevant to the future of international politics.

Relations with Moscow began to strain after the Russian invasion of Georgia in April 2008. Trouble first brewed when the Georgian army entered the capital of the breakaway region of South Ossetia in response to violent attacks committed at the hands of South Ossetian separatists. To protect its own peacekeepers stationed in the breakaway territories and to shore up its South Ossetian allies, Russia sent over 9,000 troops to the region in a full-scale ground invasion and bombarded Georgia's military infrastructure with airstrikes.[5] The United States and its allies were quick to condemn the actions of Russia, which were viewed as a serious breach of Georgia's territorial integrity. In a harsh warning to Moscow, President George Bush exclaimed, "Bullying and intimidation are not acceptable ways to conduct foreign policy in the 21st century."[6] As punishment for bad behavior, the United States issued sanctions on Moscow, froze a civil nuclear cooperation agreement, and withdrew its support for Russia's accession into the World Trade Organization.[7]

Since US–Russian relations had become considerably strained by the end of Bush's second term, President Obama sought a "reset" with Moscow once he moved into the Oval Office in 2009. His desire for a "reset" with Russia was driven by one of his major foreign policy objectives, namely to curb Iranian nuclear ambitions. To accomplish this objective, the United States would need Russia's assistance, which would be possible only if the frayed relationship were mended. In April 2009, President Obama met with his Russian counterpart, Dmitri Medvedev (Vladimir Putin was Prime Minister at the time), in London where both parties pledged to "deepen cooperation."[8] As a testament to the spirit of partnership, the two powers worked together to decrease the nuclear arsenal, signing a new START treaty that reduced nuclear warheads by 30% on both sides. Moreover, the Obama administration pledged its support to Moscow concerning Russian efforts to join the WTO and authorized the permanent normalization of trade relations with Russia.

FYI

Innopolis is a brand new "innovation city" in the Russian region of Tatarstan. Designed by Russian authorities as the center of many high tech start-up companies, Innopolis has yet to achieve its stated mission; there are but a few companies in the city and only about 350 students in the university that was built as a training ground for youthful innovators. Russia has historically been unsuccessful in encouraging innovation and innovators. While Russians have made many important technological breakthroughs like laser and hydraulic fracking, they have been unable to translate that spirit of invention into successful business plans and a diversified economy. Loren Graham, an historian of science from MIT, visited the St. Petersburg Economic Forum in 2016 and was unconvinced about the prospects for innovation cities like Innopolis. As he said at the time, "The Russians have the ideas and the business talent" but "at the same time they (the government) prohibit demonstrations, suppress political opponents and independent businessmen, twist the legal system and create a repressive, authoritarian regime. . . . They want the milk without the cow."

Source: *The Economist*, October 22, 2016

After Putin recaptured the presidency in 2012, relations between Moscow and Washington began to sour again. For one thing, the decreasing human rights conditions in Russia unnerved the Obama administration. Putin heightened a crackdown on Internet freedom, increased fines for Russians who protested against government policies, and passed a law requiring non-governmental organizations, including those from the United States, to register as foreign agents. To make matters worse, the United States Agency for International Development was expelled from Russia in 2012 because of unfounded allegations that the organization was attempting to influence local elections. Moreover, Russia's actions on its eastern borders grew increasingly hostile once a political crisis began to engulf neighboring Ukraine in 2014.

In the Ukrainian capital of Kiev, university students began protesting President Viktor Yanukovych's refusal to sign a trade deal with the European Union that would have strengthened economic ties between Ukraine and its prosperous western neighbors. Yanukovych, a former governor of the Russian-speaking region of Donetsk Oblast, instead chose to accept a Russian loan bailout and pursue closer ties to Russia. In February 2014, clashes between police and protestors grew increasingly violent, ultimately leading to Yanukovych's ouster. In a hasty response to the unforeseen removal of the

Russian-allied Yanukovych, Putin moved to seize the Ukrainian autonomous region of Crimea. In February 2014, Russian troops forcibly annexed the peninsula by taking over its main legislative body, capturing strategic sites in the peninsula and declaring Crimea's independence. By March, Putin had held a referendum that asked Crimean citizens—60% of whom self-identify as Russian—whether they wanted the region to remain a part of Ukraine or join Russia as a federal subject. More than 95% of those who voted supported leaving Ukraine and joining Russia. But many outsiders viewed the referendum as illegitimate and illegal, considering pro-Kiev Crimeans boycotted the vote in large numbers.

Russia's annexation of Crimea was quickly and authoritatively condemned by Western powers. In testifying before the Senate Foreign Relations Committee, Brookings Institute Senior Fellow Steven Pifer explained, "Russia's actions constitute a fundamental challenge to the post-war order in Europe. The illegal seizure of Crimea is the most blatant land-grab that Europe has seen since 1945."[9] Many have disagreed on the motives behind Putin's Crimean annexation, with some arguing that the operation was a "response to the threat of NATO's further expansion" along Russian borders, while others see it as an attempt to restore Russia's place on the world stage by recapturing former territories.[10] Nonetheless, it was clear to many in the West that Russian aggression could no longer be ignored. In response, the United States and the European Union imposed travel bans and asset freezes on several Russian officials.

After the capture of Crimea, the situation in Ukraine grew more volatile. Pro-Russian separatists in the eastern Ukrainian cities of Donetsk and Luhansk began to occupy government buildings, pledging declarations of independence in referendums soundly rejected by Kiev and other Western powers. In the months that followed, separatists fiercely battled Ukrainian forces in two eastern regions, aided by Russian military equipment and Russian combat troops. The crisis in Ukraine became increasingly urgent after a Malaysia Airlines flight from Amsterdam was shot down in rebel-held territory near the village of Grabove, killing the 298 persons on board and causing outrage in Europe.

The United States has responded to the Russian aggression in Ukraine through a combination of targeted sanctions and military aid to Ukrainian forces. Originally, the sanctions largely affected those Russians with close ties to the Kremlin but were expanded after the downing of the Malaysian Airlines flight to include banks, arms manufacturers, and state firms. The intention was to target Russia's oil and gas sector—the heart of its revenue stream—and undermine "an implicit social contract that Putin has with the Russian people" that barters "diminished individual political space in return for economic stability, growth and rising living standards."[11] The sanctions were effective in temporarily decreasing the value of the ruble, leading to problematic rates of inflation. But even with a falling GDP, the Kremlin refused to change course in Ukraine. It appears the sanctions imposed were not coercive enough to change Russian behavior, and Russia was successful in circumventing them by turning to China as an energy buyer. US aid to Ukraine has encompassed mostly "non-lethal" military supplies, such as communications gear and radar, and training in defensive tactics in order to "help the Ukrainians be more effective in defending their territory without escalating the conflict."[12] In order to show its support for its non-NATO ally, the United States has hosted Ukrainian officials in Washington, D.C., sent US officials to Kiev, aided the International Monetary Fund in crafting a suitable aid package for Ukraine, and helped the country to reduce its dependence on Russian natural gas.

Many in Washington considered the targeted sanctions and the military aid to Ukraine as weak responses to Russian aggression. Some felt that the Obama administration was overly restrained in its use of sanctions, preferring to "move in concert" with the European Union, which has hesitated to endanger its trade ties with Russia.[13] Meanwhile, many congressional Republicans were sharply critical of Obama's reluctance to arm Ukrainians with better equipment; most military bases in Ukraine are located near Kiev and eastern bases are considerably lacking in infrastructure. Duncan Hunter, a Republican member of the House Armed Services Committee, explained, "If you're there, why not train them in the way Ukrainians need to be trained to counteract the Russian offensive. How nice can you be while Putin takes over the world?"[14] Even the president's Defense Secretary, Chuck Hagel, was ultimately critical of Obama's delayed response to the Ukrainian crisis, suggesting that, while the United States needed to avoid a direct confrontation with Russia over Ukraine, it also should have sent a stronger message to Moscow and increased military aid to Ukraine. "The world, including our NATO partners, were watching to see how we would respond," Hagel explained.[15]

On the Record

Russian President Vladimir Putin has, in the last few years, been at the center of a war of words with the United States and European nations, in part because of his invasion and annexation of Crimea, his connection to cyber hacking activities during the 2016 presidential election, and his threatening military buildup that has unnerved many in the West. Below are some samples of Putin's comments related to his antagonistic attitude toward his adversaries.

> Russia never lost the Cold War . . . because it never ended.
> Maybe they have nothing else to do in America but to talk about me.
> Hitler wanted to destroy Russia—everyone needs to remember how that ended.
> I don't regret anything. I did everything absolutely correctly.

Sources: TASS Russian New Agency

The most significant thorn in US–Russia relations, however, does not concern Russian actions in Eastern Europe but rather Russia's continued military involvement in the Syrian conflict. Following protests inspired by the 2011 Arab Spring events, a civil war erupted between Syria's government forces and a collection of rebel groups, many of whom have been supported by the United States and others that maintain ties to al Qaeda. After the conflict became stalemated, Moscow intervened to support the government of Bashar Al-Assad with significant military aid, bolstering the capacities of government troops and helping to keep Assad in power.

In September 2015, the Russian parliament unanimously granted Putin the right to conduct airstrikes in Syria. The strongholds of the Islamic State of Iraq and Syria (ISIS) were the intended targets of the air campaign, but observers noted that strikes were largely aimed at the command and communication centers of other, less extreme, rebel groups fighting the Assad regime. Throughout 2015 and 2016, Moscow gradually increased its military presence in Syria, even deploying ground troops for several months in order to aid Assad's forces in combating "terrorism."[16] Meanwhile, the death toll from the conflict continued to swell. The UK-based Syrian Observatory for Human Rights estimated that Russian airstrikes had killed 4,408 people (including 1,733 civilians) between September 2015 and March 2016.[17] In December 2016, Russian air offensives helped the Assad regime capture the city of Eastern Aleppo, the rebel group's last urban stronghold.

Scholars and policymakers have disagreed on why Moscow has chosen to intervene in Syria. Ostensibly, Russia has a geopolitical interest in Syria, since its only Mediterranean naval base, Tartus, is located there. Others suggest that Putin intervened on behalf of Assad to seek the kind of domestic political support that short, successful military campaigns usually bring, especially since the protracted Ukrainian conflict was proving to be a depleting challenge for Moscow. Moreover, action in Syria gave Moscow the chance to demonstrate to the United States "that it had the ability and will to intrude into areas that the United States regarded as its own area of operations."[18] In fact, many argue that Russia's saber-rattling in Syria is primarily an attempt to challenge American leadership in the region and can be viewed as part of a larger grand strategy to restore Russia's great power status.

The United States' response to the actions of the Assad government and its Russian partners has been notably restrained. The Obama administration consistently argued against a military solution to the Syrian crisis, insisting that a political accord between Assad and the fractured opposition is the only viable path forward. As such, President Obama was steadfast in his refusal to conduct airstrikes against regime targets, a path that many in his administration—including Secretary of State John Kerry—believed would encourage the Assad government to come to the table. Instead, the United States has worked diplomatically with Western allies, the United Nations, and Russia to negotiate a cessation of hostilities and begin working on a political framework to end the conflict. However, every effort to work with Russia in crafting temporary cease-fires has ended in collapse, leaving the

United States with "little influence over the course of the Syrian civil war" and Russia with renewed confidence in its military capabilities.[19]

At times, cooperation between Moscow and Washington on the Syrian conflict have been successful. In 2013 Secretary Kerry and his Russian counterpart Sergei Lavrov negotiated a framework for the removal of Syria's chemical weapons arsenal, which President Obama saw as pivotal to avoiding a US military strike. Moreover, the United States has repeatedly considered engaging in military cooperation with Russia to coordinate airstrikes against ISIS forces—a group only tangentially involved in the Syrian civil war—and the al Qaeda-linked Jabhat al-Nusra, a group directly opposing the Assad regime that operates in Idlid and Aleppo provinces (close to US-backed opposition forces). In fact, in July 2014, Secretary Kerry met directly with President Putin in Moscow to outline a proposal for joint counterterrorism operations in Syria. The plan involved the sharing of intelligence information on "actionable" al-Nusra targets, including logistical depots, headquarters, and training camps followed by coordinated US–Russian airstrikes. The proposal hinged on Russia's ability to use its influence to curb the Syrian regime's air attacks against civilian and moderate opposition forces. The joined efforts failed to come to fruition; analysts suggest that Moscow believed US-backed opposition forces coordinated efforts with al-Nusra at times (a claim US officials deny). In addition, they perceived US tepidness in directly targeting al-Nusra forces in the past as de facto support for the group. Moreover, any plan for joint counterterrorism operations fell by the wayside after Syria and Russia's repeated violations of temporary cease-fires and the Assad regime's refusal to allow humanitarian aid into besieged areas for the hundreds of thousands of civilians lacking access to food and medical care.

With the civil war raging on and peace negotiations repeatedly stalling, President Obama began to receive sharp criticism from a cross section of American policymakers who believe his Syrian policy—or lack thereof—has strengthened Russia at the expense of American power. They argue that his disengagement from Syria, and the region in general, has left a void, which Russia is all too willing to fill. Florida Senator Marco Rubio warned that American inaction threatens our relevance in the Middle East because other regional powers will begin looking toward Russia for help in the future. Some have called attention to the Saudi Minister's 2015 visit to President Putin's estate in the Black Sea as a warning sign of Russia's rise in the Middle East and the United States' declining influence. Most of these critics called on the Obama administration to confront Assad and Putin with military action, lest the fighting continue to threaten American interests and destabilize the region. The chair of the Senate Foreign Relations committee, Bob Corker, has warned that Putin will continue to escalate Russia's role in Syria because the Obama administration has simply let him do so. "He sees no pushback," Corker explained, "no price to pay."[20] As Danielle Pletka from the American Enterprise Institute explained, the real lesson to be learned from the Syrian conflict is that "US deterrence is dead."[21] Meanwhile, Wisconsin Senator Ron Johnson noted that the administration's inaction in Syria has destroyed the promised

Russian reset since "Putin only respects strength and is adroit at perceiving weakness and fully exploiting it."[22] Even some international allies have been critical of Washington's "wait and see" approach to Syrian–Russian aerial bombing, including the French foreign minister, Laurent Fabius, who called Obama's response "ambiguous" and absent a "very strong commitment."[23]

The chair of the Senate Armed Services Committee, John McCain, has been particularly critical of Obama's "misguided" and "toothless" Syria policy. McCain has warned that the US approach to Syria is undermining our credibility with Middle East partners and will create a dangerous "anti-American alliance of Russia and Iran."[24] "As in Ukraine," McCain explained, "Putin perceives the administration's inaction and caution as weakness, and he is taking full advantage."[25] In an October 2016 op-ed he penned for the *Wall Street Journal*, McCain suggested an alternative approach that would not only ground Assad's air power but would also channel "robust military assistance to vetted Syrian opposition groups." Moreover, it would send a clear warning to Moscow. McCain writes, "If Russia continues its indiscriminate bombing, we should make clear that we will take steps to hold its aircraft at greater risk."[26]

Obama was quick to defend his policies toward the Syrian conflict and put forward his own interpretation of Moscow's relationship to Damascus. In comparison to Washington's "Russia hawks," Obama perceived Moscow's position as fundamentally weak. In a 2016 interview with *The Atlantic's* Jeffrey Goldberg, Obama noted that Russia is a country with worrisome structural problems, both demographic and economic. Their actions in Syria are a "strategic blunder" that will drain them of their resources. But, more importantly, Putin's decision to bolster the Assad government is a signal of a regime desperate to maintain a relationship with its only real ally and not a show of strength. To suggest that Russia is now in a stronger position as a result of their military action in Syria and Ukraine is to "fundamentally misunderstand the nature of power in foreign affairs or in the world generally. Real power means you can get what you want without having to exert violence."[27]

Data Bank

Despite its military power and its international ambitions, Russia is a country with serious domestic challenges that are best seen in terms of standard socio-economic data points. Below is a list of some of Russia's most important and revealing data. As can be seen, Russia faces some serious domestic challenges.

Life expectancy from birth—65.3 years
Population growth rate—.2% (on a steep decline over the last ten years)
Elderly population—13%
Average annual growth rate—1.8%

Average annual rate of unemployment—7.5%
Average annual inflation rate—7.7%
Divorce rates—4.7 per 1000 population (#2 in the world)
Death rate per 1000 population—15.5 (#7 in the world)
Investment in fixed assets—declined by 37% from 2012–2016
Corruption level—#119 out of 167 countries (1 being least corrupt)

Source: OECD, *The Economist*, World Bank, and Transparency International

Those in Obama's administration did not always agree with his assessment of Russian ambitions. Many would have liked to have seen a more assertive response to Putin in Syria, including Secretary Kerry who called for establishing a "no-fly zone" in Syria. But Obama repeatedly rebuked Kerry's suggestions for limited military action. One former Obama official explained, "The optics are that we're backing off. It's not like we can't exert pressure on these guys, but we act like we're totally impotent."[28] Frustration over Obama's response to the Russian engagement in Syria caused a rift in the White House. Some noted that many Russian specialists on Obama's foreign policy team began to feel isolated for expressing more hardline views. They argued that, while the president was firm in his view that engagement with Russia was a more productive approach to ending the Syrian conflict, in reality, Putin and Lavrov were simply "stringing along" or misleading the United States.

Russia specialists also suggested that the United States could both avoid entanglement in Syria and challenge Moscow's increasingly hostile foreign policy. This strategy would involve steadfastly confronting Russian aggression in other theaters. While the world has kept its eyes on Russian military activity in Syria and Ukraine, Moscow has subtlety attempted to extend its geopolitical reach from as far as the Baltic to the Black Sea. For example, Russia has been involved in basic incursions into NATO air space, including a series of 2016 violations into Bulgarian airspace that the country's defense minister described as "provocations toward Bulgaria and its air forces."[29] In October 2014, Sweden announced reports of Russian "underwater activity" in the archipelago that surrounds the capital of Stockholm. Also, in November 2015, Turkish F-16s shot down a Russian military jet that encroached upon Turkish airspace along the Syrian border. In a speech at Oxford University in 2016, Obama Defense Secretary Ash Carter noted that such incursions in air, sea, and space were indicative of "unprofessional behavior" and "have demonstrated that Russia has clear ambitions to erode the principled international order."[30]

In response, the United States augmented its military support to various Eastern European nations in order to reassure NATO allies that felt threatened by potential Russian encroachment. This action included an American-built ballistic missile defense system constructed in Romania as well as significant American participation in major NATO military exercises in Poland and the Baltic countries. NATO's missile defense system has unnerved Kremlin officials, who have called the deployment of the system a "threat to the Russian federation" as well as to global and regional security. President Putin perceived such operations as attempts to enclose Russia and limit its influence on the international stage. In fact, Putin has said that Russia will respond to alleged NATO encirclement by creating new military divisions on its Western border; he's even threatened to fasten Russian Iskander missiles with nuclear warheads and place them in Kalingrad. However, the United States and its allied partners have been quick to assert that the purpose of the missile defense system is solely to protect NATO allies and US forces in Europe from ballistic missiles coming out of the Middle East, and in particular, Iran. As Deputy Secretary of Defense Robert Work explained, "It was never, ever about Russia."[31]

While relations between Washington and Moscow during the Obama administration were dominated by geopolitical friction, other tensions surfaced. Both the Obama administration and Congress have chided Russia on its deteriorating human rights record, especially its treatment of whistle-blowers and members of the press who are critical of the Kremlin. In 2012 the US Senate passed a law in honor of Sergei Magnitski, a young lawyer who exposed large-scale theft among a group of Russian officials and later died, suspiciously, in police custody. The Sergei Magnitski Rule of Law Accountability Act imposed US visa and financial sanctions on officials connected to his death and sent a clear reprimand to Russia over its human rights record. The legislation angered the Kremlin, which retaliated by imposing a ban on American adoption of Russian children. The Obama administration has also been critical of Russia's failure to provide equal rights for the LGBT community. During the 2013 G-20 Summit in St. Petersburg, Obama even met with nine Russian civil rights activists to discuss new anti-gay laws in Russia and openly criticized this legislation in the media. Aside from concerns over human rights, relations between Moscow and Washington were also soured by Russia's decision to grant political asylum to former National Security Agency contractor, Edward Snowden, who is wanted on espionage charges.

While President Obama's "reset" with Russia ended in failure, Donald Trump's election to the White House promises to bring a new chapter in US–Russian relations. During the 2016 campaign, questions about US–Russian relations—and Moscow's global ambitions—dominated debates on foreign policy. Democratic nominee Hillary Clinton warned of Russia's capacity to interfere with the integrity of our election after evidence surfaced that Russian hackers had infiltrated the computer systems of the Democratic National Committee headquarters and distributed compromising e-mails and other documents. Meanwhile, Mr. Trump expressed admiration for the leadership skills of President Putin and noted a desire to ease tensions with America's former Cold War enemy. In a September 2016 televised forum focusing on national security issues, Trump stated, "I think I would have a very, very good relationship with Putin, and I think I would have a very, very good relationship with Russia."[32] Mr. Trump received considerable pushback from Democrat officials, the Clinton campaign, and many security experts in the

Republican establishment who consider Russia to be a dangerous foe. Members of the GOP found themselves in the compromising position of having to clarify the party's views. During a weekly news conference, Paul Ryan exclaimed, "Vladimir Putin is an aggressor that does not share our interests" and insinuated that he was complicit in state-sponsored cyberattacks on the US political system.[33]

Since his election victory, Trump has continued to signal that his administration will work to thaw the icy relationship that has developed between Russia and the United States. For example, in December 2016, President-elect Trump nominated Rex Tillerson, the chief executive of Exxon Mobil, to the post of Secretary of State. Tillerson has worked for many years in Russia on behalf of the oil company and, purportedly, has extensive ties to Vladimir Putin. Many Congressional lawmakers expressed serious concern about Tillerson's relationship with Russian officials and potential conflicts of interest. Florida Senator Marco Rubio called for a thorough vetting process noting, "The next secretary of state must be someone who views the world with moral clarity, is free of potential conflicts of interest, has a clear sense of America's interests."[34] Nonetheless, many GOP hard-hitters, such as Senate Majority Leader Mitch McConnell, expressed their support of Tillerson, who was subsequently confirmed.

Regardless of his intentions, achieving rapprochement with Russia may be a difficult task for President Trump as tensions continue to balloon over accusations of Russian interference in the US election. In December 2016, the Central Intelligence Agency presented lawmakers with an intelligence briefing that concluded "with high confidence" that Moscow had acted covertly, with the help of Russian hackers, to increase the chances of a Trump victory. According to intelligence sources, the US Federal Bureau of Investigation was in agreement with the CIA's analysis of the interference. President Trump has been quick to dismiss the accusations, portraying the CIA as incompetent and biased. But a growing contingent of lawmakers from both sides of the aisles, such as Senator John McCain and the ranking Democrat on the House Intelligence Committee, Adam Schiff, expressed outrage at the alleged Russian actions. The Obama administration chose to take decisive and provocative action in response by expelling 35 Russian intelligence operatives working in the United States and imposing new sanctions on individuals and agencies tied to the hacks. The expulsions prompted vows of retaliation on the part of angered Kremlin officials, but soon Vladimir Putin had announced his decision that Russia would not retaliate against President Obama's actions out of a desire to build a cooperative relationship with the incoming administration. As he had during the campaign, Trump praised Mr. Putin's decision as level-headed. At the start of 2017, tensions between Moscow and Washington had reached fever-pitch, resembling the most tense periods of the Cold War. But evidence suggests that the Trump administration may, in fact, change the trajectory of this old rivalry.

The controversy over the Russian hacking during the 2016 election did change the trajectory of US–Russian relations, but not in the way that President Trump may have anticipated. As the administration took control of the reins of power, the Putin hacking scandal did not diminish but intensified despite President Trump's unwillingness to take aggressive action to get to the bottom of Russian involvement and the question of whether Putin ordered the hacking. Despite numerous statements and tweets in which he denied any link to the Russians during the campaign, President Trump faced mounting pressure to support investigations into the Russian role in the election.

The political blowback from the Russian hacking scandal began to have an impact on the Trump White House, including a) the firing of National Security Adviser Michael Flynn for his ties to Russia, and b) questions about the financial involvement of campaign chair Paul Manafort and Trump son-in-law Jared Kushner with a Russian bank (tied to Putin and others like Carter Paige and Roger Stone, who also had ties to the Russians). A constant media frenzy was created as leaks and unnamed sources sought to link the Trump administration, and perhaps Trump himself, to the Russian hacking effort.

The controversy took a more serious turn when President Trump fired FBI Director James Comey for what many outside of the White House circle felt was an attempt to end the investigation of Russian hacking and possible collusion by the Trump campaign. In a dramatic hearing before the Senate Intelligence Committee, Comey testified that he was convinced the president was seeking to quash the investigation and wanted Comey's consent. Comey did not leave quietly as he admitted that he leaked the private conversation with Trump to the press in order to ensure that it would not fade from public view.

The firing of Comey only deepened the investigation of collusion with newspaper and media stories raising questions about the role of Putin, the financial ties of Trump and his business empire to Russian business groups, and regular presidential tweets that denied involvement and collusion and, at one point, placed the blame on the Obama administration for the hacking. The Congress in the summer of 2017 had enough of President Trump's unwillingness to challenge Russia and Russian interference in the 2016 election process when it passed an expanded sanctions bill. Russian President Putin responded to the sanctions bill by expelling 755 U.S. diplomatic personnel. For his part President Trump reluctantly signed the bill but stated that it was "unconstitutional. The drama kept building and building as the entire controversy took on the character of the Watergate scandal during the Nixon administration. No one can accurately predict where the scandal is headed.

The Great Debate

Russia is attempting to expand its influence in the Middle East through its military support for the Syrian regime. But the European theater is of great importance to Russian foreign policy and that raises questions about United States foreign policy in this area of geostrategic importance.

Debate topic

Should the United States strengthen its commitment to protect NATO allies in Eastern Europe or hold back its activity in the region in order to prevent provoking Russian counter-aggression?

Critical Thinking Questions

1. Why do you think Vladimir Putin decided to annex the Crimean peninsula?
2. Do you believe that US inaction in Syria has increased the influence of Russia in the Middle East?
3. How should the United States respond to allegations that Russian officials illegally interfered in the 2016 US presidential election?
4. Should the United States apply diplomatic pressure on Russia to encourage the Putin regime to improve its human rights record?
5. Do you think relations between Russia and the United States will improve under the Trump administration?

The Davis Center for Russian and Eurasian Studies at Harvard University provides resources on Russian politics and US–Russia relations. Their website can be accessed at: http://daviscenter.fas.harvard.edu

The Kennan Institute at the Wilson Center also provides resources on US–Russian relations. View their website at www.wilsoncenter.org/program/kennan-institute

The Council on Foreign Relations compiles opinion pieces on US–Russia relations from major world publications on its website. It can be accessed at www.cfr.org/region/russia-and-central-asia/ri168

The Office of the Director of National Intelligence's report on Russian hacking can be accessed at www.intelligence.senate.gov/sites/default/files/documents/ICA_2017_01.pdf

The State Department has compiled information on current US sanctions on Russia on their website. View the information at www.state.gov/e/eb/tfs/spi/ukrainerussia/

Some Books to Read

Legvold, Robert, *Return to Cold War* (New York: Polity Press, 2016).

Mankoff, Jeffrey, *Russian Foreign Policy: The Return of Great Power Politics* (Lanham, MD: Rowman and Littlefield, 2011).

Martin, Malia, *Russia Under Western Eyes: From the Bronze Horseman to the Lenin Mausoleum* (Cambridge, MA: Harvard University Press, 1999).

Stent, Angela E., *The Limits of Partnership Relations in the Twenty First Century* (Princeton, NJ: Princeton University Press, 2015).

Zygar, Mikhail, *All The Kremlin's Men: Inside the Court of Vladimir Putin* (New York: Public Affairs, 2016).

Notes

1. Russell Leng, *Bargaining and Learning in Recurrent Crises: The Soviet-American, Egyptian-Israeli, and Indo-Pakistani Rivalries* (Ann Arbor, MI: University of Michigan Press, 2000).
2. Robert G. Kaiser, "U.S. Soviet Relations: Goodbye to Détente," *Foreign Affairs*, Vol. 59, No. 3 (1980), pp. 500–521.
3. Seweryn Bialer and Joan Afferica, "Reagan and Russia," *Foreign Affairs*, Winter, 1982/1983 Issue.
4. "Resolution Condemning Russian Aggression Against Republic of Georgia Passes Foreign Relations Committee," Embassy of Georgia to the United States of America, May 20, 2008.
5. "Bush Slams Russia's Invasion of Georgia," *CBS News*, August 11, 2008.
6. "Bush to Russia: Bullying and Intimidation Are Not Acceptable," *Los Angeles Times*, August 15, 2008.
7. Steven Pifer, "George W. Bush Was Tough on Russia? Give Me a Break," Brookings Institution Op-Ed, March 24, 2014.
8. "Obama, Medvedev Say Nuke-Free World Is Goal," *The Wall Street Journal*, April 1, 2009.
9. Steven Pifer, "Ukraine, Russia, and the U.S. Policy Response," Congressional Testimony, June 5, 2014, www.brookings.edu/testimonies/ukraine-russia-and-the-u-s-policy-response/
10. Daniel Treisman, "Why Putin Took Crimea: The Gambler in the Kremlin," *Foreign Affairs*, May/June, 2016.
11. Steven Pifer, "Ukraine, Russia, and the U.S. Policy Response."
12. Michael Carpenter, Deputy Assistant Director of Defense, "Russia's Violations of Borders, Treaties, and Human Rights," Testimony Before the United States Senate Committee on Foreign Relations, June 7, 2016, www.hsdl.org/?view&did=795363
13. Ibid.
14. Jim Michaels, "U.S. Limits Training in Ukraine to Avoid Provoking Russia in the Region," *USA Today*, April 11, 2016.
15. Dan De Luce, "Chuck Hagel: The White House Tried to Destroy Me," *Foreign Policy*, December 18, 2015.
16. "Putin Uses Assad Visit to Talk Up Kremlin Role as Syria Broker," *Reuters*, October 21, 2015.
17. "Russia's Military Action in Syria—Timeline," *The Guardian*, March 14, 2016.
18. George Friedman, "Why Putin Went Into Syria," *Geopolitical Futures*, March 15, 2016.
19. David Sanger, "Russian Intervention in Syrian War Has Sharply Reduced U.S. Options," *New York Times*, February 10, 2016.
20. Kristina Wong, "Corker: Putin Sees 'No Pushback' on Syria," *The Hill*, September 30, 2015.
21. Dave Boyer, "Russian Aid to Syria Latest Example of Obama's Inability to Confront Putin, Critics Say," *The Washington Times*, September 15, 2015.
22. Ron Johnson, "Putin's Push for Power," September 11, 2015, www.ronjohnson.senate.gov/public/index.cfm/2015/9/putin-s-push-for-power
23. David Sanger, "Russian Intervention in Syrian War Has Sharply Reduced U.S. Options."
24. John McCain, "Stop Assad Now—Or Expect Years of War," *The Wall Street Journal*, October 5, 2016.

25. Taylor Wofford, "Senate Republicans Blast Obama for Russian Involvement in Syria," *Newsweek*, September 20, 2015.
26. John McCain, "Stop Assad Now—Or Expect Years of War."
27. Jeffrey Goldberg, "The Obama Doctrine," *The Atlantic*, April, 2016.
28. Michael Crowley, "Rift in Obama Administration Over Putin," *Politico*, October 13, 2015.
29. "Bulgaria Calls Rise in Airspace Violations by Russian Aircraft a 'Provocation,'" *Reuters*, July 24, 2016.
30. Steven Erlanger, "NATO Ratchets Up Missile Defense Despite Russian Criticism," *New York Times*, May 5, 2016.
31. Andrew E. Kramer, "Russia Calls New U.S. Missile Defense System a 'Direct Threat,'" *New York Times*, May 12, 2016.
32. John Wagner, Jose A. DelReal, and Anne Gearan, "Trump Praises Putin at National Security Forum," *The Washington Post*, September 8, 2016.
33. Kristen East, "Trump in Hot Water After Putin Embrace," *Politico*, September 9, 2016.
34. Steven Mufson, Philip Rucker, and Karoun Demirjian, "Trump Picks ExxonMobil CEO Rex Tillerson to Be Secretary of State," *The Washington Post*, December 13, 2016.

24

CONFLICTS **IN** THE
MIDDLE EAST

Issue Focus

Conflict and the Middle East often are linked together. Whether Afghanistan, Iraq, Syria, Yemen and the pseudo-state of ISIS, the Middle East has been a region wracked by war, destruction, human suffering, and often little hope. Major powers have attempted to bring order to the region, only to find their troops and officials bogged down in a quagmire of unending involvement. While some of the states in the region like Jordan, Saudi Arabia, and the tiny United Arab Emirates have remained relatively stable, in part because of either oil wealth or strong royal government, they have been overshadowed by the constant state of instability and unrest in the rest of the Middle East. Currently, the focus of conflict is on Syria, where the bloody regime of Bashar al Assad has crushed the rebellion with unbelievable cruelty, and in the diminishing so-called radical Islamic caliphate of ISIS in parts of Syria and Iraq. Hundreds of thousands of people have been killed, and hundreds of thousands more have been left homeless to seek peace and security, primarily in Europe. There is little evidence that the conflict in the Middle East will come to an end or at least diminish. Diplomats have tried to bring peace to the region but have failed to find a recipe for a cessation of hostilities. The only certainty is that the conflicts will continue and perhaps spread to those countries that have been spared the chaos to date. Discussing conflict in the Middle East is an important topic, but one that begs for solutions that are elusive if not hopeless.

Chapter Objectives
This issue chapter will seek to:
1. Explain the historical context within which the conflicts in the Middle East have developed over time.
2. Discuss the country-specific conflicts and the impact of the conflict on the citizenry.
3. Examine the efforts to bring peace and stability to the region, despite years of failure.

SOME BACKGROUND

In the twenty-first century, the United States has become entangled in various conflicts throughout the Middle East and North Africa. Our complicated engagement with the region started with an invasion of Iraq two years after the September 11th attacks. But when President Bush spoke to the American people on March 19, 2003, announcing that the United States had begun the attack on Iraq to remove the dictator Saddam Hussein from power and then proudly stood before the "Mission Accomplished" banner aboard the USS Abraham Lincoln two months later, few Americans (and certainly few in the Bush administration) anticipated that the United States would, for the next decade, be engulfed in a sectarian civil war that would claim the lives of over 4,400 American soldiers, injure over 30,000, and cost, by most estimates, at least $1 trillion. What had started out as a bold move to secure weapons of mass destruction, replace an authoritarian government with democracy, and change the political and governing climate of the Middle East had become one of the most divisive and controversial foreign policy actions in modern American history.

As American forces attempted to stabilize sectarian flames in Iraq, they were fighting another war to the east of the Iraqi border, in Afghanistan. Shortly after September 11th, the United States invaded Afghanistan, the country in which mastermind Osama bin Laden had planned the attacks. As a result of the invasion, the United States ousted the repressive Taliban, a Sunni fundamentalist group that had been in power since 1996, and drove Osama bin Laden into the mountainous region bordering Pakistan. The United States has maintained a presence in Afghanistan—along with allied NATO forces—since the invasion in 2001. The objective has been to "disrupt, dismantle and defeat" both the al Qaeda network and the Taliban, to assist Afghan military and police forces in building counter-insurgency capacity, and to construct a government that is capable of securing its own territory.[1]

President Barack Obama inherited both of these wars when he moved into the Oval Office in January 2009 and spent much of his eight years as president adjudicating them. During his first year in office, the debate over the US presence in Iraq shifted from war fighting and counter-insurgency to seeking a prudent and effective means of drawing down its military commitment to Iraq. Since those heady days in 2003 when President Bush pronounced "Mission Accomplished," the government and the people of the United States have engaged in a dialogue about how to end US involvement while retaining American influence in the Middle East. Ultimately, President Obama chose to withdraw US military forces from Iraq, with the final battalions leaving in December 2011. But by 2013, Iraq had collapsed back into political crisis and sectarian violence and was facing a new enemy in the Islamic extremist group known as the Islamic State of Iraq and Syria (ISIS). Faced with renewed civil war and terrorist threats from ISIS, Americans began to question if leaving Iraq was a costly blunder. In Afghanistan, however, President Obama chose to increase troop presence, noting that the real enemies of the United States are hiding in the rugged mountains between Afghanistan and Pakistan. In December 2009, Obama announced his approval of a short-term surge of 33,000 troops to the country, marking July 2011 as a date for withdrawal. With the focus on disengagement from the region under President Obama, the number of troops stationed in Afghanistan has steadily declined to approximately 12,000 in 2015.

While the United States was mired in war in Iraq and Afghanistan, another conflict was flaring in Syria and threatening stability in the region. Bashar Al-Assad has ruled Syria as president since July 2000, extending the authoritarian rule of his father, Hafez al-Assad. After the Arab Spring uprisings in Tunisia and Egypt during the winter of 2011, demonstrators in Syria began to protest the Assad regime in the city of Daraa. When protests spread to other cities, the Syrian government responded with brutal repression. The United States and European Union swiftly condemned the violent crackdown on political opponents of al-Assad, instituting economic sanctions on the regime as well as bans on the import of Syrian oil. However, the conflict only worsened with time, deteriorating into a full-blown civil war between the Assad regime and several different factions, including the Free Syrian Army, rebel forces aligned with al Qaeda, the Islamic State of Iraq and Syria, and groups of Kurdish forces.

The United States has not assumed a large role in the Syrian conflict, aside from arming moderate rebel groups in their fight against the Assad regime. As the civil war has intensified, the United States has attempted to broker peace deals between the Syrian government and rebel groups, with the help of its NATO allies and Russia, which has been disbursing extensive military aid and air support to the Assad regime for the past several years. In general, President Obama erred on the side of caution with respect to intervention in Syria, favoring a political solution in which President Assad would agree to relinquish power. America's disengagement from the Syrian conflict was one of the most controversial aspects of President Obama's foreign policy record. Throughout the course of the civil war, the administration actively debated launching air strikes on the Assad regime, especially after US intelligence found evidence that the regime had used chemical weapons against civilians. But, ultimately, President Obama was steadfast in his decision to forgo military action, even as the Russians amped up their military support to Assad, thus bolstering the Syrian regime's position. The civil war in Syria continues to rage, with nearly 400,000 Syrians having been killed, over 4 million having fled, and over 6 million having been displaced internally since the beginning of the war.[2]

Conflict between Israel and Palestine has also shaped America's relationship to the region. Since declaring independence on May 14, 1948, Israel has fought a series of wars—the Arab-Israeli war of 1948 against Egypt, Syria, Jordan, Lebanon, and Iraq; the Six-Day War of 1973 against Egypt, Syria, and Jordan; and the Yom Kippur War of 1973 against Egypt and Syria. In each instance, the Israelis were successful in defeating their enemies. In addition, as a result of the Six Day War, Israel annexed the West Bank of the Jordan River from Jordan, the Gaza Strip and the Sinai Peninsula from Egypt, and the Golan Heights from Syria. Since declaring nationhood, the Israelis have also been locked in a constant confrontation with the Palestinian people, who lay claim to the land controlled by Israel, and the Hezbollah fighters in Lebanon (a militant group aligned with the Palestinians), who have on numerous occasions been engaged in battle with Israel on the border between the two countries.

Despite its highly effective security apparatus, Israel faces a lingering anxiety and uncertainty associated with constant threats by adversaries in the region and unyielding positions by terrorist groups. Israel has engaged in preemptive strikes against targets in neighboring countries such as Iran and Syria that were deemed potentially threatening to its security. Israel also remains at war with terrorist groups such as Hamas and Hezbollah, who have shown little interest in solving long-festering problems through diplomatic negotiations. As a result, Israel and its society are always on guard against attack. Despite the normalcy that is often seen in its major cities, Israel remains a nation under siege with regular threats from those in the region who hold the view that the Jewish state has no legitimacy and must be pushed out of the Arab world.

Throughout Israel's sixty years as an independent and sovereign nation, the United States has maintained close diplomatic and military relations with it. Israel is the closest ally of the United States in the Middle East and the largest recipient of both American economic and military assistance. Israel's foreign and military policy have often meshed with US objectives in the region—such as counterterrorism—since Israel has been a force against extremists and terrorists. United States and Israeli intelligence agencies work closely together to gather and share information about threats in the region, and the leaders of both nations inform each other regularly about military actions that might be necessary to ensure the security of both Israel and the United States. American presidents have historically pledged to defend Israel against attacks and have pursued numerous avenues of negotiations to bring peace to the region and end "the Palestinian problem." Issues related to Israel and its security have consistently been at the forefront of American foreign policy and will likely remain at the forefront for the immediate future.

DEBATES, DIFFERENCES, DIVISIONS

Iraq and Afghanistan have anchored debates about US foreign policy in the Middle East for the past decade. Discussions about American hegemony, relevance, and decline start and end with these two seemingly intractable conflicts. Even after withdrawing from Iraq, liberals and conservatives continue to debate the wisdom of invading these countries and how history will judge the occupation and nation-building actions of the United States. From the perspective of the Bush administration, it seemed in the best national security interests of the United States to remove a dictator supposedly hiding weapons of mass destruction and then to establish a democratic-like state, even though it was in the midst of Middle Eastern authoritarianism and radical Islamism. Indeed, these actions sent a strong signal to both dictators and terrorists that this country was willing to use military force to face them. But the ghosts of Iraq have animated public debates about "intervention" as foreign policy and have shaped the Obama administration's responses to conflicts in Syria, Yemen, and Libya.

President Obama began his presidency with a profound interest in getting out of both Iraq and Afghanistan. Withdrawal had been a chief element of his foreign policy platform during the 2008 campaign and, making good on his promises, he pursued this agenda after inauguration. The Iraq War had seriously drained American resources, he argued, and the United States should be careful to avoid promising victory in conflicts that might be unwinnable. Many congressional Republicans, however, were wary of Obama's withdrawal plans. Their position was based on the belief that any quick and massive withdrawal from Iraq would send the wrong signal to Iran, the major supporter of radical Shi'ite groups, Palestinian militants, and terrorist insurgents in Iraq. From this perspective, the United States would be viewed as weak and unwilling to influence the direction of government and security interests in the Middle East. Without a sizable American military presence, Republicans believed that Iran would quickly fill the power vacuum in the region, turn Iraq into an Islamist state, and push toward its ultimate objective of destroying Israel. In their opinion, the United States had to remain active and present in the region to continue to protect itself from Islamist extremists and continue to change the political environment in the Middle East. To do otherwise would only embolden the enemies of the United States and, in the words of Senator John McCain, "allow the terrorists to follow us home."[3]

From the perspective of the Democrats, conservatives were only following a failed policy and keeping US troops in the middle of a sectarian civil war. Their primary objective was to develop a speedier timetable for withdrawal while sending clear signals to the Iraqi leadership that they needed to take aggressive steps to solve a range of political issues that have divided Shi'ites and Sunnis. Obama stressed that the answer to the Iraq imbroglio was not a long-term military commitment but a political solution built upon effective governance. He accused the Iraqis of becoming dependent on the US presence and unwilling to make tough political compromises because of their view that the American military would remain in large numbers for years to come. By setting a firm timetable for the withdrawal of a large segment of the 140,000 troops in Iraq, the United States would send a clear signal to the Iraqi government that the occupation was over and that Iraq had to meet its own security challenges.[4]

President Obama eventually won cautious support among members of the GOP for his exit strategy. In February 2009, Obama announced a plan to reduce the number of US troops in Iraq to 50,000 by August 2010, with the remainder of forces leaving by 2011. By 2012, only 150 troops remained in Iraq. Having disengaged from Iraq, the Obama administration shifted attention to neighboring Afghanistan, where the president took the position that the United States must defeat the Taliban terrorists. Obama argued that while the United States was placing its emphasis on defeating the insurgency in Iraq, the Taliban in Afghanistan were regrouping and becoming a serious threat to the government of Hamid Karzai, the pro-American president of Afghanistan. After weeks of internal discussions among Obama, his national security team, and the Pentagon, the president ordered an Iraqi-style surge of an additional 30,00 troops, which would increase the total United States military presence to nearly 100,000. Obama did qualify the commitment of the new troops to eighteen months, and he presented the new commitment as not open-ended but designed to force the Afghan government to build the institutional structures necessary for stability and sustainability. In addition to the troop surge in Afghanistan, Obama ordered a raid on Osama bin Laden's Pakistani compound in May 2011, which resulted in the death of America's most wanted enemy.

While Obama was praised for bringing down bin Laden, his decision to remain in Afghanistan faced intense criticism from liberals in Congress who felt he was letting the United States become entangled in a war that could last for years. Concerns were raised over the mounting cost of the war—over 1,000 soldiers dead, growing budget commitments, the weakness of the Afghan army, the unpopularity of the government, and the skepticism of the American people about a long-term presence in Afghanistan. The president, however, was convinced that the United States and its allies fighting in Afghanistan could not afford to let the Karzai government fall to the Taliban. A Taliban victory would only embolden the terrorists and provide al Qaeda with a new site for its operations.

For a time, the Afghan surge worked. It helped secure some areas of the country under the control of the Taliban, and a number of key Taliban leaders were killed in drone strikes along the border with Pakistan. But there remained serious problems of governance and corruption. While the current Afghan president, Ashraf Ghani, is viewed as a more trusted partner than his corrupt predecessor, Hamid Karzai, the institutions of government remain in shambles and the economy is dependent on illicit drugs and foreign assistance. Moreover, the Taliban made a resurgence in the waning years of the Obama presidency, launching an offensive in the spring of 2015 that helped them make strategic gains in the Helmand and Kunduz provinces. The deteriorating security situation in Afghanistan postponed the president's plans to drastically reduce troop presence there.

Data Bank

The countries of the Middle East have in modern times all suffered with low economic growth rates and stagnating economies. Such poor growth potential coupled with rising populations has created a toxic mix of unemployment and unrest. But amidst the poor economic prospects of some countries, there are some signs of growth in the region. Below are the projections for the growth of the economies of the major Middle Eastern countries for 2017 as determined by *The Economist*:

GDP Growth

Algeria—1.7%
Egypt—4.8%
Iraq—4.0%
Israel—3.7%
Jordan—2.4%
Lebanon—1.9%
Libya—3.7%
Morocco—3.3%
Saudi Arabia—1.7%
Syria—2.1%

Source: The Economist 2016 Handbook of Statistics

At the same time, violence was engulfing neighboring Iraq. Just three years after disengaging from the country, the United States watched as Iraq began to collapse under the weight of renewed sectarian violence. The political bargain struck in 2010—which had kept Shi'ite Prime Minister, Nouri al-Maliki in power—had unraveled. Sunni leaders claimed that the Shia-dominated government in Baghdad had severely marginalized Sunni and Kurdish groups as al-Maliki consolidated an increasingly authoritarian stronghold on power. As a result, Sunni insurgency groups began to contest his power throughout the country and, in a vicious cycle, the violence committed by Sunni insurgency groups led to violent government repression and retaliatory attacks on the part of Iraqi Shi'ites. But it is the rise of the Islamic State of Iraq and Syria (ISIS) that has most alarmed policymakers and the public in the United States. The political vacuum in Iraq permitted the Sunni extremist groups to gain significant territory in parts of Iraq and have succeeded in winning the hearts and minds of many Sunni Iraqis who have experienced repression at the hands of the Shi'ite-led government. By 2014 ISIS had taken control of the cities of Fallujah, Ramadi, and Mosul, although they have since lost much of this territory to the Iraqi army's counter-offensive.

The rise of ISIS has deeply troubled Americans. Not only has the group wreaked havoc on a nation that thousands of Americans soldiers had sacrificed their lives to protect, but they've also engaged in vicious terrorist attacks throughout Europe and the United States with an army of willing recruits (many of whom were radicalized through Internet platforms in the very countries they attacked). Many conservatives have placed the blame for Iraq's collapse—and the subsequent rise of ISIS—on the Obama administration's hasty plans for withdrawal. As Obama's fiercest foreign policy critic, John McCain, recalled, "[Obama] decided to pull everybody out once the surge had won at great sacrifice and squandered all the gains there, which then gave birth to ISIS."[5] The US military had provided a buffer in Iraq, preventing ethno-sectarian violence by "guaranteeing Maliki against a Sunni coup d'etat and guaranteeing the Sunnis against a Shi'ite campaign of militarized repression."[6] Withdrawal had removed that buffer, and with it, much of the political leverage Americans had in Iraq. The Obama administration, however, was quick to place blame for Iraq's collapse squarely on the shoulders of the Iraqi government. His deputy national security advisor noted that "it was the failure of [al-Maliki] and Iraq's various political factions to govern in the spirit of national unity" that led to the renewal of conflict.[7] The administration argued that the continued presence of American troops would not have changed Iraq's political trajectory. Moreover, the rise of ISIS, the president argued, had caught even the most well-versed analysts by surprise, deflecting criticism that US withdrawal had precipitated its territorial gains. Conservatives also criticized Mr. Obama for downplaying the threat posed by ISIS, especially after making comments that referred to the radical group as a junior varsity basketball team.

But as ISIS advanced toward the Kurdish city of Erbil and began to threaten the Yazidis—a Christian minority group living near the Sinjar mountains of Kurdistan—the Obama administration took action by authorizing airstrikes. Nonetheless, Obama was quick to call on the support of NATO allies in waging an offensive against ISIS, emphasizing the need for a multilateral approach to the threat. He was also emphatic in stating that that the United States had no intention of "being the Iraqi air force" and that America would be successful in eliminating ISIS only if "we know that we have got partners on the ground who are capable of filling that void."[8] It seems that while President Obama entered the Oval Office with plans to end the war in Iraq and win the war in Afghanistan, he left office having achieved neither of these objectives and handed over the legacies of these dual wars to his successor, Donald Trump. As 2016 drew to a close, the United States was continuing to send troops to assist Iraqi security forces in battling ISIS, while 8,400 American troops still remained in Afghanistan.

Once in office, Trump benefited from the collapse of ISIS in the key city of Mosul and the fall of the capital city of the caliphate Raqqa. The rejuvenated Iraqi army and other groups, such as the Kurds, ended the terrorist state that they had started in Iraq and Syria. As to Afghanistan, President Trump showed no reluctance to support an expansion of US presence, especially when a number of Taliban attacks proved that the national army was unprepared to defend key cities and regions. The longest war in the history of the United States became longer with no real end in sight.

FYI

In 2014 while representing Bridgewater State University in northern Iraq—commonly called Kurdistan—I (MK) was asked to accompany some of my hosts to a refugee camp outside the city of Dohuk. The camp was run by the United Nations High Command on Refugees, commonly called UNHCR or simply the UN Refugee Agency. The huge camp housed over 80,000 refugees, mostly displaced Syrians. A barbed wire fence surrounded the encampment, but movement in and out was fairly fluid as some of the refugees were permitted to work in jobs in nearby Dohuk. When I arrived, I was encircled by young women with babies begging to intercede for them with the authorities so they could leave the camp for an unknown but much better destination. The camp was organized along "streets" of tents and make-shift houses with no plumbing or water. I talked with a family of eight who lived in one of these tents; they smiled half-heartedly, masking the pain. At one end of the camp was a UNHCR tent that housed offices of child protective services as human traffickers were known to kidnap children and sell them to the sex trade. When I left the camp, I knew that I had visited the saddest place on earth.

The ghosts of Iraq and Afghanistan deeply affected the Obama administration's Syria policy. President Obama was wary of repeating the mistakes of his predecessors and being saddled with a negative foreign policy legacy. For these reasons, he repeatedly warned of American overextension in the Middle

East when confronted with demands for more assertive action against the Assad regime. Citing foreign policy realists like George H.W. Bush and his National Security Advisor Brent Scowcroft, Obama argued that there are few conflicts in the Middle East that warrant direct intervention. In contrast to his "liberal internationalist" secretaries of state, Obama was strident in his belief that one should put the lives of American soldiers at risk only in situations where American interests are directly threatened—such as al Qaeda operations in Afghanistan or dangers to Israeli security. The conflict in Syria, by his estimation, did not directly threaten US interests; therefore, a diplomatic solution had to be pursued.

Since the start of the Syrian conflict, the United States has for called for the removal of the Assad regime and for the establishment of an inclusive and democratic government in Damascus. However, the Obama administration failed to achieve this goal and, some argue, refused to actively work to remove Assad. Part of Obama's hesitancy to become more involved in brokering the conflict is explained by his general orientation toward a more cautious foreign policy, but also a genuine miscalculation about Assad's resolve, since he assumed that Assad would eventually fall, just as Egypt's Hosni Mubarak had during the first phase of the Arab Spring.[9] When it became clear that Assad would neither be driven out of power nor relinquish it willingly, President Obama agreed to send arms and logistical support to moderate rebel groups fighting the Syrian government. The decision to support Syrian rebel groups was criticized by many in Washington. Some were wary of such an action because it was reminiscent of the US support of the Mujahedeen in 1980s Afghanistan—which inadvertently led to the rise of al Qaeda and the Taliban—while others argued that the United States should have increased the levels of training and equipment provided to moderate rebel groups. Secretary Clinton suggested that the United States should amplify its efforts to arm rebels, arguing that working with opposition groups might "convince Assad's backers to consider a political solution."[10] Moreover, if the United States neglected to properly support moderate groups, jihadists would surely fill that vacuum. But President Obama disagreed with the strategy, suggesting that arming rebels wouldn't have "changed the equation" on the ground in Syria.[11]

Policymakers on both sides of the aisle have balked at Obama's resistance to military intervention in Syria, especially his decision to forego airstrikes after the Assad regime was found to have used chemical weapons against Syrian civilians. In 2013 President Obama had drawn a figurative "red line," in which he promised military action against the Assad regime in the event of a chemical attack. "It's important for us to recognize that when over 1,000 people are killed, including hundreds of innocent children, through the use of a weapon that 98 or 99 percent of humanity says should not be used even in war and there is no action," he explained, "then we're sending a signal that that international norm doesn't mean much. And that is a danger to our national security."[12] However, on the day before a planned attack on key government sites in Syria, Obama backed down, citing his doubts about the legality of such a strike and his trepidation about intervening in Syria without the approval of Congress. Conservatives railed against the decision, claiming that US credibility had been seriously damaged by the president's about-face. Key allies in the Middle East, including Jordan and Saudi Arabia were also frustrated by the decision and began to doubt whether the United States was committed to maintaining stability in the region. Even those within the Obama administration were both surprised and critical of the move. Secretary of Defense Leon Panetta explained, "Once the commander in chief draws that red line, then I think the credibility of the commander in chief and this nation is at stake if he doesn't enforce it."[13] But even though the fallout from the "red-line" controversy was fierce, Obama was able to quickly remedy the situation by working with Russian president Vladimir Putin and President Assad to negotiate a deal that successfully removed Syria's chemical weapons arsenal from the country (thus avoiding the need to take military action).

As the war dragged on, President Obama continued to eschew military options in Syria, remaining steadfast in his pursuit of a political solution even after multiple rounds of failed cease-fire negotiations. Administration officials like Secretary Kerry and UN ambassador Samantha Power pushed for more aggressive action in Syria, citing serious concerns about the gross atrocities committed by the Syrian and Russian militaries. Both Kerry and Powers invoked the "responsibility to protect" doctrine, which implied that the United States could violate norms of sovereignty if a government was found to be committing acts of war against its own people; but such a principle was not enough to persuade Obama to utilize military action against the Assad regime. Russia's entry into the conflict complicated the US position and emboldened White House critics, who claimed that the Obama administration's Syria policy boosted the geopolitical influence of the Kremlin in the Middle East at the expense of the United States. But even as Russia continued to encroach on the US sphere of influence in the Middle East, administration officials warned against overextension in the Arab world, which would "ultimately harm our economy, harm our ability to look for other opportunities and to deal with other challenges, and, most important, endanger the lives of American service members for reasons that are not in the direct American national-security interest."[14]

As for President Trump, he took a much more aggressive tact with regard to Syria, especially when Assad used chemical weapons on rebel groups in Aleppo. Trump ordered an airstrike, using sophisticated Tomahawk missiles, to attack Syrian airbases. Trump was praised for his quick and decisive actions, but the attack did little to limit Assad's desire to eliminate the rebels and solidify his ties to Russia. Nevertheless, it was clear that Trump was not afraid to use military might as a tool of foreign policy. Diplomacy took a back seat.

While policymakers in Washington have continually debated the utility of intervention in Iraq, Afghanistan, and Syria, the United States has remained committed to its staunchest ally, Israel. But that does not mean that there are no areas of disagreement between these two friends, or that the United States has not taken policy positions that have caused tensions with government leaders in Tel Aviv. At the top of the list of areas of tension is the longstanding criticism of the Israeli construction of settlements on the West Bank, often termed by the Jews as the biblical area of Judea and Samaria. The Palestinians see these settlements as proof that Israel is an expansionist nation and is unwilling to negotiate a homeland for the Palestinian people. US presidents in recent years have gone on record in opposition to the settlements and the frequent removal of Palestinians and other Arab people who occupy the land where the settlements are being built. The United States has also been uneasy about Israel's human rights policies regarding the Palestinians and its less-than-stellar international reputation as an abuser of Palestinian rights, particularly the killing of innocent civilians when it has retaliated against Hamas or Hezbollah leaders or terrorist targets. Many international human rights organizations such as Amnesty International have castigated the Israelis for their harsh measures against the Palestinians. US officials have openly criticized the Israelis for the policy of responding to violence with violence and their justification for attacking civilian sites that they see as often harboring terrorists.

Obama took office in 2009 with a strong intention to advance the cause of peace in Israel. During his first term, he vigorously pursued a peace deal grounded in the vision of a two-state solution. However, his ambitions were hampered by his rocky relationship with the right-leaning Israeli Prime Minister, Benjamin Netanyahu. Those close to Netanyahu suggested that "Bibi"—his often-used nickname—was eager to work closely with the incoming US president since he had difficulties with President Clinton during his first period as Israeli Prime Minister in the 1990s. However, Barack and Bibi seemed to have a shaky relationship from the start. In their first White House encounter—a meeting generally reserved for "breaking the ice"—Obama reportedly stunned Netanyahu by demanding a total freeze on the building of Israeli settlements in disputed territory. As former Israeli ambassador to the United States, Michael Oren, notes, Obama's request disregarded a "core principle of Israel's alliance with America"—that is, there will be "no surprises."[15] Netanyahu, and other Israeli officials, were also angered by a speech the president gave in Cairo during his first official trip to the Middle East. In his speech, Obama expressed support for the Palestinians and underscored Iran's right to pursue nuclear power. The content of the speech was less problematic for the Israelis than the Obama administration's refusal to share advanced copies of the speech with Israeli officials, a common practice. Moreover, Obama chose to skip a visit to Israel during the visit, which Netanyahu and company perceived as a slight.

Obama's actions led to the impression that the president lacked a true commitment to defending the sacrosanct alliance between Israel and the United States, at least among Netanyahu and his allies in the Knesset (the Israeli parliament). Among certain officials in Tel Aviv, there was uncertainty as to what lay ahead with regard to US–Israeli relations under the Obama administration. Following a 2009 non-binding United Nations resolution that urged Israel to join the Nonproliferation Treaty, there was even some speculation that the administration would put pressure on Israel to submit its nuclear arsenal to international inspection. Such an act would retract a 40-year-old covert agreement signed by Richard Nixon and Golda Meir that permits Israel to "maintain an active nuclear facility without inspection."[16] Even the Israeli public began to doubt the Obama administration's dedication to the alliance; public opinion suggested that only eight percent of Israelis believed that relations between the two countries would improve during a second term.[17] As Amir Tobin and Tal Shalev, Israeli media correspondents, explained, there was a certain narrative put forth by the Israeli media that President Obama "cared more about improving US ties with the Arab World than strengthening relations with Israel."[18] This narrative was equally persuasive among conservative policymakers and analysts across the Atlantic, who believed that the actions of the Obama administration were seriously damaging the relationship between Washington and Tel Aviv.

On the other hand, many analysts believe Netanyahu's missteps contributed to the weakening of US–Israel relations, in particular his support of settlement construction. Seeking the electoral support of settlement communities and right-wing Israelis, Netanyahu has continuously championed the construction of settlements on the West Bank, after initially supporting a temporary freeze in 2009. His actions have angered Washington officials who perceive the continued construction on the West Bank to be the most serious impediment to achieving a negotiated agreement with the Palestinians. Netanyahu, on the other hand, views the building of new settlements as an outcome of a natural growth process and rejects the notion that the settlements are the main stumbling block to peace.[19] The disagreement between Tel Aviv and Washington over the Israeli settlements was aggravated by a 2010 diplomatic faux pas on the part of the Netanyahu government. During Vice President Joe Biden's trip to Tel Aviv—in which he had reaffirmed the United States' steadfast support for Israel—Israel's interior minister announced the construction of 1,600 housing units in East Jerusalem. The announcement took Netanyahu by surprise; more importantly, it infuriated the Obama administration, including Vice-President Biden, who remarked that the move was "precisely the kind of step that undermines the trust we need right now."[20] The rift relationship between Netanyahu and the White House only worsened when Netanyahu, not so subtly, threw his support behind Obama's rival, the 2012 GOP candidate for president, by hosting a private dinner at his home for Mitt Romney during the Republican challenger's visit to Israel four months before the election.[21]

On the Record

Israeli Prime Minister Benjamin Netanyahu has often taken a hardline approach to those countries and terrorist organizations that seek to destroy his country. He usually is outspoken in his commitment to Israeli sovereignty and to those who threaten that sovereignty. Here are three quotes from Netanyahu regarding his hardline approach:

If the Arabs put down their weapons today, there would be no more violence. If the Jews put down their weapons today, there would be no more Israel.

(continued)

On the Record   (continued)

> Peace is purchased from strength. It's not purchased from weakness or unilateral retreats.
>
> You can make peace with an enemy, if the enemy abandons the idea of destroying you. That is the critical test. Democracies fail to understand that.

Sources: Jerusalem Times

The relationship between Obama and Netanyahu did not seem to improve during the president's second term in office, even as the alliance between the United States and Israel remained strong. While President Obama continued to pursue a peace agreement in the Arab–Israeli conflict—this time with his new Secretary of State, John Kerry, at the helm—the peace process was largely abandoned after talks between the Israelis and Palestinians collapsed in April 2014. The talks failed for a number of reasons. On the one side, Israel had purportedly refused to commit to halting the construction of new settlements in disputed territory and had reneged on its promise to release certain Palestinian prisoners. But the death knell sounded when the Palestinian Liberation Organization announced that it had negotiated a pact with the militant group Hamas in Gaza to form a unity government. Since the collapse of the talks in 2014, Prime Minister Netanyahu has renounced his support for a two-state solution, arguing that the PLO has not met basic requirements for the acceptance of Palestinian statehood, including demilitarization and recognition of Israel as a Jewish state. Netanyahu has said that he began to question the viability of a two-state solution during the fated Arab Spring, which he perceived to be fundamentally "anti-west, anti-liberal, anti-Israel."[22] Moreover, Netanyahu perceives the peace process, and Washington's role in it, to be fundamentally flawed. In his view, the Obama administration gave a "free pass" to the Palestinians for their actions to undermine the peace process, including their decision to boycott negotiations, reconcile with Hamas, and bypass Israel by seeking statehood at the United Nations.[23] At the same time, Obama openly and publicly condemned Netanyahu's actions on the settlement issue.

Perhaps the largest point of contention between the United States and Israel has been the Iran deal. While the Obama administration perceived the negotiations to be its greatest foreign policy triumph, Netanyahu fervently condemned the deal, calling it an "historic mistake" that will create "a sure path to nuclear weapons" for the Islamic state of Iran, a country openly hostile to Israel.[24] Tensions between the United States and Israel over the Iran deal came to a head when Netanyahu accepted an invitation from Republican leaders to address a joint session of Congress on the dangers of the Iran Deal for both Israeli security and global stability. Accepting such an invitation, without consulting the White House, flouted standard diplomatic protocol.

While relations between the White House and the Netanyahu government seemed to reach a nadir after the Iran deal, many analysts have suggested that the rift was nothing more than "political bickering" and that the "strategic ties" between the United States and Israel remained "robust."[25] Moreover, Obama was quick to remind conservative critics how American engagement with Israel had strengthened during his presidency. He pointed to the funding that the United States had provided for the Israeli Iron Dome missile defense system and the myriad times the United States used its veto power in the United Nations to block condemnations against Israeli for its settlement policy. Furthermore, Obama administration officials pointed to a 2016 deal in which the United States agreed to spend $38 billion dollars on Israeli military aid in the next ten years as proof of the US commitment to Israel and reiterated that "the bond between the United States and Israel is unbreakable."[26] As Donald Trump entered the Oval Office in 2017, evidence suggested that the bond between these two allies may grow stronger. In public announcements, President Trump has expressed strong support of Tel Aviv and appointed David Friedman, an American lawyer aligned with the Israeli far right, as his nominee for ambassador to Israel. Friedman has long been a supporter of making Jerusalem the capital of Israel, a position that would enrage the Arab people and certainly heighten violent reactions in the West Bank territory and in Israel itself. For his part, President Trump supported the idea of making Jerusalem the capital, but this position faded as the attention of the administration turned elsewhere, in particular to North Korea. Nevertheless, Trump continued to stress his favorable relations with Netanyahu and his commitment to support positions that were pro-Israel. For example, Trump ardently condemned the American abstention on a December 2016 UN resolution condemning Israeli settlements that, as John Kerry explained, was meant as a last ditch effort to defend a crumbling two-state solution. Given that President Trump and Mr. Netanyahu are more ideologically aligned on security issues, it is likely that the US–Israeli alliance will only strengthen over time.

The Great Debate

The Syrian Civil War has been described as the "greatest humanitarian crisis in a lifetime" because of the massive loss of life and the significant political repercussions from the displaced Syrian population. But US policymakers debate the effectiveness of an intervention that might not be in America's best interest.

Debate Topic

Should the United States deploy ground troops and/or conduct airstrikes in order to force the Assad regime out of power, or should it continue its policy of solely arming moderate rebel groups without direct military intervention?

Critical Thinking Questions

1. Should the United States recommit ground forces to Iraq in order to help the Iraqi government deal with the threat of ISIS?
2. Do you believe the United States should maintain a long-term presence in the Middle East?
3. Do you believe that the deaths and injuries of thousands of American soldiers have been in vain or a valuable contribution to freedom and democracy in the Middle East?
4. Should the United States demand that Israel make significant diplomatic efforts and land concessions to solve the Palestinian problem?
5. Do you agree with the current US position that the United States is pledged to come to the military assistance of Israel if its sovereignty and very existence is threatened?

Connections

The Saban Center for Middle East Policy at the Brookings Institution is a valuable resource for understanding Iraq and the Iraq war. See www.brookings.edu/saban/iraq-index.aspx

The Middle East Research and Information Project is another key source of policy analysis on Iraq, Afghanistan, and the Middle East. See www.merip.org

The United States Institute of Peace is an informative resource for analysis of the Syria conflict. See www.usip.org/category/countries/syria

The US Embassy in Israel provides a good overview of the relationship between the two countries. See http://usembassy-israel.org.il

Shmuel Rosner is one of the most influential journalists and bloggers in Israel. View his opinion pieces at the *New York Times*, www.nytimes.com/topic/person/shmuel-rosner

Some Books to Read

Al-Ali, Zaid, *The Struggle for Iraq's Future: How Corruption, Incompetence and Sectarianism Have Undermined Democracy* (New Haven, CT: Yale University Press, 2014).

Bacevich, Andrew J., *America's War for the Greater Middle East: A Military History* (New York: Random House, 2016).

Dueck, Colin, *The Obama Doctrine: American Grand Strategy Today* (Oxford: Oxford University Press, 2015).

Jones, Seth, *In the Graveyard of Empires: America's War in Afghanistan* (New York: W. W. Norton, 2010).

Mearsheimer, John J. and Stephen M. Walt, *The Israel Lobby and U.S. Foreign Policy* (New York: Farrar, Straus, and Giroux, 2008).

Laqueur, Walter and Barry Rubin, eds., *The Israel–Arab Reader* (New York: Penguin, 2007).

Notes

1. "Remarks By the President in Address to the Nation on the Way Forward in Afghanistan and Pakistan," December 1, 2009.
2. "Syrian Civil War Fast Facts," December 22, 2016, *CNN*, www.cnn.com/2013/08/27/world/meast/syria-civil-war-fast-facts/
3. See a critical discussion of McCain's position on "cutting and running" at www.huffingtonpost.com/paul-abrams/McCain_cut-and-run-from-a_b_129755.html
4. See Barack Obama's position on Iraq during the presidential campaign at http://content.usatoday.com/news/politics/election2008/issues.aspx?1&c=12
5. Kristina Wong, "Obama's Unsettled Legacy on Iraq and Afghanistan," *The Hill*, February 10, 2016.
6. Frederick Kagan and Kimberly Kagan, "Is Iraq Lost?" *The Weekly Standard*, January 2, 2012.
7. Wong, "Obama's Unsettled Legacy on Iraq and Afghanistan."
8. Michael D. Shear and Julie Hirschfeld Davis, "While Offering Support, Obama Warns That U.S. Won't Be 'Iraqi Air Force,'" *The New York Times*, August 8, 2014.
9. Jeffrey Goldberg, "The Obama Doctrine," *The Atlantic Monthly*, April, 2016.
10. Rebecca Kaplan, "Hillary Clinton Still Wouldn't Give Up on Training Syrian Rebels," *cbsnews.com*, September 22, 2015.
11. Goldberg, "The Obama Doctrine."
12. Frederick Pleitgen and Tom Cohen, "War Weary Obama Says Syria Chemical Attack Requires Response," *CNN.com*, August 30, 2013.
13. Goldberg, "The Obama Doctrine."
14. Ibid.
15. Michael B. Oren, "How Obama Abandoned Israel," *The Wall Street Journal*, June 16, 2015.
16. "Obama Won't Press Israel to Reveal Nuclear Arsenal," *Haaretz*, October 3, 2009.
17. Amir Tibon and Tal Shalev, "Bibi and Barack: Scenes From a Failed Marriage," *Huffington Post Highline*, November 12, 2015.
18. Ibid.
19. Jodi Rudoren and Jeremy Ashkenas, "Netanyahu and the Settlements," *The New York Times*, March 12, 2015.
20. Ethan Bronner, "As Biden Visits, Israel Unveils Plan for New Settlements," *The New York Times*, March 9, 2010.
21. Jordan Michael Smith, "After Favoring Romney, Netanyahu Hurries to Make Nice With Obama," November 8, 2012, www.msnbc.com/msnbc/after-favoring-romney-netanyahu-hurries-m
22. Barak Ravid, "Netanyahu: Arab Spring Pushing Mideast Backward, Not Forward," *Haaretz*, November 24, 2011.
23. Oren, "How Obama Abandoned Israel."
24. Isabel Kershner, "Iran Deal Denounced By Netanyahu as 'Historic Mistake,'" *The New York Times*, July 14, 2015.
25. Christi Parsons and Joshua Mitnick, "Obama's Tense Relationship With Netanyahu Colors His Legacy on Israel," *The Los Angeles Times*, September 21, 2016.
26. Emily Harris, "Kerry Touts U.S.-Israel Bond After Israeli Angst Over Iran Deal," *NPR News*, December 5, 2013.

GLOBALIZATION
AND TRADE

Issue Focus

The world is no longer made up of isolated countries and separate regions with limited contacts. Today the operative term to describe the new world situation is globalization. In the globalized world, countries and regions are increasingly linked in ways never imagined just thirty years ago. Expanded trade in goods and services, the movement of people from one country or continent to another, the exchange of ideas and cultural mores, and the electronic interconnection of banking, currency, and stock market positions and investment policies are now commonplace and drive this relentless push to create a global system. The Internet and mass communication have contributed to the advance of globalization as the new world order becomes just a mouse click away or the redirection of a satellite dish. Globalization offers countries and people new opportunities to grow and prosper, but there are downsides to this new phenomenon, especially for those without the education, the skills, and the competitive entrepreneurial spirit to ride the wave of change. The election of Donald Trump to the presidency was in part a reaction by his supporters to globalization and its negative impact on their lives, their jobs, and their futures. There are thus winners and losers in the globalized environment, which creates the basis for debates, differences, and divisions.

Chapter Objectives
This issue chapter will seek to:
1. Explain the new global economic system and the involvement of the United States in that global environment.
2. Discuss the policy disagreements that have arisen over how the United States can best compete in the global economy, with particular emphasis on job loss in this country.
3. Describe the challenges faced by globalization in a political arena where nationalism, protectionism, and anti-global sentiment is gaining ground.

SOME BACKGROUND

As the children's ride at the Disney theme park proclaims, it is indeed "a small world." Although the planet is large, with people from many different cultures, speaking many different languages, and believing in many different religions, an interconnectedness of people and places makes a diverse world a small one. We call that interconnectedness *globalization*. We live in a time in which advances in communication, transportation, and information transmission have made the world smaller and, in the process, billions and billions of new connections are created every day, from the movement of capital and people to the trading of goods and services and the expansion of Internet contacts, along with the introduction of new ideas, new products, new lifestyles, and new values throughout the world. It is not an exaggeration to state that globalization has revolutionized the way we live, bringing both enormous change and significant challenges as nations and people seek to adjust to a smaller and smaller world.[1]

This enormous expansion of worldwide contacts that has come to be called globalization is most pronounced and influential in the economic and financial sectors of countries. We now live in a global economy in which exports and imports play a prominent role in the shape and growth of nations. Governmental leaders are championing the benefits of more open trade, foreign investment, relaxed corporate regulations, tax incentives for businesses, and the benefits of the capitalist market system as the keys to making globalization a success. The United States has been one of the major proponents of globalization, and since the 1980s, during the Reagan administration, it has advocated, within governing and business circles both domestically and internationally, for a reformulation of the rules of economic development and financial expansion. Often called the Washington Consensus, political leaders, corporate heads, economists, bankers, and other advocates of a more liberalized approach to national growth and international integration have pushed for the acceptance of a series of changes in the manner in which economies and governments work, which can be summed up as follows:

1. Establishment of the private sector as the source of economic growth
2. Elimination of tariffs on imported goods (free trade)
3. Expansion of exports and a de-emphasis on traditional sectors of production
4. Openness to foreign investment and an end to the nationalization of key economic assets
5. The movement of work and the production of goods to foreign sites (outsourcing)
6. Privatization of state enterprises
7. Deregulation of bureaucratic controls on businesses
8. Maintenance of a low rate of inflation
9. Elimination of corrupt practices in public and private sectors
10. Reduction in the number of government workers[2]

At its core, the Washington Consensus was the triumph of the capitalist ethic over the statist system that was not only used by the former communist countries, but also served as the basis of national development in many less-developed countries. With the fall of communism and many less-developed countries desperate for new ways to stimulate their economies, the prospect of moving to a global system with new rules quickly became attractive. Four countries—South Korea, Singapore, Hong Kong, and Taiwan—became known as the Asian Tigers as their economies moved forward with huge spurts of growth and development.[3] Later, Brazil, Russia, India, China, and South Africa (BRICS) followed suit as they opened their countries to free trade, foreign investment, and the market system. Many other countries in the former Soviet Union, Eastern Europe, and other Asian countries such as Vietnam and Thailand accepted the globaliztion rules and began to enjoy significant upswings in their economies. By the new millennium, globalization had become firmly established and was enhancing economic development in those countries that embraced the Washington Consensus.

However, although the principles of globalization were being implemented, the downside of this new form of economic and financial interconnectedness was beginning to be experienced in the same countries that were enjoying enhanced growth and personal wealth. Signs that a globalized economy could create deep divisions between those who benefitted from it and those who saw little change in their lives began to surface in a number of countries.[4] Huge job shifts from wealthy countries to poorer countries where labor was cheaper angered many workers who become unemployed. There were frequent news stories of workers who were treated unfairly as they toiled for low wages in modern-day sweatshops owned by multinational companies. Moreover, data pointed to rising levels of income inequality, which showed that globalization had some winners but many losers. All of this evidence spurred demonstrations and violent protests by a rising chorus of anti-globalization activists. The message delivered by these anti-globalists was that the new rules of the international economy were stacked against the poor, the unskilled, and those who worked in the old-line manufacturing jobs. More troubling, too often governments and multi-national corporations ignored many of the human problems and class separations that accompanied this modern-day form of doing business and enhancing national growth. Globalization thus became a cause for economic optimism, yet a serious threat to income and job security.[5]

DEBATES, DIFFERENCES, AND DIVISIONS

Although the globalization paradigm was heavily influenced by the Washington Consensus and promoted by US leaders, its implementation in the American economy has caused extensive controversy and negative reaction. Perhaps the best place to begin the discussion of the debates, differences, and divisions surrounding globalization and its effect on the US economy is the passage of the North American Free Trade Agreement (NAFTA). Signed by President George H.W. Bush, Prime Minister Brian Mulroney of Canada, and President Carlos Salinas of Mexico in 1992, NAFTA was seen as the beginning of what was envisioned as a region-wide free trade zone that would allow goods, services, and capital to move without the imposition of tariffs or other economic controls. Such a liberalized economic system envisioned heightened economic growth for the three countries, creation of new jobs, and the spread of prosperity to a broader spectrum of the population. On the signing of the NAFTA agreement,

President Bush stated that the three nations were embarking, "on an extraordinary enterprise [that would create] . . . the largest, richest and most productive market in the entire world: a $6 trillion market of 360 million people that stretches 5,000 miles from Alaska to the Yukon to the Yucatan Peninsula."[6]

The agreement was presented to the American people as a huge economic benefit because it could create hundreds of thousands of new export jobs, grant greater access to the Canadian and Mexican markets, allow cheaper Mexican goods to enter the United States, and enhance the profits of both large-scale multinationals and small- and medium-sized businesses that would enjoy enhanced opportunities for growth. However, the NAFTA agreement was not without its problems, which organized labor, environmentalists, and those political leaders who advocated for more protectionist trade policies quickly pointed out. Many argued that that the American worker would lose on account of NAFTA and that jobs would leave the United States for Mexico where wages were less, unions were weak, and labor and environmental rights were negligible.

After the passage of the NAFTA agreement in 1994, both Presidents Clinton and Bush sought to expand trade agreements in the western hemisphere, with President George W. Bush successfully renegotiating the Dominican Republic–Central American Free Trade Agreement (DR–CAFTA) and Congress approving it in 2005. Clinton and Bush both stressed the economic successes they attributed to the new free trade environment, highlighting the significant growth in exports, foreign direct investments, and job creation. Business supporters of NAFTA pointed to a jump in US employment from 110 million jobs in 1993 to 137 million in 2006, with manufacturing output increasing by 63% between 1993 and 2006.[7] Moreover, other proponents argued that NAFTA had made a significant impact on poverty, life expectancy, literacy, and infrastructure formation in the poorest parts of Mexico. Such an argument was part of a larger narrative that globalization leads to socio-economic growth and prosperity for those countries that embrace it; in short, globalization "lifts all boats."

On the Record

Pulitzer Prize-winning journalist Thomas Friedman has been one of the most prolific and prescient writers on globalization and its impact on national economies. He has also served as a kind of prophet on how globalization will affect the lives and futures of individuals, even those in his family. Friedman writes on the impact of globalization on his daughters.

When I was growing up, my parents told me, "Finish your dinner. People in China and India are starving." I tell my daughters, "Finish your homework. People in India and China are starving for your job."

Source: YouTube video, August 20, 2013

Although free trade and enhanced foreign investment were strongly supported by the Bush administration and its allies in the business community, there was growing opposition from the same sources that were active during the NAFTA legislative debate in 1994, only this time there was ten years of data and experience with NAFTA that gave labor unions, environmentalists, and protectionists ammunition to convince Congress to end its unqualified support for the key foundations of globalization. Critics of NAFTA, CAFTA, and other bilateral free trade agreements stated that, since 1993, over 900,00 jobs—many in the manufacturing sector in the United States—had "gone south, outsourced to countries that paid much lower wages and offered little or no benefits."[8] Although supporters of free trade agreements declared that millions of new jobs had been created in the export sector as the United States expanded trade, unions and other opponents of these agreements were not swayed by the claims of employment benefits. The liberal Economic Policy Institute stated, "If the United States exports 1,000 cars to Mexico, then American workers are employed in the production. If, however, the United States imports 1,000 cars from Mexico rather than building them domestically, then a similar number of Americans who otherwise would have been employed in the auto industry will have to find other work."[9]

Environmentalists were also active in criticizing the free trade system put in place since NAFTA. They pointed to lax environmental standards as United States and other foreign companies working in the maquiladoras (free-trade zone industrial parks) polluted rivers, dumped toxic waste, and failed to implement clean air standards. The result was growing environmental decay that posed a health hazard to the workers and those living near the factories. Although the DR–CAFTA agreement did have more rigid environmental safeguards, there was general skepticism that these safeguards would be enforced. Environmentalists also feared that, ultimately, an environmental or human disaster would occur in these loosely regulated industrial free zones.

These are the fault lines of globalization that President Obama encountered upon taking office in January 2009. On the campaign trail, he had responded to both the uncertainty and ire surrounding the processes of globalization by promising to open up the NAFTA agreement for renegotiation in order to address its shortcomings with respect to labor and environmental protections.[10] However, once in office and facing a massive recession that had destabilized the American economy, the Obama administration abandoned plans to reopen trade talks with NAFTA members and worked to solidify trade ties with a host of nations. But unionist and environmentalists remained steadfast in their opposition to both NAFTA and other free trade deals on the horizon. President Obama was also receiving pushback on his trade agenda from Congressional Democrats whose constituents were particularly hard-hit by the outsourcing of jobs that has come with globalization. As North Carolina Congressman G.K. Butterfield explained, "NAFTA was a disaster—in my district, anyway. In some places in the country it may have been a bonanza, but in my district it was a disaster."[11] Policymakers like Butterfield wanted to ensure that Obama's trade deals create jobs in his district, not just contribute to economic growth as a whole.

But concerns over NAFTA did not disappear. Obama tried to assuage the frustration of anti-NAFTA activists by promoting the potential benefits of a new trade regime on the horizon: the Trans-Pacific Partnership (TPP). The TPP is the largest trade deal ever negotiated, encompassing twelve nations that border the Pacific Ocean, including the United States, Japan, Mexico, and Canada. The agreement was intended to boost trade between the economies of Asia and the western hemisphere by lowering tariffs on everything from trucks to textiles. But it has also served to rewrite some of the rules of the global economy since the agreement requires signatory countries to "adopt strict environmental and labor rules, provide stronger legal protections to drug companies, lengthen the term of copyright protection, give foreign investors a new way to challenge countries' law and regulations, and much more."[12] The Obama administration attempted to sell the Trans-Pacific Partnership to the American people as an "upgrade" of the NAFTA agreement; since the TPP would include both Mexico and Canada as signatories, it would replace NAFTA's shortcomings with more encompassing provisions. President Obama explained, "NAFTA failed to require a minimum wage, ban workplace discrimination, protect the right to form a union and bargain collectively, or prohibit child and forced labor. TPP includes every single one of these standards, along with enforceable trade sanctions for any country that violates them."[13] Moreover, the TPP would solidify the American economic relationship to the fastest growing region in the world, which would only benefit the American worker and the American consumer. Finally, supporters of the TPP touted the geo-political importance of the agreement, which, incidentally, excluded America's most significant economic rival, China. By strengthening economic ties with allies in Pacific countries, the United States could encourage China to embrace free trade and to institute economic liberalization reforms—in short, to play by the new rules written by the United States and its partner nations.

The agreement was signed in February 2016, after years of tough negotiating between the trade representatives of the nations involved. But even as the deal was being signed, the Obama administration faced pushback in Congress, where opposition to the agreement had already formed. One of the most vocal opponents of the TPP was Vermont Senator Bernie Sanders, who argued that the agreement would result in massive job loss in the US manufacturing sector because American workers would be forced to compete against low-wage labor in Asia's emerging economies. He also expressed concern about the lack of transparency in the drafting of the deal and the influence of multinational corporations in the content of the agreement. In a public statement after the historic deal was reached, Sanders explained, "Wall Street and big corporations just won a big victory to advance a disastrous deal. Now it's on us to stop it from becoming law."[14] For Sanders, the Pacific Rim deal had been drafted by corporate America, who would be its main beneficiary (and not the American worker). Massachusetts Senator Elizabeth Warren also criticized the TPP for its dispute settlement architecture because the agreement contained a provision that would allow foreign investors to lodge complaints against the United States. Such specification, she argued, would "tilt the playing field in the United States further in favor of big multinational corporations" and, ultimately, "undermine US sovereignty."[15]

Some conservative policymakers were also critical of the TPP, especially those from states whose industries would be affected by the deal's provisions. For instance, Senators Thom Tillis and Richard Burr of North Carolina and Senate Majority leader Mitch McConnell from Kentucky—both tobacco-producing states—expressed reservations about a TPP provision that would bar tobacco companies from using special tribunals to sue nations that adopted antismoking laws. Republican lawmakers in the Rust Belt were also wary about some aspects of the agreement. Facing pressure from an electorate plagued by job loss in the manufacturing sector, Ohio Senator and former US trade ambassador Rob Portman announced his opposition to the deal on the campaign trail. "I cannot support the TPP in its current form because it doesn't provide that level playing field," Portman stated. "I will continue to urge the Obama administration to support American workers and address these issues before any vote on the TPP agreement."[16] The complex and multi-dimensional battles over the Trans-Pacific Partnership illustrate that globalization has become a political issue that does not conform to traditional left-right divides in American politics. The ways in which lawmakers have responded to trade policies has been partially dependent upon what industries are located in their districts, and therefore, whether their voting base of constituents will be the winners or the losers from trade deals. Regarding the TPP specifically, the US International Trade Commission projected that the industries that would profit from the deal include passenger cars, apparel, dairy production, and retailers and wholesalers, while those industries that would face economic losses include auto parts, soybean production, and chemicals and drugs.[17]

The battle over the TPP was also set against the backdrop of an election campaign that featured anti-trade rhetoric from both sides of the political spectrum. Recognizing the potential electoral costs of being on the wrong side of the TPP debate, some Republican lawmakers from manufacturing states reversed course on the TPP, expressing opposition to the deal after previously supporting it. In Pennsylvania, Republican Senator Patrick Toomey "flip-flopped" on the Pacific Rim deal because he was facing a tough re-election bid and was wary of losing the support of anti-trade voters in steel towns and coal country. His challenger, Democrat Kate McGinty, capitalized on Toomey's inconsistent trade record in order to portray herself as the "fair trade" candidate, calling the TPP "an agreement that even its supporters admit will cost Pennsylvania tens of thousands of jobs."[18] Moreover, the 2016 presidential candidates placed the issue of international trade front and center in the campaign. Vermont Independent Bernie Sanders drew significant campaign support from anti-globalization activists concerned about the byproducts of deals like the TPP in the United States and around the world, including weakened labor rights, environmental decay, and heightened inequality. Sanders supporters also drew attention to the role that Wall Street and large multinational corporations played in the drafting of the Pacific Rim deal and used it to portray the US system as increasingly oligarchic. His challenger in the Democratic primary, Hillary Clinton, expressed her own reservations about how the TPP might hold down wages for some working families in the United States. Her stance on the TPP on the campaign trail was controversial, however, since she had previously stated her enthusiastic support for the agreement, praising it as a deal that "sets the gold standard in trade agreements."[19] As Secretary of State during Obama's first term, Clinton had helped to design his signature "Pivot to Asia" foreign policy agenda, of which the TPP was the economic cornerstone. Her detractors saw her 2016 opposition to the TPP as mere political posturing and accused her of "flip-flopping" on trade in order to win over white working-class voters.

But it was the precipitous electoral rise of billionaire populist Donald Trump that catapulted globalization into the center of American political debate. On the campaign trail, Trump took a stance that separated him from much of the pro-free-trade Republican establishment. He railed against NAFTA, claiming that the agreement had made it easier for US companies to relocate their production facilities to Mexico. For Trump, NAFTA was one of the main factors contributing to the decline of American manufacturing, and the political elite in Washington had actively facilitated this decline through policies that supported their free-trade agenda—policies that had ultimately led them to abandon the working class. In a June 2016 campaign speech outside of Pittsburgh, Trump exclaimed, "Our politicians have aggressively pursued a policy of globalization—moving our jobs, our wealth and our factories to Mexico and overseas . . . this wave of globalization has wiped out our middle class."[20] Mr. Trump viewed the Trans-Pacific Partnership as yet another betrayal of the American worker, calling the agreement a "rape of our country."[21] He promised to abandon the TPP and renegotiate the NAFTA agreement once in office. In many respects, Trump's campaign slogan "Make America Great Again" partially reflects his pledge to lure manufacturing firms back to US soil, which he claimed would produce massive job expansion in the industrial sector and relieve the downtrodden American worker.

Trump's detractors were quick to point out that he, himself, had been a beneficiary of US trade policies. Liberals accused Trump of building his business empire at the expense of American workers, outsourcing the production of his various merchandise lines to labor in developing countries. In response to Trump's blistering attack on Washington's free trade policies, the Clinton campaign tweeted a photo of a Donald J. Trump Signature Collection golf shirt with a "Made in Bangladesh" label on its collar. Moreover, Mr. Trump was accused of utilizing undocumented Mexican workers for the construction of portions of his hotel chain; therefore, his anti-globalization rhetoric, liberals argued, was both hypocritical and self-serving. Despite his business practices, Trump's populist stance on globalization seemed to appeal to many blue-collar Americans who have experienced job loss in the manufacturing sector. Trump enjoyed surprising Electoral College wins in the heart of the rust belt, including victories in Michigan, Pennsylvania, and Wisconsin.

Mr. Trump was not only critical of particular US trade agreements, but he also criticized Washington for creating a hostile environment that worsened the ill effects of globalization by encouraging US businesses to move their operations overseas. During the campaign he pledged to both cut corporate tax rates and loosen government regulations. On one of his first days in office, President Trump met with the executives of some of America's largest corporations—including Johnson and Johnson, Dell, Ford, Dow Chemical, and US Steel—to present his plan to reduce the corporate tax rate to as low as 15%. As for regulation, President Trump explained, "I think we can cut regulation by 75%, maybe more."[22] Incidentally, President Trump has also "talked tough" to the American business community, threatening serious consequences for companies who leave the United States. For Trump, the reward of a less-regulated private sector should be made available only to those companies who keep American jobs within US borders.

Trump and other conservatives have also claimed that the Obama administration had fallen short on trade enforcement. The Chinese government has been accused of intentionally undermining the value of its currency. By doing so, Beijing is giving itself an unfair trade advantage since an undervalued currency keeps Chinese exports inexpensive in foreign markets. Such practices, critics claim, directly impact the profitability of American exports and, therefore, unfairly undermine the welfare of American workers. Beijing has also been accused of intellectual property theft, unfairly subsidizing its industries, and dumping its exports on foreign markets at a price below its cost of production. Throughout his two terms in office, Congressional conservatives blasted President Obama for not taking decisive action to penalize Beijing for its predatory trade practices, while liberals suggested that tough action would only spark a tit-for-tat reciprocation from the Chinese government and, possibly, a trade war. In response to criticism from Trump and other Republicans on the 2016 campaign trail, the Obama administration attempted to ardently defend its trade enforcement record. The administration cited the 20 enforcement cases it filed (and won) at the WTO since 2009, winning billions of dollars for the American aircraft, automobile, agriculture, and clean energy sectors; 11 of those cases were against China.[23]

On the campaign trail, Donald Trump promised to instruct the US trade representative to label China a currency manipulator and to bring even more cases against China to the World Trade Organization. Outlining his economic plan in September 2016, Trump pledged, "If China does not stop its illegal activities, including its theft of American trade secrets and intellectual property, I will apply countervailing duties until China ceases and desists."[24] In Trump's view, China is "winning" the globalization race; in the zero sum game of international trade, China's unprecedented growth is directly related to America's own economic stagnation. Many Americans seem to agree with this assessment as 53% of respondents in a 2012 Gallup poll claimed that China was the leading economic power in the world today (followed by the United States, Japan, the European Union, India, and Russia).[25] In response to a rising China, Trump has seemed to advocate greater trade protectionism—even suggesting as much as a 45% tariff on Chinese exports to the United States—as opposed to greater negotiation and engagement with Beijing. Mr. Trump's critics have grown increasingly concerned about his potential reversal of decades of US foreign economic policy, which has encouraged free trade in order to promote economic growth and prevent conflict among nations. Many note that increasing tariffs on Chinese goods would not encourage the substantial job growth in American industrial sectors that Trump envisions. Economists have noted that American manufacturing output is already at its highest levels in history and that unemployment in industrial sectors has been a consequence of efficiency gains and technological automation, not Chinese competition. Imposing tariffs on Chinese exports, they argue, would only provoke a trade war in which Beijing would impose reciprocal tariffs leading to a rise in the prices of Chinese consumer goods that Americans have come to rely on.[26]

While Republicans and Democrats have clashed over US trade policies, many have found common ground in recognizing a need to reform taxation of international business. Both conservatives and liberals have decried the increasing number of US multinational corporations—including Google, Microsoft, Cisco, and Apple—that have engaged in tax inversion, a practice in which firms "shift earnings to low-tax jurisdictions"—often through a merger with a smaller company—to avoid high statutory tax rates. According to Richard Lane of Moody's financial services company, "US companies outside the financial sector held $1.2tn of cash overseas at the end of 2015."[27] Those critical of this practice have called attention to the reality that, as multinational corporations circumvent the US tax system, American citizens are denied essential public funding for infrastructure, schools, and other services. Also, because the US recovery from a devastating recession has been tenuous, it cannot afford for corporations like Apple to "cheat" on its tax obligations. The Obama administration has attempted to curb tax inversion through a set of tough rules established by the Treasury Department. President Obama called on Congress to rewrite portions of the tax code to prevent one of the "most insidious tax loopholes out there," but has received pushback from some Congressional Republicans who believe such a move would undermine investment and, ultimately, harm US companies.[28]

Data Bank

Forbes Magazine presents a yearly list of the ten most powerful international brands as a way of showing the extent to which private corporations have developed a global presence and reap the profit rewards from their global brand. Below is the list for 2016 with the brand value.

> \# 1 Apple—$154.1 billion
> \# 2 Google—$82.5 billion

(continued)

Data Bank   (continued)

> # 3 Microsoft—$75.2 billion
> # 4 Coca-Cola—$58.5 billion
> # 5 Facebook—$52.6 billion
> # 6 Toyota—$42.1 billion
> # 7 IBM—$41.4 billion
> # 8 Disney—$39.5 billion
> # 9 McDonald's—$39.1 billion
> # 10 General Electric—$36.7 billion

Source: *Forbes Magazine*, February 2016

In addition to trade and taxes, another issue related to globalization has also become a political flashpoint, both in the United States and in the less-developed world. Agricultural subsidies, which are designed to support the domestic agricultural sector, have angered many poor countries. Congress has consistently passed pro-agricultural legislation that includes billions (nearly $4 billion in recent fiscal years) in subsidies to make American farm products cheaper to sell abroad. These subsidies make it extremely difficult for less-developed countries to compete with American farm products, and they raise the price of imported goods from the United States on essential commodities. Numerous international meetings (the so-called Doha Round of trade negotiations) have been held under the auspices of the WTO to solve the subsidy issue and bring some trade relief to the less-developed countries, but the agricultural lobby in the United States (and also in Europe and Japan) is so powerful that there has been little movement to reduce the subsidies. As foreign critics of US agricultural policy point out, the United States is for free and open trade except when it comes to protectionist subsidies that benefit a key economic sector.

FYI

The national retail chain Walmart, with its headquarters in Bentonville, Arkansas, is in reality a hugely international operation, the largest company in the world, and an example of how the global economy is organized. As of December 2016, Walmart had 6,345 stores in 26 nations employing over 800,000 people. International sales topped US $32.7 billion; domestic sales were $129.7 billion. Walmart's largest business presence is in Latin America with nearly 4,100 stores in operation, with its Mexico division consisting of 2,400 stores.

Source: Walmart corporate report, December 2016

These political flashpoints have shaped the way that Americans view globalization, a trend that has, indeed, changed over time. After an initial positive response to free trade and free trade agreements such as NAFTA, TPP, and expanded investment in countries such as China and Mexico, American public opinion has soured on the new global economy. In a poll conducted by CBS News in July 2016, Americans were evenly divided on globalization, with 53% responding that the United States has lost more than it has gained because of globalization, while 48% of respondents had claimed that trade with other countries creates job loss and not job gain. Americans also seem skeptical of particular trade agreements, with 44% of respondents in a 2016 Bloomberg Poll stating that the NAFTA agreement has been "bad for the US economy."[29] In a 2016 poll, Americans also showed concern over foreign investment in the United States with 44% stating that such investment was "dangerous" and only 36% viewing foreign investment as "necessary and positive."[30] Increasingly, Americans are seeing foreign countries, such as China and the oil sheikdoms of the Middle East, use sovereign wealth funds (state-managed investment capital generated from successful trade or oil revenues) to invest in—or purchase outright—US corporations, banks, and investment houses or gain substantial stock control in those entities. This foreign investment influence has begun to hit a nationalist nerve in the United States with fears that foreign countries may, in the future, have undue influence on the American economy.

The current negativity in the United States and the hostility of President Trump toward trade agreements like NAFTA and the TPP are not likely to diminish in the short term, but then neither is the new global economy going to collapse and be replaced by a new paradigm. Globalization, despite its deficiencies, is firmly in place and being embraced by more and more countries.[31] American political leaders are aware that the voting public has seen enough of "Made in China" products, jobs going south, and foreign countries buying US assets. In the coming years, protectionist legislation is certain to be debated in Congress and placed high on the agenda of the president as pressure builds to redesign globalization so as to ensure that the American manufacturing sector has the ability to survive and perhaps even be reborn. However, to many who have studied the globalization model and have seen how it benefits the corporate bottom line, the redesign of the new global economy will be a difficult task. There remain in this country, and in the world, powerful economic and financial interests that continue to insist that globalization is the key to prosperity and general national development. Some adjustments may be made to the globalization regime, such as more job training programs, protection of certain industries, and demands that nations trade not just freely but fairly. However, even if these reforms do occur, the foundation of free trade and free markets upon which globalization was built is secure and lasting.

While the debate over the future of globalization and the American economy simmers, people in the United States will continually be reminded that the world has changed and the new global economy is a reality. They will still get Indian customer service personnel when they call for advice on their computers or cell phones, notice "Made in China" on most of the goods they buy, see a flood of foreign tourists coming to the United States to buy goods because of a weak dollar, and find that the world has indeed become smaller, or as Thomas Friedman calls it, "flat," as more and more countries compete with, and in some cases surpass, the United States. Globalization has indeed changed the world, and strangely, an idea and system of economic rules that started in the United States and was promoted by the US government and business community has now come back to challenge the economic supremacy of the United States.

The Great Debate

Despite its clear benefits to the world economy profit margins, there is no doubt that the globalization regime has its downsides, especially when it comes to job security, environmental protection, and worker pay. This clear separation of benefits and drawbacks can be the basis for a debate.

Debate Topic

Should the United States rewrite the rules of the globalization system regarding worker rights and environmental protection, even if such actions have a detrimental effect on corporate competition in the world economy?

Critical Thinking Questions

1. Do you support the rules of the new global economy as outlined in the Washington Consensus?
2. Should the Trump Administration have abandoned the TPP and demanded a renegotiation of trade agreements like NAFTA to protect domestic manufacturing jobs?
3. Supporters of the new global economy have said that globalization will "lift all boats" and eventually bring prosperity to an ever-wider group of workers both in the United States and in the less-developed world. Do you agree with this analysis?
4. Globalization has created powerful multinational corporations with significant economic international influence. Is this a positive development?
5. How can the United States best combat the problem of tax inversion?

Connections

The World Bank has numerous studies of globalization that can be accessed from its website. See www.worldbank.org

The website of the Office of the United States Trade Representative contains information about US free trade agreements and bilateral investment treaties. View the website here: https://ustr.gov

The World Growth Institute provides balanced analysis of globalization. See www. worldgrowth.org

The Economic Policy Institute is one of the more respected critics of globalization. See http://epinet.org

The American Enterprise Institute has provided analysis of the TPP on its website. Access it here: www.aei.org/tag/trans-pacific-partnership/

Some Books to Read

Bhagwati, Jagdish, *In Defense of Globalization* (New York: Oxford University Press, 2007).

Eichengreen, Barry, *Globalizing Capital* (Princeton, NJ: Princeton University Press, 2008).

Findlay, Ronald and Kevin H. O'Rourke, *Power and Plenty* (Princeton, NJ: Princeton University Press, 2009).

Rodrik, Dani, *The Globalization Paradox* (New York: W.W. Norton, 2012).

Stiglitz, Joseph, *Making Globalization Work* (New York: W.W. Norton, 2007).

Notes

1. For background see Manfred Steger, *Globalization: A Very Short Introduction* (New York: Oxford University Press, 2003).
2. For a discussion of the Washington Consensus see Maggie Black, *The No-Nonsense Guide to International Development* (London: Verso UK, 2002), pp. 50–70.
3. The most widely read and influential book on the new global economy is Thomas Friedman, *The World Is Flat* (New York: Farrar, Straus, and Giroux, 2007).
4. See Gary Burtless, Ribert J. Laurence, Robert Litan, and Robert Shapiro, *Globalphobia: Confronting Fears About Open Trade* (Washington, DC: Brookings Institution Press, 1988).
5. Robert E. Scott, "The High Price of Free Trade," Economic Policy Institute, November 17, 2003, www.epi.org/publications/entry/briefingpapers_bp147
6. See this discussion of NAFTA in Michael Kryzanek, *U.S.-Latin American Relations*, 4th edition (Westport, CT: Praeger, 2008), pp. 284–286.
7. Robert Pastor, "The Future of North America," *Foreign Affairs*, July/August, 2008.
8. Jyoti Thottam, "Is Your Job Going Abroad," *Time*, March 1, 2004, pp. 26–30.
9. Scott, "The High Price of Free Trade," op. cit. See also "Debating the Central American Free Trade Act," 2005, www.pbs.org/now/politics/caftadebate.html
10. Claude Barfield and Philip Levy, "In Search of an Obama Trade Policy," American Enterprise Institute, 2009, www.aei.org/publication/in-search-of-an-obama-trade-policy/
11. Russell Berman, "Are Democrats Prepared to Abandon Obama on Trade?" *The Atlantic*, June 1, 2015.
12. Timothy Lee, "The Transpacific Partnership, Explained," *Vox*, July 25, 2016, www. vox.com/cards/trans-pacific-partnership/what-is-the-trans-pacific-partnership

13. "President Obama Explains the Difference Between TPP and NAFTA in Layman's Terms," *Forbes*, October 28, 2016, www.forbes.com/sites/quora/2016/10/28/president-obama-explains-the-difference-between-tpp-and-nafta-in-laymans-terms/#2f81a4b36485

14. Jackie Calmes, "Trans-Pacific Partnership Is Reached, But Faces Scrutiny in Congress," *The New York Times*, October 5, 2015.

15. Elizabeth Warren, "The Trans-Pacific Partnership Clause Everyone Should Oppose," *The Washington Post*, February 25, 2015.

16. Paul Kane and Kelsey Snell, "Portman to Oppose Trade Deal as Opposition Back Home Builds," *The Washington Post*, February 4, 2016.

17. William Mauldin, "Ten Winning and Losing Industries From the Pacific Trade Deal," *The Wall Street Journal*, May 19, 2016.

18. Jackie Calmes, "T.P.P. Faces Rough Road in Congress," *The New York Times*, September 1, 2016.

19. Michael Memoli, "Hillary Clinton Once Called the TPP the 'Gold Standard,'" *The Los Angeles Times*, September 26, 2016.

20. "Full Transcript: Donald Trump's Jobs Plan Speech," *Politico*, June 28, 2016, www.politico.com/story/2016/06/full-transcript-trump-job-plan-speech-224891

21. Jose A. DelReal and Sean Sullivan, "Trump: TPP Trade Deal 'Pushed By Special Interests Who Want to Rape Our Country," *The Washington Post*, June 28, 2016.

22. Bourree Lam, "Trump's Promises to Corporate Leaders: Lower Taxes and Fewer Regulations," *The Atlantic*, January 23, 2017.

23. For more, see Office of the United States Trade Representative fact sheet, https://ustr.gov/about-us/policy-offices/press-office/fact-sheets/2015/january/fact-sheet-obama-administration's

24. For transcript of speech, see http://time.com/4495507/donald-trump-economy-speech-transcript/

25. See pollingreport.com under International Trade/Global Economy

26. For more see Mark J. Perry, "An Economic Analysis of Protectionism Clearly Shows That Trump's Tariffs Would Make Us Poorer, Not Greater," American Enterprise Institute, 2016, www.aei.org/publication/an-economic-analysis-of-protectionism-clearly-shows-that-tariffs-make-us-poorer-not-greater/

27. Sam Fleming and Barney Jopson, "U.S. Companies Braced for Tax Shake-Up as Apple Feud Escalates," *The Financial Times*, August 25, 2016.

28. Richard Rubin, "Obama Renews Call for Congress to Limit Tax Inversions," *The Wall Street Journal*, April 5, 2016.

29. See pollingreport.com under International Trade/Global Economy

30. See www.americans-world.org/digest/global_issues/globalization/general.cfm

31. For a critique of globalization see Robert Skidelsky, "Gloomy About Globalization," *New York Review of Books*, April 17, 2008, pp. 60–63.

CONCLUSION

AMERICAN DEMOCRACY: DECAY AND DECLINE OR RENEWAL?

At the conclusion of the Constitutional Convention in Philadelphia in 1787, citizens gathered outside Independence Hall to find out what the Founders had decided. A Mrs. Powel approached Benjamin Franklin with what are now these famous and prescient words: "Well Doctor, what have we got, a republic or a monarchy?" Franklin answered, "A republic, if you can keep it."

Franklin's warning is certainly appropriate for the times we live in. The United States is awash in division and differences, and each policy issue we have examined is colored by intense partisan debate. Congress is viewed with disdain and marked by so-called "gridlockracy"; President Trump entered office with the lowest approval rate in modern history; and the American people are not only mistrustful of their government and leaders but are increasingly taking to the streets to register their displeasure with a fragile and failing democracy.

Although the current turmoil in our republic is directly connected to the victory of Donald Trump in the Electoral College, even though Hillary Clinton received 2.9 million more votes than the president, the debates, differences, and divisions that now define our politics are not new; there have always been periods in our history when leaders clashed, parties refused to cooperate, social movements challenged the status quo, and public polls reflected deep fissures in our democratic system. As Alexis de Tocqueville remarked when he visited this country in 1840, he was "stunned by the tumult."

Despite our history of tumult, present day tumult is worrisome, if not dangerous. Some see our republic as coming apart; some see our republic as leaning toward authoritarianism; some see our republic as dying a slow death culminating in eventual decline.[1] The growing perception among more and more Americans is that our government doesn't work or works only for the rich and the well-born. Nagging economic and social problems are ignored, while politicians become captive to special interests, all in the name of campaign contributions. Most seriously, the hallowed words of our Preamble to the Constitution, "We the People" now ring hollow as elections fail to bring real change and policy promises are mere words to be forgotten after elections.

Hope and confidence have now been replaced with cynicism and anger and those entrusted with running our government are viewed with suspicion. Gone are the days when Americans idolized political leaders as heroes and role models. Now there is only constant shouting at rallies and cruel snipes on social media. Calm, reasoned debate has been left behind as more and more Americans choose to participate by questioning what would normally be considered indisputable facts or following media charlatans from the left and right who spew only hate and prosper through division. If democracy were a passenger train pulling American democracy forward, it could rightly be defined as "going off the rails and headed into a deep ravine."

So the obvious question would be: How did we get this way? How did we as nation and a people drift apart and fall prey to what one analyst described as chaos syndrome?[2] As with any major shift in American life and politics, there are no easy and simple answers as to why we drifted apart and are stuck in this chaos. But there are some critical cultural and governing developments over the last twenty years that have contributed to the intense debates, the passionate differences, and the deep divisions. Francis Fukuyama, a noted political scientist, in a recent book entitled *Political Order and Political Decay*, traces the national political malaise to the fact that there are too many veto holders in our system of government. Our Founders purposely set up a governing system of separation of powers and checks and balances, but Fukuyama believes that in our modern society these veto holders have fostered a decision-making climate that is chock full of institutional roadblocks and special interest power grabs. Moreover, Fukuyama also faults "adversarial legalism" where disputes are resolved by state and national courts (too often in 5–4 decisions) rather than through quiet consultation and compromise within the bureaucracy or the party system and by much less aggressive legislative bodies. Fukuyama, in his own words, suggests reforms such as "curtailing the power of senators to hold up presidential appointments, reducing the ability of members of Congress to lumber government with unfunded or incoherent mandates, increasing presidential power over independent government commissions and regulatory bodies and cutting back on court interference and supervision of government bureaucracies."[3]

Although, on the surface, these reforms do not appear to be terribly dynamic, what Fukuyama wants is the beginning of a movement in government to become an "efficient, responsive, capable state." If our democracy is to be saved from itself, Fukuyama believes that this country must move away from what he terms "vetocracy" and toward a governing system that provides for the capacity to get things done and, in the process, regain the trust of the American people. There is no need to move to a parliamentary system where the national leader can be removed through a vote of confidence, or a national term limits amendment that guarantees new faces in government, or a drastic reduction in the size and power of the bureaucracy. Rather, the answer is in small steps to push aside the roadblocks and reduce the power of special interests. Failure to do so will, in Fukuyama's view, lead to political decay and democratic decline.[4]

Also weighing in on the question of "How did we get this way?" is Jonathan Rauch in an article in *The Atlantic* entitled "What's Ailing American Politics." Rauch bases his analysis on the fact that what ails American politics is the decline of political parties and the role they used to play as "middlemen" in the political process. Rauch readily admits that the old party system was often a bunch of men in smoke-filled rooms making decisions on candidates, campaigns, and most of all, policymaking. Those party-dominated days are gone and have been replaced by more democratic but more divisive reforms such as open primaries where fringe candidates can win nominations, unlimited campaign contributions that put billionaires in control of candidates, a Congress of divisive cliques who disregard loyalty and challenge party leaders, open and transparent decision-making that weakens close-door compromise, and a decline of so-called earmarks (usually termed pork barrel) that in the past led to cooperation.[5]

Although these changes and reforms can be described as democratic in nature and did promote transparency and openness, Rauch also bemoans the fact that these changes and reforms weakened political parties, the electoral process, and Congress by fostering an internal climate of extremism, mistrust, disloyalty, and refusal to compromise and led to his original description of our democracy as beset with "chaos syndrome." Rauch's answer to the chaos syndrome is likely not to be attractive to the current wave of American public opinion. He sees a need to strengthen political parties and build new political networks with centrist views and calls for a return to a responsible political elite—what he terms the middlemen who controlled politics in a less then democratic way but also ensured that extremism, disloyalty, intransigence, and intense partisanship did not rule the day. Such a return to the old days of American politics is a long way off as the American political psyche is currently not attuned to such a shift and glories in the new form of democracy—populism—with its accent on advancing the interests of the common person and ridding the country of a corrupt and privileged elite.[6]

Although Fukuyama and Rauch are by no means optimistic about the future of traditional democratic behavior and governing, a recent book by John R. Hibbing and Elizabeth Theiss-Morse called *Stealth* reflects the current thinking of many Americans. Through their use of polling data and focus groups, Hibbing and Theiss-Morse found that between 25% to 40% of Americans have little understanding of how American government is constitutionally organized and functions. These Americans seem to care little that our constitution is a sacred document that has guided our country since 1787. Furthermore, they see politicians as corrupt and wedded to destructive partisanship. The solution that Hibbing and Theiss-Morse find among this group of Americans is control of the policy process by what they term ENSIDs—empathetic, non-self-interested decision-makers—individuals who could be politicians, bureaucrats, or perhaps autocrats; democracy is less important to these Americans than pushing aside a system that is completely broken. It is the option to accept an autocrat as the answer to our current governing malaise that has caught the attention of academics and pundits as they fear that traditional democratic values and practice could fall to be replaced with ENSIDs, perhaps an autocrat who promises to get things done. Of course, the sub-text of the ENSIDs option is the presidency of Donald Trump, which those not in that 25%–40% of Americans believe is a disturbing development that could spell the end of democracy as we know it with all its flaws and disappointments.[7]

Amid all this gloom and doom about the state of democratic governance in this country, there is an article by James Fallows, also in *The Atlantic*, entitled "How America is Putting Itself Back Together." Fallows and his wife flew their small plane across America in 2013 and 2014, visiting small towns and big cities, and talked to hundreds of Americans about what they are doing to improve their communities. Expecting to hear stories of intense debates, serious differences, and deep divisions, Fallows found that the vast majority of Americans he talked with had a far more optimistic view of their communities, their neighbors, and their future. In his travels, Fallows found that there was a deep-seated commitment to reinvent their town, city, or state; there was little connection to the divisive character of Washington, D.C. and the national political conversation based on partisan differences. Fallows found confident entrepreneurs, vibrant start-ups, respected local political leaders, an acceptance of racial, ethnic, and religious diversity, and a strong belief that America will rise once again.[8]

The Americans that Fallows talked with and those that communicated with him by email or letter are no wide-eyed idealists with rose-colored glasses. Fallows found that "many people are discouraged about America. But the closer they are to the action at home, the better they like what they see." The future of democratic resurgence thus is likely to happen not in our nation's capital or in political party enclaves but at the local level where Americans are remaking this country and, in the process, remaking democracy. As Philip Zelikow of the University of Virginia stated in the Fallow's article, "There are a lot more positive narratives out there—but they're lonely and disconnected. It would make a difference to join them together, as a chorus that has melody."[9]

So if democracy is to enter a new period of revival and renewal it will, if Fallow's airplane trip is accurate, come from the work of Main Street Americans and the confidence they have about the future of this country. There is no way to predict whether this revival and renewal of America and American democracy will be successful or that, in the process, trust in government, support for elected officials, and an effective and efficient policymaking process will return, but change from the grassroots has often been a hallmark of American democratic reform. The coming years will be critical for defining the destiny of our capacity to reform the governing system. In response to Benjamin Franklin, let us keep and protect our Republic.

The Great Debate

There are many signs that point to our country and our system of democracy as facing its most serious challenge since the Civil War. Multiple examples of institutional decay and systemic failure can be found throughout our government and in the political arena. These examples call into question the ability of our nation to fix our democracy and save our republic from a period of decline.

Debate Topic

Does the United States have the capacity to address the problems facing our governing system, or is our nation headed into a period of political decline?

Critical Thinking Questions

1. What do you consider the most pressing governing challenge facing the United States?
2. How will it be possible to bring the nation together in the midst of this period of differences and divisions?
3. What level of blame do you place on our elected officials for these governing challenges?
4. Present one reform that you think will help move the governing system toward renewal and revival.
5. How much of the blame do you place on the American people for this period of governing dysfunction? Are we at fault?

Connections

Journalist Bill Moyers often discusses the need for reform in our governing system. Visit his site at www.billmoyers.com

Citizens for Political Reform is a bipartisan organization committed to reforming our political and governing system. See www.bipartisanpolicy.org

There is a Reform Party in American politics dedicated to bringing change to our democratic system. Visit their site at www.reformparty.org

See the site Democracy Matters for proposals on governing reform at www.democra cymatters.org

For a conservative view on political and governmental reform see the site www. newamerica.org

A Few Books to Read

Fukuyama, Francis, *Political Order and Political Decay* (New York: Farrar, Straus and Giroux, 2015).

Grumet, Jason, *City of Rivals: Restoring the Glorious Mess of American Democracy* (New York: Lyons Press, 2014).

Hibbing, John R. and Elizabeth Theiss-Morse, *Stealth Democracy: Americans' Beliefs About How Government Should Work* (New York: Cambridge University Press, 2002).

Murphy, Cullen, *Are We Rome? The Fate of an Empire and the Fate of America* (New York: Mariner Books, 2008).

O'Connor, Karen and Larry J. Sabato, *American Government: Roots and Reform*, 12th edition (New York: Pearson, 2013).

Notes

1. Cullen Murphy examines the current malaise in American society and politics and makes comparisons to the decline of the Roman Empire. See Cullen Murphy, *Are We Rome: The Fate of an Empire and the Fate of America* (New York: Mariner Book, 2008).
2. This term, chaos syndrome, is discussed in Jonathan Rauch, "What's Ailing American Politics?" *The Atlantic*, July/August, 2016.
3. See Francis Fukuyama, *Political Order and Political Decay* (New York: Farrar, Straus and Giroux, 2015).
4. Michael Ignatieff comments on Fukuyama's analysis of American Democracy in "Doubling Down on Democracy," *The Atlantic*, October, 2014.
5. Rauch, "What's Ailing American Politics," op. cit.
6. Ibid.
7. See John R. Hibbing and Elizabeth Theiss-Morse, *Stealth Democracy: Americans' Beliefs About How Government Should Work* (New York: Cambridge University Press, 2002).
8. James Fallows, "How America Is Putting Itself Back Together," *The Atlantic*, March, 2016.
9. As quoted in Fallows, "How America Is Putting Itself Back Together," op. cit.

INDEX

CPSIA information can be obtained
at www.ICGtesting.com
Printed in the USA
LVHW040142270820
664360LV00019B/2263